Expectations of Justice
in the Age of Augustine

Expectations of Justice
in the Age of Augustine

Kevin Uhalde

PENN

UNIVERSITY OF PENNSYLVANIA PRESS

Philadelphia

10   9   8   7   6   5   4   3   2   1

Published by
University of Pennsylvania Press
Philadelphia, Pennsylvania 19104-4112

Library of Congress Cataloging-in-Publication Data

Uhalde, Kevin, 1971–
Expectations of justice in the age of Augustine / Kevin Uhalde.
p.   cm.
ISBN-13: 978-0-8122-3987-1 (alk. paper)
ISBN-10: 0-8122-3987-3 (alk. paper)
Includes bibliographical references (p.) and index
1. Christianity and justice. I. Title.
BR115.J8 U33   2007
270.2—dc22   2006050945

For my family

Contents

Introduction

Expectans expectavi Dominum et inclinatus est ad me et
audivit clamorem meum.
Patiently I awaited the Lord and he turned to me and
heard my cry.
—Vulgate Psalm 39:2

This doubled word deserves attention, for such a
graceful repetition is not mere embellishment.
Certainly we are able to be expectant, but in a grudging
mood. Still we may be patiently expectant when we
bear something calmly and with powerful longing.
—Cassiodorus, *Expositio Psalmorum* 39.2

THE LIFE OF Flavius Magnus Aurelius Cassiodorus Senator (485/90–ca. 580), best known simply as Cassiodorus, epitomized the age of transition in which he lived. One foot rested in the ancient past, for Cassiodorus had impeccable credentials as a late Roman aristocrat. While still a young man, he served as assistant to his father, the praetorian prefect, and then as quaestor. In 514 he was the sole consul in the empire, then master of offices from 523 to 527, and praetorian prefect in Italy for four years until 537. His other foot, however, was in the Middle Ages. He wrote Latin letters on behalf of King Theoderic the Great (ca. 452–526) of the Ostrogoths, the Germanic occupants of Italy whose relations with the imperial court in Constantinople deteriorated into open warfare during Cassiodorus's public career. He began his commentary on the Psalms while still in Ravenna, probably around 538, at a moment of personal transition. He had known what it meant to serve in public life and to wait "grudging" but "expectantly" through its vicissitudes, and now he was facing a new life. It was a whole other life, in fact, for he would live fifty more years, most of them as a recluse on the monastery he founded in Southern Italy, called Vivarium after its pools stocked with fish.[1]

In the "Explanation of the Psalms," the book his medieval readers would know best, Cassiodorus acknowledged his debt to Augustine of Hippo (354–430). Indeed, Cassiodorus's future spiritual and literary career owed much to Augustine and other members of his generation a century earlier. For in their hands, as Mark Vessey has argued, the interpretation of scripture had become a new form of authorship, in which one's public and spiritual lives were equally invested and measured out for posterity.[2] Cassiodorus was attuned to Augustine's intellectual universe and especially to his sensitivity with regard to human expectations and divine justice in the Psalms. Nonetheless, Cassiodorus, this former adviser to a barbarian king, lived in a world different from the bishop of Hippo's. Studying, reflecting, and writing at his retreat at Vivarium, his fingers stained with ink (we have his marginal notes penned in a few manuscripts),[3] Cassiodorus enjoyed a leisure Augustine and many of his contemporaries had hardly known. For although they too might have wished to measure their lives by the books they wrote, the bishops with whom this book is primarily concerned also had their hands full with the mundane affairs Cassiodorus had left behind in Ravenna.

The bishops who held office during Augustine's adult life, between roughly 370 and 430, lived and worked through massive changes in politics, society, and religion that would affect their successors, directly or indirectly, for generations to come. This book is concerned particularly with the way these bishops explained the failure of justice to themselves and their followers. Augustine and his near contemporaries were no more or less successful at handling justice than other late antique or early medieval bishops. However, perhaps in part because the challenge of representing divine justice while simultaneously engaging in and even presiding over the mess of worldly justice was still novel for church officials, we can find ample evidence of their frustration and whatever measures they sought for relief.

The Christian intellectuals who figure prominently here were no ivory tower recluses. On the one hand, their elite status connected them with other elites around the Roman Empire, within both the church and secular government. On the other hand, their professional occupation as bishops forced them into contact with the middling and lower ranks of society and filled their days with the sorts of activities that made communities hum — business deals, litigation, gossip, and violence. In this respect, bishops in Augustine's day were not so different from those Cassiodorus would have known.

During the fourth through the sixth centuries, Christian bishops were intellectuals, legislators, patrons, judges, and pastors. To adequately fulfill just some of these roles meant juggling disparate skills and responsibilities that fit together awkwardly more often than not. Bishops' broad occupational experience with both the philosophy and the exercise of justice shaped not only the ideal of the episcopal office, but also created a practical sounding chamber for Christian notions of justice and salvation. Theory and practice—one affected the other. So on the one hand, for example, in his *De civitate Dei* ("The City of God"), Augustine employed a classical text as an *intellectual* sounding chamber for a Christian theory of justice. By substituting Christ for the ideal statesman whom Cicero (106–43 BC) had described in *De re publica*, Augustine redefined the place of justice in human society. "The City of God" then demonstrated the result in historical and theological terms, as Robert Dodaro has shown with meticulous care.[4] On the other hand, though, Augustine and other bishops also lived with the result of the Christian transformation in their own communities. Their experience with the way legal procedures and judgment worked on the ground compelled bishops to question whether anyone could be guaranteed justice on earth even from bishops, God's own representatives. As a result, Christian ideals of divine justice fundamentally changed to accommodate the unpleasant reality of worldly justice and its failings. The implications of this transformation resonated within Christianity for centuries and directly affected religious life, from the performance of penance to the way people conceived of the Final Judgment.

This book illuminates the decisive but subtle processes by which this happened. It focuses on the age in which Augustine lived, a slice of time across which we may trace the complexities and contingencies of those processes. Keeping them in focus will also require that we sometimes move backward and forward in time, examining the different ways church leaders represented their own authority, conducted mundane and sacred affairs, and communicated with lay Christians about justice. The sources resist this project in a number of ways. From a very rough estimate of a thousand bishoprics in the western regions alone of the Roman Empire, the experiences of only a handful of bishops are sufficiently represented in the written record for us to be able to discern not only their professional ambitions but also something of their personal success or failure. Those thousand or so Western bishops lived and worked among as many as twenty million laypeople, the smallest fraction of whom now enjoy even an oblique reference in the sources. Did these ordinary people ever expect to receive justice? Where did they look for it? Were they ever satisfied? We must content ourselves with exploring the vestiges their expectations and experiences left in the material that survives: secular and ecclesiastical law, theological treatises, sermons, saints' vitae, liturgical prayers, letters, and inscriptions.

Because of these limitations in the evidence, the present investigation is in equal parts an intellectual history and a social history, building on and sometimes departing from contemporary scholarship in both these areas. As an intellectual history, it examines legal structures and customs within the church and surrounding the church in the world at large. Caroline Humfress's work has been important in this context, for it demonstrates with clarity and precision the ways in which Roman law shaped Christian doctrine with regard to the definition and proscription of heresy.[5] The legal expertise of bishops—whether real, imagined, or exaggerated by bishops themselves—is important to this study. But so is the application of this expertise in mundane society. Beyond the intellectual developments of the Christian clerical world, this study is an attempt to sense the presence of a lay world, which "waited expectantly" (*expectans expectavi*), in the words of the psalmist, for justice.

So this is not a book only about bishops. If bishops figure prominently in its pages, it shows them from an unusual viewing point. For, unlike much of the current attention given bishops, this book considers the impact of bishops' incompetence rather than their competence. Bishops were challenged to carry out what was, after all, an impossible task—to harmonize the conflicting demands of spiritual purity and worldly administration within Christian communities. These local communities were complex, and they continued to grow larger and more complex over the course of the period under examination, often sharing space, overlapping, and conflicting with communities that followed different traditions and even different leadership, including Jewish and polytheistic communities. Unlike conventional intellectual histories, this book puts less stress on the discourse among religious elites than on the discourse between religious elites and the rest of society. The experience of bishops with a range of judicial situations was often frustrating for themselves and their followers, but ultimately it was productive. On the edge of failure, adaptation took place. During this period, perhaps more than any other until the sixteenth century, a combination of historical factors and institutional conditions lowered the screen between religious beliefs and social practices. Christian society changed as a result.

Change and Continuity

The following chapters encapsulate a broad span of time in order to explore continuities related to religious leadership, the crafting of law, judicial procedures, and popular responses, where such responses are discernible. These continuities give coherence to an otherwise tumultuous age. Few historical periods furnish us with less information about the conduct of daily life and the experiences of people outside of a narrow elite than this—the beginning of the proverbial Dark Ages, the last centuries of antiquity, the first centuries of the Middle Ages, the postclassical, post-Roman, or sub-Roman world.[6] Yet one thing can be said. The more we come to know this period, the more we realize that, in certain crucial respects, the world of the later Roman Empire—a world so different from the ancient world before it that we call it by a different name, Late Antiquity[7]—lived on in Western communities deep into the sixth and even the seventh centuries.[8] This book traces some of these slow processes across the long span of Late Antiquity and examines them more closely during the age of Augustine.

All the same, if late antique society knew only continuity, there would be no history to write.[9] Until fairly recently, this era in Western history was far more famous for its discontinuities, still made most memorable for us in images of barbarian hordes rushing down from the frosty North to spoil the sun soaked South. J. B. Bury's lectures on "The Invasion of Europe by the Barbarians," for example, remain in print more than seventy-five years after their publication in 1928. One suspects that they attract readers less for their nuanced argument about gradual barbarian assimilation than for their vivid descriptions of the "dismembering" of the Western empire.[10] Of course, considerable evidence exists, and articulate proponents remain, to support the argument that foreign peoples did indeed destabilize the Roman Empire decisively during the fourth and fifth centuries. Yet it is something more romantic, surely, that explains why titles of otherwise sober scholarly works continue to evoke notions of sudden invasion and utter collapse.[11]

Less popular than the barbarian hordes but easily as influential is a narrative of religious discontinuity within Christianity, epitomized in two related myths that still inhibit our understanding of this transitional period. One is the myth of Christianity's decline, according to which the general quality of humanity sunk steadily toward its Dark Age nadir. Its plot, like that of invading barbarian hordes, is compelling and familiar from its repetition by countless authors and so can be sketched in broad strokes here. Almost simultaneously with the conversion of Constantine (r. 312–337) and the triumph of Christianity in the fourth century, churchmen and laypeople set to work devastating a spiritual landscape that once had been fertile. Christians after Constantine, so the story goes, watched while a Golden Age receded into the past, a lost moment when pastors had been sensitive to the needs and abilities of their followers and ordinary Christians were committed to spiritual excellence.

For evidence that at least the myth of an early Christian Golden Age was operative in antiquity, we may detect nostalgia for Christianity's imagined heroic past in the sermons of bishops from throughout the period, such as Pacian of Barcelona in the fourth century and Caesarius of Arles in the sixth century.[12] The roots of the myth of decline are almost as deep, appearing in early medieval writers, including the monk Jonas of Bobbio. His biography of Columbanus, written in 639–43, described how that saint brought the hope of salvation to Northern Gaul, a region Jonas claimed was devoid of spiritual promise before Columbanus arrived.[13] Those roots of the myth sustain a hearty tradition flourishing still today in the work of distinguished historians such as Arnold Angenendt and Jacques Le Goff. Their visions of the Middle Ages rely in part on a bleak view of its origins in what Angenendt calls the "eclipse" and Le Goff calls the "stagnation" of Christian intellectual culture that accompanied the fall of the Western Roman Empire.[14] In his *Birth of Purgatory*, Le Goff cuts even the invading barbarians slack for their part in launching the Dark Ages, because "the 'responsibility' for the decline in the general cultural and spiritual level was not borne by the 'barbarians' alone." He goes on to explain that "the fact that the peasant masses, the 'barbarians' within, took up the Christian religion was at least as important as the fact that invaders from outside the Roman world took up residence inside it. The 'barbarization' of Roman society was in part a democratization." The 'barbarization' or 'Germanization' of Western Christianity has its own story with its own authors. It is enough for us to agree with Le Goff that "here matters become still more complicated" and then to leave such generalizing narratives alone.[15]

Nevertheless, the fifth century was *not* the end of a Golden Age. For one thing, the Christian Golden Age never existed. It was no more real than the Roman Golden Age, when Saturn ruled the earth and Justice dwelled in person among humankind—although both Golden Ages had meaning for some Christians living in the late Empire.[16] The historians who have perpetuated the notion, moreover, have used the myth of decline to help explain another, corollary myth—that of ecclesiastical rigorism. This myth insists that the fifth century was the beginning of a long period of neglectful rulership when Christian leaders became caught up in the machinery of their institution and disregarded its spirit. The notion is most discernible in modern histories of the sacrament of penance and its development during Late Antiquity and the Middle Ages. Cyrille Vogel was the most prolific commentator on what he alleged to have been the church's "systematic refusal of any indulgence adapted to human weakness" during this period, but Vogel was hardly alone.[17] More recently, medievalists have worked at revising the entire history of penance.[18] The fifth through seventh centuries remain a crucial period of transition, and Mayke de Jong, Peter Brown, Éric Rebillard, and Robert Meens have led a reconsideration of both the decline and rigor myths in the context of understanding how sin and forgiveness worked.[19] We seem close to being able to write a new history of Christianity, one no longer bound by the old myths whose "grand narrative," as De Jong calls it, still persists.

The tenacity of these myths is understandable. Following the history of Christianity from its earliest centuries to the Middle Ages and the age of reformations, moving from council to council and heresy to heresy, from one reform movement to another, through successive alliances and conflicts with secular princes, perhaps it is easy to get caught up in the apparent momentum of its progress. In reality, however, more or less after the conversion of Constantine, like a heavy truck hitting a steep grade, the processes of Christianization had shifted into a lower gear, moving with greater traction and slower velocity than before, and our attention must shift accordingly. After Christianity became an imperial and later a royal religion, church leaders, willingly or not, locked pace with slower developments in the life of religious communities, developments that were less interesting to later generations of spectators focused on institutional, sacramental, and theological mile-marks looming in the distance. But these slower developments were where the expectations of bishops and their followers came into closest contact, especially over timeless questions of justice.

To emphasize continuity over disruption, to argue for what Peter Garnsey and Caroline Humfress have called "creeping change" and "'creative' evolution" between antiquity and the Middle Ages, is to join company among many historians of the late ancient and early medieval worlds.[20] Legal historians, for example, may have once emphasized dramatic changes in law resulting from Christianization and Germanization during this period, but now Maurizio Lupoi and the late Patrick Wormald have written about smooth transformations and "shared culture" leading directly to a European "common law."[21] Similarly, this was not the first time in history that everyday people hoped to win judicial satisfaction or at least enjoy some degree of personal security. These were stable desires that political upheaval, social disruption, and religious revolution hardly affected. Christianity made very little difference, moreover, in the devices, techniques, and procedures that supplied and controlled justice in real life. The single most outstanding factor of change in the way elites handled justice and the way ordinary people experienced it was the rise in the person of the bishop as an official who bridged the theory and practice of justice. This is the subject around which the following chapters revolve.

Calumny: Well-Known Reasons Why Justice Fails

By the late fourth century, bishops were actively engaged in worldly justice in the capacity of judge, arbiter, plaintiff, and defendant. In the late Roman Empire and in the kingdoms that followed in the West, secular rulers allowed bishops varying degrees of judicial authority in religious and worldly affairs. For the Western successor kingdoms, bishops were among the expert custodians of Roman laws, procedures, and administration.[22] Of course, we must be careful not to exaggerate the degree to which the idea of judicial expertise translated into institutional reality. For one reason, as Richard Helmholz observes in his survey of church law and administration in medieval England, most regional churches lacked the Roman Empire's institutional resources for implementing the laws their leaders esteemed. "The institutional life of the church could not be securely tied to legal rule, no matter the aspirations of its bishops," Helmholz writes. "The short of it was that the laws so highly regarded by many of the church's leaders did not add up to a regime of government by law."[23] Perhaps not, but we also should not discount the evidence that legal expertise did not expire altogether and that clerics continued to practice the law alongside secular lawyers, even if on a diminished scale—all of which Detlef Liebs has demonstrated for the Merovingian kingdoms.[24]

There is another reason, however, for us to look beyond the laws in order to understand how justice worked. For at the same time that the church preserved some familiar judicial forms, a variety of other ways for settling arguments, cementing relationships, and getting what people wanted existed outside of courtrooms and audience chambers.[25] Options ranging from legalized venues of arbitration to the illicit use of trickery, magic, or violence provided both alternatives and supplements to regular courts, contributing to what Jeffrey Bowman, referring to a later period, recognized as a "kind of ordered irresolution in the judicial process" that maximized the range of options for potential litigants, even if it could not guarantee them success.[26] Here, too, bishops played important roles. Within most local communities, they were a more accessible source of judicial authority than any imperial or royal official.

Although informative documentary evidence for actual business conducted in bishops' courts during this period is scarce, we get a sense of what both bishops and disputants expected by examining the problem of calumny (*calumnia*), a perennial topic of Roman law and later of ecclesiastical law. Bishops joined emperors and their legal experts in trying to confront the problem of calumny as a juridical dilemma, capable of a juridical solution. Calumny included false accusations as well as spurious litigation intended to harm or harass defendants. In edicts and canons spanning centuries of legislation, authorities repeatedly attacked calumny with a limited arsenal of weapons: procedural requirements, rules of evidence, prohibition of certain types of accusations, and sanctions for convicted violators.

Calumny, however, was also a social problem, catching bishops uncomfortably between the abstract certainty of divine justice and the inescapable uncertainty of human society. This timeless trap was a byproduct of human interaction and what Augustine of Hippo followed Cicero in describing as "social bond" (*socialis necessitudo*).[27] Centuries later it continues to draw the attention of philosophers such as Martha Nussbaum, who describes how "our insecurity is inseparable from our sociability." Shame, vulnerability, self-doubt: these aspects of uncertainty are as important as trust and certainty to holding a society together. For, as Nussbaum suggests, "if we think of ourselves as like the self-sufficient gods, we fail to understand the ties that join us to our fellow humans. Nor is that lack of understanding innocent," for it leads to the breakdown of social bond.[28]

Set against the demands of "social bond," the campaign against calumny was a failure by any realistic measure. Juridical solutions could not work; in fact, they made things worse by adding further layers to judicial complexity that likely favored crafty calumniators over naïve innocents. When we trace the problem of accusations through a sample of ecclesiastical sources, we shall find that various bishops reacted differently to the fallibility of their own procedures and institutions. Yet, at the end of the day they did not ignore or isolate calumny as an incurable disease of the secular world. Instead, the ideology of Christian unity and leadership absorbed the prevention of calumny as a religious virtue. Thus our attention to the procedures of fairness brings us to the heart of what made the episcopal office distinctive and what makes it central to this study: bishops straddled the theory and the practice of justice, the letter of the law and its application.

"Judge like God": What Bishops Claimed to Expect of Themselves

From their first emergence as spiritual leaders in the early centuries of Christianity, bishops administered justice in the daily lives of their followers. Justice also served as a key attribute of their spiritual authority. Like late antique emperors, who adopted the Hellenistic concept that a sovereign is "living law" (*empsuchos nomos*), bishops represented divine justice in all its impeccable, indefatigable, unyielding, but merciful glory. The ideal bishop-judge was a manufactured personality that came to be associated with the episcopal office and its occupants, an identity which made sense of their disparate qualifications and obligations—ascetic, pastoral, and judicial authority, which Claudia Rapp examines with an admirable balance between clarity and nuance.[29] In its purest form, this personality provided individual bishops with a sense of professional and spiritual continuity. Their office supplied them a profile, moreover, to match what freshly ordained bishops soon would discover to be a dissonant chorus of demands and expectations that were impossible for them to fulfill.

For at the same time, more like middle-level government officials than princes, bishops could not escape the pathetic failure of justice within human society, among good Christians, and in their own churches and courtrooms. To their chagrin, bishops were unlike most other lawmakers of the time. Although they celebrated their own stellar attributes of justice as much as any emperor or king, their authority was also sunk deep in the vagaries and failings of human society. We shall weigh the ideal against reality by looking at how Ambrose of Milan, one of the key early proponents of episcopal justice, responded to its failure in a particular judicial case. Although the ideal of the bishop-judge persisted throughout this period and beyond, real bishops were caught between the "glory of forgiving," as one imperial edict characterized episcopal justice, and "a demand for justice that far outstripped the bishops' ability to satisfy it."[30]

That bishops made exceptional judges became a commonplace in late antique and early Byzantine Christian literature. In treatises, vitae, and epitaphs, authors embroidered their subjects with scriptural allusions and suggestions of aristocratic refinement. For their part, bishops were likely to grumble about the time they lost when handling legal matters, none more famously than Augustine, who—at least according to his fellow bishop and biographer, Possidius of Calama—viewed his role in resolving disputes "as forced labor that took him away from better things."[31] In order to place such perceptions in a broader context, we must have a sense of how justice worked outside of episcopal audience chambers. Fortunately, studies by Jill Harries, Tony Honoré, Christopher Kelly, Detlef Liebs, and Caroline Humfress have explored how law, administration, and legal science worked and sometimes failed to work in the fourth- and fifth-century empire.[32] Bishops were part of a larger world that had both its own legal culture that did not revolve around their anxieties and its own, persistent problems they had to learn to handle. The provision of justice was one of those problems that bishops, partly out of necessity and partly of their own volition, made their own. Regardless of whether bishops resented the reputation they earned over time for being exceptional judges or whether that reputation was deserved, it became a fundamental component of episcopal authority.

One specific attribute of the ideal bishop-judge was the power to discern obscurities (*discretio, diakrisis*)—an attribute that had a range of religious, social, and legal applications. In polite society, letter writers might address difficult questions to a bishop as a "spiritual brother who judges all things," being imbued with the "spirit of revelation," as Paulinus of Nola (ca. 354–431) addressed Augustine before joining him in the episcopal ranks by becoming a bishop himself.[33] Indeed, bishops began to resemble the jurists Ulpian (d. 228) had once called "priests" because both bishops and jurists were charged with "distinguishing (*discernentes*) lawful from unlawful, aiming to make men good not only through fear of penalties but also indeed under allurement of rewards."[34] Reactions to this expectation were not uniform. "How am I an 'oracle of the law'," Augustine of Hippo responded to a person asking for clarification on a scriptural matter, "when I do not know many more things than I do know about its latent and hidden secrets?"[35] Sincere or not, his reservations do not appear to have been shared widely among bishops. Dionysius Exiguus (d. 526/556), himself a legal expert, hoped his editions of church law would restrain bishops otherwise inclined "to respond from within themselves, just as from a hidden oracle."[36] Emperors, however, had recognized bishops' power to discern secrets and "judge like God," a power that "searches out and reveals many things" that could not be disclosed in ordinary courts of law.[37]

The promotion of this attribute in letters, laws, sermons, treatises, epitaphs, and biographies provided bishops with a means for reconciling the spiritual and secular demands of their office. At the same time, the claim to discernment increased the scope of their religious authority, for reading the secrets of hearts was an ability the desert fathers claimed as well. In the late fourth and fifth centuries, ascetic authority and episcopal authority overlapped, interacted, and came into conflict. Discernment has never been the primary focus of the scholarship, but it has been a recurring theme; Claudia Rapp, Conrad Leyser, Andrea Sterk, and George Demacopoulos have made important contributions to this subject, and Philip Rousseau's 1978 study remains the essential starting point.[38] Understanding this specific aspect of the relationship between asceticism, pastoral care, and religious authority in turn helps us better to comprehend bishops' stake in the legal tradition of discernment. By fusing discernment with judgment and associating this singular ability with the power to absolve sinners, bishops claimed a unique position of authority over their rivals.

Christian Oaths:
A Case Study in Practicality over Doctrine

Calumny, failed leadership, and the prevalence of sin were reminders of an unchanging fact: uncertainty was endemic in human communities, Christian or otherwise. The swearing of oaths was one method of controlling uncertainty within society. All sorts of political, social, ethnic, and religious elements contributed to individual and group identities in Western communities during the late empire and after.[39] However, as we shall see in the case of the late fourth-century landowner Publicola, a Christian whose overseers accepted "demonic" oaths from his "barbarian" employees, these sorts of identities were of less consequence than the particular terms on which people formed relationships.[40] The political oaths that scholars have studied most, similar to the oaths clergy swore upon ordination, served to identify the relationship of those who swore allegiance with the state or institutional hierarchy to which they swore.[41] Examining other kinds of oaths, however, can move us beyond the ordered appearance of hierarchies and increase our analytical control over "the lability of the relations and trajectories" that the cultural historian Roger Chartier has said "define identities."[42] Within and outside of their immediate social circles, people made agreements and alliances that sometimes reinforced, sometimes contravened, and sometimes ignored political, social, ethnic, or religious boundaries.[43]

Oaths were more than simple instruments. The swearing of oaths established the terms of interaction, the language of community, and the limits of trust between individuals and between groups of people.[44] Oaths were malleable in ways that political, social, ethnic, or religious identities often were not: formulas, vocabulary, gestures, and names could be changed to fit the occasion, much the same as the legal tablets Elizabeth Meyer has studied so brilliantly.[45] In part because they were flexible, oaths occurred in almost every aspect of social conduct. A theologian like Augustine of Hippo, who spent almost half his long life as a bishop, involved with the mundane affairs of ordinary Christians, was unable to keep his theoretical position against oaths separate from the persistent demands of real society, where oaths were commonplace. Conveniently for the purposes of this study, oath-swearing was both a discrete and persistent source of aggravation for Augustine, with the result that he helped generate a considerable trail of evidence. At the same time, it was a problem with larger implications for the ways Christians should understand the workings of justice on heaven and earth, as the bishop of Hippo was well aware.

Augustine's complex opinions about Christian oath-swearing, traced closely over the span of two decades, reveal something unexpected: the indelible impression that commonplace expectations of justice made on a powerful intellect. This impression was the product of continuous negotiation conducted throughout an entire career between a bishop and his congregants over what measures for controlling uncertainty and securing trust were acceptable, given the limits of worldly justice. It was a subtle impression, of course, for Augustine never budged on what mattered most to him—his belief that justice existed only in Christ. Robert Dodaro observes that "Augustine's views on justice and society stem more from his analysis of the capacities and limits of the human soul than from his thinking about social and political structures."[46] He was a philosopher, in modern terms, not a political scientist. Yet, what we learn from studying Augustine on oaths is also what Augustine learned, that *thinking about* social and political structures was not the same as *living with* those structures and explaining their effect on everyday human life. Oath-swearing challenged Christian writers to explain their philosophy's relevance to the real world. In this case, theology, far from smothering social history, takes us deep into the risks of ordinary human interaction.[47]

Mercy Not Justice:
How Penance Became a Worthy Act of Self-Incrimination

Even when bishops gathered in council among the company of their colleagues in what we may consider a legislative environment, justice was a difficult affair. The records and decrees surviving from church councils that met throughout Western Europe and North Africa during Late Antiquity occasionally capture the noise of bishops at work. They envisioned themselves to be hammering out the principles of justice hot from the forge of pentecostal consensus—for bishops said the Holy Spirit was active in their assemblies. But in the midst of the very same councils, we also catch glimpses of justice sometimes failing and sometimes producing a mess—what they would have called a "scandal." This could be the case when bishops had to judge one of their own colleagues. At a council in Marseilles in 533, for example, the bishop of Riez, whose improbably apt name was Contumeliosus ("abusive"), threw himself at the feet of laypeople, an abbot, and fifteen of his fellow bishops, confessing to the unspecified but "many foul and disgraceful acts" for which he had been summoned. Along with financial reparations, his colleagues charged him to do penance in a monastery for his crimes.[48] Mercy was an important component of episcopal justice not least because bishops were among its common recipients.

Penance was the most subtle and perhaps successful means by which spiritual leaders negotiated the tensions between divine and worldly justice. First, penitents shared the burden of these tensions with their bishop by becoming judges in their own guilt or innocence. Second, the show of mercy did more than hint at a bishop's power to withhold that mercy should he deem fit. It also blurred the lines between guilt and innocence, and thus between certainty and uncertainty. Penance produced truth through painful interrogation, much the same as whips and scalpels were believed to work on criminals. Agony helped to crystallize essential truths out of the chill fog of doubt and deception. Yet, unlike the tortured subjects of ordinary judicial inquiry, when the suffering was over penitents found themselves refreshed and even reborn as heroes. The mercy of the church was a salve for the wounds that worldly justice so often inflicted and for the spirits torn and the expectations shattered in its hard, precise, uncompromising gears. Penance, moreover, provided an occasion to rise above human uncertainty, to momentarily transcend "the shared frailty of human flesh," in Peter Brown's words, and to glimpse the union of salvation and justice.[49]

Long ago in the third century, the bishop Cyprian of Carthage (d. 258) famously insisted, *salus extra ecclesiam non est*—that there existed no salvation and, by extension, no truth or justice outside the church.[50] A half century later another native of Africa, Lactantius (ca. 250–ca. 325)—rhetor, author, and tutor to a child of the first Christian emperor—was the first to claim outright that Christians owned justice. Lactantius drew on scripture as well as classical texts, especially Cicero's *De re publica*, as Augustine would a hundred years later, in order to make his argument that justice could not exist without Christian piety.[51] Later, between the fourth and sixth centuries, whether in Augustine's North Africa or Cassiodorus's Italy, theirs was hardly a widespread belief. Also remote but looming in the future were the ages of Carolingian, Lateran, and Protestant reform, when nostalgia for the Golden Age of early Christian devotion was matched only by contempt for the alleged apathy of lukewarm Christians in the three centuries following the conversion and rule of Constantine. Then and only then did certainty revive and boundaries resurface between ecclesiastical rigor and spiritual decline, between episcopal responsibility and personal liability, between public humiliation and private confession, between divine and worldly justice, and between expectation and practice. The discrepancy between ideology and reality remained, of course, to plague reformers and frustrate historians. What distinguishes this period is that some Christians had confronted that gap head on. Although their efforts to bridge divine and human justice ultimately failed, they incidentally exposed to examination a substratum of ordinary religious, social, and judicial expectations.

I

Calumny: Well-Known Reasons Why Justice Fails

CHRISTIANS EXPERIENCED JUSTICE the same as everyone else in the ancient and medieval worlds. For ordinary people, this meant that the laws that protected them could also cause them injury if the laws were manipulated by crafty people, perverted by corrupt officials, or bungled by inept judges. For administrators of justice, including lawmakers and judges in the church, the empire, and the successor kingdoms of Western Europe, this meant that traditional means of legal reform (usually the addition of new laws to the old) also contributed to the complexity of the law. By tracing the history of calumny and calumny reform through later Roman legislation and early medieval canon law, it is possible to see how Christian leaders came to terms with the limits of their own ability to offer security and the hope of justice to ordinary Christians.

Judicial Culture

As members of an elite culture that valued education in rhetoric and the law, many bishops during the fourth through the sixth centuries carried legal experience with them into office as a token, as one attribute among many, of their cultural background.[1] Priscus of Lyon (573–585/589), for example, served in the household of King Guntram before becoming a bishop. He was remembered in his epitaph as a man,

Progenie clarus felix generosus opimus
Mentis et arbitrio iustitiaque potens
Indulsit prudens mixto moderamine causis
Iurgia componens more sereniferi
Concomis et dignus regisque domesticus et sic
Promeruit summo mente placere Deo.

In descent, brilliant, fortunate, noble, rich;
With force of intellect in both judgment and justice,
He was indulgent in lawsuits, adept at tacking rudder,
Resolving quarrels with a settling manner;
He was his king's courteous and worthy servant, and so
He showed himself with utmost concern worthy of satisfying God.[2]

But alongside this elite culture, of which legal acumen or rhetorical polish might be an attribute, the law had a culture all its own. Within that culture, most working bishops soon would come to distinguish between an ideology centered on the triumph of justice and procedures intended to absorb the shock of its failure.

Historians have devoted much attention to late antique and early medieval bishops, meticulously mapping their careers and their interactions with other elites wherever possible, most notably in Gaul.[3] Others have focused their efforts differently: Claude Lepelley, for example, celebrated the rediscovery of the bishop as a "private person," a theme that runs through his and Claire Sotinel's edited volume *L'évêque dans la cité du IVe au Ve siècle: image et autorité*.[4] With experts drawing on prosopography, epigraphy, archaeology, cultural and legal anthropology, the sociology of elites, and textual criticism, the scholarship on bishops is rich and diverse, perhaps on the verge of sprawling. One persistent element in our understanding of bishops, however, deserves more critical attention: the new and improved bishops as a group, according to the scholarly literature, enjoyed virtual autonomy in crafting their image to fit the social, political, and religious terrain of the emerging postclassical world, even though as individuals they were less successful at crafting the terrain to their liking. That is, we can see that bishops during this period deliberately worked at defining what it meant to be a bishop, both for their own understanding and for laypeople's understanding. No doubt the payoff of their efforts in terms of the social or political clout they enjoyed was contingent on a range of circumstances. Indeed, the bishops who succeeded both in mastering their environment and in generating respect for their authority most famously did so, in the words of Neil McLynn, only by "hectic improvisation."[5]

Even this, though, assumes that bishops generally were in control of their professional faculties most of the time. In short, bishops appear to have controlled what it meant to be a bishop. What about when they were not in control? The American documentary filmmaker Errol Morris once told an interviewer from the *New Yorker* that he constructs all his films around "the idea that we're in a position of certainty, truth, [and] infallible

knowledge, when actually we're just a bunch of apes running around." Our approach to bishops and their professional conduct does not need to be as zoological as that. All the same, there is traction to be gained by setting our wheels down in the deep, well-worn ruts of administrative failure, for surely bishops learned as much through failure and disruption as through plan and design. We know the law sometimes failed bishops, just as it does everyone. By necessity, then, they learned to cope with both the failure and success of justice through the course of their professional and religious lives. Bishops' experience with the rules and procedures of secular law would determine the appearance of medieval canon law, the vocabulary of ecclesiastical administration, and even the formulation of heresy, as Caroline Humfress has shown.[6]

But the influence of endemic administrative and judicial failure went deeper than vocabulary, forms, and techniques. Legal culture—in particular formal devices such as rules of evidence and various testamentary oaths and judicial reform—introduced bishops to another, older, and less controllable culture: a culture of judicial uncertainty, where the possibility of failure and triumph hung more or less evenly in the balance. It became the responsibility of the church and its leaders to explain what difference they made to this balance. As we shall see in this chapter, doing so was an uphill battle. Outside the church, justice ruined innocent people. Groundless accusations, slander, forged or missing evidence, anonymous denunciations, procedural violations: these were the means by which malicious people worked the system to their advantage. Sometimes the law did not seem capable of delivering justice—certainly not to all people equally. "If the transgressor of the law be of the monied class, it is not likely that he pays the penalty of his wrongdoing," complained a Greek who had so detested the unfairness of Roman justice that he settled permanently among Attila's Huns, where the historian Priscus of Panium claimed to have found him in 449. If, on the other hand, the transgressor "should be poor and ignorant of how to handle the business," the man continued, "he endures the penalty according to the law—if he does not depart life before his trial. For the course of these cases is long protracted, and a great deal of money is expended on them. Probably the most grievous suffering of all is to obtain the rights of the law for pay. No one will even grant a court to a wronged man unless he lays aside some money for the judge and his attendants."[7] Priscus was quick to defend both the cost and pace of imperial justice; he claims to have done this so persuasively that the renegade even shed tears over the excellent design of Roman laws. Still, though the Greek conceded the good intent of the laws' designers, he suggested that good intentions did not translate necessarily into good practice. At this moment, an interruption required Priscus to abandon the conversation. The renegade did not join Priscus and his companions on their return to the empire, so he seems to have remained unpersuaded in the end.

Late Roman emperors in fact sustained a campaign against the abuses that had driven this citizen to live among the Huns, abuses they sometimes addressed collectively under the rubric calumny (*calumnia*). This was a technical term, meaning false accusation, but its usage in literary and legal sources, both secular and ecclesiastical, was often much broader and took in whatever might threaten the judicial system and foster uncertainty over its ability to deliver justice.[8] Emperors attacked malicious informers, corrupt judges, and inefficient bureaucrats all with equal fervor, if unequal punishments. In large part the campaign was rhetorical, part of what Jill Harries has called a general "culture of criticism" among late antique emperors and their legislators, which, we shall see, directly influenced the administration of justice within the Christian church as well. This campaign was a mode of imperial authority, and is by no means proof that justice actually had become more corrupt or emperors more honest.[9]

However, while we can appreciate the campaign against calumny as a facet of legal culture and as a rhetorical posture on the part of emperors and kings, it existed in neither a juridical nor a political vacuum.[10] The following points are well known to historians working with documentary evidence from the earlier empire; we should keep them in the front of our minds when turning to episcopal justice in the West, where the testimony of both papyrus and stone is sparse when it comes to the law. First of all, the legislation tapped a real problem in contemporary society. Indirect evidence that calumny caused popular anxiety is abundant, and direct evidence sporadic from throughout this period. Second, the mechanisms that rulers and their jurists put in place in order to prevent injustice sometimes actually discouraged people from seeking justice, repelling them either by its cumbersome procedures or by its severe sanctions. Most of those people could choose instead to use a limited but viable range of alternatives to imperial courts—arbitration, oath-swearing, magical devices, or violence, for example—and they did so readily. Third, the mechanisms for controlling false accusations in imperial courts even influenced some of these alternative sources of justice. In episcopal courts, for example, secular rules of evidence applied not only in the civil disputes bishops might arbitrate but also in purely religious affairs. Procedural regulations simultaneously defined and limited what bishops were able to do; thus they limited what laypeople could expect from episcopal justice.

Finally, the legal culture of the later empire—its forms, its mechanisms, and its professed concern for its own shortcomings—affected bishops from the late fourth century onward, at the same time that they found themselves unable to fulfill all the expectations of their followers. Even bishops gifted with the most brilliant minds for theological speculation, debate, and theorizing had little choice but to dirty their hands in the practice of justice. They were professionally obliged to deliver both salvation and justice to Christian men and women. So how, their followers asked, could the offer of salvation be fixed and certain while the promise of justice appeared to twist in the winds of calumny? Although no easy answers were forthcoming, we can follow the earnest attempts some bishops made at relieving the burden of uncertainty.

Juridical Solutions: Roman Law

The concept of calumny provided rulers with an inexhaustible opportunity to voice their concern over institutional corruption and the uncertainty that troubled their citizens. The threat of falsehood lurked in every relationship, every contract, and every trial. Wealthy people lost their property because of false accusations; the poor were oppressed or became slaves; and just people suffered from unjust accusations.[11] Meanwhile, legislators railed against calumny, virtually without rest.[12] The "culture of criticism," in Jill Harries' apt phrase, which supplied a context and vocabulary to late Roman calumny legislation, thrived on the uncertainty inherent in judicial process. Under the law, calumny covered false accusations as well as vexatious litigation—groundless lawsuits, that is, with little or no chance of succeeding, pursued in order to catch off guard, wear down, or simply perturb an opponent.

A Problem Categories Cannot Contain

In the Theodosian Code, which made its official debut in the Roman Senate on 25 December 438, accompanied by twenty-eight successive acclamations of the emperors as "destroyers of informers, destroyers of calumnies,"[13] rules pertaining to calumny cropped up in various legal categories. It is precisely this slippage that makes calumny an important historical subject, for it reveals a dilemma that sometimes confused the academic interests of jurists and exceeded the professional interests of judges. Nothing had changed a century later. Gallo-Roman legal experts in the late fifth century, probably bishops, compiled a collection of Roman laws for the Visigothic court, a collection commonly known as the "Breviary of Alaric." Their lengthy gloss (*interpretatio*) of a decree by Arcadius and Honorius from 398 was effectively a checklist of calumnious incidents that numerous late Roman decrees had addressed separately. Calumniators here included those who initiated cases on another's behalf without written permission, who renewed closed cases, who fraudulently claimed property on behalf of the government so that innocent people could not enjoy peace, and who made false accusations. What all these offenders shared in common was that they "dared to stir the minds of the emperors to wrath."[14] Once an imperial official detected calumny in a criminal case, he was immediately to terminate the case for good, lest the "innocence and security of another be terrorized."[15] When the calumny involved a false accusation in a criminal court, the accuser would be tried in a special proceeding; convicted calumniators suffered infamy and deportation.[16]

Beyond whatever deterrent effect these sanctions might have had, however, and except for the regular requirements related to filing accusations and presenting witnesses to support a legitimate case,[17] Roman legal experts had discovered few methods for preventing calumny. An edict of Valentinian and Valens in 368 referred to "the strongest provisions against calumnies" that already should have allayed any fear or uncertainty in the minds of their subjects. Nevertheless, the same emperors also found it opportune to proclaim, "Let the madness of defamatory suits (*furor famosorum libellorum*) perish, as we often have decreed (*saepe ut constituimus*)."[18] Generations later, at Constantinople in 533, the emperor Justinian declared the suppression of calumny to be one of an emperor's primary objectives. "The prince of Rome should stand victorious," declared Justinian—"conqueror of the Alamanni, Goths, Franks, Germans, Antes, Alans, Vandals, and Africans"—not only on the battlefield but also "by driving out the iniquities of calumniators through the conduits of the law."[19]

CALUMNY OATHS

The task of detecting calumnious intentions even before a trial began was beyond the capacity of ordinary judges, but it was well within the scope of divine justice. This was a fact long recognized not only by experts in supernatural devices such as curse tablets, as we shall see later, but also by lawmakers.[20] The oath of calumny (*jusjurandum calumniae*), like oaths generally, exploited the religious force inherent within Roman law in order to bring the threat of divine revenge to bear on the perjurer. It was one of the earliest means of preventing false accusations and vexatious litigation. The oath appeared in civil proceedings during the Roman Republic, first in criminal law, then in private cases; it was included in title nine (*De calumniatoribus*) of the Perpetual Edict, which the jurist Salvius Julianus codified for Emperor Hadrian around 130; and the calumny oath became the subject of subsequent juristic commentary, as did calumny itself.[21] In criminal cases, an accuser was required to swear an oath to the effect that he believed his charge to be true (*non calumniae causa agere*). A defendant could also be a calumniator—for example, someone who knew he had no case but proceeded in the hope that some fortuitous miscarriage of justice would work in his favor. In private cases, therefore, the defendant also might be required to swear that his case was legitimate (*non calumniae causa infitias ire*).[22] The *jusjurandum calumniae* appears gradually to have displaced or absorbed most other means of preventing calumny. The Perpetual Edict, already mentioned, required the calumny oath in a variety of circumstances beyond the scope of regular judicial procedures, in situations where a person needed to demonstrate that he had no malice aforethought. Someone seeking to insure his own property against potential damage from a derelict building on adjoining property (*cautio damni infecti*), for example, had to swear a calumny oath.[23] So did someone demanding that a banker produce his accounting records, "lest perhaps [the plaintiff] should demand either unnecessary accounts or ones which he [already] has [in his possession], for the purpose of harassing (*vexandi causa*) the banker."[24] The legal campaign against calumny moved on multiple fronts, within and outside the courts, and the *jusjurandum calumniae* traced a commensurate path through classical and postclassical law.

The calumny oath endured into the sixth century (and indeed, long after), when it was subject to further modification and new applications.[25] In 529, Justinian required that a *juramentum de calumnia* precede the admission of any and every piece of evidence requested by either party in the course of a trial, because "the contentious activity of litigants is restrained by fear of the oath."[26] Jurists almost immediately recognized the insurmountable disruptions this requirement might cause, and so they tried to limit trial evidence to the essential items that both parties agreed to be necessary to their case.[27] Two years later, in 531, the emperor required both parties to swear calumny oaths in all lawsuits. The advocates for both parties also swore, upon the Gospels; no judge was allowed to conduct hearings without the presence of the Holy Scripture in the room.[28] Finally, in 534, Justinian filled in the details: what to do in the case of women and people whose rank did not allow them to appear in court, in the case of minors and their guardians, in the case of people who had a third party conduct a case on their behalf, and in the case of plaintiffs or defendants who refused to take the oath (plaintiffs forfeited their case, defendants effectively confessed to everything alleged against them).[29]

Justinian's calumny reforms were not dramatically innovative. More than anything else, they placed a high value on judicial clarity, which late antique emperors had venerated as well. Justinian formulated his "clear and comprehensive constitution" in order to displace "the ancient oath of calumny, together with all its subterfuges." By preventing calumny through the regular administration of the *jusjurandum calumniae*, the emperor aspired to create a world in which citizens would "think that they are in sanctuaries rather than in courts of justice."[30]

THE COSTS AND PERILS OF JUSTICE

It is doubtful that anyone in Late Antiquity ever mistook a courtroom for a sanctuary, although a person might reasonably have mistaken some sanctuaries for law courts. Public trials were cultural events of high entertainment value, capable of evoking elements of sacred ritual.[31] The trial, however, was only one stage in the judicial process. Even when it worked smoothly, imperial justice could be slow.[32] Distance between judges and contestants required time for travel, resulting in trials that might last up to four months and much longer in the case of appeals. Every stage of the process involved paperwork, which required legal expertise. Although there were usually fees to be paid along the way and, in addition, advocates charged for their services, the costs were not beyond the means of people with at least modest resources. However, public justice also required social currency: litigants could draw on favors and influence if they had the right connections, or else they could try to create new lines of patronage. As for people who lacked access to cash and clout, public justice "could be," in

Jill Harries' words, "an expensive, unpredictable, perhaps risky and often futile indulgence."[33]

When Justinian tried to cleanse the judicial system of calumny, he faced the same odds as the emperors before him, and he enjoyed as little success.[34] One major obstacle to all legislative solutions to calumny was that each additional edict pitched at reform contributed another layer to the complexity of the law, what Justinian derided as its "subterfuges," and in turn created new opportunities for savvy calumniators to edge out innocent contestants for advantage within the law. Justinian and his jurists were not the first to recognize the dilemma. In the opinion of Nazarius, a panegyrist in the reign of Constantine, laws themselves became "mazes that produce calumny (*calumniosae ambages*)."[35] That ambiguity was also behind Theodosius II's initiation of the great organization project that produced the Theodosian Code a century later.[36] Until then, according to Theodosius and his legal staff, even the experts despaired of successfully winding their way through the maze of imperial constitutions, "submerged in thick clouds of obscurity."[37]

Emperors and their legal experts were sensitive to the unpleasant fact that knowledgeable calumniators could turn their laws upside down, even using imperial prohibitions of calumnious activities as helpful indices to just what maneuvers were possible within the shadows of justice. Calumniators conspired to co-opt even the calumny oath for their own devices, or so Justinian believed.[38] The paradox touched on the conflicted relationship between princes and the law more generally. As the orator Themistius put it to Theodosius I the Great, an emperor was at one and the same time "the animate law" and a "refuge" from its severity.[39] He revealed himself to be the living law whenever he issued a rescript or edict; he proved himself to be a refuge from law's severity whenever he exercised clemency. It was a simple matter to show mercy toward the guilty, toward those whom the machinery of justice had captured; emperors forgave convicted criminals on an almost regular basis. It was more difficult to provide refuge for the innocent who were the potential victims of justice and the ones who most deserved a refuge. Without diligent and accurate administration, the rules of process might injure the people they were meant to protect. Calumny, therefore, amplified the dissonance between the promise of justice and the reality of its execution, dissonance which Roman emperors and their jurists decried. It revealed the terrible gap that loomed between theory and practice, a gap both secular and ecclesiastical rulers endeavored to fill with laws, procedures, and sanctions.

Popular Responses

In most places, at most times, throughout the ancient and medieval worlds, people could try to protect themselves from calumny through means just as venerable, less costly, far more accessible, quicker, and much more final than public courts, imperial officials, and the calumny oath. They had good reason to do so, for while emperors encouraged officials and citizens alike to be on the lookout for connivers, cheats, and false accusers and, indeed, to bring accusations against such people themselves, everyone was on some level aware of a larger, more shadowy culture—a popular culture of judicial uncertainty. Imperial tirades against calumny would have found little resonance and no political purchase without this popular culture. It was much older and involved many more people than any legal rhetoric that emperors and jurists could contrive. As we have seen, the law might have inadvertently provided calumniators with a sort of navigational chart to help them steer through the "subterfuges" and "ambiguities" of the judicial system and reach their illicit landfalls. Other sorts of tools also helped chart judicial uncertainty, whether one's goal was to calumniate against others or to defend oneself against calumniators.

ORACLES AND CURSES:
INSURANCE AGAINST INJUSTICE

We find both goals reflected in oracle texts (*sortes*) that provided advice to inquirers willing to roll the dice.[40] The most famous of these texts, the *Sortes Astrampsychi*, emanated from Egypt around the third century, but similar texts appeared elsewhere. One of these is the *Sortes Sangallensis*, a collection of oracles preserved in a manuscript produced in Merovingian Gaul during the sixth or seventh century. What makes the St. Gall collection so exciting is that it well may be a direct reworking of the third-century collection, far removed in time and space from its archetype.[41] William Klingshirn has traced a similar complex of translation and adaptation between non-Christian and Christian, Greek and Latin oracular responses in his study of the *Sortes Sanctorum*.[42] Although the oracular source (Christian, non-Christian, or unidentified) and the particular language in which secret knowledge was conveyed changed according to time and place, what was on the minds of people who sought such knowledge was remarkably consistent; they were searching for reassurance in the face of uncertainty. For example, in the Merovingian *Sortes Sangallensis*, advice on property issues and legal procedures of various forms and at various stages looms large, affording us a rare glimpse of accusers contemplating action. Questions regarding calumny elicited frank responses: "Sure you deserve it, but there is no calumny against you: you are safe." "You are under suspicion. Do not calumniate now; do something else." "You are a nuisance to yourself. Do not calumniate against anyone."[43] Sometimes the oracle left the matter up to God; once it promised immediate intervention: "Have no fear. God will avert your misfortunes and the calumny you endure."[44] Everywhere in the oracle texts lurks the fear of what others are thinking. Is a friend loyal or giving false testimony behind one's back? Is a business alliance reliable or a swindle? When should one accept a pledge? How far should one distance one's own true intentions from a promise? "Why do you trick people? You cannot trick God with your deceit."[45]

However simple the anxieties reflected in such collections may be, they demonstrate an undeniable continuity between Greco-Roman communities and their Christianized successors. Perhaps adherents to the new faith could leave the old anxieties behind on occasion, while on pilgrimage, for example, when Christians were more likely to contemplate the biblical past than "to cast a suspicious gaze into the future and detect hidden vice."[46] Yet, at home some healthy suspicion was prudent, for Christians as for anyone else. Devices like the oracle texts made it possible for them to gaze into the future to protect their own interests.

Advocates and jurists were far from being the only experts in the law. One of the most common types of curse tablets (*defixiones*) extant from Greek and Roman antiquity is the judicial curse.[47] Although their appearance and formulas varied over the centuries and across different regions, most judicial curses emanated from a set of similar circumstances. A person anticipating a trial engaged a professional to inscribe the names of the opposing party on a scrap of lead or other material, occasionally including a description of the matter in dispute. This curse, usually rolled and sometimes pierced or fixed with a nail, then would be deposited in a place with some supernatural significance—a grave, a temple, a well. The texts of many surviving tablets include the targets' names and little else, but the rolling of the tablet and even the direction of the spelling or script (either backwards or retrograde) probably symbolized the desired result: mental confusion. In numerous *defixiones* from the classical period, people asked that the thoughts of their opponents (and sometimes those of their opponents' accomplices, witnesses, advocates, and anyone else who might be involved in the trial) be scattered or their tongues frozen so that they would be physically inhibited from presenting their cases effectively.[48]

The pressure of judicial uncertainty on litigants was perhaps most intense in the interval between the filing of an inscription and the day of the actual trial, the same time when we find them contracting for the help of experts in supernatural justice.[49] A cache of tablets from Cyprus, for example, includes a number of curses from between the late second and mid-third centuries; remarkably, they were inscribed by a single hand. One of them invoked the *daimones* to "bind and put to sleep the tongue, the passion and the anger [my opponent Aristôn] holds toward me, Sotêrianos also called Limbaros, lest he oppose me in any [legal] matter (*pragma*)."[50] Another tablet, perhaps from the fourth century, named only the client's opponents "in the matter concerning the slaves and concerning the personal property and concerning the papers and concerning the things of which they might accuse me."[51] It was prudent to be both specific and exhaustive: this litigant identified not only the subject of the upcoming trial (a dispute over slaves), but also the documents (*grammata*) which his accusers would use against him. He also anticipated the possibility that other allegations might arise in the course of the trial and sought to prevent these as well.

Curses cast by people whom public justice had left in the lurch survive among more than a hundred tablets discovered at the spring of Sulis Minerva in Bath and dating from the imperial period. Usually, the people behind these curses were victims of theft. They had no witnesses to summon, no known opponents to prosecute, and no way other than the supernatural to recover their possessions; many of them might have belonged to the lower social orders.[52] In short, these were the people public courts could not serve because they lacked both cash and clout. Such people used magic, not to increase their odds of obtaining justice in the courts, but instead of the courts, and in order to achieve unambiguous closure. "The one who has stolen my bronze bowl is accursed," reads one curse. "May the man who did this pour his own blood into the very bowl."[53]

"If God Is for Us Who Is Against Us?"

Christians had the same reasons as anyone else for using supplementary measures to improve their odds in public courts or for evading those dodgy odds altogether. There were other factors, of course. Some, for example, might have taken to heart Paul's injunction against seeking judgment outside of the religious community: "If any of you has a dispute with another, dare he take it before the ungodly for judgment instead of before the saints?" (1 Cor 6:1; also Mt 18:15–17).[54] This might well have convinced some early Christians to turn to their bishops as mediators rather than to governors and their subordinates, the established sources of public justice. Even so, by the end of the fourth century, in a Christian empire, the immediate relevance of Paul's prohibition had changed dramatically. The judges were no longer ungodly, or at least they were likely to be Christians; at the same time, Christians and non-Christians shared similar reasons for suspecting worldly justice. Inscribed on the lintel of a home in Tigzirt in modern Algeria was a commonplace invocation against covetous guests: "Envy, live, look: so you can see better things." The goal of this sort of inscription was to prevent an injurious thought from even entering the mind of a present friend, who might well become an enemy in the future. Here, however, the engraver had joined the old-fashioned mantra with words from the apostle Paul: "If God is for us who is against us?" (Romans 8:31). Furthermore, in this liminal inscription, a chrism was carved between the adjoined phrases, so that a symbol of Christ could serve the apotropaic function a phallus more commonly accomplished.[55] The apostle Paul's confidence in divine justice sounded with crystal clarity against the uncertainty of daily life, the same uncertainty that troubled followers of Christianity and more ancient religions alike.

Christian leaders shared the concerns as well as the remedies of ordinary people. When a barrage of hideous accusations ranging from fornication to homicide threatened his reputation, even the bishop of Rome covered his bases. Thus Damasus (366–84) composed an inscription for the basilica of Saint Felix of Nola. It was a votive offering for the church's namesake, who was a reputed expert in matters of uncertainty. The saint's intervention had relieved Damasus from an illness and helped "the purgation of a false accusation (*purgatione falsi criminis*)" he had faced in a secular court.[56] The shrine of Saint Felix endured for generations as a prime location for defeating calumny. Augustine of Hippo sent two of his clergy there from North Africa around 402 in order to test the accusations one had made against the other. As was the case with Damasus, fornication was the charge, so there were no witnesses to the alleged, secret acts. The saints might not monitor the sex lives of the clergy, either, but they were believed to be able to catch out perjurers who dared to deny the truth in the presence of their relics. We do not know whether either of Augustine's clerics failed to pass the test.[57]

Once their success was demonstrated, instruments for defending against uncertainty were slow to disappear, whether they were spells, curses, or prayers to saints for intervention. Ordinary people and elites, Christians and non-Christians: most people worked the system to their greatest advantage, whether rapaciously at the expense of others or defensively in order to protect themselves. Whenever possible, they changed venues, sought appeals, curried influence and patronage, avoided fines or sanctions, and invoked the supernatural. On that count, Christianity did not change the nature of justice and the way it worked, or failed to work, on the ground.[58] Rather, the experience of justice, along with its failings and its alternatives, made a great impact on Christianity, as we shall now see.

The Bishop's Court

As spiritual leaders, bishops tested allegations of sin within their congregations; as administrators, they investigated cases of misconduct among their clergy; as arbiters or mediators, they heard disputes between parties who preferred to avoid secular courts.[59] It is this last activity, the episcopal hearing (*audientia episcopalis*), that has attracted the most attention from scholars interested in bishops and justice.[60]

Given the subterfuges and ambiguities in the law, and the potential costs of public justice in time, cash, and social currency, people had good reason at least to research their alternatives. Religious leaders had acted as judges in spiritual matters and mediators in private conflicts within Christian communities from the beginning. In the later empire, their function gained a new sort of legitimacy (as also in contemporary Jewish communities) when citizens were permitted to submit disputes to a bishop for a settlement that was binding in secular law and did not allow subsequent appeal to secular officials.[61] The evidence indicates some problems of jurisdiction and enforcement that arose from pursuing justice in episcopal courts, but the same evidence is far too lacunary for us to establish what the norm was, if there ever was one. More importantly, we are unable to tell whether people who sought out a bishop's arbitration were satisfied or felt better served than they would have felt in an imperial court or with a different arbiter. However, these apparent shortcomings in the documentation may not be purely accidental.

It is important to remember that the *audientia episcopalis* was a legal conceit, a way for emperors and jurists to integrate judicial activities of bishops into the imperial system. Behind the conceit lay an avenue of justice that played an important part in Christian society before, during, and after the official conversion of the empire. The closest thing we have to enabling decrees for the *audientia episcopalis* are laws from Constantine's regime, but they are textually problematic.[62] Although there has been extensive debate over these sources, it appears clear, at least, that the emperor expanded episcopal jurisdiction beyond what it had been, although how far beyond and whether he did so "brashly" remains open to argument.[63] In a 333 edict addressed to Ablabius, the pretorian prefect of the East, Constantine allowed bishops a degree of judicial authority so anomalous by comparison with all other late antique legislation that some scholars have been understandably skeptical of its authenticity, and otherwise rightly dubious of its relevance to contemporary reality. According to its terms, and contrary to normal requirements in arbitration proceedings, one party could transfer a case to the bishop's court without the other's agreement (*compromissum*). This edict also required public judges to accept a bishop's testimony in ordinary proceedings as gospel truth, even when that testimony was uncorroborated. According to the edict, their religious authority (*sacrosanctae religionis auctoritas*) enabled bishops to uncover details in a trial that could never emerge in secular courts, where these essential facts were caught up in technicalities and fast talk (*captiosa praescriptionis vincula*).[64] Constantine pushed the limits of what could be asked both of bishops and of public officials, who were obligated to cooperate with these newcomers to the judicial system. The edict of 333 would have read much differently, no doubt, had Ablabius not been a Christian himself, "replete with justice and the approved religion."[65]

As Olivier Huck has argued, the success of this edict's provisions would have meant a tidal wave of casework for bishops.[66] We should recognize nonetheless that from a juridical perspective this edict could fit sensibly within a rational, familiar legal program: bishops' courts were another component in an imperial campaign against calumny, another mechanism for "crushing out the mischievous seeds of litigation," in the language of the edict to Ablabius, and therefore another device which was bound to fail. Constantine expanded episcopal authority and introduced it into the course of public justice in order to free "wretched" citizens from the "long and seemingly eternal snares of lawsuits." Confident in the capacities of religious leaders, or at least in the value of providing a more expedient alternative (*maturo fine*) to the public courts, the emperor aspired to free his subjects from "vile petitions and perverted greed."[67] As a legislative solution, however, like any other legislative solution we have discussed here, the *audientia episcopalis* added to the complexities of both the law and the judicial system. In a lengthy edict on the subject in 452, Valentinian III observed that the *audientia episcopalis* was raising complaints from a number of quarters. He spelled out the conditions under which a bishop could judge a case—basically, only when both parties, cleric or lay, filed a *compromissum*, or mutual agreement, to accept the bishop's decision. The terms of the edict suggest that either bishops had been overstepping their jurisdiction or litigants had been taking advantage of bishops.[68] From the time of Constantine to that of Valentinian, the *audientia episcopalis* was a bugbear for emperors, jurists, and judges alike.

The reality was quite distinct from the letter of the law, although that does not mean that theory and practice were always in contradiction with each other. Bishops from Constantine's day onward were increasingly and deeply involved in popular expectations of justice. As with calumny and imperial law, however, neither the courtroom nor the legislation was where most people grappled with judicial uncertainty, nor were they the places where expectations of justice were shaped. What may be the most important fact to keep in mind with regard to episcopal courts is that they were only one component of the modest array of judicial options available to people. That array of options existed not simply because any single option might be deficient, but because judicial uncertainty arose in a wide range of contexts. No one solution or device could protect individuals from every threat to their legal security. Bishops here become particularly important for gauging the real extent of uncertainty in daily life. This was not because they offered the best source of legal security, but because, along with legal security, they also attempted to provide spiritual and social security.

Well aware of both their predicament and the opportunity it presented for distinguishing themselves from ordinary judges and administrators, bishops crafted their professional image around the claim to practice justice on a plane entirely removed from this realm of uncertainty. In the phrase of the *Didascalia*, an older collection of allegedly apostolic precepts reworked and translated in the 370s, bishops might "judge like God." We shall return to that text and to bishops' judicial image in the next chapter. Now, however, we must move on to consider what impact judicial uncertainty made on the church's laws. What we shall discover is that the concept of calumny did not only occupy ecclesiastical legislators as it had imperial jurists and lawmakers. Calumny also became a way for leaders of the church to vent their own anxieties, both professional and personal, and to demand protection from threats they perceived against themselves, their church, and their faith. Bishops treated calumny as a legal problem but also as a broader, social problem. Just as homeowners had carved the apostle's words on their doorframes to protect them from covetous neighbors, so clergy used familiar legal devices to stave off attacks on their authority.

Juridical Solutions: Canon Law

The prevention of calumny was as central a component of episcopal authority as it was of imperial authority, and its legislative record in the church was similarly thick. The bishops who gathered together at Elvira around 306, in the earliest council whose proceedings survive, were already experienced in dealing with accusations. Their severest sanctions punished accusations against clergy, while Christians who accused other Christians in imperial courts faced perpetual excommunication for accusations of capital crimes and five-year excommunication for accusations of lesser crimes, even if the accusations were valid. At this point, five or six years before the Edict of Toleration, also known as the Edict of Milan from 312, the bishops' concern was not only to prevent calumny but to keep Christian affairs inside the church and out of public courts, where their religion was still illegal.[69] In 314, bishops at Arles prescribed excommunication until death for clergy who falsely accused other clergy. Christians who denounced others for betraying the faith during the persecutions were required to produce documentation from the public records, not merely rumor and allegations (*verbis nudis*).[70]

Canons from church councils, many of which were convened in order to hear complaints or accusations against bishops, addressed the problem of testing the grievances of laypeople against clergy in private cases over property or legacies.[71] To prevent spurious accusations, bishops at Carthage in 390 prohibited any person who was implicated in misdeeds (*sceleribus irretitus*) from making accusations.[72] Another council at Carthage in 419 prohibited a more extensive list of people from accusing clergy: excommunicates; slaves or freedmen of the accused; persons who were legally infamous including actors; heretics and pagans (*pagani*); and Jews. A cleric who could disprove just one of the accusations brought against him by an individual would be cleared of all of the same accuser's remaining allegations.[73] Many of these restrictions were read into the proceedings of the last council in Roman North Africa, on 24 September 427, at Augustine's city of Hippo.[74]

The 419 council of Carthage had lasting importance for defining regular procedure in the case of clerical accusations. Twenty-three years later in Gaul, bishops dealing with accusations between bishops tried to steer clear of the messy scandal that such internal affairs could produce should they become public. The members of the council at Vaison in 442 described a situation in which one bishop was privy to the misbehavior of a colleague but lacked the evidence to make an accusation. According to this canon, he should first urge the culprit toward remorse by "wearing him down with private rebukes" (*secretis correptionibus elaboret*). If matters degenerated and the offensive bishop continued to share in public communion, even though there still was no proof (*probationibus deficiat*), his fellow bishops would require his "withdrawal for a time" (*secedere ad tempus*), in deference to the authority of his accuser. The authors of this canon tried, without violating the rule of law, to establish a mechanism for defusing conflicts that were aggravated by competing claims to justice and authority by rival bishops. The accused and the accuser were to avoid each other—that is, not share communion—but the accused remained otherwise unaffected, so long as no proof against him emerged.[75] Even when proof was forthcoming and led to either a voluntary confession or a formal conviction, bishops endeavored to contain the potential fallout by imposing penance on their colleague, as we shall see in the final chapter of this book.

Subsequent councils repeated and elaborated on the calumny legislation. A fifth-century compilation of canons included, from the first council of Arles in 314, the penalty of exclusion from communion until the point of death for people who made false accusations leading to capital punishment.[76] In Gaul, the 465 council of Vannes treated false witnesses in the same category with murderers.[77] At Agde in 506, clergy were forbidden to initiate cases in secular courts without their bishop's permission. They could respond in court, however, if they were charged (*pulsatus*). Any layperson, meanwhile, who tried *per calumniam* to hassle (*fatigare*) the church or any one of its officials but lost his case would "be shut out of the church and catholic communion unless he should do a worthy penance."[78] Bishops at Orléans in 549 tried to avoid "vexation and lawsuits" for the church (*quibuslibet modis molestiam aut calumniam patiatur ecclesia*) by insisting that slaves who sought its asylum be returned to their owner, provided the owner would swear an oath not to injure them subsequently.[79] At Clichy in 626/27, bishops again prohibited slaves from making accusations and rejected accusations from anyone whose accusations had failed in the past.[80] The council at Clichy also excommunicated secular officials who tried clergy without their bishop's permission, or subjected them to calumnious or unjust law-suits (*calumniis vel injuriis*).[81] So here we see church officials suffering more than three hundred years of anxiety over specious litigation and false accu-sations, from before the conversion of the first Christian emperor to long after the last Western emperor was deposed.

Calumny Beyond the Boundaries of Audience Chambers

The threat of calumny and the abuse of justice were as difficult for church officials as for emperors and jurists to control and contain. Despite legal safeguards against calumny, the later empire anticipated the failure of its own systems by inviting vigilance on the part of its administrators and subjects. This climate of suspicion and watchfulness reached deep into the church where—as legislators, arbiters, and pastors—bishops focused their attention and their capacities on the "craftiness of calumniators" (*versutiae calumniatorum*).[82] On all of these fronts—legal, social, and spiritual—the same contingencies and procedures constraining imperial lawmakers and judges also limited the ability of bishops to dispel uncertainty. The implica-tions of this uncertainty reached beyond the courtroom, especially for bish-ops, whose responsibilities exceeded the absolute boundaries of the law.

In Christian communities where the church was likely to hold sub-stantial property and moveable wealth, where most clerical and religious members probably had social, economic, and familial ties with lay society, where business took place in the courtyards in front of churches and where, as we shall see in the final chapter, Christian oaths sealed contracts of all varieties, many cases that found their way into bishops' courts were con-nected in some way to the church, but that did not mean that they were religious disputes.[83] Nor did church affairs, however litigious, spare religious leaders face-to-face encounters with the failure of worldly justice. Bishops at Vaison in 442 crafted a lengthy canon describing the church's role in establishing custody over abandoned children. The "collectors"—that is, whoever discovered such children and would be willing to support them—were to notify their pastor. He was then to make a public announcement and allow ten days for any surviving relatives or guardians to come for-ward. It was not the charity of the church that made clerical intervention appropriate in these adoption proceedings. What the churchman supplied was public notice, so that the fear of a lawsuit might not frighten away potential guardians.

This was necessary because the threat of calumniators had intimidated anyone from taking in foundlings and, as a result, wild dogs were devouring children who might otherwise have enjoyed the kindness of strangers.[84] It is worth contemplating the possibility that alleged calumniators who claimed foundling children as their own might have been telling the truth and, in that case, making a perfectly reasonable legal claim by demanding the return of their legitimate wards. One person's legal claim was another person's calumny: this is precisely the ambiguity—or perhaps relativism— that made calumny not only a juridical but also a social problem. The bishops assembled in Vaison, members of a profession accustomed to protecting its members from accusations and litigation, sympathized with the guardians and despised those who would threaten them. The council considered any persons who launched lawsuits against people taking responsibility for abandoned children after the ten-day waiting period to be calumniators and treated them with the same contempt and sanctions as if they were homicides.[85]

Eighty years after bishops at Vaison tried to rescue orphaned children from lonely, gruesome deaths, bishops at the council of Clichy (626–27) confronted the problem of slavery—not as an institution, but as an unjust misfortune that befell some freeborn and freed persons. They treated those who stripped others of their rightful freedom as calumniators.[86] Once again, it was possible for a legitimate claim to property (for slavery was not illegal in the eyes of Frankish kings or the church) to be treated as a calumnious action. A calumnious action, moreover, was more than a legal trespass. This was a religious society, after all, where God's own primordial enemy was the devil, the "grand calumniator." People—especially those hit by lawsuits, which would include members of the church—believed that calumny, at its core, was antisocial in a real, dangerous, and completely uncompromising way. Calumny, such persons seemed to claim, jeopardized the basic human relationships on which the existence of society relied.

Social Bonds and Boundaries

Not very long after he had become bishop of Hippo in 395, Augustine wrote that "in each and every religion, true or false, people can cohere to one another (*coagulari*) only if they are bound together by some union (*consortium*) of visible signs or sacraments."[87] The sacraments of the church were its binding rituals; the liturgical calendar insulated participants and marked

the outsiders. One January, people in the streets of Carthage enjoyed the
feast of Kalends, a celebration of the new year and the appointment of the
consuls. For several days, the festivities continued outside the ecclesiastical complex, as patrons and clients exchanged gifts and staged lavish ban-
quets.[88] Augustine, meanwhile, delivering a guest sermon, commended
those inside the basilica for their resolve. The strength of their community
provided warmth against the perverse fires beyond, fanned by blustery
winds and threatening to consume Christian hearts.[89] The "perverse solemnity" of the outside hardened the strong core of pious life within the community. Augustine would not begrudge his congregation their grief when
a popular young man died before receiving baptism; nevertheless, the youth
could not be buried near the altar, the nexus where the sacraments brought
living Christians closest to divine justice.[90] The bonds of community were
also its boundaries: those who chose not to participate or had been excluded from Christian society were like buoys, easy for good believers to
spot, floating on the surface of the deep waters of ignorance, animosity,
and alienation that surrounded the catholic community.

CAUGHT BETWEEN POPULAR PRESSURE AND DUE PROCESS

However, during the course of Augustine's episcopate and by the time of
his death in 430, that assurance vanished, nowhere more dramatically than
in North Africa, where waves of former Donatists entered catholic congregations at Hippo and, we may suppose, in other cities. The result was
an epidemic of uncertainty and, along with it, a large-scale procedural problem for bishops and their courts.[91] Augustine constantly used the story of
Noah's ark as a plea for toleration and endurance among his followers:
"There were both pure and impure animals there; thus good and bad people engage in the sacraments of the church."[92] He assured them that an un-
worthy infiltrator who tried to siphon the liquid energy of the sacraments
would ingest deadly poison instead of clean fuel.[93] Such a person could
make all the right moves—sign himself, kneel, pray; these were only the
"false signs of a living man: he is dead."[94] God, the great "retributor," would
not hesitate on any of the counts where the bishop was constrained, because God did not require a witness to know someone's deeds.[95]

Due process, however, restricted Augustine and the members of his
community. Good Christians might be standing next to a greedy land-
grabber or a known thief: "Let him carry his burden, you your own."[96]

Sometimes, more scandal might come from confronting such a person than avoiding conflict, and a bishop might discourage a trial "out of necessity for peace." The fact was that some people "are known to be bad, and cannot be convicted. To be emended and degraded, to be excluded, to be excommunicated—they cannot be convicted."[97] And even though bishops like Augustine stressed the medicinal, remedial purpose of excommunication— a tool for healing rather than condemning—their hands were still tied, unless an offender had "willingly (*sponte*) confessed, or been named and convicted by either a secular or an ecclesiastical trial."[98] All the usual forms of compelling evidence were necessary for a conviction, and without a conviction the bishop could not excommunicate. Thus bishops at the 419 council of Carthage agreed to shun any of their colleagues who excommunicated a person on the basis of an alleged private confession, if the subject denied the confession. In that case, the demand for incontrovertible evidence trumped the word of a bishop even among his fellow bishops: "It is more important that the bishop be wary of saying something against someone that he cannot prosecute with other documents."[99]

Rumor was not enough. There had to be a trial, there had to be evidence, and there had to be a proper accusation from an actual accuser. A bishop had to resist the influence of scandalous gossip and personal vendettas within his congregation and his court. Allegedly a reluctant judge,[100] Augustine was acutely concerned with the problems due process created for the administration of justice. He acknowledged that manifest offenders should be disciplined. But discipline was serious and demanded precision, and precision meant proof. "By all means," Augustine advised, "if you are a judge, if you take on the power of judging according to the ecclesiastical rules, if there is an accusation before you, if there is a conviction with valid documents and witnesses, then use force, go to trial, excommunicate, degrade. This is how endurance is vigilant, so that discipline does not sleep (*sic vigilet tolerantia, ut non dormiat disciplina*)."[101] The requisite criteria of proof for conviction in an ecclesiastical hearing were no more or less rigorous than those demanded in a tribunal.

As spiritual advisors, religious leaders, and mediators, bishops frequently got caught in uncomfortable positions, pressed between popular anxiety over judicial uncertainty and the practical limits of justice. What mattered most to people involved in any judicial process was the ruling and whether or not it was enforced. Bishops faced limits to their authority on multiple fronts, and it was impossible for their followers not to notice when they left justice to all appearances unserved. They rendered judgments and

passed sentences ranging from rebukes to monetary fines to recommenda-
tions for corporal punishment.[102] Ultimately, however, the only means of
coercion officially at their disposal was excommunication—a powerful sanction to be sure, which threatened offenders with not only alienation but a
horrible curse, whose threat Christian preachers would wield for centuries
to come. Thus in 1622, at a London mansion called Sion, John Donne tried
to convey the trauma of spiritual alienation to a group of nobles: "That
that God, who, when he could not get into me, by standing, and knocking,
by his ordinary meanes of entring, by his Word, his mercies, hath applied
his judgements, and hath shaked the house, this body, with agues and
palsies, and set this house on fire, with fevers and calentures, and frighted
the Master of the house, my soule, with horrors, and heavy apprehensions,
and so made an entrance into me . . . what torment is not a marriage bed to
this damnation, to be secluded eternally, eternally, eternally from the sight
of God?"[103] What we notice most is that the sense of damnation Donne
evokes in fact finds little echo in our period. Even exile and alienation need
historical context if we are to understand what they meant in Augustine's
age, and we shall return to these subjects in the final chapter. Nevertheless,
the procedures restricting the use of ecclesiastical sanction, even when bishops knew it was warranted, and the simple fact that excommunication did
not always work, suggested limits to episcopal authority and consequently
for episcopal justice. [104]

THE LIMITS OF COERCION

Sometimes bishops needed help.[105] Unlike imperial sanctions, excommunication was medicinal. In the realm of law, the sort of soft authority a bishop
worked with was limited at best: he had no recourse "except the glory of
forgiving."[106] Emperors who occasionally lavished their subjects with the
same compassionate glory—their *clementia*, the "privilege of imperial *phil-
anthrôpia*"[107]—were represented on the ground by administrators with more
forceful means of persuasion at their disposal. Force backed justice, not only
against criminals, but against judicial abuse and sometimes in support of
bishops. Like bishops, for example, municipal defenders (*defensores civita-
tum*) were responsible for protecting defenseless groups (children, women,
and the poor) against exploitation, not least by the government.[108] Writing in 420 to his friend Alypius, the bishop of Thagaste and an envoy of
the African church to the imperial court at Ravenna, Augustine smoothly

shifted topics from the lack of men suitable for the clergy to the lack of secular officials protecting weak citizens.[109] Augustine wanted more municipal defenders with a mandate to defend the less fortunate against the more fortunate. Although *defensores* and other imperial officials might have seemed in short supply to a bishop, even relative to his own inadequate staff, a representative of the imperial government may have at least represented physical force, even if he had none at his disposal. The surviving legislation did not describe any retinue, armed or otherwise, for the municipal defenders and it explicitly forbade them from one form of violence—judicial torture; however, one edict from 392, issued within a month of the edict prohibiting their use of torture, did specify that defenders should be those who are "the most tested and the most stringent (*districtissimi*)," so that they might not hesitate from stifling injustices.[110] In any case, bishops like Augustine, in the daily execution of their office, were constantly, tediously, maddeningly reminded that they lacked the persuasive muscle imperial officials might flex.

If a bishop with Augustine's clout and experience could not trust his leverage against powerful laypeople, other bishops had much less hope, even when it came to counting on their own colleagues' support. Sometime between 427 and 430, a young bishop named Auxilius excommunicated a distinguished official (*vir spectabilis, comes*) named Classicianus.[111] Classicianus was pursuing the prosecution of a group of debtors. They had worked out some sort of agreement with their guarantor (*fidejussor*), sworn to it on the Gospels, and then balked. After deceiving Classicianus and their guarantor by this ruse (as well as "disregarding the sacraments of Christ" by their perjury), they took asylum in Auxilius's church. According to Auxilius, when Classicianus arrived on the scene with an armed retinue (*comitatus milites*) and intimidated the refugees into coming out, he also violated the sanctity of the church. Enraged, Auxilius excommunicated Classicianus and his entire family. The nobleman sought Augustine's intervention, and Augustine complied by urging Classicianus to seek reconciliation in one letter and upbraiding his junior colleague in another.

Episcopal sanction was a spiritual weapon, Augustine assured Classicianus—a powerful curse not to be used lightly, and never against people guilty only by association.[112] Augustine promised to make this argument at the next church council, but no record of such a discussion survives in the conciliar records (perhaps because this was soon before the Vandals swept across Roman Africa). Nevertheless, the lack of an official canon on the subject did not diminish the authority of his pronouncement. Augustine's rationale against group excommunication bore the weight of a conciliar decree among later generations of North African bishops and subsequently passed into medieval canon law.[113]

Beneath the theology and scriptural texts that comprised his argument against group excommunication, Augustine also laid out a series of points by which he might explain, perhaps to the assembly of fellow bishops he was anticipating, why he had decided to side with a layman against one of his own. The offenders, he wrote, were perjurers, and scarcely worth mention; they even had "perjured against the Gospels (*perjuraverunt contra evangelium*)," a point Augustine emphasized twice in a single sentence.[114] Classicianus, meanwhile, had once been a catechumen beloved by Auxilius. He enjoyed honorific titles, and he came in armed company only because his occupation required it. No doubt, these were the points Classicianus had made in his petition to Augustine. The bishop of Hippo repeated them back, not for the official's sake, but for Auxilius, to whom Classicianus was sure to brandish the letter as proof of his own vindication. Augustine also suggested that the perjurers might have forfeited their right to asylum. In fact, if these were public debtors, as seems likely, the law required Classicianus to remove them.[115] This pertinent point of law, however, is curiously absent from Augustine's letters. Instead, he finally advised Auxilius to be merciful and remove all the sanctions he had imposed, including the one against Classicianus. It would have been difficult for the young bishop not to comply. If he had expected his colleague's support against a powerful layman, Auxilius was mistaken.

Auxilius's position as guardian of a sanctuary, effectively managing a fault line between human law and divine law, was not novel to the Christian world. Anne Ducloux and Stefan Esders have studied ecclesiastical asylum in Late Antiquity and the Early Middle Ages, when bishops in church councils staked out the church's jurisdiction within the broader realm of civil and criminal law.[116] Yet there also was an old tradition of priests discerning the hidden motivations and intentions of those who fled from human justice to divine justice. A millennium before in classical Greece, where relatively new secular laws had run up against the older holy laws of sanctuary, priests also found themselves monitoring the thresholds of the temples and testing the characters of fugitives. Particularly in the matter of runaway slaves, as Angelos Chaniotis has demonstrated, priests established whether the slave was eligible for sanctuary and then judged whether he or she would be sold to a new owner or become temple property.[117] There is no direct connection, of course, between Greeks of the age of Demosthenes and bishops of the age of Augustine,[118] but Christian bishops would have found this process very familiar.

Auxilius wound up deciding whether or not to offer sanctuary to fugitives in part because he was obligated as a pastor to help the oppressed, but also because he was a mediator between divine justice and human justice. Imperial law was thorny enough, but when perjurers fled an imperial agent and invoked the sanctuary of the church, then imperial law, canon law, and divine law became a thicket that not only Auxilius had trouble penetrating, but so did Augustine, even with the privilege of hindsight, seniority, and objectivity.

Augustine might have been prudent to recommend forgiveness over punishment. He also had experienced the same frustration in his own career, however, sometimes occasioned by individuals far less distinguished or powerful than Classicianus. When a priest of curial rank abducted a woman sworn to the church (*sanctimonialis*), a group of other priests beat him. Because of this affront, the priest sought redress directly from the bishop of Rome. Beating a *curialis* was wrong, as Pope Celestine (422–32) agreed. Augustine was outraged nonetheless and decried the privileges that constrained the church from enforcing even its own spiritual sanctions. A bishop's hands were tied, and excommunication alone was simply not a threat against people who "are not Christians or Catholics, or [else] live in such a way that they might as well not be." Nevertheless, Augustine was also able to use the letter of the law to serve his own ends; because the priest had withheld evidence from the pope when making his appeal, Augustine called his actions calumnious.[119] On another occasion Augustine had to deal with an estate manager (*procurator*) who raped a sworn religious woman. Because he confessed only after his crime had been proved, the manager was excommunicated, but Augustine believed further punishment was necessary.[120] He wrote to urge the man's boss, a respectable landowner named Dorotheus, to strip him of his title, "in which his freedom from punishment is puffed up." Augustine asked for punishment commensurate with what a cleric in his church would receive, because "if he had been a cleric he would have lost the honor of his rank."[121]

Everyone endured uncertainty in their daily lives. Their membership in the Christian community demanded considerable dues for admission, so surely it should bear some of the load. On the one hand, therefore, purity and integrity were as often the subject of popular demand as they were an official imposition, and some Christians expected quite a lot from their community and from their bishop. On the other hand, not all bishops shared either Augustine's stance on the subject of mixed congregations or his candor regarding the limits of episcopal justice. For centuries, the leaders of the church complained, harangued, and legislated over the requirements of due process, particularly when accusations involved clergy in public or episcopal courts, as we have seen.

Far removed from Augustine in temperament as well as time, the bishops gathered at Clichy in 626/27 encouraged each other to excommunicate first and worry about the fallout later. They refused to watch spiritual discipline be constrained by the fear of litigation and appeals. If synods existed to correct unjust excommunications, then let them do so. "A bishop should not be afraid of excommunicating anyone," they pronounced. Any excommunicant who felt mistreated could bring a complaint to the next gathering of bishops, which would grant absolution if it was persuaded that the bishop was wrong.[122] Most ordinary laypeople did not take that route. Later in the Middle Ages, certainly, and perhaps already during the period under investigation here, bishops used excommunication less often to "medicate" sinners than to deal with stubborn people who bluntly refused to cooperate with ecclesiastical courts.[123]

Calumny could slow down the machinery of any administration and threaten its most powerful members. False accusations jeopardized the security of individuals, local communities, and institutions, up to and including the political (or ecclesiastical) body as a whole. Both secular and religious efforts to provide personal security tended toward juridical solutions, consisting of procedures that were meant to dissuade spurious litigation, weed out calumny, and avoid punitive sanctions that could do little to compensate the damage a victim might have already suffered. All the legal, literary, and anecdotal evidence confirms that the rules of process could not wipe out calumny. It also demonstrates that the same rules sometimes inhibited bishops from administering justice, even within their own churches.

The demands of worldly justice, therefore, simultaneously defined and limited what people could expect from episcopal justice. Uncertainty was already an inescapable part of social life, and became a fact of Christian religious life as well. A realistic bishop who was sensitive to the real anxieties of ordinary people, as Augustine was, did not try to hide this fact from his congregation. "Among your many inner-most thoughts, uncertain and flighty, human conjecture and human error, when does something false not creep up on you, who are put here in the land of falsehood?"[124] The laws of emperors and the laws of bishops were equally corrupt—or polluted,

in the memorable phrase of the Hebrew prophet Isaiah: "We all have become impure, all our justice like menstrual rags, and we all fade like leaves
and our iniquities like the wind have swept us away."[125] Both kinds of laws
offered protection from uncertainty and made people vulnerable by one
and the same means. It is against this background of unrelieved uncertainty—a social problem that that the legal concept of *calumnia* represented
for a very long time—that we may best appreciate how important the episcopal personality could be for winning the trust of laypeople.

2

"Judge like God": What Bishops Claimed to Expect of Themselves

CHRISTIAN LEADERS CRAFTED THEIR AUTHORITY around the promise of justice. Bishops' social background, elite culture, and ascetic discipline were all important factors in the formation of their image as religious leaders, and all of these have been well treated in recent scholarship. Here, however, we discover how negative factors also determined the way bishops represented themselves to each other and their followers. By unpacking the common notion that bishops possessed a divine power of discerning the truth and then following the evolution of that notion in discrete situations over time, we shall see how bishops recast their image to allow for the failure and shortcomings of justice.

Between Perfection and Failure

Not every bishop became a saint. Some were exiled or put to death by princes; many more were cursed by fellow bishops; still others were lynched, some of these by their own disaffected followers (for if some bishops were less than holy, others were less than tolerable). The vast majority of bishops passed quickly and forever into obscurity. The "powerlessness of good intentions," in Conrad Leyser's words, "and the vulnerability to error of those in authority" compounded the possibility that a bishop simply might be incompetent or otherwise fail to live up to expectations.[1] These are good reasons for historians, especially those with an eye toward the Middle Ages, to keep what Neil McLynn has called, most appropriately, our "heavily episcopocentric" inclinations in check.[2] We must exaggerate neither the popularity nor the importance of bishops in society. "But in general," Sir Henry Chadwick wrote for a 1979 colloquium whose minutes still make worthwhile reading, "the bishop was a figure that people wanted to like, and of whom they hoped that their expectations would be realized."[3] This book aims to substantiate some of those expectations; to understand which expectations, if any, were unique to Christian society; and to determine whether bishops fulfilled those expectations. Meanwhile, likeability, fuzzy though it is as a category, may indeed have utility for us: it was not the same as sanctity, of course, but likeability implies some threshold of competence. To be liked might have been a lofty enough goal for average bishops.

This chapter traces an important view of episcopal behavior that is manifested everywhere in the sources from between the fourth and sixth centuries: bishops make exceptional judges. It was a simple ideal rooted in a thick soil of scriptural, philosophical, and ascetic traditions. The first part of the chapter introduces the literary dimensions of the ideal, which include both the old, third-century texts that justified episcopal claims to divine judgment and the new, fourth- and fifth-century texts—sermons, treatises, and written correspondence above all—that propagated the ideal among clergy and a wider audience as well.

Then we will turn to the ways in which this ideal related to major transformations in religious authority that were taking place around the turn of the fourth to the fifth century. Only suggestions are possible here, for even this much requires reference to the relationship between ascetic and institutional authority, monks and bishops, holy men and priests. This is a vast subject, multifaceted and well studied, and we still have a long way to go before we can comfortably claim to understand it. Nevertheless, what is certain is that bishops emerged out of the fourth century as more extraordinary judges than ever before. What their "asceticization" might have changed was the way in which they turned a key attribute of divine judgment, the power of spiritual discernment, toward the pastoral care of ordinary Christians, in a manner most reminiscent of the mentoring relationship between desert fathers and their disciples.[4]

Finally, having drawn as clear a sketch of the ideal bishop-judge as the sources will allow us, the final sections will "set these figures in motion," as Philip Rousseau has urged us to do—first by observing a bishop at work under the most flattering light available to any bishop, the otherworldly glow of hagiography, then by watching a bishop at work in the real world, where the ideal did not always prevail.[5] Together these case studies reinforce the conclusion that a bishop's capacity to judge was essential, both to the Christian ideology of justice, and to a bishop's likeability.

Traditions of Judgment and Discernment

Although it is difficult to get at the values of ordinary Christians around the end of the fourth century, the handling of the much older *Didascalia Apostolorum* (Doctrine of the Apostles) at least shows us something of the way church leaders could imagine themselves and their responsibilities. The different recensions and translations of the *Didascalia* are as revealing as its content, which presses a case for episcopal power more forcefully than most texts during this period: the image of the bishop we find here might represent the loftiest aspirations of some leaders, but they are by no means anomalous.[6] The authority of the text derived from its alleged provenance in the assembly of the apostles at Jerusalem in 48 CE (Acts 15).[7] Originally composed in Greek during the second half of the third century, the *Didascalia* enjoyed at least a modest revival in the last quarter of the fourth century, when it was incorporated into a larger conglomeration, the *Apostolic Constitutions*, which in turn was translated into other languages and became very influential in its own right.[8] This cluster of texts reveals how vibrant the biblical age remained in the minds of some late antique Christians. It also reveals the effort churchmen put into sustaining their own lifeline to the apostolic past.[9]

THE APOSTOLIC KEYS

The apostles, the alleged authors of the *Didascalia*, were the predecessors of the bishops, and their spiritual gifts provided the church with a good reason to propagate this and similar texts. Episcopal authority derived from the keys that Jesus had bestowed upon the apostle Peter and the church. A Spanish priest named Juvencus, writing during the reign of Constantine, encapsulated this tradition in hexameter verse:

Caelestique tibi claues committere regni
Est animus. Terrisque tuo quae nexa relinques
Arbitrio, caelo pariter nodata manebunt;
Soluerit et rursus tua quae sententia terris,
Haud aliter uenient caeli sub sede soluta.

The keys of the heavenly kingdom are entrusted to you.
What by your arbitration is left bound on earth,
Likewise will remain bound in heaven;

And what your judgment looses on earth,
Likewise will be loosed beneath the throne of heaven.[10]

The "apostolic keys" became central to early ecclesiology and became a subject of controversy in centuries to come.[11] In the *Didascalia*, a bishop discovered his place among the apostles, whereby he inherited the power to "bind and loose" (*ligans et solvens*). This "great and celestial and godlike power (*potestas*)" meant that his judgment on earth would be mirrored in heaven: whom he punished, God would punish; whom he forgave, God would forgive.[12]

While the *Didascalia* was full of detailed rituals, procedures, and sanctions associated with diverse aspects of Christian life, what would most impress a bishop was the scope it allowed his spiritual authority. The *Didascalia* bound that authority inseparably with the ability to provide justice, to relieve anxiety and uncertainty, and to protect innocent Christians against calumny. A king governed the body of his subject, but a bishop reigned over body and soul. People should not only fear their bishop as they would their king, but also love him like a father and honor him as they would God.[13] A bishop discovered an even older legacy in the *Didascalia*: his was the same role as the ancient Levite high priest, who acted as minister, mediator, king, teacher, and father to his people. The bishop held God's place, presided as a figure of God (*in typum Dei*), and commanded the veneration due to God.[14]

A bishop's privilege was also his burden. The *Didascalia* paid far less attention to the power of binding than it did to the power of loosening; that is, it preferred to address forgiveness over punishment. The bishop had authority so that he might show mercy and had power so that he could protect his people from calumny and sedition. Jesus had defended an adulteress caught in the very act of sin and invited whoever among her assailants was without sin to cast the first stone (Jn 8). As we shall see later, this served as an important lesson to bishops who would be judges. The *Didascalia* invited the bishop to follow Jesus's example, to be an "investigator of the heart" (*scrutator cordis*), and to search out hidden truths.[15] This power of discernment was critical to the image of the bishop-judge, something real bishops, adopting the language of philosophers and ascetics, would invoke for centuries to come under the rubrics *dioratikon*, *diakrisis*, and *discretio*. Here we find the alleged apostolic origins of discretion shimmering like an electrical strand in the long cable of spiritual authority, tying bishops still more firmly to the past. The bishop was part of a legacy, a tradition of authority that grounded divine charisma in human communities, a personality larger than any human being, which could see beyond the dangerous uncertainty of ordinary existence.[16] Therefore, even while it warned against mundane weaknesses such as bribery, corruption, personal predilections, and the traps set by calumniators, the *Didascalia* also assured the bishop of his extraordinary capabilities and instructed him, "Judge, bishop, with confidence like God."[17]

THE SPIRITUAL SWORD

The discerning power had a history, as did its attributes; one image for representing spiritual discernment was the "sword of the spirit" (*gladium spiritus*), which enjoyed wide and diverse application from the pens of Christian writers. They naturally drew on Scripture: in Ephesians 6:17, the spiritual sword represents the word of God; in the Gospel of Luke (2:35), when Mary and Joseph present the infant Jesus in the temple, Simeon prophesies to Mary that a sword will pierce her soul, "so that secret thoughts from many hearts will be revealed" (*ex multis cordibus cogitationes*); finally, in Hebrews 4:12, the word of God is more penetrating than a double-edged sword. It sunders the soul and the spirit, and exposes the thoughts and secret intentions of the heart. Ambrose of Milan, for example, identified the spiritual sword with the wisdom of Solomon. When asked to decide who between two women was the mother of a living child (1 Kgs 3:16–28), the king had listened to the "voice of her womb." As a judge, he had descended to the visceral testimony of the women.[18] The truth lay hidden, and it was necessary that his inquiry penetrate, like a sword, "not only the viscera of the womb, but even of the heart and mind."[19]

As in the *Didascalia*, the tools of episcopal authority were also burdensome. One who wielded the sword of discernment must be certain to harbor no deception in himself, so that none might suspect him of fraud or error.[20] A single sword cleaved knots of ambiguity and agents of deception, and in the most common usage it revealed heresy and destroyed heretics.[21] Thus the late fifth-century epitaph for the priest Claudianus Mamertus, author of an important philosophical tract and brother to the bishop of Vienne, granted him an episcopal style of authority, for he served as a sort of vicar for his brother.[22] Claudianus "was adept at solving (*soluere*) knotted questions," it read, "and skewering sects with the sword of the word."[23] Finally, where the law of the Hebrews required some sinners be put to death, the spiritual sword enabled bishops to excise sinners from the community by means of excommunication, while allowing them the opportunity for redemption up until their physical death.[24] The double use of the sword, which could both destroy and revive, was crucial because discernment was what drew people to the bishop as an arbiter and a councilor. The biblical allusions, the metaphors, the vocabulary, and the applications of spiritual discernment provided the ideal bishop with not only flesh but also muscle mass, while "the ancient traditions lent [him] a density, a third dimension."[25] More pragmatically, such traditions gave bishops a handle to help grasp the dimensions of their own authority and translate that authority into useful activity.[26]

Spiritual Discernment at Work

To "judge like God" was not only a matter of inheriting extraordinary equipment, such as the spiritual sword; it also required style. Whereas the *Didascalia* explicitly employed judicial terminology to describe the traits that commended clergy to others, Ambrose of Milan wrote about *usus consiliorum*, the ability to give good advice. In his treatise, *De officiis*, which he wrote within a couple decades or so of the Verona translation of *Didascalia*, Ambrose reshaped Cicero's philosophical treatise on social obligations around the Christian clerical office. According to Ambrose, following Cicero, *usus consiliorum* depended on prudence and justice, both of which were "expected by many."[27] The adviser Ambrose envisioned, unlike Cicero's, was a religious leader whose pastoral obligations would saddle him with a wide range of activities and demands. Ambrose addressed a hypothetical group of Christians and advised them, "If you find someone who excels in natural vivacity and intellectual vigor and authority, whom experience and habit show to be well prepared, who dissolves immediate threats, warns against those to come, who moves debates along, brings remedy when appropriate, and is prepared to provide not only advice but practical assistance, have faith in him!"[28] Those elite who still followed the old religions of Rome had no reason to respond positively to this "attempt at cultural takeover," but they would have understood the professional ground Ambrose was staking out.[29] This *usus consiliorum*, the essence of episcopal authority, was intrinsically judicial, as Ambrose demonstrated by associating the giving of advice with the power of spiritual discernment: the ability to see things as they truly were. Through their proper conduct of office, bishops would reveal the church to be the true "image of justice."[30]

GIVING ADVICE, RENDERING JUDGMENT

The power to discern obscurities had its place in polite society as well, where many late antique bishops felt most at home and counted their friends. Like Ambrose, Augustine of Hippo came to know both the advantage and burden of *usus consiliorum*. Although the power and originality of his writings earned him his wide reputation, correspondents addressed Augustine in the language appropriate to his office and to one who was endowed with extraordinary powers of discernment. Learned people, for example Paulinus of Nola (ca. 353–431) and his wife Therasia, who wanted to know how the voices of the angels sound, wrote to Augustine. More specifically, they called on a "spiritual brother who judges all things" (1 Cor. 2:15) and was imbued with the "spirit of revelation" so that he could probe the mysteries of the past, present, and future.[31] We of course must be aware that the endearing touches writers like Paulinus added to their letters came not only from the heart but also from generic traditions, as Klaus Thraede traced in an important study.[32] Nevertheless, the appeal to soulful examination was not merely formulaic deference, peculiar to elite epistolary circles. Christians were happy to remind bishops of their obligation to serve them. In particular, they summoned their bishops' expertise in metaphorical language that converged with the language of real judicial inquiry.

Moreover, while friends like Paulinus and Theresa might couch their demands in friendly language, considerate of a bishop's time and reputation, a layman named Consentius felt little inclination to be tactful. Writing from Minorca, his claims on a distant bishop's gifts were as blunt as his questions were expansive. In a letter written around 410, Consentius insisted that Augustine give him a glimpse of something "ineffable" and mysterious, if indeed God had "granted to [Augustine the ability] to penetrate the structure of the heavens and 'with open face behold the glory of God,' [and] to the extent that the One who gives the power of reckoning of this sort should give [the bishop] power of revelation."[33] Augustine might have expected courtesy from Consentius: he dedicated his treatise "Against Lying" (*Contra mendacium*) to him; Consentius is even one of the first people we know to have read Augustine's *Confessions*. (What would one day gain wide regard as a literary masterpiece left that reader rather cold.)[34] Although

he probably expended some of his discerning powers untangling the pro-
tases and apodoses of Consentius's request, the bishop dutifully responded.
After all, these were erudite inquiries, which Augustine's own renowned
erudition had earned him.

However, between sounding angels' voices and testing heaven's fabric,
the bishop of Hippo would have spent more time responding to less ethe-
real questions that would have been standard fare for most of his colleagues
as well. Not surprisingly, the issues prompting people to seek the expert
advice of a bishop often involved the law, whether worldly, ecclesiastical,
or divine. Knowledge of the law, not simply its just application, was itself
a mark of divine judgment and spiritual discernment—not exclusive, of
course, to bishops or to Christians. Thus the jurist Ulpian had written, "Of
that art we are deservedly called the priests. For we cultivate the virtue of
justice and claim awareness of what is good and fair, discriminating between
fair and unfair, distinguishing (*discernentes*) lawful from unlawful, aiming
to make men good not only through fear of penalties but also indeed under
allurement of rewards, and affecting a philosophy of which, if I am not
deceived, is genuine, not a sham."[35] More than a skill, "the virtue of justice" was an attribute of the ideal bishop and therefore a burden as much
as a privilege. Absent diaries or stenographic records from their audience
chambers, we are again reliant on bishops' correspondence for gauging
their reaction to legal work, although surely much more was conducted
in person. Even this uneven record demonstrates mixed reactions among
bishops to the demands placed on them.

To the bishops in this period, law was more than an academic or administrative matter, it was a matter of salvation. We shall look more closely at
this convergence of judicial and pastoral functions in the final chapter. For
now it is enough to observe that bishops perceived a convergence between
theology and their pastoral duties, on the one hand, and law and administrative obligations on the other. The convergence of religious and mundane tasks made a hard job harder, not easier. Augustine of Hippo, for
example, responding to a person asking for private clarification of some
scriptural matter, once wrote, "How am I an 'oracle of the law,' when I do
not know many more things than I do know about its latent and hidden
secrets? Even if I wanted to, I could not reach and penetrate its many folds
and opaque recesses. The only thing I know is I am not capable."[36] To his
friends, Augustine lamented the arduous task of probing the undisclosed
sins of the Christians under his care, a responsibility that could surely blur
with his other judicial tasks. "I admit that I err daily in these things," he

confessed. "What dread in all of this, my Paulinus, holy man of God! What dread, and what shadows!"[37]

We must offset these striking disclosures, which taken by themselves might suggest a paralyzing failure of confidence on the part of the bishop or else be dismissed as rhetorical postures, with the ample evidence that Augustine was at the very least a competent judge. More importantly, perhaps, Augustine had his own connections, which allowed him to forward complex or obscure questions of law to the appropriate experts.[38] In any case, his reservations may not be characteristic of men in his position, for other bishops showed no hesitation claiming superhuman expertise in the law. Dionysius Exiguus (who died between 526 and 556) complained about this confident sort. Dionysius was himself an expert, a Scythian who had settled in Rome where he collected legal materials and made Latin translations, including a translation of the *Apostolic Constitutions*, the extended version of the *Didascalia* from the 370s.[39] In the prefatory letter to his second collection of Greek church councils, which he dedicated to Bishop Hormisdas of Rome in the second or third decade of the sixth century, Dionysius scorned bishops who claimed not to need his handbooks. He clearly had particular individuals in mind, for their tone exasperated him as much as their apparent indifference to the fruits of his labor. Beset by none of Augustine's qualms and instead propelled by "a certain temerity," these bishops answered any and all questions of church law definitively: they "fancy themselves most expert on the Greek canons," Dionysius reminded Hormisdas, and "seem to respond from within themselves, just as from a hidden oracle."[40]

By that time, a hundred years after Augustine's death, the language of spiritual discernment had seeped outside of treatises, polite letters, and church councils; news of its judicial application had entered official discourse long ago. Emperors in the fourth century alread had acknowledged bishops' power to discern secrets and complexities, and their capacity to "judge like God." Their religious authority "searches out and reveals many things" that could not be disclosed in ordinary courts of law, Constantine declared in a famous (and controversial) edict from 333.[41] When in 378 Bishop Damasus of Rome—survivor of a contested election, bloody riots, and accusations that ranged from adultery to homicide—received backing from a Roman synod to request episcopal immunity from secular judgment, the bishops supporting him (Ambrose of Milan surely among them) could remind the emperor what they expected he already knew: bishops relied on their discernment to obtain the truth where ordinary judges had recourse to torture, and bishops' success rate was better by far. "Finally," they wrote, "should not a person who wants to punish a religious offence search it out, not in innocent people's flesh (*lateribus* [literally in the flanks, which would be pierced or torn under torture]), but in the behavior (*moribus*) of the accused person? For how often has it been shown that people the courts (*iudicia*) would have let off were condemned by bishops, and people the courts would have condemned were let off?"[42] Getting bishops to agree with each other over what they discerned in the law was another matter entirely. The efforts to which clergy went to get accurate copies of church councils is just one hint of the limits to which any single bishop could persuade other bishops to trust his instincts on the basis of his authority alone, especially when it came to the letter of the law.[43]

LIFT UP YOUR HEARTS: DISCERNING SACRED MYSTERIES

Whereas bishops, like other legislators, might become entangled in the interpretation and application of their own laws, matters of divine law made the need for spiritual discernment and divine judgment all the greater. Bishops believed the will of God and the mysteries of the world were hidden in sacraments. This Latin word (*sacramenta*) enjoyed many meanings in ecclesiastical usage: alongside the old meaning of "oaths," *sacramenta* also translated the Greek *mustêria* and applied to the mysteries of Scripture as much as to the mysteries of the Mass. Bishops must be able to control all these forms.[44] The handling of the mysteries might inspire awe in even their youngest followers. In a story well worn among church historians, a bishop of Alexandria watched out his window as young boys played on the beach, pretending to act out the mysteries of the Mass. One of them, who assumed the role of bishop and even began baptizing his playmates, later succeeded to the see of Alexandria as Bishop Athanasius (ca. 296–373).[45] Even this story was used to convey a pointed lesson. Christians who were divinely endowed to interpret the sacraments were adamant that unqualified people not attempt the activity, for the consequences could be deadly.

Priscillian of Avila, for example, warned of the landmines waiting beneath the surface of scriptural mysteries to destroy the sort of incompetent exegetes who would misread the "griffins, eagles, asses, elephants, serpents, and unnecessary beasts" as innocuous creatures, not as dangerous symbols of demonic power.[46] At the time he issued this warning, Priscillian was a lay ascetic, not a bishop or even a cleric, and he was under examination for heresy, especially for reading forbidden books and making erroneous interpretations of scripture. After becoming bishop of Avila despite powerful opposition, Priscillian was executed for sorcery by imperial command in 385. Nonetheless, Priscillian and his opponents were in agreement on one matter—the sacraments were not for everyone. A clear and penetrating intellect was necessary to understand their meaning and to keep them from the "uninitiated," just as ancient priests had protected their own sacred rites.[47] "Not everyone sees the depths of the mysteries," Ambrose wrote in *De officiis*, probably within a few years of Priscillian's death, "for they are hidden by the Levites so that those who should not see them do not see them, and those who cannot keep them do not handle them."[48]

It was the particular charge of the priesthood to preside over the Mass, where ancient mysteries and eternal sacraments converged at the altar. However, just before the celebration of the eucharist in masses since at least the third century, priests extended to all Christians the offer to have "conversation in heaven" (Phlm. 3:20), that is to walk regularly among God's elect: *Sursum corda*, "Lift up your hearts"; *Habemus ad Dominum*, "We lift them up to the Lord."[49] In part, the refrain was intended to draw the attention of the congregation away from chatter and distractions and toward the altar.[50] But for the spiritually ambitious, a truthful response to the refrain *sursum corda* was the first step to comprehending things that otherwise surpassed human faculties. A person whose heart truly was with God might know the most intimate connection with divinity that was possible for humans on this earth. This is what Augustine told Consentius, the layman who had asked him to use his "power of revelation" to explain something "ineffable." Augustine instructed Consentius to "pray ardently and faithfully that the Lord may give you understanding." For God revealed things to those whose "conversation" was in the heavens, and if Consentius was to join Augustine there, it would be when "our mouth responds truthfully, 'We lift up our heart.'"[51]

According to some pastors, however, few people actually meant the refrain they spoke, thus opening up a gap between the *spirituales*, who had their conversation in heaven, and the *carnales*, mired here in the world. Most Christians never turned their attention away from the noisome chatter, as bishops were still complaining a century after Augustine and Consentius wrote.[52] There were also important differences among the *spirituales*, between ascetics and clergy, priests and bishops. In 394 Jerome (ca. 345–420) wrote to Nepotian, a former soldier who had joined the clergy, and emphasized the importance of priests being "expert and highly erudite" in sacraments and mysteries.[53] Naturally one would expect the same skills in bishops, who were clerics like their priests and deacons. However, Jerome took this occasion to chide bishops who had forgotten their clerical roots, as it were, and, where another writer might distinguish a bishop from his priests, Jerome emphasized their proximity to each other. For example, the figure of the bishop was often associated with Moses, who went up Mount Sinai and received the divine law directly from God; meanwhile Aaron and his sons, who were priests and also served as figures for Christian priests, remained below.[54] In his letter to Nepotian, however, Jerome associated the bishop with Aaron, and the bishop's priests with Aaron's sons. All were close to God, but none looked God in the face. Still, Jerome acknowledged that clergy owed their bishop a different sort of respect than he owed them, and he encouraged Nepotian (whose uncle, Heliodorus, was a bishop and an old friend of Jerome's) to take note of how many different hats his own bishop wore. For in the person of the bishop, "several titles should be observed: monk, pontiff, uncle."[55]

Alternative Traditions of Discernment

In 405, Jerome tried to avoid giving advice requested by a man who had traveled all the way from Gaul to Bethlehem to see him. Jerome thought him confused, "as if I held the bishop's throne and was not shut up in a cell, lamenting past sins and trying to avoid present ones, far removed from the crowds."[56] Jerome was clearly (and characteristically) touting his own reputation here, but still he provides important commentary on the episcopal ideal, not least because his perspective was oddly conflicted. Generally, Jerome was skeptical whether most bishops lived up to the ideals they professed and so he tried to keep his distance. This was the mild Jerome. Genuine antipathy toward bishops had peaked in him much earlier, long before he settled in Bethlehem, before even his stay at Rome enjoying the hospitality of wealthy virgins and widows. In 374, Jerome had tried to withdraw himself from circulation completely, abandoning secular and ecclesiastical society alike for the desert of Chalcis near Antioch. That same year Jerome wrote to Heliodorus, Nepotian's uncle; if somehow we could find the autograph copy, according to its author, we would see it blotted with Jerome's tears. The tone of the letter, by turns remorseful and accusatory, must have puzzled Heliodorus, for he was hardly the prodigal friend

Jerome's moralizing might suggest. Although unwilling to share Jerome's monastic retreat, Heliodorus aspired to the clergy and eventually would become bishop of Altinum in Italy. Singing the praises of monastic life and questioning the ability of priests and bishops to live up to the demands their offices placed on them, Jerome wrote for himself, not for Heliodorus. In the words of one modern commentator, it was Jerome's "last ditch attempt to justify his own ambitious repudiation of the world, and to recall to the East a man who had already foreseen the folly of so completely rejecting the past."[57]

So it is all the more remarkable that even here, with Jerome putting forward his strongest case for abandoning social life altogether and choosing the desert over the basilica, we recognize the effect episcopal authority and the expectation of spiritual judgment had on the way people understood Christian society. "Not all bishops are bishops," Jerome wrote. It was up to each bishop to judge whether or not he was up to the job, for "the dignity of the church does not make a Christian."[58] Jerome's greatest doubts stemmed from the distractions clergy faced, living in cities and towns among the ordinary people they were obliged to protect. Nevertheless, he was careful to acknowledge the authority of those "successors to the apostolic rank" who protected all Christians, including a monk like Jerome; "because they hold the keys of the kingdom of heaven, in a certain respect they judge us before the Judgment Day."[59] The combined privilege and burden of apostolic authority made it difficult even for Jerome to present a compelling case for Heliodorus to choose seclusion over ordination: "If a monk should fall, a priest will intervene for him; who will intervene for the fall of a priest?"[60]

What we see in even this brief glimpse at Jerome's correspondence is not only that bishops were not universally liked, but that the relationship between monks and clergy was ambiguous, particularly when monks did not stay in their cells but engaged in scholarship and debate, as Jerome did. So it is time we addressed the relationship directly, also as Jerome was forced to do. While living as a recluse in Chalcis, the monk was caught up in a schism, a rivalry between two different claimants to the bishopric of Antioch. Even more to the contrary of the advice he sent Heliodorus, Jerome received ordination as a priest in that city. When he left Antioch, it was not for the desert but for Constantinople, where he engaged in church politics on an ecumenical scale. His patron there was Gregory Nazianzen, a bishop of three different cities by either ordination or default, and at that time one of the people most capable of showing a skeptic like Jerome, whose resolve was rapidly weakening, how a priest might balance ascetic devotion and pastoral responsibility.[61]

MONKS, BISHOPS, AND DESERT FATHERS

By the time Jerome went to Constantinople, newly ordained as a priest, he would have discovered that not only was it hard for a monk to escape the snares of ecclesiastical life completely, but actually a monk could feel at home and be effective within the church. Bishops like Gregory Nazianzen and the other "Cappadocian Fathers," including especially Gregory's friend Basil of Caesarea and Basil's brother Gregory of Nyssa, brought ascetic discipline with them to the bishop's throne, the same discipline that drew Jerome and many others into the deserts, a discipline reflected in their power of spiritual discernment. They fused two very different kinds of authority, one derived institutionally from ordination and the receipt of the apostolic keys, another derived experientially from hard labor at self-discipline and training. The result was the "monastic episcopate" or "monk-bishop," as scholars have called it. This ideal, which would become the prevalent model of church leadership in the medieval Greek church, was important around the Christian world already in the fifth century. The Cappadocians described and advocated the fusion of institutional and ascetic authority in sermons, letters, and treatises. They did not pursue a systematic campaign; rather, they praised those qualities they respected in each other on the occasion of an ordination, a death, or the anniversary of a death, and only later in treatises devoted to the subject. The final product, however, was a composite portrait of an ideal monk-bishop. At the same time, these bishops were appointing or influencing the appointment of ascetics to the office of bishop, ensuring that the ideal became reality in some towns and cities.[62]

The power of spiritual discernment runs through the sermons, poems, orations, and treatises on the public life of ascetics like a refrain. Basil looked for the gift of discernment in bishops and abbots alike; both were the "eyes" to the body of believers in their care. Gregory of Nyssa described how the third-century bishop of Caesarea, Gregory Thaumaturgus ("Wonderworker," ca. 213–ca. 270), used his powers to probe the divine mysteries when he could enjoy seclusion like Moses, and to pick out an unlikely candidate for the episcopate, a lowly coal deliverer, when other people were taken in by mere appearances.[63] Jerome might have remained ambivalent about the ascetic authority of bishops throughout his life, but others suffered no such doubts. John Chrysostom, whose life provided the basis for a literary portrait of the "monk-bishop par excellence," was a devoted practitioner and eloquent proponent of the new ideal,[64] but it is important to notice where Chrysostom maintained clear distinctions between monks and clergy. Like Jerome in his cell at Chalcis and Ambrose on his throne in Milan, Chrysostom observed that while monks might hide away in secret, priests were exposed to the entire world, like performers on a stage.[65] The fact that they were accountable to God for the sins of other people, the sins of entire cities, the sins of the entire world (*oikoumenê*), was one of the reasons why Chrysostom insisted that the priest (*hiereus*) had a much greater need for spiritual refinement than monks: "The soul of the priest," like the soul of the apostles, Chrysostom wrote, "should be pure as the rays of the sun."[66] According to Palladius, for whom Chrysostom struck the perfect balance of institutional and ascetic authority, the bishop of Constantinople could discern the plots being orchestrated against him. After those plots had worked to drive him from his bishopric and into the desert, the same power allowed him a vision of a martyred bishop who announced Chrysostom's own impending death.[67]

Yet the power of spiritual discernment had other claimants besides bishops and those ascetics who left the desert for a social life. In Egypt the recluse Pachomius, whose purity of heart enabled him to perceive "the invisible God as if in a mirror,"[68] stood trial in 345 before an assembly of bishops and monks in Latopolis, charged with claiming the power of spiritual discernment (*to dioratikon*). Pachomius was at pains to distance himself from any exaggerated rumors (*huper ta metra*), and made it clear that his ability was a "gift from God" (*to charisma tou theou*) that he could not invoke at will but which moved inside him by divine inclination.[69] He even rationalized the power, claiming any thoughtful person could come to know and interpret the movements of familiar people—his powers were not so different.[70]

Pachomius did not think it likely, however, that spiritual discernment would proliferate throughout human society. His familiar people were a community of monks, and by a thoughtful person he meant someone with a pure heart. Just because the power of spiritual discernment was not the prerogative of any person or type of person did not make it common, either. Discernment (Latin *discretio*, Greek *diakrisis*) was a dual process of perception and evaluation that allowed people to "discern the ideal and distinguish the differences from that ideal,"[71] whether the object were the mysteries of the universe or the heart of another human. In theory, just as priests offered all Christians "conversation in heaven" during the *Sursum corda*, all Christians might enjoy such discretion, but in practice experts had long since staked their claim on it.[72]

Bishops Turn Discernment into Judgment

Nevertheless, some adepts were willing to spread the benefits of their discretion around. In the West, bishops and monks came to infuse the pastoral care of laypeople with traditions of ascetic direction that were refined in monastic communities, and none did so with more polish and influence than Gregory I the Great (ca. 540–604).[73] Closer to Pachomius's world, some ascetics, most famously the "holy men" of Egypt and Syria, shared their discretion with admirers from all walks of life.[74] The desert fathers, for example, read the hearts of those who came to seek their wisdom so that their words of advice would be always appropriate and profound. Written down, detached from the private interviews between master and disciple that produced them, and later collected together as the "Sayings of the Desert Fathers" (*apophthegmata patrum*), these words were instruments "to solve problems in human relationships."[75]

If there was a difference early on between the powers of discernment claimed by monks and bishops, it is to be found in application, not pedigree. Many of the remotest desert monks enjoyed a historical ancestry, just as bishops enjoyed a direct link to the apostles. However, even in the earliest literature the precise lineage became hazy within a generation or two, after disciples identified their masters and possibly their masters' masters. More than a pedigree of lineage, asceticism valued a pedigree or "typology" of behavior.[76] But it is the application of spiritual discernment that is most revealing. The most important relationship addressed by the "Sayings of the Desert Fathers," for example, was increasingly considered to be the monk's relationship with himself; hence the common slogan in the ascetic literature, "watch yourself" (*proseche seautôi*).[77]

The story of a desert father or early monk caught in the act of discernment, as Claudia Rapp skillfully demonstrates, became "something like an event with its own spiritual force," drawing readers back (or the subject forward) in time, engaging them directly in the activity of holiness. A traditional form of philosophical dialogue (*diêgêsis*) became a medium for portraying philosophers, now transformed as Christian saints, who turned a traditional tool of philosophical inquiry (*discretio*, *diakrisis*) into an instrument of penitential self-awareness.[78] The focus of this activity was above all spiritual direction, less spectacular and singular than some of the miracles that spice later reminiscences by the likes of Theodoret of Cyrrhus or Cyril of Scythopolis, but of greater overall importance for "the gradual improvement of sinners."[79] This contrast reinforces the particular importance the activity of judgment had for the identity of the ideal bishop. Though by the fifth century Christian asceticism had become a life of imitation rather than an exercise of sheer charismatic force, and though some of the sheen was fading from the "charismatic brilliance" that had once illumined monks like Pachomius, bishops positively glowed.[80]

A fine and famous demonstration comes from the life of Abba Macarius the Egyptian, a desert father who exuded such authority that he was called a "god on earth" (*epigeios theos*), the epithet that *Didascalia* and related texts attributed to bishops.[81] No doubt this title was partly in recognition of his discerning powers, revealed in his words and his actions. His administration of those powers could be quite subtle, as when parents brought their virgin daughter to him in the shape of a horse, a victim of sorcery or so they believed. Macarius could see that the daughter had not become a horse: "there [was] nothing barnyard about her" (*nihil in se pecudis habentem*), he assured her parents, she only appeared to have been changed; anything equine was in the eyes of her beholders (*in oculis intuentium*). What they were seeing were "demonic phantasms, not the truth of things," but after some concentrated prayer people saw the virgin human being she truly was.[82]

If Macarius looked like a bishop and saw like a bishop, he did not judge like a bishop. One day a man fled to Macarius's cell swearing his innocence in a murder that had taken place nearby. His accusers were unimpressed by his oaths and Macarius endured their arguments back and forth for a while before asking where the victim's corpse was buried. The party relocated to the tomb, where Macarius knelt and invoked the testimony of the deceased under oath, calling in a loud voice, "Through faith in Christ I call you as witness to say whether you have been killed by this man who is suffering calumny." (The last clause, which would seem to be leading the witness, here may mean simply "who is under accusation.") From the tomb a voice distinctly responded that he had not been killed by the accused. The stupefied spectators dropped to the ground and rolled around at Macarius's feet before realizing there was still a chance for satisfaction. They urged Macarius to ask the victim who the real murderer was, but the holy man shocked them once again. "'This I shall not ask,' he said. 'It is enough for me that an innocent man is set free, it is not my job to reveal the guilty man'."[83]

A bishop would not have been likely to disappoint in this situation, particularly not a bishop "set in motion" by the pen of a competent biographer. Although there was little difference between the "kind of authority" commanded by Macarius and a contemporary soldier turned ascetic from Pannonia named Martin, their styles were worlds apart.[84] As a monk, an exorcist, and finally a bishop in Gaul, the activities of Martin of Tours (ca. 316–97) covered the gamut of what we have seen the expectations of episcopal authority to have included. Sulpicius Severus, a monk and a priest like Jerome, completed a vita not long after Martin's death. There Martin's gifts of insight enabled the saint to unravel the mysteries of Scripture, to ferret out demons, phantasms, and false prophets, and to lead the people of Tours toward salvation. When everyone else had forgotten what martyr rested beneath a nearby monument, Martin, who "did not lightly give credence to uncertainties," stood on top of the grave and asked God to reveal the occupant. A "foul and grim" ghost, invisible to all but Martin, gave a full deposition in words only he could understand: not a martyr, but a robber and murderer who had been executed for his crimes now rotted in the grave.[85] If Martin was cut from the same cloth as the desert fathers, by serving as a bishop he fulfilled his potential to the benefit of everyone—monks, clergy, laity, and even pagans.[86] That potential continued to grow along with Martin's legend, which added yet another link in the long chain of episcopal authority. In subsequent stories of his life and virtues, Martin assumed the mantle of the Hebrew prophets, a mantle he passed on to later bishops, including his distant successor and one of his hagiographers, Gregory of Tours.[87]

The Exemplary Life of Bishops

By the end of the fourth century, saints were rapidly gaining a legitimate role in spiritual life, thanks in no small part to the efforts of bishops, including Damasus's embellishment of shrines around Rome during his episcopate (366–84), Ambrose of Milan's miraculous discovery in 386 of relics belonging to martyrs named Gervasius and Protasius, and sermons on the saints such as the one Victricius of Rouen delivered in 396, to single out only a few landmarks.[88] The futures of bishops and relics were closely intertwined, and yet, similar to the important differences that distinguished bishops from monks, episcopal authority remained different in kind from the intercessory power of the martyrs and confessors. As Victricius (ca. 340– ca. 410) hoped on behalf of himself and his congregation in Southern Gaul, one expected the holy dead to "excuse our sins with the pious compassion of an advocate, not search them out in the spirit of a judge (*animo iudicantis*)."[89] Not everyone would agree that the saints should be dragged back down to earth, with its weary inhabitants still caught up in sin. Vigilantius of Calagurris, a priest and contemporary of Victricius whom Jerome verbally throttled for opposing the veneration of relics, was not the only cleric in Gaul left cold by Victricius's sort of enthusiasm.[90] Meanwhile, no one questioned whether or not bishops should search out sins with a judging spirit. Bishops were most definitely judges, as Victricius and Vigilantius's contemporaries were making emphatically clear.

AN EXTREME EXAMPLE OF THE IDEAL BISHOP

Bishops were sentinels, heralds, and active inquisitors for their communities. They were not advocates whose sympathies were for hire, nor were they like revenue collectors, charged with chasing down delinquent taxpayers. Bishops were the "watchmen," in Greek *skopoi* or *episkopoi*, in Latin *speculatores* or *episcopi*.[91] Commenting on Ezekiel 33, the textual basis for the tradition of episcopal oversight, Jerome had heralded bishops as the watchmen of the new Christian era. Both biblical watchmen and then bishops interpreted scripture and saw into the future in order to testify to the people and correct those who strayed.[92] Julian Pomerius argued in the late fifth century that a spiritual leader should have a higher vantage point than his followers, as well as "the grace of greater knowledge (*maior scientia*)" in order to protect them.[93] When Gregory the Great wrote of discretion, as we saw above, he was prescribing a spiritual exercise by which Christians with pure hearts might emulate the saints and desert fathers. Judgment was something different and bishops surveyed from another plane entirely, so that Gregory explained the word *speculator* to mean "one to whom the care of others is committed. . . . That way he may reside loftily in the mind and the title itself may derive from the virtue of his action."[94]

A generation earlier, far to the north of Gregory's Rome and far from his own native country in Southern Gaul, one bishop took the idea of superior surveillance to literal extremes. In 526, the Frankish king Theoderic (r. 511–33) recruited a monk from the south named Nicetius to serve as a bishop in his realm. Nicetius (d. 566) assumed the episcopacy of Trier, located in Northern Gaul between vine-covered slopes and the Moselle River. Trier had once been a capital city in the Roman Empire, and its massive gates and multiple basilicas still preserved the memory of imperial munificence, although intermittent turmoil in centuries since had left destructive marks in the urban fabric.[95] Theoderic perhaps had some indication of his recruit's intrepid and fiery temperament, for as an abbot his chosen prelate had "often laid [the king's] sins bare."[96] Nicetius also threatened to excommunicate his own royal escort on the way to his ordination, before even reaching Trier. As bishop, he settled down to the mundane responsibilities of the episcopate, including the administration of justice, as well as numerous extensive building projects, among which the construction of his own fortified residence, perched on a prominent point looking over the city, was the most remarkable.[97]

After Theoderic's death in 533, when Trier came under the rule of his brother, Chlothar (511–61), Nicetius repeatedly threatened the new king with excommunication, unperturbed by reciprocal threats of exile from the kingdom.[98] Like many of his Western colleagues, Nicetius also was enraged at what he knew about the theological debates taking place in the Greek East, known as the Three Chapters controversy. So from Trier, a northern city that had passed decisively out of the political orbit of the Roman world a hundred years earlier, the bishop addressed a letter of stern rebuke to Constantinople, reprimanding none other than the emperor Justinian himself.[99] It was no empty compliment, therefore, for his biographer to write that Nicetius of Trier had "no respect for the person of power."[100]

This incendiary bishop, however, brought more than a predisposition for trouble with him to early medieval Trier. The shock of his forceful personality passed through contact points that Nicetius shared with generations of spiritual leaders before him: he honed his skills in monastic training, but they became manifest in his judicial activities as a bishop.[101] Gregory of Tours, the bishop and author who supplies much of what we know about the politics of Gaul in the sixth century, was a generation younger than Nicetius, their lives just overlapping in years and through some common acquaintances. Gregory shared his elder's dedication to renovating church buildings. Also like Nicetius, Gregory knew what it was like to be the subject of a full-scale judicial inquiry conducted by his fellow bishops. Yet their political styles were quite different: where Nicetius's impulses moved him toward confrontation, Gregory's tended toward diplomacy, at least as far as he portrayed himself in his *Histories*. Nevertheless, writing

about the life of Nicetius years after his death, and after the deaths of many
of those who might object to any softening of his image, Gregory was able
to focus on those personality traits that he, as a fellow bishop, could best
understand and commend. They revolved around divine judgment and spiritual discernment.

In Gregory's mind and through his prose, the essential qualities of
ideal spiritual leadership appeared to be solidly settled within Nicetius
despite or, indeed, perhaps by virtue of his forceful personality. Gregory
presented a composite portrait of the perfect spiritual leader in what he
called (deliberately using the singular) the *Life of the Fathers*—a collection
of miracle stories drawing on the lives of many pious individuals that
together provided a single model for exemplary conduct. His was, in other
words, a deliberate project, in contrast to the ideal of the monk-bishop,
which scholars have constructed from various writings of the Cappadocian
Fathers.[102] In the preface to the chapter on Nicetius, Gregory defended
the reliability of what followed against those who "disbelieve what is written, scorn what is given in testimony, and recoil from what they see as if
it were counterfeit." As not only a bishop and an author but also a pastor,
Gregory lamented that such skeptics had "ripped the very foundation of
belief from their breasts." The life of Nicetius thus bore particular importance, for Nicetius dramatized the special ability of holy people to discern
the "foundation of belief" where it was concealed in both honest and deceit-
ful people—the credulous and the skeptical alike.[103] This probative ability,
the power to see past deceit and to uncover the truth, was the foundation
of Nicetius's judicial authority. Nicetius perceived the world with a clarity
of vision that revealed the fate of kings as easily as it penetrated the surface of a stream to locate tasty fish for supper.[104]

Like other holy persons, Nicetius displayed his complete capacities
most dramatically when people swore oaths in his presence or, after he died,
at his tomb. "What shall I say about perjuries?" asked Gregory in another
of his miracle collections, *The Glory of the Confessors*. He had described miracles that revealed perjurers at the shrine of Maximinus, one of Nicetius's
fourth-century predecessors as bishop of Trier, and then moved on to
Nicetius's own tomb. "If anyone dared to swear a false oath there, immediately he was corrected by divine retribution. Nor does anyone dare to
say either these things or that he intends to resolve a suit there, if because
of his tormented conscience he knows that he is guilty." It was to the living
Nicetius, moreover, that other religious leaders had turned for help convincing monarchs to keep their solemn promises.[105] The bishop exercised

a "single cure," a cure which pacified, purged, and healed the contests perturbing Christians under his care.[106] The cure reflected the organic unity of his pastoral and judicial roles, while the power of spiritual discernment gave it potency. Nicetius of Trier had easy and familiar access to the highest levels of supreme justice because he held his "conversation in the heavens." Gregory himself elicited first-hand memories of Nicetius from one of his understudies, the abbot Aredius of Limoges (d. 591), because the young bishop of Tours enjoyed a similar "conversation" (*conversatio*) himself—a simplicity of heart that might allow him to attain "the height of God's miracles."[107] In all his activities, regardless of his own tendency or taste for confrontation, as far as Gregory of Tours was concerned Nicetius behaved as an ideal bishop. The episcopal personality even at its most cantankerous promised accuracy and justice.

THE LONG LIFE OF THE BISHOP-JUDGE

The ideal of the bishop's essential judicial attributes had considerable staying power. Thus we are told how Bishop Epiphanius of Pavia (467–97) brought Scripture to life by assuming the virtuous attributes he found there. Depending on his day's reading, the bishop became a prophet for his people, led them like Moses along the path of God's law, or imparted to them the sweetness of Paul's well-tempered justice.[108] The power of episcopal discernment also retained its potent scope, penetrating the secrets of the universe as much as the secrets of the heart, so that a Merovingian author in the late seventh century remembered Gregory the Great as one "to whom the secrets of heaven lay open."[109] As for the burden of episcopal authority, a pseudonymous and widely influential work from seventh-century Ireland called "The Twelve Worldly Abuses" (*De XII abusivis saeculi*) addressed the neglectful bishop (*episcopus neglegens*), the tenth "abuse" of the dozen.[110] *Episcopus*, the text observes, is a Greek word best translated as *speculator*. There follows a quotation from Ezekiel (3:17–19), according to which the power of foresight obliges the pastor to notify his congregation of the impending divine judgment, represented by a sword. Negligent bishops are therefore warned that as watchmen they must be diligent and perspicacious, constantly evaluating the moral standing of their flock in order to judge and correct trespasses before it is too late. When the end comes, they will be personally responsible for the conduct of their office.[111]

Finally, within the Gallic hagiographic tradition that Sulpicius Severus and Gregory of Tours did so much to shape, all the elements of the ideal bishop-judge continued to make heroes out of bishops.[112] In northern Francia, for example, Eligius of Noyon (588–660), a "Roman" by descent—that is, not a Frank—and a native of Aquitaine, served loyally and well in the court of King Dagobert before becoming a bishop. In his vita, composed by a friend who was himself bishop of Rouen, we see that the divine power moving inside Eligius, as inside Pachomius, followed its own inclinations.[113] Whereas Macarius of Egypt's adjuration was enough to make a dead man speak from his grave, Eligius's abjuration evicted a powerful demon from the deepest innards of a living woman.[114] Like Martin of Tours, Eligius was a worthy successor to the Hebrew prophets, as he demonstrated with the confident boom of his voice when he preached and the casual manner in which he foretold the deaths of kings and queens.[115] Eligius was fierce toward perjurers, as Nicetius had been, and people who bluffed their way through regular trials found it impossible to conceal secrets in the presence of the bishop or his tomb.[116] Even after death, Eligius would not abandon Christians who sought his protection from the harsh sentences of worldly justice, but instead his spirit sat beside princes and moved them to mercy. Many necks were saved from nooses thanks to his miraculous interventions, good reason for Eligius's cult to enjoy popularity.[117] Finally, the only surviving sermon known to have been preached by Eligius was, appropriately enough, on the Final Judgment and included quotations from Ezekiel and Isaiah. It was in a bishop's interest to remind them constantly of divine justice, Eligius assured his audience, for as their bishop he would face the ultimate tribunal with them.[118]

This was how successful bishops behaved: they were constantly vigilant, channeling their spiritual, philosophical, and pastoral training through the act of judgment. The ideal of episcopal authority relied not only on the notion of divine justice, but on the act of judging itself. As we have seen, the bishops who wrote to the emperor in Damasus's defense in 378 juxtaposed their own, careful inquiry with the hastier, scattershot, and always bloody inquisition of ordinary judges. Eligius's hagiographer made the same contrast between Eligius's posthumous prudence and the faulty rulings of public judges. Treatises such as the *Didascalia* and Ambrose's *De officiis*, as well as letters, sermons, and miracle stories, reveal a widespread belief that the process of inquiry was intrinsic to the preservation of justice, and the logical point where bishops, as administrators of justice, would focus their efforts. That was the advice Augustine of Hippo passed on to a Roman official overseeing the trial of religious offenders in 411. Although we have seen Augustine worrying to Paulinus over the possible errors plaguing every sort of examination, he encouraged Count Marcellinus to be a Christian judge, for whom "there is a greater need for inquiry than for punishment. For even the gentlest of men examine hidden crime diligently and persistently so they might find some whom they can spare."[119] As for forgiveness, so long as bishops had sincerely offered the opportunity for reconciliation and made its importance clear, they could confidently hold up their hands and announce, "We have fulfilled our episcopal duty towards these people."[120] Well within the limits of episcopal duty, however, their pastoral and judicial responsibilities were closely entwined. This convergence of pastoral and judicial functions, this dual identity of protective shepherd and judging prophet, was the distinguishing feature of the ideal bishop.

The Ideal Fails

So the episcopal ideal grew over three centuries and moved from Syria to the English Channel. The focal point of this book—the decades around the end of the fourth century—was a critical period in its evolution but neither the start nor the finish. Having now reached the limits of the ideal bishop-judge, we must turn to application and practice, and this means contemplating the failure of the ideal. In the first chapter we looked at the failure of justice in broad terms, as both a legal problem and an issue of concern for Christian leaders and the community as a whole. For the remainder of this chapter, we shall focus on a particular topic which frequently involved bishops throughout this period: accusations of sexual misconduct. As this chapter has already demonstrated, the ascetic movement made an impact on the conceptual development of episcopal authority. It also affected the day-to-day administration of the episcopal office, as bishops found themselves responsible for growing numbers of virgins and widows within their congregations, not to mention the married couples who sanctified their unions with Christian vows.

Apace with sexual renunciation came accusations of sexual misconduct. Few areas of law were so in need of spiritual discernment as these types of cases. The difficulty of disproving sexual libel drove more than one bishop to swear his innocence before holy relics, as we have seen already in the case of Damasus, bishop of Rome. We shall begin here with a concrete case that went sour. Then, just as we explored the long history of divine judgment and the attributes that empowered bishops, we shall survey the history of sexual calumny, which at times threatened to confound bishops' success. Finally, we shall juxtapose these histories and discover how one bishop, an extremely important individual for the articulation and propagation of episcopal authority, chose to respond to the failure of justice.

CALUMNY, FORNICATION, AND GENDER

Around the year 394, Bishop Ambrose of Milan (337/39–397) wrote to his colleague Syagrius in Verona.[121] Ambrose was interceding on behalf of a woman named Indicia, who shared a house in Verona with her sister and her sister's husband. Indicia came from a wealthy family; she was close friends with Ambrose's sister, Marcellina, and both women were consecrated virgins. But someone had filed anonymous charges against Indicia, charging that she was having sexual relations in violation of her oath. Ambrose had learned that everyone figured Indicia's brother-in-law was behind the charges, hoping to ruin the reputation of his wife's sister and gain control over her property.[122] Even such speculation should have been moot, because the case was so weak. Under the law, it was no case at all, so long as no one was willing to sign a formal accusation. Despite the shoddy case against her, though, Indicia's bishop, Syagrius, trying to avoid a formal confrontation, had created a scandal instead. Indicia was subjected to a vaginal examination in order to check whether her virginity remained intact.

Ambrose was furious. He wrote a sharp letter to Bishop Syagrius saying, "Will everyone be free to make accusations? When they lack evidence, will the way be wide open for them to seek the inspection of the most intimate genitalia?"[123] On Indicia's appeal, a panel of bishops, including Ambrose, cleared the woman and excommunicated the two witnesses against her. Indicia's social connections had saved her—not her piety, and certainly not the skill or religiosity of her bishop.

Whether in the loftiest circles of elite society or in the smallest rural communities, sexual offenses lent themselves especially well to false accusations and general abuse, because it was easy for accusers to explain why they might lack convincing corroboration for their story: the offensive act took place in private. As Martha Himmelfarb has shown, apocryphal texts such as visions of hell, popular throughout Late Antiquity and into the Middle Ages, placed sexual crimes and slander close together because of their common "invisibility."[124] In narrative histories from Tacitus through Ammianus Marcellinus to Gregory of Tours, where false accusations were common weapons in political intrigue (church politics included), the allegations frequently involved adultery.[125] Nicetius of Trier accused his own archdeacon of adultery: the man tried to enter the crypt of Saint Maximinus to clear himself by an oath, but before he even made it through the door he was gripped by a fierce fever. Confessing his crime, the archdeacon was "restored to the love of his bishop."[126] Even without ever approaching a courtroom or a saint's shrine, whispers, glances, gestures, and bawdy songs ruined reputations and put lives in jeopardy.[127]

Opportunities for sexual slander were embedded in the justice system. Within Roman law, the broadest and most significant changes in the later empire came under Constantine the Great, the first Christian emperor. Taken as a whole, Constantine's legislation against informers and illicit denunciations may hint at a personal "distaste" for calumniators, which also showed through in his marriage legislation.[128] His edict in 320 reforming Octavian Augustus's longstanding law on celibacy and childless marriages, for example, was an attempt to protect innocent people from calumny: it targeted informers who were manipulating antiquated procedural details to make a profit. Some informers would obtain property that was not rightfully theirs by raising technicalities, by legal cunning, and by brutally wearing down their innocent opponents in costly, embarrassing, and slow-moving lawsuits; others accepted cash payoffs from opponents who preferred to avoid the mess altogether.[129]

Six years later, Constantine dealt with adultery. Under the old law (*Lex Julia de adulteriis coercendis*), again dating back to Octavian, any member of the community in good standing could bring accusations against a woman—the usual terms of accusation in criminal statutes (*jure extranei*). Once convicted of adultery, the woman lost a portion of her dowry and other property, suffered relegation to an island (presumably only temporarily, but for an unknown duration), and was reduced to the status of a prostitute.[130] Under Constantine, only family members were allowed to file accusations, "because some persons use the right of accusation wantonly and ruin marriages by false slander."[131] The emperor, however, deplored vexatious litigation and groundless defenses as much as he did wanton accusations. Constantine therefore sought to expedite legitimate accusations of adultery. He encouraged the suspecting husband to be an "avenger of the marriage bed" and allowed accusers to withdraw their accusation if they changed their opinion or, more likely, reached a financial agreement; this also freed them from potentially suffering the penalties of calumny if their case fell apart.[132]

Later emperors in the fourth century followed Constantine's lead, smoothing the channels for accusations of adultery and punishing adulterers who tried to evade due punishment.[133] One alleged stratagem had illicit lovers claim that they were close relatives or good friends, for which reason sex between them was unthinkable. If they won their case but then married each other once the smoke from the trial had cleared, the couple would "be punished as if the crime had been clearly proved and confessed."[134] Adultery was a capital crime. Although judges appear to have had latitude in assigning penalties, contemporary literary sources record the use of the death penalty, especially in high-society cases.[135] Like other capital offenders—homicides, magicians, and sorcerers—adulterers were denied the right to appeal.[136] According to the particularly graphic and probably hyperbolic prescription crafted under Constantine's son Constans in 339, "the judge must sew up alive in a leather sack and burn the sacrilegious violators of marriage as though they were manifest parricides."[137]

Expectations of regularity similar to the requirements of secular law obtained inside the bishop's audience chamber, where in various circumstances he might act as judge, arbiter, mediator, or counselor. When handling accusations against virgins and widows, which very well might involve both moral propriety and physical property, bishops straddled religious and civil jurisdictions. What may be the earliest surviving papyrus document emanating from an episcopal hearing comes from Hermopolis and involves an accusation against a virgin named Thaësis. The woman was accused of stealing books, and the bishop Plusianon conducted her hearing inside the church atrium, with the presence of the local magistrate, a deacon, and two other men. The case against her does not appear to have been strong. The bishop, acting as an arbiter, suggested that the accused offer to swear an oath to her innocence if no witnesses could prove the alleged crime.[138] The intercession of a bishop and the sanctity of an oath added legal weight to Thaësis's moral reputation.

These deterrents only protected the innocent against calumny when officials enforced them, however, and Christians were fully aware of the threat false accusations posed to women in particular. Male advisers to sworn virgins and widows often advocated a preemptive strategy: present an impeccable character and an unassailable, transparent daily routine, never allowing the opportunity for insinuation. "To be sure, it was impossible for anyone to traverse the course of this life while avoiding the bites of other people," wrote Jerome.[139] He also reminded the virgin Principia about the dangers she and her companion, the widow Marcella, had faced when they lived in Rome, before its sack in 410. "In a slanderous city, in a town where once there were people from around the world, and the palm of vices, where they falsely accuse upright persons and pollute the pure and spotless, it is difficult not to contract some tale of wicked rumor."[140] Jerome knew the dangers of rumor first hand. Anyone "might have to run the gauntlet of accusing fingers," as Philip Rousseau observes, and sexual scandal clouded Jerome's own departure from Rome.[141] However, Jerome was not a bishop. He wrote in order to defend the virtue of female celibacy against its detractors.[142] His contemporaries, meanwhile, were defending celibate females against accusations made by their own neighbors and family members.

Modesty Versus *Temeritas Calumniae*: A Problem of Proof

Ambrose of Milan was born to protect chaste women. According to his biographer, as a boy Ambrose liked to play at bishop, much like Athanasius and his friends in Alexandria. For Ambrose, instead of performing mock baptisms, being bishop meant offering the women in the household, including his widowed mother and virgin sister, his hand to kiss.[143] As a real bishop, Ambrose gave such women the same advice as Jerome, that a solid reputation warded off innuendo and gossip. Perhaps the advice was sociologically sound, a part of displaying the right "body for the job," but there surely was a more urgent rationale behind it, best understood as pragmatic self-preservation.[144] Whatever the wisdom of the advice, Ambrose's own experience called the real value of such passive, preventive techniques into question. In one treatise he lamented the sadness of human life, the "countless calumnies, so much trouble, and the many tears of those who grieve over such trouble, and 'there is no one to console' them" (Lam 1:2).[145] In another he admitted that wherever there were wealth and honor, there would be calumny, defamation, and malicious informers. Yet he still encouraged widows to defend themselves through a pristine manner of life.[146]

Even if they were accused of fornication, the fact that widows had been married and presumably sexually active saved them some discomfort. Once accused, virgins might have had to submit to another form of proof, as Indicia had discovered. There is no way to know how often midwives performed vaginal examinations at the insistence of a judge. Although even

Jesus's mother Mary was asked to submit to a vaginal exam (in the apocryphal *Protoevangelium of James*), there was a lot of scientific skepticism over the validity of this type of evidence.[147] In Mary's case, the hand of the examiner shriveled on contact; but most women, even elite women like Indicia, could not rely on such an intervention. Unlike Syagrius, Ambrose counted himself among the skeptics on more than just this occasion.[148] He further contended that the true proof of a virgin's virtue was "reliant not upon the inspection of hidden and secret places, but upon her modesty transparent to all."[149] It is hard to imagine a more careful conduct of oneself and one's reputation than that with which Ambrose credited Indicia, the virgin in Verona, yet neither her conduct nor her reputation had saved her, as Ambrose well knew. Indicia had run up against a fundamental failure of justice to protect those who most deserved protection.

Men and women alike were powerless in terms of proof when it came to crimes committed in secret, and the increasing veneration of celibacy in clerical and aristocratic circles from the fourth century onward also stimulated commentary on adultery. Recounting the biblical story of Joseph and the adulterous wife of the Egyptian officer Potiphar (Gn 39) as a demonstration of chastity's ultimate reward in the middle of the third century, the bishop Novatian had gone on to draw attention to chastity's more immediate vulnerability: "Unobserved, in a secluded area of the house, a hiding place suitable for wicked acts, the incontinent, brazen woman thought she could overcome by means of blandishments and threats the young man's purity. . . . The imprudent woman did not hesitate to add the temerity of calumny to the crime of immorality."[150] The secrecy of the place made her accusation possible and Joseph's defense impracticable. The "temerity of calumny" (*temeritas calumniae*) that impelled her was the same temerity the Roman jurist Marcian had reviled in his commentary on false accusations.[151] In the specific matter of adultery and fornication, of course, women were more likely to fall victim to false accusations, and their legal status made their defense more difficult. This was the case for Novatian's second example of the power of chastity: Susanna. Her nature was guileless (*simplex*) and the alleged crime against her took place in secret, without witnesses other than her accusers.[152]

The story of Susanna did not exist in the Hebrew Bible; it was chapter 13 in the Septuagint version of Daniel and in the *Theodotion*, a separate translation that passed into the Old Latin Bible. Late antique Christians knew the story well. Susanna was a beautiful woman and a faithful wife. Two old men lusted after her and stole peeks at her bathing. But when they failed to seduce her, they submitted official accusations of adultery against her and testified according to Judaic law, which required at least two witnesses. Susanna was convicted and sentenced to death. She cared for her fidelity more than her life—or as Ambrose would tell the story, with a legal turn of phrase, *castitatis calumniam, religionis injuriam ploravit*.[153] Therefore, Susanna resigned herself to God, who inspired the prophet Daniel to take over the case, although he was still only a boy. Daniel separated the two old men and interrogated them individually. When their stories did not match, he declared the accusation false, and the old men were executed.

Susanna was a popular figure in Late Antiquity and the Early Middle Ages, appearing in religious literature, painting, sculpture, liturgy, and prayers. The "Commendation of the Soul," a prayer for the dying or deceased (probably from the third century) that later solidified into liturgical orations for the dead and other applications, invoked the assistance of God after the specific fashion of certain figures, mostly from Hebrew scripture. Susanna, whose own situation seemed hopeless until the moment she was saved, was an apt model for intercession in this world and the next, where humans would confront demons charging them with sins they had committed, as well as ones they had not. "Save this spirit, o Lord," the prayer pleaded, "just as you saved Susanna from a false accusation of crime."[154] Alternatively, as a symbol of marital chastity and feminine virtue, Susanna served pastors well. On the walls of catacombs and on sarcophaguses from the fourth and fifth centuries, Susanna appeared flanked by her accusers and raising her hands to invoke God's witness. But though her chastity might have inspired viewers to be loyal spouses and to put their trust in God, as Kathryn Smith has argued well, Susanna also taught an unsettling lesson about justice: virtue was vulnerable, and the law could be a weapon.[155]

CHRIST RAISES THIS HEAD WHEN THERE IS NO ACCUSER

The lesson made its biggest impact on bishops, who now found themselves in the position of Daniel.[156] In the case of Indicia, the bishop of Milan had taken his colleague Syagrius to task for violating proper procedure in the hearing. Things never should have gone so far as a physical inspection. For his part, when Indicia's case finally came to trial before himself and a group of other bishops, Ambrose followed Daniel's solution to the letter. The primary witnesses were interviewed separately, and their stories were found to differ. In this case, they did not lose their heads but were excommunicated.

Ambrose observed to Syagrius that Indicia was far worse off than even Susanna. For Susanna at least had faced actual accusers, while no one filed a formal inscription against Indicia.[157] It was a smear campaign, to which Syagrius's presence lent false judicial pretenses. The fact that the accusation against Indicia remained officially anonymous, however, also furnished Ambrose with his main artillery against his colleague. Even Jesus Christ made no qualms about getting an accused adulteress off on the basis of invalid procedure, regardless of innocence or guilt (Jn 8): "When a woman is accused, Christ lowers his head," the bishop observed, "He raises it, however, when there is no accuser." [158] Ambrose was one in a long line of commentators who used this passage to support a person's right to confront a known accuser.[159]

In a perfect world, in a world without sin, there would be no calumny. "The nature of beasts," Ambrose commented, "is *simplex*, it does not know the calumny of truth." Among beasts, mutual and unconditional affection preserved the integrity of the family.[160] As Novatian had suggested, Susanna was also *simplex*—she had no guile. However, because she lived among human beings, her virtue had to serve as a defense against malicious attacks. The example of Susanna might have given some Christians hope that their God would protect them, if not in this world, then in the judgment to come. Her virtue was so powerful, in fact, that Ambrose cast her as an active participant in her own absolution. He described how, "when she was finally condemned to death, she exclaimed like a judge of the guilty, like an arbiter of calumniators (*quasi judex reorum arbitra calumniantium*). By the authority of her innocent conscience, she summoned divine investigation (*cognitio*) to her own judgment. She was not stirred by the fear of death; she was exalted by the power of a compelling case (*arguentis censurae potestate*)." Nevertheless, the only complete escape from slander and calumny was an utter departure from society. "So Susanna fled this world and gave herself to God, fleeing to the pinnacle of the eternal city that enfolds the whole universe. For all things are within God."[161] Stuck on earth, Indicia more recently had both suffered and benefited from episcopal justice.

Ambrose's enthusiasm over the eventual rewards of divine justice sat uneasily with his practical experience, and must have left some Christians feeling abandoned. Whether in treatises on widowhood or in letters pertaining to real sex scandals, Ambrose ultimately placed the responsibility for personal security on the victims. Writing on John 5:30 ("I can of mine own self do nothing: as I hear, I judge"), Ambrose once speculated on what God would say to a Jew pleading for mercy: "The judge replies to him:

"I can do nothing on my part. In the act of judging [there is] justice; in the act of judging there is not power. I do not judge but your deeds judge in your case. They accuse you and they condemn [you]. . . . I offer nothing from myself; rather, the sentence of judgment emanates from you and against you."[162] Brent Shaw, refering to Ambrose's days sitting in judgment as a governor, before he became a bishop, suspects that Ambrose himself "must have uttered much the same words to some poor defendant facing his tribunal."[163] Virtuous people did not need to fear attack or suffer uncertainty; by implication, those who were afraid must have something to hide. This principle encompassed far more of Ambrose's outlook than merely the view from his audience chamber: this was what he taught his followers to expect from divine justice in the Final Judgment, as Éric Rebillard has demonstrated marvelously.[164] It was a harsh prospect, as foreboding as those calumnious demons of apocalyptic visions—"a view of the world," in the words of Peter Brown, "marked by sharp antitheses and by hard boundaries."[165]

Where in this landscape would one locate the ideal bishop portrayed with such charismatic vigor in the *Didascalia*, or with such compelling charm in Ambrose's own *De officiis*? Indicia's horrible examination was testimony to the incompetence of Syagrius, revealed to be one bishop likely to have failed Henry Chadwick's likeability test, and one who would perhaps have preferred passing into obscurity rather than the afterlife he actually enjoyed in Ambrose's letters. However, Indicia's eventual exoneration thanks to the intervention of the holy bishop of Milan raises much more troubling questions about the ideal of episcopal judgment, for we can scarcely image a bishop more capable and competent than Ambrose.

It seems clear that there was a "fundamental imbalance" in Ambrose's sense of justice and his role in it. Neil McLynn has offered a frank character assessment pertinent to our present analysis: "Unsparing in his denunciations of sin and immorality, he was nevertheless prepared to defend his friends and clients to the hilt."[166] Susanna had nothing to hide, therefore she was unafraid; Indicia had at least one ally who knew the law, therefore she was vindicated in the end. Ambrose does not appear to have drawn any larger lesson about justice from this experience, at least not one he shared in his treatises or letters. His attitude and actions toward female vulnerability together demonstrated the limits theological notions of justice and the ideal of episcopal judgment could attain, while still remaining distant from the reality in which ordinary people lived.

Ambrose, who was experienced in law both inside and outside the church, who carefully crafted his own image as a bishop and a judge, and who steered the training and conduct of other bishops in Northern Italy, deliberately and consciously contributed to the development of an episcopal personality.[167] He preferred to emphasize the capabilities that gifted officials could bring to the courtroom, however, rather than dwell on the limitations that bound the hands of even the best judges. Nevertheless, even Ambrose sometimes had no choice but to sweat through the mundane details of ordinary justice, and on such occasions, like all bishops, Ambrose rediscovered how clumsy the tools at their disposal could be. In the final analysis, then, Ambrose was content to have left the tension between the ideology of divine justice and the reality of worldly justice not only unresolved, but virtually unacknowledged. This issue was, however, too important to episcopal authority for bishops to ignore it for long.

3

Christian Oaths: A Case Study in Practicality over Doctrine

ALTHOUGH POPULAR RESPONSES to intellectual and institutional developments are difficult to trace, we are able to reconstruct the demands that led one famous church leader to bend his ideology to accommodate social reality. Here Augustine of Hippo's attitudes toward the swearing of oaths is examined over the course of his long career as a bishop. During this period, Christians accepted oath-swearing as a necessary method of establishing trust in communities where justice was otherwise uncertain and relationships were dangerous.

Oaths Are Social Bonds

In any community, trust may exist at different levels, between family members, business partners, neighbors, allies, leaders and their followers, and be manifested in a range of verbal, written, symbolic, and practical forms, including oaths. Throughout antiquity and the Middle Ages, trust shared an intimate history with the swearing of oaths. As we have seen, calumny drew so much fire from emperors, jurists, bishops, and professional spell casters because it was dangerously, pathologically antisocial. By perverting the safeguards that kept uncertainty contained, calumniators threatened to destroy the basic relationships constituting society. No procedural or legislative antidotes, as we have seen, worked effectively against calumny's destructive tendency. Trust alone prevented the annihilation of relationships and thus of society itself. Trust was neither a disposition, nor a belief, nor an expectation, all of which might exist isolated in the mind of an individual and be unaffected by context, circumstance, or reality. Instead, trust was intrinsically social and involved inclinations opposite to calumny—namely, the willingness to create relationships with other people, to maintain them over time, to forego the chance of one-time windfalls and instead opt for long-term security, and thus to sustain society.[1] Communities relied on trust, and oaths defined communities.

In the opinion of some modern scholars, however, the sort of trust that swearing involved blended with Christian values like water and oil— not at all, that is to say, at least not until "Germanic influence" wore pious sensibility down to an irrational, superstitious nub. Hasso Jaeger made an eloquent contribution to this widely held view in proceedings of the Jean Bodin Society published in 1963: "The oath, just like the ordeal, corresponds to a 'selfish' attitude and to a feeling of biological membership to a community of blood; it is opposed, by its very nature, to the spiritual and self-less principle of charity."[2] We shall not find much evidence for this sentiment among ordinary late antique or medieval Christians, with the possible exception of some so-called Pelagians, as we shall see, or Cathars centuries later.[3] Nor did this condemnation represent a consensus among their religious leaders. Some prominent voices, it is true, forbade or restricted the swearing of oaths.[4] Christian scripture justified their position: "Do not swear at all (*nolite omnino jurare*)," said Jesus, "either by heaven, for it is God's throne, or by the earth, for it is his footstool, or by Jerusalem, for it is the city of the great king. And do not swear by your head, for you cannot make even one hair white or black. Let your oath be yes [for] yes, no [for] no; anything beyond this is from the evil one" (Mt 5:34–37; Jas 5:12). Bishops' expectations of community, charity, trust, and justice, nonetheless, were not far removed from the ordinary men and women of their society. And ordinary people swore oaths. While a handful of intellectuals and hardliners debated the legitimacy of oaths, the Christianization of swearing was already well underway.

Augustine of Hippo was one of the intellectuals who thought, wrote, preached, and debated about oaths—more so, probably, than anyone else— and in his earliest writings he even pursued hard-line arguments against swearing. As a bishop, however, who handled matters of trust and uncertainty on a daily basis, he soon developed his own theology of swearing. What makes Augustine's opinions on oaths so remarkable is not how far or how little he was able to sway fellow theologians to his way of thinking. Rather, it is how much, and with what sympathy, his thinking swayed before the needs and practices of ordinary Christians. Of course, as James O'Donnell has observed in his biography, we must be aware that the elderly Augustine, looking back on his life's work in the *Retractationes* ("Reconsiderations," a sort of annotated auto-bibliography), would not have us focus on this development. The *Retractationes*, O'Donnell writes, "replaced the living, breathing, quarreling cleric with Augustine the author," thus creating the image of a career author that was attractive to later authors including Cassiodorus and Bede the Venerable, as Mark Vessey has argued.[5] But Augustine's grappling with oaths throughout his career reveals to us the living bishop—sometimes frustrated but willing to question his own ideas. As early as 398 (the date of a letter in which he addressed the swearing of oaths as a social fact), Augustine stopped writing about oaths for academic purposes and began supplying lay people with pragmatic advice. Swearing put the philosophy of justice in starkly human and pressing terms, as he preached to his congregation some fifteen years later in 415. Every time a person confronted the mundane question of whether or not to swear an oath in a particular situation, "it is as if [God] has set you against your own reflection."[6] And, when it was necessary, especially in situations where trust was lacking, the bishop himself swore oaths.

In their experience with oath-swearing, bishops like Augustine also absorbed a critical, subtle lesson about justice. Whether oaths cemented trust between people where it already existed or fabricated trust where it was absent, oaths invariably relied on a sturdier trust in divine justice. When people swore, they invoked supernatural precision and accountability into their own lives, merging their low expectations of worldly justice with their higher expectations of divine justice. Such a convergence had both professional and philosophical relevance for bishops. Whereas experience with the administration and reform of law had revealed to bishops how due process or the threat of calumny could impede their authority, the accomodation of oath-swearing expanded it. Already by the fifth century, saints were standing in the place of—or alongside—the gods who once had guaranteed oaths (and continued to do so, alongside the newcomers). Soon bishops themselves, as we saw when considering Nicetius of Trier and Eligius of Noyen above, ensured that oaths sworn in their names or in their presence would receive justice.

We shall see in the final chapter how bishops used the power of forgiveness to teach ordinary Christians the limits of episcopal justice, the importance of mercy, and the extent of their own accountability for the sins of their followers. But first, in this chapter we shall witness a different process of education working in the opposite direction. For oaths revealed to bishops an expectation of accountability, certainty, and justice their followers would never forego. In short, oath-swearing is one of the few instances—alongside the practice of granting asylum, for example, as studied

by Anne Ducloux—where we clearly can see that social practice contributed to changes in institutions and ideas.[7]

The Public Life of Oaths

Oaths were adaptable, flexible, and ubiquitous. Their formulas could be
elaborate or curt, their performance a mere gesture or an elaborately orchestrated ritual, with a respected official mediating or else no mediator at all.
Oaths brought divine intervention to bear on daily life; they fulfilled social
necessities; and they responded to the common desire for personal security. The habit of swearing (in the view of some theologians) may have
tended to inure Christians to the danger of perjury, but trust and security
in human society required vows all the same. Not even bishops passed
through life without offering oaths, and nothing alerted Christian intellectuals to the dangers of swearing more acutely than their firsthand experience. But even when they sought out biblical guidance on the troublesome
issue, they faced an entire history—their own, sacred history—inscribed
from its genesis by oaths.

What Is at Stake: Truth, Judgment, Justice

Jerome, the famous translator, ascetic, and spiritual advisor, was a moder-
ate in the matter of oaths. He grumbled when people swore by anything
other than God's name (*nisi per dominum deum nostrum*). Those types of
oaths, secular oaths, he believed, were what Matthew 5:34 prohibited. Oaths
were sacred, and therefore should invoke only the source of all holiness.[8]
And yet Jerome understood ancient oaths perfectly, whether or not they
were Christian. In his commentary on Jeremiah, he pinpointed what gave
oaths their compelling, binding force: they encompassed truth, judgment,
and justice, and "without these there will be no oath, only perjury."[9] The
action of swearing might be as complex as a surety binding multiple parties in a written contract or as simple as one person uttering a promise
heavenward. When making any oath, however, a person submitted his or
her vow to transcendental standards. Should the promise be kept, he or
she would expect to benefit from those standards; should it be violated,
to suffer them. Oaths offered ordinary people an association with these
divine ideals—truth, judgment, and justice.

THE ROOTS OF SWEARING

The double function of every oath was to bind and to judge. In some ancient societies, swearing developed out of ordeal trials.[10] "Ordeal" (from Old English *ordal*) is a ritual that invokes a supernatural revelation of the truth. At the request of human beings (usually a priest will mediate) and through some sign (that may require priestly interpretation), a divinity reveals whether or not a person is lying. The most notorious ordeals in Western history are the medieval "trial by fire" and early modern witchcraft tests.[11] Various types of ordeals are well known from the legal and literary sources of the ancient Near East, as well, such as one in the name of Marduk, the chief deity of Babylon.[12] The purgative oath (by which the act of swearing exculpates a person), moreover, corresponds to "medial judgment" in early common law, or *Beweisurteil* (the German "Urteil" corresponding to English "ordeal") among historians of ancient law. In such a process, disputing parties negotiate the most appropriate terms by which to swear; a divinity then stands as the guarantor of the resulting oath. This hearkens back to the oldest surviving depiction of oaths in Western literature—the swearing scene on the Homeric shield of Achilles.[13] In fact, all oaths involved divine inquiry and compulsion. Although direct evidence for ordeals is relatively scarce from the imperial and late Roman periods, oaths continued to carry out many of the same functions.[14] The terms of an oath were inescapable. This was the most basic fact about oaths, and the one Christian authors like Jerome could understand most readily, even when criticizing oaths that did not invoke their God.

Oaths—and ordeals for that matter—were also closely related to curses. The power of the oath relied on the implicit or explicit curse to befall one who broke it or swore falsely. For Augustine, the gravest oath a person could utter was a curse (*exsecratio*) against oneself: "If I do this, let me suffer the same" (*si illud feci, illud patiar*).[15] Oaths and curses both invoked the ancient sense of sacred (especially Greek *anathêma*, Latin *sacer*)—what was given over to a divinity was off-limits for human beings.[16] In the same way, Jewish and Christian excommunication bound the subject directly to God (Hebrew *herem*).[17] These relationships are, admittedly, difficult to distinguish absolutely (oath, curse, and excommunication); in practice, however, all that mattered was the active bond between human and divine that protected fidelity, uncovered deception, and punished transgression: truth, judgment, and justice. To people throughout much of antiquity and the Middle Ages, appeal to those divine activities offered better odds for satisfaction than reliance on social institutions.[18]

JUSTICE IN AND BEYOND THE GRAVE

The types of evidence for oaths, ordeals, and curses are as varied as the formulas themselves, and just as challenging to coordinate. The most intriguing specimens may be ancient funereal epitaphs, which often bore imprecations against tomb violators. Inscriptions ranging across the first through the fourth centuries make terse appeals to divine activity on behalf of the deceased. These are expectations of justice in extremis, boiled down to bare bones.

One famous assemblage of grave curses is from Phrygia, and it delivers a couple of pointed lessons to students of Western oath-swearing.[19] Many grave curses promised divine judgment to tomb violators (*estai autôi pros ton theon* or *pros tên krisin*). Those who erected the monuments counted on supernatural, spiritual discernment: there would be no deception (*mê lathoito ton theon*).[20] Justice, too, was expected, where dedications to the "Holy and Just" in the masculine or feminine were frequent (*hosios kai dikaios* or *hosia kai dikaia*),[21] though it might be slow in coming (*dôsei logon tôi theôi en hêmerai kriseôs*, "will render an account before God on Judgment Day"). One formula guaranteed that the guilty would be accountable before the hand of God (*pros tên cheira tou theou*), which surely recalled that most common and ancient oath gesture, the raised hand.[22] It is difficult, often impossible, to tell for certain whether there was a religious orientation to these formulas.[23] Some seem clearly polytheistic in origin and many were Jewish; eventually, definitely Christian formulas appeared.[24] But activating the divine predilection for truth, judgment, and justice in the form of ordeals, curses, and oaths was the prerogative of no single religious culture. Whoever erected the tombstones had entrusted the deceased to divine protection, and the inscriptions physically reinforced the solemnity of that pact.

BUSINESS AND POLITICAL OATHS: SLOW CHANGE

The religious transformation of swearing (its "Christianization") was slow, subtle, and never complete. Not surprisingly, the process also was not uniform across time or space. Just like in society generally, dramatic change took place first, maybe only, at the political level. Social and economic habits resisted change, yielding to influences from the new religion only with reluctance. Our most abundant and best-studied sources for swearing are business contracts surviving from Egypt. The oaths that bound the parties in these documents usually referred to the current emperor or emperors, making them valuable as dating devices to papyrologists.[25] They incidentally reveal Christians, long after the official conversion of the empire, casually swearing by the good fortune of the emperor—business, after all, is business. There are references to the "Father, Son, and Holy Spirit" from around 439, not earlier; the "Trinity" (*trias*) appears in these oaths only from the reign of Justinian onwards, even later than it does in grave inscriptions, and can later be found in an oath confirming an amicable divorce.[26] Basil of Caesarea had argued to his governor in 372 that tax collectors should not compel destitute farmers to swear an oath when they could not pay their taxes. Basil's concern was not that they might be swearing in the name of an emperor or a false divinity. Instead, he anticipated the great temptation for the farmers simply to lie and avoid payment; that would get them in the habit of swearing. The fact that a perjurer always ran the risk of divine and swift retribution (*oxeian epagei tên antapodosin ho kyrios*) was the gravest concern: the collector would lose revenue, and the farmer his soul.[27] Finally, in other forms of sworn arrangements (Latin *stipulatio*, *sponsio*), the witnesses themselves might serve as "oracles and avengers" to the settled terms, a tradition that would find echoes in the Early Middle Ages as far away as Ireland and Wales.[28]

As for political oaths, Virgil had warned the first Roman emperor that he had better get used to being invoked in oaths, even while he was still alive.[29] Public inscriptions, such as the one erected during Octavian's lifetime in the Iberian province of Baetica, joined later oaths in business contracts, such as those we have seen recorded on papyrus, in proclaiming the emperor's good fortune (Greek *sôtêria*, Latin *salus*).[30] In the third century Tertullian could tolerate swearing by an emperor's fortune(Greek *tychê*, Latin *genius*), if not his tutelary deities.[31] Wooden tablets record oaths sworn by the current emperor along with the spirits (*numina*) of his predecessors.[32] Citizens and soldiers alike swore loyalty oaths, complete with caveats against perjury.[33] An inscription from western North Africa is a remnant of a ceremony in which soldiers offered sacrifice to Jupiter Optimus Maximus and swore loyalty to the emperor before his image, which was attached to a shield.[34] Altars from such ceremonies survive in Britain, where they were buried on the parade ground each January, when oaths were renewed and a new altar erected.[35] Servants of the state, within five days of entering office, swore to preserve new imperial statutes as well as the old. When they swore, they swore as publicly as possible, on the temple steps above the forum, facing the rising sun.[36] By the end of the fourth century, the annual military oath added the members of the Trinity before the greatness of the emperor (*jurant per deum et per christum et per spiritum sanctum et per majestatem imperatoris*).[37] The political value of these practices was not lost on Western successors to the emperors.[38] Christianity affected the form of oath-swearing, but not its omnipresence.

Solemn Promises plus Some Exemptions

Although it was difficult for some late antique Christians to accommodate contemporary swearing practices, their most ancient sacraments (*sacramenta*) were in essence oaths.[39] These shared their history, moreover, with Judaic and polytheistic traditions of ritual swearing. Baptism, for example, was an oath, and not just in a vaguely symbolic sense. Tertullian, concerned as he was over the terms of proper conduct, had described religious initiation with the technical vocabulary of sworn agreements (*stipulatio*, *sponsio*): baptism was nothing other than a "consensual contract" between God and the new Christian.[40] Even if the church would not control the sacrament of marriage until the High Middle Ages, conjugal vows were sacred. It was their oath that bound Christian spouses to each other and their union to Christ as its witness. Severing that union would figuratively "tear apart" the body of Christ. Bishops, moreover, witnessed the dotal contracts between newlyweds (*tabulae matrimoniales*).[41] During the fourth century, oaths to abstain from sex had become not only more common, but also more public.[42] Spouses, for example, might decide to swear a mutual vow of chastity. It bound them as tightly as their marriage oath (*te obstrinxisti*); again, God preserved its record (*tenetur apud Deum sponsio*).[43] Melania the Younger and her husband, Pinianus, were among the most prominent citizens of Rome to swear such an oath, as we shall see later. Pinianus, it turned out, was far more successful at keeping this vow than another he made later on. Because of the religious tutelage he and Melania shared, however, he doubtlessly knew that all vows worked the same way: God summoned oaths like a lender called in debts (*et debita exigit et promissa persolvit*).[44]

    When unwed or widowed people pledged their chastity, they engaged God in a contract, much like people who made votive offerings in return for divine benefaction.[45] Such offerings might take the form of promises to be on good behavior, specific acts like erecting a shrine, or gifts—either symbolic, material, or cash. The records of votives survive from countless inscriptions on monuments, gravestones, and the gifts themselves.[46] One tangible result of Christianization is the appearance of votive offerings from people buried close to the shrines and relics of saints (*ad sanctos*)—the privilege, after all, had a cost. As we shall see later, in the Christian Middle Ages as throughout antiquity, any sort of occasion might elicit a vow, from an aggravating headache to an invasion by barbarian hordes. Sometimes, however, vows and gifts did not win satisfaction, and disappointment could test the credulity of anyone who put their faith in divine activities. A sense of betrayal hovers around the grief in this epitaph: "Marcus Antonius Augustanius Philetus, most innocent son, who lived 3 years, 8 months, 10 days, a little boy whose life the gods (whose names one dare not utter) stripped away, against the vows (*contra votum*) of his parents."[47] Such melancholy outcomes, nevertheless, emphasize the shared solemnity of oaths and the general expectation of their fulfillment. It did not take a Christian theologian to explain that, as unreliable as human beings were even when under oath, God was the most opaque participant in any act of swearing.

God swore, and not always by the rules.[48] For example, when God told Abraham to spare Isaac's life, there was no doubt about it: God had altered his own oath. This did not surprise Ambrose of Milan, according to whom God frequently changed his mind (*sententiam*).[49] The bishop's larger point here, in the treatise *De officiis*, was that, in contrast to God, humans were far too inept to engage themselves in the uncertain wagers of oaths. Nervous excitement or muddling inebriation was all it took for them to make a vow they would later regret; perjury was a wicked thing, but one might swear to perform an act yet more wicked. To demonstrate, Ambrose drew on examples of imprudent oaths by biblical figures. Herod, for example, had murdered John the Baptist rather than break his foolhardy promise to the contemptible Salome. He thus compounded stupidity with wickedness.[50] Basil of Caesarea suggested that modern princes might learn from Herod. Their own oaths might have hidden consequences for their subjects, so it was better to violate bad oaths than to sin in fulfillment of their obligation.[51] Moreover, in one of his "canonical" letters (guidelines on Christian behavior composed during 374/75) Basil took off five years from an eleven-year term for penitents who had committed perjury because of violence or force (*ek bias kai anagkês*).[52]

If oaths were sacred and fundamentally binding, how could Ambrose and Basil treat them as if they were negotiable? Both men were willing to count some oaths less sacrosanct than others, even providing loopholes for impetuous people and drunkards. Ambrose, at first glance, appears to have

contradicted himself in this regard. During his famous clash with Symmachus, an old-fashioned senator and polytheist, when presenting his side
to Emperor Valentinian, Ambrose acknowledged all oaths to be dangerously solemn and binding, even those sworn on a pagan shrine.[53] Nevertheless, Ambrose was determined throughout his career to establish clearly
defined boundaries around the Christian community and within it as well,
between what was sacred and what was trivial, for the benefit of its faithful members.[54] These boundaries represented new priorities, the talking
points of the religion, which sometimes conflicted with what only recently
had been the easy and unproblematic rules of social interaction. Keep all
communications simple, Ambrose admonished Christians in *De officiis*, talk
straight and do not try to trick neighbors with circumlocution. But, in the
event of an unfair promise, "it is more tolerable not to carry out a promise
than to do something shameful."[55]

Exegetes on Swearing

Isolating inviolable from spurious oaths was an immense challenge for
pastors like Ambrose: they were determined to direct the behavior of their
followers along paths removed as far as possible from regions of moral
ambiguity. The challenge, perhaps, explains why every Christian who wrote
on oath-swearing during the late fourth century used similar rationale to
explain away a nettling and obvious conflict in the Bible regarding oaths:
Oaths and curses are common in the Old Testament, but the New Testament
appears to prohibit them. Once exposed, the discrepancy begged explanation; this was not a unique problem for Christian exegetes, and we find a
number of responses in the literature.[56] So, for example, in a letter of 390
to Chromatius of Aquileia (the only surviving correspondence between the
two bishops), Ambrose found it worthwhile to ponder the academic but
popular question of whether God could commit perjury.[57] The answer was
unequivocally negative, but the question itself begged a series of less tract-
able dilemmas.

Chromatius of Aquileia: "Anyone Who Speaks Truly Swears"

Chromatius, who became bishop of Aquileia in 387 or 388, enjoyed high
regard among theologians, especially his friends Jerome and Ambrose.

Like his older colleague in Milan, Chromatius was ambivalent about oath-swearing. He explored the sacred and social aspects of oaths in his commentary on Jesus's censure of swearing during the Sermon on the Mount (for example, Mt 5:31–37).[58] At the same time that he affirmed their solemnity, Chromatius was troubled by their implications for modern Christian society, and so he, too, had recourse to biblical exegesis. Scripture itself was a series of oaths—"pledges about the truth to come" (*sacramenta futurae veritatis*)—and, like the oaths God swore in the Old Testament, existed solely as a result of "human incredulity." Because of his inherent truthfulness, God was not only unable to lie, but everything he said had an oath's same power (*pro juramento habetur*). It was human "treachery"—specifically, for Chromatius, the "treachery of Jewish infidelity"—that required anything more than the truthful words themselves. The Jews of scripture would believe and obey only what was sworn by oath; God therefore acquiesced, repeatedly, on their behalf by making solemn promises.[59] Oath-swearing thus reinforced the difference between the Old Law and the New, between the "error" of the Jews and the correct faith of Christians. Chromatius found a "double meaning" (*duplex intellegentia*) in the evangelical prohibition of swearing, half of which was for Jesus' followers to forego the Jews' naïve reliance on the power of oaths.[60]

That Chromatius and his contemporaries knew little about Jewish oath-swearing, whether biblical or contemporary, is hardly surprising.[61] They were determined to distance Christian conduct from the moral, spiritual, and exegetical ambiguities swearing raised. God did not need oaths, but Jews demanded them relentlessly. Christians should be more like God and less like Jews. "The Lord wants no difference to exist between the oaths we swear and the words we speak," Chromatius advised. "Just as no treachery should enter an oath, there should be no lies in our speech, because both perjury and lying (*perjurium et mendacium*) are condemned by the punishment of divine judgment. . . . Anyone who speaks truly swears."[62] Any Christian, in turn, who swore truthfully and often, might feel free to lie when not under oath. Crafty Christians, moreover, might imagine that oaths sworn by something other than God's name offered them a loophole. Therefore, Jesus had proscribed a list of oaths: "neither by heaven, for it is God's throne, nor by the earth, for it is his footstool; nor by Jerusalem, for it is the city of the great king, [nor] by your head, because you cannot make one hair white or black" (Mt 5:34–6). To Chromatius, unlike Jerome, this prohibition was inclusive and absolute: do not swear at all, by God or anything else, whether falsely or in truth.[63]

Chromatius was not alone in suspecting that ingenious humans would evade simple prohibitions against swearing. Augustine of Hippo had received his catechesis from Ambrose while Chromatius was still a priest in Aquileia. By the time he joined his elders in clerical vows, Augustine was exploring similar routes through the exegetical problem of biblical swearing as his colleagues and, like Chromatius, he wound up at the error of the Jews. They had believed that oaths not rendered to God, but instead sworn by heaven or by earth, did not oblige them to God. "The fault lay not with [God] giving the instructions," Augustine hastened to add, "but with those [Jews] who understood poorly."[64]

Within his exegesis of the Gospel's prohibition, however, Augustine made different emphases than had Chromatius. God's throne, his footstool: these things represented divine judgment. The hair on one's head accentuated just how far its jurisdiction extended. What, he entertained, could have less to do with God and belong more clearly to oneself than hair? Yet that was precisely where the Jews went astray. "Nothing is so vile in the creatures of God," Augustine insisted, "that anyone should decide to commit perjury by it." Everything, in reality, is sacred, so every oath belongs to God.[65] Jesus had not forbidden oaths entirely; rather, Jesus had entirely taken over possession of oaths. Augustine, therefore, stood apart from both Chromatius and Jerome in his interpretation of *nolite omnino jurare*. He used the error of the Jews as his contemporaries did, to be sure, but making sense of Jewish behavior generations before the advent of the Messiah was one thing. It was something else entirely to explain why oaths existed in the Bible after Christ's passion and ascension—why, especially, Paul swore oaths repeatedly, as we shall see. The matter was one that demanded careful consideration (*diligenter considerandum est*).

Young Augustine: "Be the Sky, So That You May Carry God"

Augustine wrote his commentary on the Sermon on the Mount during 394 and the early months of 395, several years after entering the priesthood but before he had succeeded Valerius to the episcopal throne of Hippo. Like Jerome and Chromatius, he took the sacredness of oaths very seriously. He was also aware of their meaningful presence in Christian life, from the adjurations that exorcized demons at baptism, to the vows that bound married couples together with Christ.[66] Augustine's writings are the most important Western source for swearing, not least because they span much of his long career and reveal a shift in his attitude toward oaths within that period. His responsibilities as a community leader, along with his involvement in various cosmopolitan circles, continually exposed him to practices of swearing. That may help to explain why he appears to have sustained his theoretical inquiry far longer than anyone else in his generation. In his last relevant thoughts recorded on the subject, although he had residual reservations, Augustine had placed oaths firmly within the bonds of Christian society. Early in his career, however, it was only his relentless insistence on precision that set him apart from and also led him to conflict with his peers.

In the same commentary on Matthew 5:33–37 that argued for Jewish incredulity and the power of oaths, Augustine paused to enunciate the possessive relationship between all things and their divine creator. He had already demonstrated that Jews misunderstood God's instructions on oaths. Would the metaphor of God enthroned that Jesus derived from Isaiah 66 clarify matters for Christians? Augustine spelled it out: heaven is God's throne, the earth his footstool. God did not sit like a human on a chair, his limbs stretched out between earth and heaven. Instead, the throne represented the "divine force" of infallible judgment, which symbolically resided in the heavens to demonstrate its source, God's "most perfect beauty." Meanwhile, although they were subject to this constant appraisal, humans remained at a distance, bound to earth while they were yet sinners, because "justice applies according to merit."[67] Ironically, oath-swearing was an action born out of human incredulity, a product of the sinful state, but it also bound its subjects to the "divine force" (the same double bond key to most oaths, ordeals, and curses, regardless of their religious context, as we have seen).

Elsewhere, moreover, Augustine turned this relationship between divine justice and weak-willed humans into an invitation, one he would continue to extend years after he became a bishop. During a sermon preached in the small town of Boseth in 404, for example, he encouraged his audience, "If the sky is God's throne, be the sky, so that you may carry God. When you begin to carry God, you will be the sky."[68] The people who heard these words doubtlessly used oaths on a regular basis, just like people in Carthage, Hippo, and anywhere else in the ancient world. They did not become the sky simply by swearing, of course, but by swearing they began to carry God. That, for Augustine, was what made oaths both solemn and dangerous.

Just as his methodology (scriptural exegesis) was common at the time, so the advice young Augustine had offered on swearing followed familiar lines. Habit was the thing most to be feared. "What could be said to be more taxing and toilsome," he asked, "than when the mind of a believer exercises all the energy at its disposal towards overcoming a pernicious habit?"[69] The matter was important enough to address in another treatise he composed around the same time, *On Lying*. Swearing led to a facility for swearing, he explained, and that was the first step toward habit, itself a slippery slope into perjury.[70] Ideally, a person's good conduct would speak to his or her personal trustworthiness better than oaths could. That might not be possible on earth, but Christians at least could reach for the sky, "take refuge in the fortress of the Christian army, and from that higher ground cast down the innumerable hordes of all the wicked habits rebelling" against them.[71] Like his contemporaries, Augustine tended to treat oath-swearing and perjury in tandem, and to justify their elision by invoking the specter of habit. He also was careful at this stage not to stray far from the biblical texts into the less certain realms of social bonds or human behavior.

Did Paul Swear or Did He Lie?

Within those parameters, however, Augustine held his own and others' exegeses to rigid standards of consistency and precision. For example, theologians of this time generally divided types of lying into three categories.[72] While generally agreeing that outright lies were sinful and that fabrications not intended to be believed were not, they disagreed over the third type. This was the polite or expedient lie (*mendacium officiosum*) a person told not to cause harm but for a neutral or even a good purpose—to spare a person tragic information, facilitate a complex argument, or avoid a long explanation. The expedient lie, nevertheless, functioned by deception, and Augustine, for one, counted it a sin. Others did not, including Jerome who, in a commentary on Paul's letter to the Galatians, claimed that even the apostle would tell an expedient lie. Augustine would not have it. "If we admit polite lies into the holy scriptures," he wrote in a letter sent to Jerome in Bethlehem in 397, "what authority will remain there?"[73] Both men defended their positions on exegetical grounds. But when an apparent conflict emerged, rather than accept the possibility of a contradiction within the scripture (that is, that Paul might tell a lie now and then for the sake of his doltish audience), Augustine insisted the exegesis was wrong. According to the bishop of Hippo, when Jerome believed Paul told polite lies, Jerome was misreading Paul.

The same principle steered Augustine's consideration of the Gospel's prohibition, "Do not swear at all" (*nolite omnino jurare*). "At all" (*omnino*) did not leave much ambiguity. So what about the fact that Paul, who, because he was divinely inspired, could not even tell an expedient lie, openly swore oaths, although they were prohibited? As with the phantom polite lie, there was no way around the fact that Paul swore. So Augustine, sticking to the rule of scriptural integrity over exegetical cleverness, concluded that Matthew 5:34 must not prohibit oaths.

This conclusion was not innovative in itself, but Augustine contemplated the circumstances, motives, and language of Paul's oaths with a visible curiosity that reflected his interest in swearing as a social fact and a necessary device for signifying trust. Paul enforced his assertions with oaths, there was no way around it: "God is my witness" (*testis enim mihi est deus*, Rom 1:9); "God the father of our Lord Jesus Christ . . . knows I do not lie" (*deus et pater domini nostri Iesu Christi . . . scit quia non mentior*, 2 Cor 11:31); "before God I do not lie" (*ecce coram deo quia non mentior*, Gal 1:20). "God is my witness" was an oath just as much as "by God" (*per deum*); it was the sense, not the letter, of the formula that constituted an oath—to suggest otherwise was ridiculous.[74]

Furthermore, the manner in which Paul swore diminished neither the solemnity nor the simple fact of his oath. For a brief moment, Augustine considered whether perhaps Paul swore only in writing, when he had the luxury of careful consideration to prevent an imprudent promise, and whether this would matter. To swear in such a fashion would indeed be safer than making a verbal oath when, presumably, all the spontaneous twists, turns, and digressions of ordinary conversation might result in an ill-considered vow (recall Ambrose and Basil's comments on Herod, for example). But Augustine did not entertain a distinction between written and spoken oaths for long. First of all, there was no real basis for comparison, because scripture naturally recorded only Paul's written oaths— Augustine showed himself a good source critic.

Secondly, a written oath was as much an oath as any other oath.[75] Augustine and his correspondents used the very same oath formulas in their own letters: "for the Lord is witness" in 395; "I adjure you by Christ to respond" in 402; "behold once again I call God to witness" in 405.[76] Once in 391, begging Bishop Valerius, his predecessor at Hippo, for more leisure time before commencing his priestly duties, Augustine repeated how

Valerius had made "Christ the Lord witness" his good intentions toward his young protégé, "as if I could not myself swear to them."[77] The ostensible reason for his critical letter to Jerome in 397, moreover, was to commend to him its bearer, a certain Paul, whose good character Augustine confirmed "before God."[78] In another letter, Augustine swore that that he had not been slandering Jerome and his scholarship (*deum nostrum testor hoc non me fecisse*), but Jerome appeared unconvinced.[79] Regarding the apostle Paul, however, the facts were indisputable. Written or spoken, oaths constituted swearing, and Paul swore repeatedly. To say that the apostle, who composed his letters "for the spiritual life and salvation" of humanity, was guilty of violating a divine precept would be wicked.[80] The prohibition, therefore, must have a different meaning, one less apparent than what Jerome or Chromatius or other commentators had made out: *diligenter considerandum est*.

Augustine concluded that there was a difference between oaths and perjury, that oaths in themselves were not sinful, and that social bonds required oaths.[81] Human fallibility and mendacity had not vanished with Jesus's sacrifice. Perhaps Christians had ceased to expect oaths from God, but they still demanded them from each other. One day this would no longer be the case, when all Christians would "be the sky" and "carry God." Until then, those of strong faith had to help those whose faith was still weak. Fallibility or weakness (*infirmitas*) was wicked, not oaths; weakness was also natural.[82] Far from being an absolute prohibition against swearing, Jesus's admonition, *nolite omnino jurare*, suggested the proper path through a society bound by oaths. "It must be understood to have this purpose," Augustine explained: "to the extent that is in you, you should not strive, not have love, not be hungry for oath-swearing with any sort of delight, as if it were for a good reason."[83] Although Augustine formulated this recommendation through conventional exegesis and in the context of criticizing dangerous habits, he had already veered away from the basic position most of his peers expressed in one fashion or another.

Socialis Necessitudo and the Need for Oaths

Swearing was a dangerous habit, but it was also a human habit: it arose not from wickedness but from what Augustine followed Cicero in describing as "social bond" (*socialis necessitudo*)—the risks that arose from contact with other human beings, from the time Adam joined Eve in sin down to the present, affecting every member of human society, including philosophers, bishops, and apostles.[84] "No one knows," Augustine claimed, "except someone who has been there (*expertus est*), how difficult it is, first, to extinguish the habit of swearing, second, never to fear doing what necessity sometimes requires doing."[85] Pressure to relapse was powerful and constant. Only a few years removed from the leisurely world of intellectualism and immersed in pastoral duties, and not even yet a bishop when he wrote this, Augustine already claimed to have "been there." In the years to come, his experience with oath-swearing would increase exponentially, and not always in areas through which his analytical powers could guide him so reliably.

EVEN DEMONIC OATHS EARN TRUST

Around 398, the bishop of Hippo, in office almost two years, received a letter from an acquaintance named Publicola.[86] Augustine addressed him as *honorabilis* in his response, and the occasion of the letter implies wealth: Publicola owned estates in North Africa, in the region where people known as the Arzuges dwelled, probably around the border of modern Tunisia and Libya.[87] Publicola was not resident on these estates, however, and relied on his representatives on the ground to keep him abreast of business.[88] Recently the landowner had been troubled by the circumstances under which his agents had been occasionally employing people who were probably nomads—representatives of the *barbarae innumerabiles gentes* who, to a large extent, negotiated their own *modus vivendi* with the officers monitoring the most southerly boundaries of the empire, and who drew the attention of bishops and governors alike.[89] Publicola knew something about the political situation, but what had piqued his interest was the intrusion of pagan gods into the social and economic interactions of the area.

The "barbarians" (*barbari*) in question worked under hire to guard Publicola's estates, protect the produce from his fields, and occasionally provide safe passage for travelers through the area.[90] When his overseers contracted their labor or services, the parties sealed the arrangement with oaths. Naturally, for the oaths to be binding, the employees swore according to their own custom—Publicola did not know the particular formulas (they were sworn *per daemones*, he writes), only that they were not Christian. No doubt Publicola's God was the intruder on transactions that had proceeded without difficulty up till then, but he was not concerned with local traditions. So the question, once an overseer accepted a pagan oath, was whether he and (more importantly, for Publicola) his employer shared in the sin of paganism. "If swearing by their demons to protect the crops does not pollute the crops themselves (which would contaminate the Christian who knowingly eats from them or makes a profit from their sale)," Publicola wrote, "then please let me know. . . . What am I supposed to do about these crops and their sale?"[91] He knew the practice was common and that nearby frontier officers also received oaths sworn *per daemones*. Oaths were necessary even when other pledges—money, hostages, or both— changed hands. The reason was that the act of swearing stood for public credit (*medium intercessit*).[92]

Once Publicola had taken the initiative to write to an authority on spiritual matters, he did not shrink from asking additional questions. These, thirteen in all, ranged across issues of cosmic belief, purity, and contamination, their common subject never veering far from the sacred nature of oaths.[93] Publicola was not writing an analytical treatise (although he did present an ordered list); his letter reflected the position of oaths in social life more naturally, with less clean precision, and with more immediacy than had the ponderous abstractions of his contemporaries in the church. Part of the immediacy was pragmatic and self-centered.[94] Publicola was worried about two things: his commercial product and his spiritual liability. Prudently, he contracted this unfamiliar dilemma out to an expert.

Publicola's "scrupulous" attention to the myriad, "nugatory" possibilities for contamination have seemed almost "pathological" to some modern scholars, but but no one in Late Antiquity would have found much peculiar in Publicola's concerns.[95] Augustine, surely, did not misunderstand his intent. Neither the landownder nor the bishop wished to end practical relations between Christians and the rest of society, but both wanted to clarify the terms of those relations. Publicola's own material interests in this spiritual and geographical frontier zone would benefit from stability, not disruption.[96] The degree of his anxiety measured his regard for his livelihood and his salvation, both of which he monitored with the amount of care appropriate to his status and condition (wealthy, noble, and Christian).

Publicola's Latinity suggests that he did not fancy letter writing to be the worthwhile craft some of his contemporaries did (a lack of interest that modern commentators find hard to believe); but, when it was read to Augustine, perhaps the bishop was to understand that by making the effort to write on this occasion Publicola was conveying his determination to have resolution.[97] If anything in the letter were to set Augustine's teeth on edge, it would be Publicola's candor. Although not long a bishop, Augustine was a bishop nonetheless, and his reputation toward 399 was growing rapidly. Publicola was not only determined to get an answer; he was also comfortable with his own, gentlemanly relationship with the bishop. Publicola addressed the bishop as *dilectus* (Augustine would respond with *dilectissimus*), and concluded the first section of his enquiry: "If you write to me with any doubt, I could fall into greater doubts than before I asked."[98]

Roughly eight hundred and fifty years later, Thomas Aquinas recorded Publicola's name, and a portion of Augustine's response to his letter, in his *Summa Theologica*. Aquinas—expert in Aristotle, "doctor" of Roman Catholicism—understood "scruples" and "contamination" perfectly well, even if he thought less about barbarians and demon-oaths than he did about Jews and usury. In any case, the bottom line Aquinas drew from this ancient epistolary exchange was that Christians did not have to worry about sharing someone else's sin.[99] When Augustine responded to Publicola, even while making it clear he understood that a sense of urgency compelled his correspondent, he did what he could to evade the commercial gist of the original inquiry.[100] Instead, he honed in on a simple statement of fact that Publicola had made in passing: oaths stood for public credit. The heart of the matter, as the bishop refashioned it, was not the risk of pollution, but instead this public credit. Was it possible that two people exchanged the same currency of fidelity when they swore to it by different divinities? The pagan who swore an impious oath and violated that oath would sin on two counts, idolatry and perjury.[101] A Christian who employed that pagan or used the product of their agreement to a good purpose did not contract any sin through association.

Augustine gave more attention to the other side of the demon-oath than Publicola probably expected (or cared), by considering the barbarian who swore a pagan oath and also kept that oath.[102] Such a person had less to fear than the Christian who committed perjury.[103] Augustine wanted Publicola to take particular notice of the immense sanctity that imbued a Christian's oath. Because a Christian invoked more holiness than a non-Christian, he increased the severity of his perjury should he violate that holy trust. Publicola, by making his problem Augustine's, inadvertently forced the subject of oath-swearing out of theoretical, exegetical thickets and onto the open ground of social life. The bishop had no choice but to confront the reality of oath-swearing in society.

Swearing in Polite Society

Publicola encountered dilemmas that Christianization itself had generated and left unsolved. At least once, while he was still a priest, Augustine had tasted the fruits that reform combined with authority might bear, when he helped put a stop to a popular tradition—carousing around martyrs' tombs.[104] As a bishop, however, his burden of responsibilities was more diverse, and he had less freedom to choose his battles. Experience revealed to him the uneven realities of the reform process at work. In the same years that the government finalized the official end of traditional (pagan) religion, Augustine faced what would be the single most important aspect of religion in the early medieval West, the "growing differentiation of the Christian community."[105] Most people who shared Augustine's theoretical bent—among them, bishops, legislators, and modern scholars—could remain oblivious or willfully ignorant of diversity. But even between only two people, the bishop and the landowner, whose social and economic backgrounds (compared to the majority of humans) shared more in common than not, the possible approaches to the same religion could be extremely different. In their determination to conduct their lives according to the fundamental rules of Christian behavior, however, both Publicola and Augustine recognized that oaths were sacred and necessary.

Augustine lived in a world where oaths were beginning to contribute to Christian society in new ways. His friend Paulinus of Nola (ca. 353–431), in a song composed for the saint whose sanctuary he had helped to expand through pious donations, described the arcades, courtyards, and fountains of Saint-Felix at Cimitile, the burial area just outside the Italian city of Nola. It was the same shrine where, as we saw in the first chapter, Pope Damasus had inscribed his gratitude to the saint for relief from illness and calumny. Paulinus contributed to the legacy.

In veteri nobis nova res adnascitur actu,
et solita insolita crescunt sollemnia voto.

In a performance long familiar to us something new accrues,
And the customary ceremonies grow by an uncustomary votive gift.[106]

Later, around 409, Paulinus would become bishop of Nola and of the pilgrimage site at Cimitile, the city's claim to fame throughout the Mediterranean.[107] For now, he and his wife Therasia were modern nobility—wealthy, Christian, and chaste. As we have seen, they cherished their correspondence with the intelligentsia of the Christian empire: Ambrose, Jerome, Alypius of Thagaste, and Augustine.[108] Between themselves and the latter two North Africans, in fact, Paulinus and Therasia shared a common acquaintance with an Italian family. These were members of the *gens Valeria*, a family then feeling its way through the highly esteemed, sometimes conflicting, avenues of propertied leisure and devoted asceticism. Their name was traceable to the early days of Rome: Melania "the Elder," granddaughter of a consul, who married into the family, was widowed at twenty-two, and enjoyed worldwide renown;[109] her granddaughter and namesake, Melania "the Younger," whose husband descended from a branch of the same *gens*;[110] finally, son of one Melania and father of the other with Caeionia Albina (daughter of a prefect), son of a consul of Rome, *vir clarissimus*, and consular of Campania (an office Paulinus had held in 381), Valerius Publicola.[111]

Only circumstantial evidence supports an identification between the Publicola who wrote to Augustine in 398 and the father of Melania the Younger: many scholars have supported their identification;[112] others, including the most recent commentator, have rejected it;[113] and, until another cache of letters or an inscription is discovered to either establish a Publicola in North Africa or close the gap in the existing evidence, there can be no positive verdict.[114] So much is the better for the reputation of Melania the Younger's husband, Pinianus, himself a descendent by blood of another Valerius Publicola, the first consul of Rome.[115] For a personal relationship to the Publicola who had written Augustine about his problems with *barbari* and their demon oaths would have given Pinianus still less of an excuse when he violated an oath he had sworn in front of the bishop and entire congregation of Hippo in 411.[116]

A THORNY MATTER OF TRUST

During what would be a long journey from Italy to Jerusalem, leaving just before the sack of Rome in 410, the couple Melania and Pinianus made an extended sojourn in North Africa. After roughly seven years of marriage and the deaths of two infants, they had sworn mutual vows of chastity, liquidated many of their assets, and were residing at Thagaste, Augustine of Hippo's birthplace and the bishopric of Alypius, Augustine's oldest living friend.[117] Melania's mother Albina was with them there. The family held property in the area, they had established a monastery complex, and Bishop

Alypius was an old family friend. Famous family, famous friends, and famous wealth and liberality made them instant celebrities. On a visit to Hippo in 411, an ebullient congregation insisted that Pinianus never leave. Although unwilling to comply, Pinianus was either too polite or too flattered to refuse outright, and soon found himself in an awkward but earnest negotiation over his future.

The final resolution to this cross-communication between the forceful expectations of a congregation and the clumsy reservations of a young man came "as a breath of fresh air" to Augustine, the wary but relenting mediator in the process.[118] In the basilica, before the bishop, the other clergy, and the congregation, Pinianus swore that he would not join the priesthood anywhere but in Hippo and that, if he should leave the city and later decide to take clerical vows, he would return here, to his favored admirers. The ceremony took place during the liturgy, after the catechumens had been dismissed, when only full members of the Christian community remained.[119] Pinianus's oath was his *oblatio*, his personal offering to God and the congregation. A scribe recorded the oath in a document, which Pinianus and the witnesses signed, although Augustine would not add his signature. With the ritual concluded and all parties seemingly satisfied, Pinianus promptly fled the city, never to return. If his sudden departure did not cause the people of Hippo to doubt the young man's fidelity, he soon jettisoned whatever might have remained of his reputation by publicly complaining that he had sworn his oath under duress, because the "mob" back at Hippo was potentially violent, and because the people there had loved him only for his money.

Time and place conspired to make the worst possible mess of this all-around embarrassing fiasco. If he had sworn his oath forty years earlier in Caesarea or twenty years earlier in Milan, then perhaps Pinianus would have come out of this clean. Bishops Basil and Ambrose, as we have seen, both believed that certain contingencies, even including inebriation, might mitigate a person's obligation to fulfill an oath. Nothing suggests Pinianus was drunk when he swore to stay in Hippo, although his wits seem to have been muddled, unless he simply was offended by the prospect of spending his life in a city like Hippo, no matter who its bishop was. In any case, although some other Christians besides Ambrose and Basil restricted or placed qualifications on the legitimacy of oaths and others forbade them entirely, all such people belonged to a very small minority during antiquity and the Middle Ages. Augustine was more conventional and took oaths extremely seriously, which bode ill for Pinianus.

It was only after other parties took up Pinianus's defense that truly dangerous tensions surfaced and threatened to tear apart an old circle of friends. Those tensions still make uncomfortable reading of the two pertinent letters that survive, especially Augustine's response to Albina. In retrospect, Augustine acknowledged, there had been a lot of pressure throughout the whole exchange; not all of it, however, had been on Pinianus. The bishop had displayed no more than lukewarm confidence in the young man's capacities. Not long after writing his last word on the whole debacle, he would recall why it was not an entirely bad thing if some people erroneously took the gospel prohibition against oaths literally, for at least then they would not commit perjury. "Only God swears safely," Augustine observed, "for he cannot be led astray."[120] The one fact on which everyone tacitly agreed, apparently, was that Melania's husband was his own worst counselor. Alypius, in rare dissent with his old friend, having been present throughout the oath negotiation and ceremony, carefully suggested to Augustine that Pinianus's perception of danger, real or imagined, might invalidate the oath.

Pinianus might have been afraid, Augustine admitted to Alypius. The circumstances, however, did not change the terms of the oath. If anything, the man was under greater obligation to fulfill his oath, because he had raised popular expectations of his fidelity. Years earlier, Augustine had warned Publicola, a nobleman dealing with the stark realities of business, that a Christian perjurer sinned more than a pagan. Now, addressing a fellow bishop, he recalled a specific pagan who was justly famed for preserving the letter of an oath to a tee. Regulus, a consul and successful general during the First Punic war, had sworn to his captors to return after delivering the terms of a prisoner exchange to the senate. He betrayed the Carthaginians, insisting that Rome not give back prisoners to the enemy, but nonetheless returned to face captivity, torture, and death rather than break his vow.[121] Regulus displayed a heroic sense of priorities, according to Augustine, honoring divine obligations over all else, even though he did not enjoy the deterrents supplied to Jews and Christians. Just as tombstones throughout Asia Minor attest, they had the biblical curse of Zachary's sickle to scare potential perjurers (and grave robbers) straight.[122] But still, Regulus, a pagan, had kept to the death an oath he swore "by the filth of demons," while Pinanus, a famous Christian, betrayed an oath that he swore inside a church, with the true God as witness.

Oaths were a fact of life for ascetics and clerics as much as for pagan laborers and Christian overseers. By the strength of his reputation, Pinianus assumed a level of spiritual responsibility similar to that of clergy. The expectations for them were higher, not lower; their obligation to fidelity was greater, not weaker. Augustine had confronted the practice of swearing among clergy already in his career. Timothy, a lector, had sworn an oath never to leave the side of his mentor Severus, the bishop of Milevis. Assigned to service as subdeacon in a smaller town, Timothy balked. He claimed that his oath bound him to his beloved bishop; leaving the nest would perjure them both. Whatever he thought of Timothy at that point, Severus was genuinely confused, and in 401 he asked Augustine for advice. Characteristically, his colleague showed the greatest possible respect for this oath, by treating it on purely logical grounds. Severus had had no knowledge of the oath; therefore, he was under no obligation. Parties to an oath were usually present in person and always had to swear willingly; indeed, even the curt oath formulas in the Egyptian papyri attested to willfulness.[123] Furthermore, Timothy would not perjure himself by taking up his assignment; he could bind his own future actions, but not those of a third party.[124] What was clear in this episode was that all parties—Timothy, Augustine, and even Severus—respected the sacrosanct terms of an oath, even if they disagreed over what precisely those terms entailed.

Reasonable bishops wanted to avoid scandal, and the potential scandal surrounding Timothy and his oath was nothing compared to the scandal Pinianus had already caused, even before he involved his mother-in-law, Albina. Far more than Alypius's query, however, Albina's charge rankled the bishop of Hippo. She aired the ugly suspicion that greed lurked behind the whole affair. She insisted that Pinianus was hardly the one to blame, just because he had buckled under the pressure of the unreasonable demands Augustine's congregation had made. As far as Augustine was concerned, this fine woman was accusing him of avarice and irresponsibility. For the bishop alone, he reminded Albina, was responsible for the behavior of his congregation, particularly when financial matters were involved. The simple fact was that Pinianus had sworn an oath he never meant to keep. That was perjury and bad enough, but more than Pinianus was affected. The charge of greed had infected the good reputation (*bona fama*) of a congregation and its bishop. A purge was necessary.[125]

Augustine's respect for Albina, combined with the severe accusations implicit in her complaints, prompted him to a grave solution. In order to allay her suspicions regarding the people of Hippo and his character, and to prove what was otherwise impossible to demonstrate—that neither they nor he had ever had any harmful or pecunious interests in Pinianus—the bishop swore. "What are we supposed to do?" Augustine asked Albina in a letter. "By what rationale do we clear ourselves with you, if we cannot even do so with our enemies? This is a matter of the spirit; it is interior, hidden away far from mortal eyes, known only to God. So what remains, except for God, to whom it is known, to bear witness? You compel us to swear . . . by threatening the death of our reputation . . . God is my witness . . . God himself is my witness. . . ."[126] No doubt Augustine expected Pinianus to hear this letter and for all of them to learn how seriously he took this matter. If this did not satisfy their resentment and sense of having been cajoled, it certainly ended the immediate conflict. Where could it have gone, after a venerated bishop had sworn under duress, in writing, with his personal reputation on the line? Once emotions cooled, these two older, more mature parties recovered their mutual regard; Augustine happily exchanged letters on philosophical topics with Albina's brother in coming years; Melania's reputation did not suffer, either: her biographer, Gerontius, reasonably shelved the entire episode, quite irrelevant to his heroine's holiness.[127] Pinianus, however, never returned to the people of Hippo, and one doubts any love was lost between them.[128]

Swearing in the Land of Falsehood

However distasteful it might have been to him, what Augustine gained in his involvement with people like the landowner Publicola, the priest Timothy, and the ascetic Pinianus was the opportunity to contemplate the problem of swearing as a social fact; removed from exegetical and even ethical imperatives, it was another feature of the territory Christians must navigate. Being human and overworked, Augustine might have preferred to eschew the scandals and stick to hypothetical dilemmas and exegetical solutions, but that was not a viable option. We know most about conflicts that happened outside his congregation, but only because necessity demanded that they be recorded in writing. He would have had his hands full with similar situations at home. Augustine was not one to take any responsibility lightly once he had turned his attention toward it.

His experience with oaths in these central years of his career reveal not so much an articulate theology of swearing as a series of compelling insights on how Christians might conceptualize and rationalize its practice. The oath was a final testament of credibility; it placed the burden of honesty or deception entirely on the one swearing. Invoking God was a formal, binding, and even liturgical action. It represented an expectation of truth, judgment, and justice (to repeat Jerome's triad). Oaths were necessary because the currency of human fidelity lay hidden (*intus est, procul ab oculis secreta mortalium*).[129] Oaths worked, Christians would understand, because God had the ability to look into human hearts and discern the truth.[130] The language of discernment—the idea that, ultimately, credibility required soulful testimony—was already becoming the Christian language of judgment, as we have seen in the preceding chapters. Oaths fit with Christian expectations of justice.

Not everyone was sold. In the latter years of his career, Augustine entered into a high-profile dispute over grace and human nature remembered as the Pelagian controversy. Incidentally, Pelagius and his admirers seem to have drawn a hard line on swearing. In 413, the same year in which Augustine revised and extended his treatment of the pagan Regulus's oath for inclusion in the premier book of *On the City of God*, Pelagius wrote a letter to Demetrias, a noblewoman who had recently sworn chastity. While extolling the powerful virtues that were now hers to exercise, Pelagius quoted Matthew 5:34 to suggest that, instead of swearing oaths, her speech might be "discreet, unassuming and infrequent."[131] Oaths introduced turmoil into the minds of the spiritual elite, minds that required tranquility—nothing "quieter, nothing purer, nothing in a word more lovely"— and freedom from the terrestial uncertainty oath-swearing represented.[132] Sweet, calm devotion to Christian principles, if nurtured and attended to properly, could withstand any pressures to swear.

This categorical prohibition of swearing was a mere grace note in a scale of spiritual self-improvement that sounded euphonious to many ears throughout the Christian world, but which Augustine found misguided at best, heretical at worst.[133] In psychological terms alone, as far as the bishop of Hippo was concerned, the notion of ascending toward salvation through sheer human effort was an audacious conceit. On the matter of swearing, to deny bluntly the incredible pressures in ordinary society that compelled people to swear was simply to fly in the face of reality. What world, Augustine wondered, did Pelagius and others like him inhabit? Wherever the bishop turned his attention, there were more oaths than words.[134] Everywhere, people scarcely opened their mouths without swearing to something.[135] Augustine asked his congregation, "If a person were to examine closely that as often as he swears throughout each day, he wounds himself as often, he strikes and runs himself through with the sword of his tongue as often, what spot on him would be found whole?"[136] One curious layman, Hilarius, wrote to Augustine from Sicily about some of Pelagius's teachings he had heard in Syracuse, including the instruction that oaths were forbidden.[137] The bishop's response was sharply dismissive; adherents of such beliefs were too inept to know what an oath even was.[138]

The recent resurrection by the Pelagians of exegetical arguments against swearing undoubtedly lay behind three sermons Augustine delivered at Hippo during 414 and 415.[139] Once again, he methodically covered the familiar but crucial ground that stretched between perjury and oaths, one sinful, the other not. By swearing, people walked the edge of a precipice and relied on unsteady feet. The human will should not be trusted with a matter so delicate as swearing.[140] Augustine worked deftly through the old exegetical dilemmas, including the reasons why God could not perjure himself.[141] Nevertheless, he made it clear that when it came to the practice of swearing, scriptural analysis by itself minimized the real moral complexity of the issue. Twenty years after his first serious essays on the subject, Augustine remained wary—*diligenter considerandum est.*

In these sermons, Augustine for the first time took the initiative in explicitly treating the practice of swearing as an issue of community. The simple fact that people swore oaths to other people, usually their neighbors, as a part of maintaining relationships became one of the reasons Augustine considered all oaths to be sacrosanct. The bishop showed no surprise that the old practice of swearing literally on the head of one's own child in a circle of townspeople was still common.[142] Their living in the "land of falsehood" (*regio falsitatis*) was the reason why all people who swore risked perjury, but it was also why oaths were necessary.[143] Membership in the fallible human community meant that Augustine had to swear for the assurance of friends and enemies alike. He did not keep this a secret from his congregation: "Whenever I see that I will not be believed unless I do it, and that I will not expedite something someone does not believe for a person who does not believe me, once I have carefully weighed the reason and balanced my consideration, with great fear I say, 'Before God,' or 'God is my witness,' or 'Christ knows it to be so in my heart.'"[144] As a moral principle, Augustine's gentle admonition to avoid swearing had the great advantage of remaining flexible to circumstances. So long as one understood this moral principle, the proper course through social interactions (whether to swear or not to swear) would usually be discernible. It stood in sharp contrast to the conclusions reached by most of his near contemporaries: Ambrose, Chromatius, Jerome, and Pelagius and other hardliners.[145]

The practical functions of swearing were easily reconciled with Christian notions of divine justice. Swearing offered truth, judgment, and justice simultaneously, when trust was necessary but trustworthiness failed, when uncertainty overshadowed the urge for security, and when the threat of "secret criminality and breakdown of connective justice" left participants no recourse but to call on the supernatural.[146] When Augustine sent Boniface and Spes—his own priest and monk, one of whom had made allegations against the other—to purge themselves before the relics of Saint Felix in 402, he was pursuing a rather conventional solution to judicial uncertainty.[147] The clergy attendant on the shrine at Nola were accustomed to this sort of veneration. Graffiti on the walls recorded the votives of other pilgrims to Cimitile, humbler versions of Damasus's inscription inside Saint-Felix.[148] Oaths marked the trust people placed not only in one another but in God, divine justice, and the agents of divine justice on earth.

The church absorbed oath-swearing. Oaths had already been a part of Christian ecclesiastical life, but swearing now reached new levels of religious significance for Christians, as martyrs and saints guaranteed the integrity of oaths, bishops monitored their ritual observance, and ordinary men and women bound themselves directly to God with solemn vows. Late antique and early medieval bishops worked hard and successfully at regulating the channels of spiritual authority by controlling access to shrines and relics, censuring rogue visionaries, refashioning the symbols of their office and the rituals of the mass, creating a new elite within the episcopal ranks, and refining the concept of rulership. Uncertainty was inescapable, trust in society was indispensable, and bishops were the crucial link to God and divine justice.

4

Mercy Not Justice:
How Penance Became a Worthy Act of
Self-Incrimination

JUSTICE WAS A LONG PROCESS whose outcome no one could be certain of surviving until the final verdict was rendered. This chapter will argue that some pastors shaped the practice of penance, the means by which Christians atoned for sins and sought redemption, around the mandate that Christians become their own judges. While bishops remained the watchmen of their communities, ordinary people could examine their own consciences and retain mercy (*misericordia*) as their "advocate and patron" before the divine tribunal. Moreover, the performance of penance in ceremonies of reconciliation demonstrated with drama and economy the fruits of contrition and the joy of forgiveness to participants and spectators alike. Liturgical penance did not need to happen often or involve large numbers of penitents to make an impact; it did not need to happen at all, for plenty of role models, ranging from renegade bishops to the first human beings of Genesis, proved the same essential lesson, that mercy rewards remorse, so people can anticipate God's justice without fear.

A Profession of Holiness

Agiulf, a bone hunter and deacon in the church of Saint Martin at Tours picking up relics from Rome in 590, brought back more than remnants of dead saints, he had reports of a new wonder-working bishop on the scene. To his own bishop, Gregory of Tours, Agiulf delivered a firsthand account of how the river Tiber had flooded the previous November: churches had collapsed and grain rotted in the storehouses; water snakes lay putrefying on the shores, and plague had threatened the inhabitants of the city. Their bishop was stricken and died early on, and his successor, Gregory the Great, had asked the people to take refuge in penance while time yet remained, to search out their own faults and punish them with tears. This was no call for leisurely introspection; like a classical orator evoking the destruction of a great city, Gregory strove to collapse time and distance and generate a sense of immediacy. While poets and pastors alike might reach for an emotional reaction from their audiences, Gregory aimed still deeper to elicit physical evidence that penance was working to win forgiveness, demanding that his congregation summon their sins from hidden depths and look at them directly (*ante oculos mentis*). All the clergy, monks, children, widows, and other laypeople together processed around the churches singing psalms, even while eighty participants dropped dead to the ground. Finally, however, the plague ended and God's mercy seemed won.[1]

Penance was about more than punishment. It involved criminals and reprobates, but also bishops, priests, monks, and all ordinary Christians who were concerned about surviving the Final Judgment. As we shall see, penitents during this period became clerics; clerics performed penance; and penitents joined lay religious, sworn virgins and widows, and even priests and bishops in the ranks of the living saints, which encompassed all those who made a profession of holiness (*professio sanctitatis*), a solemn vow to apply themselves wholly to the process of spiritual perfection.[2] Contrary to long-esteemed wisdom, which we shall address in this chapter's conclusion, penance was alive and well. In just this single display at Rome, the apogee of a series of penitential processions that Gregory of Tours recorded in his historical books, we see that a good bishop used penance, not to intimidate his congregation from committing sins, but to orient their minds past the evils of this world, through the depths of their own consciences, to God's perfect, compassionate justice while time still remained.[3]

Bishops' role in penance was directly related to the image and the attributes of the ideal bishop-judge: their powers of discernment were attuned simultaneously to divine justice on the horizon and to the immediate spiritual condition of their followers, so that judicial and pastoral care became inseparable. The most dramatic demonstration of this proximity, rarely addressed in the scholarship on penance, is the case of penitent bishops. Even bishops whose guilt for atrocious deeds became public might well have made compelling examples of the possible balance to be struck between justice and mercy when they earned their dignity back through penance. We know still more about bishops who did penance before ordination, particularly those who did so out of religious devotion rather than for a specific crime, thanks to authors who smoothed out the contradictions through the means of holy biographies, such as that of Bishop Eutropius of Orange. Although some important treatises from this period continued to distinguish sharply between monastic and lay discipline, many bishops trained in monasteries did not hesitate to broadcast their own penitential devotion and that of other reputable members of society.

Finally, bishops encouraged lay Christians to follow particular techniques for judging their own consciences that derived from ascetic discipline, and no one did this more influentially than Gregory the Great. This involved dealing with abstract processes of introspection and contemplation. To help communicate these endeavors and their rewards to ordinary Christians, a number of famous penitents, drawn mostly from the Hebrew Bible, were analyzed and even critiqued for the edification of Christian congregations. Living penitents, meanwhile, received praise for their own initiative—anticipating divine judgment and joining their bishops as active participants, not merely passive recipients, of justice.

Preachers of Penance

Bishops during the fifth and sixth centuries preached, wrote, and legislated almost as much about their own role in the penitential process as about the role of the penitents. They directed penance from a commanding promontory, sharing in a tradition that added another link to their historical chain of authority. Like the prophets and Jesus Christ, bishops were "preachers of penance" (*praedicatores paenitentiae*) first and foremost.[4] Gregory of Tours' uncle Nicetius of Lyon was a model pastor, forgiving the penitent and chastizing the delinquent.[5] Penitential direction was peculiar neither to Gregory of Tours' family nor to his writings: Hilary of Arles (430–49) had been one of a number of monks from Lérins to bring professional, monastic devotion to bear on their pastoral responsibilities as bishops. Whenever Hilary preached penance, all sorts of people flooded the church. He terrified them with the prospect of shadowy flames (*tenebrosum incendium*) and the Final Judgment. They responded with tears and groans. Like Gregory the Great, he forced them to look directly on their own "wounds" (*ulnera conscientiae ante oculos inspicienda*) before he added his own tears in supplication and fortified the "fruit of penance" with his prayers.[6]

Discernment Calibrates Discipline

The juridical administration of penance was tied directly to the spiritual gifts bishops claimed to enjoy, particularly their ability to discern the spiritual capacities of the people charged to their care. Bishops absolved Christians of their sins only twice in a lifetime, once at baptism and a second time, in the case of a serious sin, through the administration of penance and the laying on of their hands in a liturgical ceremony—the ritual demonstration of the "loosing" power imparted by the apostolic keys. The legal sources from our period do not agree precisely what sins were serious enough to require this second absolution, but always topping the list were homicide, idolatry, and adultery. Julian Pomerius, for example, a Mauritanian priest residing in Arles in the later fifth century, distinguished serious crimes (*crimina*) from slight sins (*parva peccata*). To atone for the slight— or what other authors often called "light" (*levia*)—sins, a variety of what we may call penitential behaviors sufficed, including the grand processions Gregory the Great led in Rome, but more commonly daily prayer, alms, and goodwill. Because serious sins were likely to carry secular penalties as well, Julian observed that criminals would likely undergo both human punishment and what he called "voluntary excommunication"—that is, spiritual punishment.[7] Voluntary participation was a crucial criterion of penance in sources from throughout the period and meant that the will of the sinner must be involved for his or her penance to be effective, but voluntary did not mean penance was a matter of choice for serious sins. Bishops meeting at Orléans in 541, for example, required that homicides perform penance even if a secular ruler or the relatives of their victims had already forgiven them.[8] Those guilty of capital sins who refused to perform penance were banished from all contact with Christians and lost all hope of salvation.

In practice, the administration of penance was neither so clear cut nor as limited in its scope as even these broad juridical categories would imply. Although Cresconius, an early compiler of church canons, suggested that legal knowledge might help bishops decide whether to judge sinners "according to severity or leniency," neither he nor the laws he edited described how that process worked in practice.[9] A modern expert on the same laws, Cyrille Vogel concluded from his efforts to uncover a stable penitential system that such a search missed the point of late antique penance: "It is nothing. The bishop remained the sole judge in the matter, for each particular case."[10]

Bishops might reward slack performances with longer penances, while good penitents enjoyed their pastors' "moderation and clemency" and the "humanity" of the church.[11] Bishops were to reckon the weight of sins objectively, appraise confessions, and gauge the sincerity behind the lamentation of penitents before making liturgical supplication for those worthy of forgiveness.[12] Formulating the duration and intensity of penance was an exercise of judgment (*arbitrium*) and an extension of episcopal authority (*potestas*).[13] In other words, the direction of penance was one concrete occupation that involved all the attributes of the ideal bishop-judge.

According to four bishops who stayed behind after a small council at Tours in 567 and drafted a letter to the Christian people (*ad plebem*), responsible bishops fulfilled their pastoral role—the watchful position of *episkopos* we explored in the second chapter—by calling people to penance.[14] Leo I, bishop of Rome (440–61), described the administration of penance as a power bestowed on the leaders of the church by Jesus "the mediator," who joined with them in guiding penitents through the process.[15] In 452, Leo wrote to Nicetas, bishop of Aquileia, informing him that "the length of the penance, with moderation being observed, is left to your judgment (*tuo constituente iudicio*)." A bishop should determine the duration of penance, Leo explained, "proportionate to the devoted dispositions you see in the penitents; you are likewise to be considerate of old age and take note of the requirements of sickness and of all trials. If anyone is so seriously burdened by these that his safety is despaired of while he is doing penance, it is proper that through priestly solicitude he be assisted by the favor of being admitted to communion."[16] Historians have long deliberated over whether Leo's "priestly solicitude" was exceptionally lenient.[17] Gallic bishops, at least, tended toward the same standards of pastoral care, requiring that the "remedy and hope of forgiveness by the church" be made available for everyone.[18] What Leo and other bishops seem to reveal in their sermons and letters is an active dialogue between religious leaders and groups of their followers, conducted within the established framework of episcopal authority and according to a language of guilt and confession, and entailing more of people's lives than what they shared in the liturgy alone.

PENANCE IS GOOD MEDICINE

Unlike the mere restoration of church discipline when excommunicates "rush back to peace," penance followed a broader timetable, its participants striving for a more elusive peace, one which Christians enjoyed only after death, when finally they "will have no enemy."[19] For their part, bishops demanded more from themselves than the disciplinary "power of the keys" Jesus bestowed upon the church to bind and loose sinners (Mt 16:19). As we have seen, bishops wielded a "spiritual sword," a tool for scrutiny as much as a weapon for defending the church. When sinners showed remorse, good pastors turned away the sharp edge of excommunication and offered instead a medicinal edge (*medicinale ferrum*). This excised the sin, according to a fifth-century text from Rome, and allowed "the tortures of penance [to] restore the soul wounded by iniquity."[20] Besides being a metaphor for bishops' power both to discipline and to reconcile, medicine provided preachers with their most common language for explaining penance. In Ravenna, for example, Peter Chrysologus (406–50) preached that human frailty and sin was a fever, a fiery inflamation caused by internal imbalances, and the cool humility of penance was its cure.[21]

Oftentimes, actual physical illness accompanied penance. Church leaders complained about laypeople putting off penance until the last possible minute, when they requested the "blessing of penance" along with the eucharist, which many texts refer to as the *viaticum*.[22] Contemporary critics saw deathbed reconciliation as an imperfect remedy, for without preparation through penitential works and formal absolution it could not be certain to work. What late antique bishops learned at the bedsides of the dying, however, concerned the practical constraints of their pastoral function as much as it pertained to lay devotion. The wielder of the "spiritual sword," which revealed the spiritual capacities of sinners, was baffled when the infirm lost the capacity of speech, was seized in some sort of fit, or ceased responding altogether. If possible, a mere nod sufficed to initiate the blessing, but otherwise bishops relied on friends and the family's testimony that the dying person had asked for penance. Should the patient recover, the witnesses along with the bishop were obliged to see the promise fulfilled.[23] As for their pastoral duty, bishops assumed the same array of responsibilities toward deathbed penitents as toward any other penitents under their care, from assigning proper penance to congratulating those who recovered on their new way of life.

The Penitential Lives of Religious Professionals

That hardship produced penitents was hardly surprising when bishops tied penance and the eucharist closely together with physical well-being. Bishops even suggested that these sacraments might substitute directly for illicit potions, spells, and phylacteries, which they banned on pain of penance.[24] Among the numbers of penitents who walked away healthy, moreover, might well have been future members of the clergy. Bishops at Gerona in 517 expressly allowed a person to be admitted to the clergy who had received the *viaticum* while ill, so long as he had not gone through public humiliation in the liturgy after recovering his health (*postmodum revalescens caput poenitentiae in ecclesia publice non subdiderit*).[25] While other legislation prohibited penitents from ordination, sometimes grouping them together with bigamists and men who married widows,[26] participants in the first council of Toledo in 400 specified that what they meant by "penitent" was "someone who after baptism does public penance in sackcloth for homicide or for various other crimes and serious sins and is reconciled to the divine altar." A penitent of this sort could not be ordained. The same bishops went on, however, to admit even these confessed homicides into ecclesiastical service as doormen or readers.[27] So the prohibition of penitents from the clergy was not merely an efficient shorthand for prohibiting a list of egregious sinners; the source of the prohibition was the public humiliation involved in liturgical penance, not necessarily the profession of penance, the performance of penitential works, or being guilty of serious sins. The distinction becomes important when we recognize the considerable evidence both for clergy doing penance and penitents becoming clergymen.

BISHOPS IN NEED OF MERCY

The first group is the seamier by far, and the proceedings of the Gallic church councils and the historical writings of Gregory of Tours alone provide ample specimens. Ideally the shortcomings, transgressions, and correction of church leaders could be handled internally, particularly when they involved disputes between bishops or scandalous behavior.[28] Thus bishops gathered at the council of Chalons (ca. 647–53), who had seen a written profession of penance signed by Theudorius of Arles, cautioned the bishop that anyone "who publicly professed penance" could not occupy the episcopal throne and urged him to keep out of church affairs until he received a hearing at the next synod.[29] So long as only their colleagues and select laity witnessed their tears and contrition, however, all clergy could demand or be required to seek absolution through penance, and a heartfelt confession could win immediate reconciliation and restoration to office.[30]

Reality was of course not always so kind to the public image of the clergy. For one thing, not all clergy who committed moral or civil crimes were willing to admit to them, much less seek atonement. In 419/20, Consentius, the same layman we saw in the second chapter engaging Augustine of Hippo in a philosophical discussion about the fine points of theology, wrote again to inform him of some recent events taking place in the area of Tarragona in Spain, including the death of a bishop struck down, according to Consentius, by the hand of God. Only seven days before this bishop, Saggitius of Lerida, died from a throat affliction, an episcopal council had cleared him along with at least one other bishop, other clergy, and some distinguished laypeople of serious charges that included the circulation of heretical books. Although there was written evidence against him, Saggitius was able to clear himself by a series of formal purgatory oaths—that is, exculpatory oaths—that he swore on the Gospels and the sacraments of the church, first in front of the bishop of Tarragona and then in front of a full council. As Consentius, the bishop's most dogged accuser, was well aware, failed accusations against a bishop were a very serious affair, nothing other than calumny, and Saggitius's colleagues were so outraged that a layman would discredit a bishop's solemn oaths that one of them went after Consentius with his fists flying.[31]

Nevertheless, Consentius remained convinced that Saggitius was guilty. He even suggested to Augustine that the bishop had experienced a moment of doubt when he "burned with the interior fires of a bad conscience."[32] Consentius offered this improbable glimpse into Saggitius's conscience in order to pinpoint at what point and with what clear deliberation he had chosen to lie rather than seek forgiveness from his peers. For the bishop was "powerful in the law and erudite in the literary arts."[33] In short, Consentius considered Saggitius a well-equipped calumniator, who had prepared some carefully worded oaths that could absolve himself and all other complicit parties, and had sent them to Syagrius of Huesca, the other bishop implicated in the scandal. Syagrius, however, having been summoned with Saggitius to appear before an inquiry at Tarragona, had a vision that destroyed his resolve: he saw himself standing before a tribunal where Jesus, "a judge to be feared," condemned him for his "great crime of conscience"— given the context, "conscience" here could refer either to the perjury Syagrius planned to commit, or the secrets he shared with his conspirators.[34] Deeply distressed in any case, Syagrius resolved to reveal everything he knew before the hearing at Tarragona rather than face his nightmare tribunal. He set off on foot to face his judgment, though first he would make a full confession to Consentius, who was shocked to see such a distinguished man exhausted and dirty from the road.[35]

While much about this episode is remarkable, the trials, councils, secret documents, destroyed records, and numerous bishops, priests, deacons, powerful laymen, and noble women cropping up in the course of this single letter should not obscure from our attention the long, troubled walk Syagrius made from Huesca to Tarragona or his alleged confession to a layman. No doubt, Consentius drew attention to Syagrius's walk of shame for two reasons. First, he wanted to contrast how far his own nemesis Saggitius had fallen from any hope of redemption, regardless of his official exoneration on earth. Second, he wanted to give some credibility to Syagrius, his sole source for the conspiracy and perjury charges. Although Consentius did not report on either bishop performing penance, the allusions to penitential behavior are unmistakable: the sinners' awakening to their own guilt, their mental anguish, and in Syagrius's case the disclosure of his guilt. To the historian, the whole episode is a precious window into the way judicial process caught bishops up, not only as authority figures, but as conspirators and defendants.[36] To the historian of penance, it points up what by now should be obvious: clergy, including bishops, were as much in need of forgiveness as anyone else, and laypeople like Consentius knew it.

The publicity of liturgical penance was a critical determinant in whether clergy sought formal absolution for their trespasses, so a real advantage existed in receiving ordination before one revealed one's commission of a crime. Deacons and priests who did penance for sins committed either before or after ordination were sometimes allowed to resume their offices according to Gallic and Spanish councils, with or without restrictions on their future responsibilities and upward mobility.[37] A bishop well might find himself making frequent trips to regional councils to decide whether clergy had been excommunicated rightly or wrongly and whether they should be forgiven.[38] Bishops at the third council of Orléans in 538 even reminded themselves to pay out a reasonable stipend to clerics while they were performing required penance.[39]

Although Saggitius of Lerida would go to any lengths to avoid reprimand by his peers, even risking divine vengeance for his perjuries if Consentius's story was correct, other bishops either confessed or were convicted. They did penance, often unwillingly, usually sequestered in a monastery, but in some cases still in control of the secular affairs of their church.[40] In 533, Contumeliosus of Riez confessed before the council of Marseilles and received penance in a monastery.[41] The first bishop of Clermont, seduced when his wife came to his bed like a "new Eve," withdrew to a monastery "with groaning and tears to dilute his transgression," but afterward was returned to his city.[42] Convictions for adultery and homicide did not satisfy the council of Chalon-sur-Saône (579) when it sat in judgment over the bishops Salonius and Sagittarius, whom an angry king already once had confined to monasteries to do penance, for penance could purge these sins; so it convicted and deposed the pair for treason.[43] The council of Mâcon, summoned in 585 by King Guntram of Orléans (d. 593) in the wake of a conspiracy that had implicated several important people, excommunicated Bishop Ursicus of Cahors after he openly confessed his involvement. His punishment consisted of three years hard penance, during which period he would neither shave nor cut his hair, abstain from meat and wine, and not dare to ordain clergy or perform sacraments, but would continue to administer the financial interests of his church.[44] When Fredegund (d. 596 or 597) complained to Guntram that Praetextatus of Rouen should not be able to return to his office because he had been deposed by a council of forty-five of his peers, the bishop of Paris succeeded in persuading the king that they had only sentenced Praetextatus to do penance, not to lose his see: the commonly accepted idea that bishops could do penance saved Praetextatus's career (but would not protect him from Fredegund's assassins).[45] Whatever the letter of the law, bishops knew firsthand the power of repentance and the importance of mercy for surviving the hard gears of justice in this world and the next.

ADMIRATION FOR PROFESSIONAL PENITENTS

Penance, therefore, was simply too valuable to be left to the homicides and heretics. Although clergy preferred their members not humiliate themselves with public confessions, laypeople were not surprised to find their leaders in need of forgiveness. They could also expect to discover the most respectable members of the lay community committing themselves to penitential devotion voluntarily—these would be truly voluntary penitents, not like the criminals Pomerius had described. In times of turmoil and temptation, as well as in the regular course of their daily lives, late antique pastors like Bishop Ruricius of Limoges (ca. 485–510) urged all Christians: cling to penance.[46]

In the last decade of the fifth century Ruricius wrote to Praesidius, a venerable acquaintance whose career as a public official under the Visigoths was coming to a close. Ruricius drew an admiring portrait of this "sublime and always magnificent lord" standing high on a promontory, where he looked down on the "perfidious, troublesome, and bitter sea" of public life he now left behind.[47] Ruricius had written Praesidius at least once while the latter still held governmental office, when the bishop pleaded on behalf of two criminals whom he had assigned penance for an unspecified offense. When they went to face Praesidius in secular court, Ruricius interceded on their behalf out of a twofold obligation: for the sake of these criminals turned penitents and for the sake of Praesidius's own salvation. For surely, the bishop remarked, Praesidius knew what the apostle James had written, that "there will be judgment without pity for him who does not have pity."[48] Now, by withdrawing completely from the secular world and living a penitential life, Praesidius would ready himself for divine judgment after death.

Like other pastors and laypeople between the fourth and sixth centuries, Ruricius and Praesidius shared a notion of penance broader than many later commentators would attribute to them. People like Praesidius who willingly devoted a portion of their lives toward penitential devotion deserved respect; the title "penitent" itself was worthy of record on their tombstones. One such inscription from the sixth century now rests in the crypt of a village church, north of Grenoble in France. "Here lies the penitent Ervalde," the epitaph read, "a noble woman fearful of God and hoping for resurrection in eternal life. She lived forty-two years and six months, and died 28 October in the fourteenth year of the indiction."[49] Celsus, a relative of Ruricius, was another penitent of this variety—what we may call a professional penitent. Like Praesidius, he had reached "the port of pardon through the privilege of penitence" and looked down from secure heights on the "whirlwinds of the world."[50] Throughout his career Ruricius sent encouragement to penitents, including the nobleman Agricola, whose father, Eparchius Avitus, had been a general, emperor (455–56), and bishop. Agricola had made a deathbed profession when suffering a grave illness. Once he recovered his health and his "feelings were composed," Ruricius encouraged him to be a devoted penitent the same way he had encouraged Praesidius and Celsus.[51]

Before Ruricius had written any of these penitents, while still a layman in his mid-thirties, husband to a noble woman, and father of at least five children, he had admired professional penitents and planned to follow their example. His own mentor was Bishop Faustus of Riez, with whom Ruricius exchanged letters but would meet in person only later, perhaps not until Faustus's long period of exile beginning in 477. Faustus monitored Ruricius's passage through the "tempests of this life" to solid ground and the "port of religion," whereupon Ruricius became a lay religious (*conversus*), a "spontaneous confessor of [his] own iniquity."[52] For Ruricius, however, unlike Praesidius, Celsus, and Agricola, penance was the beginning of a religious life that would culminate in the episcopate.

From Penitential Devotion to Pastoral Care

Whereas Cyrille Vogel famously epitomized the reconciled condition as "la mort civile et sociale," Éric Rebillard more recently softened it to "une façon de vivre en état de pardon."[53] Rebillard's modulation is a major departure from the scholarly chorus of penitential decline, which for many years insisted that penance could be only odious to Christians living in Augustine's generation and after, in part because penance seemed to offer a single, rigid means of atonement for all sins, great or small, and all sinners, strong or weak, and also because the condition of penitence bore too great a stigma for any but the desperate and hopeless to accept. This has proven to be a misleading account. Options existed within the constraints of penitential devotion; some respectable avenues remained open to those living "en état de pardon." For all its hardships before and after reconciliation, along with the incontrovertible and frankly unsurprising evidence that some penitents abjectly failed, there was even honor in penance.[54] The handful of epitaphs commemorating dead Christians as penitents, including that of Ervalde, could represent professional penitents or, just as feasibly, liturgical penitents who had enjoyed reconciliation.[55] Despite their occasional impatience with particularly stubborn cases, bishops allowed and perhaps encouraged respect for penitents, even those who died abroad or at sea without absolution. Christians commemorated them in the Mass through prayers and offerings; anything less would be sinful (*nefas*).[56]

Penance was too precious to leave to the criminals. It was also too precious, for that matter, to leave to the professional penitents. Moreover, although an advocate for other sinners could not himself be living in a perpetual state of pardon, he should not be harboring any unrepented sins himself. More importantly, an advocate must know what it means to need mercy. Eutropius, a native of Marseilles and the bishop of Orange from sometime before 463 until his death around 475, began religious life under the influence of his wife, whose spiritual devotion and premature death both affected him powerfully.[57] Eutropius's bishop, discerning his true capacities, pressed the grieving widower to demanding ascetic extremes. Initially, despair served Eutropius in the place of spiritual ambition. Later, however, after he became a deacon, he resolved not only to fulfill his office but also to purge himself of all his past sins through zealous penance. Verus of Orange, his biographer and eventual successor as bishop, believed that it was his contrition that earned Eutropius the distressing privilege of witnessing his own absolution. "Thus it happened one night," Verus narrated, "while deep in sleep after long nocturnal prayers, that he was assailed by a terrible vision. For he saw himself cast face up on the ground and a teeming mass of black birds stretching in a column from his genitals to the clouds. Once this stupendous situation had penetrated his dormant mind, he watched fire from the sky consume the flock of birds down to his genitals."[58] Gripped by horror, Eutropius redoubled his efforts, which won him another vision, now of a ball of flies emanating from his chest to be similarly devoured by flames. Finally, he revealed his nightmares to a pious abbot, who joyfully explained, "Do you not see, brother Eutropius, that you have earned forgiveness for not only your gloomy deeds but your innermost thoughts (*cogitationum culpis*) as well?" He was the sinner Ezekiel heralded, said the abbot, the sinner who turned from iniquity to justice and found himself absolved. Eutropius kept those visions in the front of his mind even after his reluctant ascension to the episcopate.

Penance and its satisfaction were unpredictable. In the process of burning off all residue of sin in himself, Eutropius had discovered that true penance worked invisibly as much as visibly, moving of its own accord regardless of narrow, legalistic formulas that matched sinful with redemptive actions. Verus's hero was a worthy exemplar for bishops who mediated the divide between public and private devotion. They simultaneously acted as the overseers of liturgical penitents, the counselors of professional penitents, and the pastors of the Christian majority who atoned for their sins through acts of charity, prayer, and contrition—the simple rituals of daily penance. Bishops found their role models among the prophets and saints and created new ones like Eutropius for the future. They also discovered role models for ordinary Christians, which blurred the lines still further between lay, clerical, and monastic devotion.

The Heroic Lives of Penitents

Although bishops might explore and even celebrate the nuances of redemption among themselves in hagiographic literature, such as the vita of Eutropius of Orange or the writings of Gregory of Tours, they used sturdier, more familiar models for general dissemination. Scripture provided examples of famous penitents—particularly the apostle Peter and King David, as well as the more complicated case of Adam and Eve—whose humanity was as instructive as their heroism, and preachers even compared their own followers favorably with heroes of the Bible. When it came to shaping and responding to the expectations of their followers, bishops who preached penance drew an inclusive circle around a community of heroes comprised of ordinary Christians, as virtuous as the saints and as charismatic as bishops themselves, so long as they were willing to become judges of their own iniquities.

Presented in sermons, treatises, and the liturgy, these exemplary penitents conveyed two lessons that were critical to joining episcopal and popular expectations of justice. First, the perennial uncertainty as to whether justice would work for or against a person was a problem not only of society—represented by calumny—but of humanity, for instability (*fragilitas*) threatened everyone's ability to lead a righteous life and earn the rewards of divine justice, regardless of their personal intention or sincerity. Second, by actively struggling to overcome this personal instability through introspection and self-judgment—activities analogous to the ideal behavior of bishops—every Christian might join their religious leaders, the spiritual elite, their friends and neighbors, and the entire Christian community (*ecclesia*) in a common plea for mercy. Through prayer and charitable acts on their own, by hearing about scriptural penitents, perhaps occasionally witnessing the liturgical performance of penance by an adulterer or even a murderer, and joining in penitential rituals during Easter or processions such as Gregory the Great led through Rome, individuals could share a profound spiritual experience. Penance joined the expectations of ordinary Christians, religious professionals, and the saints in a common strategy for navigating the procedures and pitfalls leading to the Final Judgment and for surviving its verdict.

PETER: CONFESSION NOT EXCUSES

Peter, the apostle and first bishop of the church, had misjudged his own spiritual capacities when he promised not to deny Christ.[59] After his third denial, however, he did not make excuses or even confess, but simply "went out and wept bitterly" (Lk 22:62). Fortunately for Peter, Augustine preached one Saturday after Easter, Jesus had known better. "In order to show Peter to himself (that is, to show Peter to Peter), the Lord turned his face from him for a time, and Peter denied him. He turned his face towards him when he 'looked,' and Peter wept. He washed his guilt with tears, he poured water from his eyes and baptized his conscience. . . ."[60] Because the diseased are often delirious and the human heart is "rough country," Augustine explained, the gift of penance depended on a spiritual diagnosis.[61] Peter revealed how far even the saints had to go before their spiritual promises became more than presumptions.

Contrition obtained absolution, while verbosity allowed opportunity for new mistakes. Ambrose of Milan had reflected, "I do not find what [Peter] said, I find that he wept. I read of his tears, I do not read of satisfaction. But what cannot be defended can be absolved."[62] Christ had first to look on the sinner before self-accusation and then efficacious remorse could take place. There was no such "look" at Judas, whose verbal confession was consequentially in vain (Mt 27:4). Maximus of Turin went so far as to allow that Judas performed a viable act of penance; nevertheless, he failed to "unbind" his conscience from his crime.[63] The poet Verecundus called Peter's contrition a "lacrymal confession," which was penance in and of itself.[64] Commenting on the psalms, Cassiodorus observed that Jesus initially turned his face from Peter because, as the divine inquisitor, he would instantaneously destroy iniquity with his gaze.[65] Judged at that moment, with justice instead of mercy, Peter would be damned. First, the sinner had to look at his own sinful state, "Peter to Peter" (*Petrum Petro*) in Augustine's words, in order to accuse himself and hope for forgiveness. Peter taught Christians that penance worked as an antidote to human fallibility and mendacity alike.

DAVID: THE POETRY OF INTROSPECTION

Like Peter, the psalmist exemplified proper penance as much by his humanity as his heroism. In Jerome's tidy equation, David taught "by his virtues, how standing I might not fall; by his penance, how falling I might rise again."[66] It had taken a prophet, after all, to persuade David to repentance: the king at first had failed to recognize his own sinfulness, until God, in the voice of the prophet Nathan, coaxed David toward introspection and self-judgment, just as bishops would later coax Christians through the poetry of the psalms.[67] So Augustine directed his congregation to listen closely: "Nathan the prophet has not been sent to you, David has been sent to you. Hear him clamoring, and likewise clamor; hear him moaning, and moan with him; hear him weeping, and add your tears; hear he is corrected, and share in his delight."[68] For Cassiodorus, who in the 540s modeled his commentary on the complete book of psalms after Augustine's work, David revealed how sinners should expect the rewards to come in the Final Judgment and petition for their share by putting the message of the psalms into action—that is, by striving to be good penitents.[69] These influential commentators on the psalms found in David the perfect model for penance, because his words and actions together provided a unified language for "the disparate moral sentiments of the entire Christian community, sentiments that individuals, steeped in their peculiar sins, find inexpressible."[70] The seven penitential psalms were especially instructive, none more so than Psalm 50, the *Miserere*, which worked almost miraculously to move people to introspection and contrition.[71] With the psalms, late antique preachers tried to move Christians toward penance, "by playing upon the Davidical harp with a plectrum of spiritual understanding."[72]

ADAM: THE SHADOW OF EXCUSES AND HOLLOW WORDS

The church's collective appeal to judgment, recompense, and forgiveness was the key to liturgical penance in Late Antiquity, but it was no easy concept to convey. Adam was an ambivalent model in this context. He was, with Eve, the first to falter on account of his humanity, a condition he demonstrated by his reluctance to face up to his sin. Nonetheless, Adam also became a model penitent, a role he fulfilled while simultaneously monitoring the penance Eve performed—unsuccessfully, as it turned out—as if he had been her bishop. The apocryphal *Life of Adam and Eve* featured its two protagonists after their expulsion from Eden. In the Latin version, which reached its extant form during Late Antiquity, Adam stands up to his neck in the Jordan for forty days, weeping along with the fluvial creatures thronging him like a late antique congregation. Meanwhile, doubting her endurance, Adam's prescription for Eve is thirty-seven days in the Tigris. The devil manages to trick her once again, this time into abandoning her penance and foraging for food. Surprisingly, because he never deviates from his penance, Adam lacks Peter's presumption and takes neither his own forgiveness nor his fortitude for granted. "Perhaps" (*forsitan*) is the leitmotif of the penitential chapters of the *Life*: "perhaps" there will be forgiveness.[73] Humility and contrition are thus shown to be inseparable.

The best evidence that these examples had meaning for ordinary people emerges in criticisms leveled at the heroes of penance themselves, above all at Adam. Three anonymous sermons or addresses, possibly composed by a single archdeacon at Rome during the fifth or sixth century for delivery during the part of the penitential liturgy known as the *postulatio*, treated Adam quite differently from the *Life*.[74] At this point in the reconciliation ceremony, the archdeacon presented the expectant penitents, prostrate at the feet of the clergy and the standing congregation, all of them weeping and moaning together, and he pleaded on their behalf to rouse the bishop's mercy—to stir his "pastoral guts" (*pastoralia uiscera*). The penitents had done most of the work already; fueled by "hidden assistance" straight from God, they had hung their minds on a cerebral scaffold and tortured themselves there (*in catasta confixus excruciet*). Now they were literally vulnerable: they stripped bare "their consciences gory with savage bites" before the bishop's own eyes (*ante tuos oculos*) and awaited his "medicinal attentiveness" (*diligentiam medicinae*).[75]

These living penitents invited direct comparison with legendary penitents. However contrite his performance in the Jordan, Adam could have hoped only to compensate for his more famous and miserable showing in the Garden of Eden where, after eating the forbidden fruit, he had chosen to hide his shame rather than to make amends. The archdeacon offered up Adam as a counterexample to the ordinary Christians of his congregation. "These people are revivified through a more prudent remedy," he said, "not by excusing, but by accusing their deeds."[76] In another address, he tested his subjects in the place of the first humans: "These are the ones, standing in church as if they were established in paradise, whom that age-old enemy begrudged. . . . Looking back and dreading the example of the ancient condemnation, however, these [penitents] do not flee from the face of God, they do not hide themselves in the shadow of excuses (*umbraculo excusationis*), and they do not cover up their shameful actions with hollow verbal defenses, like a fruitless wrap of leaves. . . ."[77] The penitents engaged sin like a criminal charge, temptation like an accuser, and the bishop like a judge. "They lay what they have done out in the open with their fruitful tears. By themselves finding fault with their own crimes, through anticipation and not denial, they overcome that enemy who would have accused them."[78]

In the ceremony of reconciliation, bishops probed the hearts of the penitents to judge their sincerity. For their part, penitents' behavior demonstrated whether they had confronted their own iniquities. Above all, the performance revealed that the penitents' submission to judgment, punishment,

and divine mercy was voluntary and wholehearted.[79] Once they came
through this process successfully, the penitents became heroes as valiant as
the martyrs and saints and worthy of emulation.

Compunction and Discernment for All

Of all the theoretical boundaries distinguishing types of sins and sinners,
the boundary that separated ordinary Christians from penitents was the least
absolute of all. Penitents provided living models for those mundane, less
sensational, and more numerous sinners comprising the Christian majority, whose gestures to obtain forgiveness might consist only of prayers and
pious works such as almsgiving. How much did ascetics, professional penitents, clergy, and ordinary Christians have in common when it came to
the ways in which they conducted their spiritual lives? Did they share a
common understanding of how their spiritual conduct might affect their
experience of divine justice, in either the present or the hereafter? In other
words, did expectations of justice find a common ground among these
diverse groups of Christians? Not only was there a common ground, but
penance was the bridge leading to it.

Writers like Gregory the Great consciously crafted a pastoral theology
around ascetic practices derived from monastic contexts and literatures but
transposed onto a spiritual agenda for all Christians by means of penitential
language—namely, confession, judgment, sanction, and absolution. Before
Gregory, bishops from a monastic background like Caesarius of Arles had
already embarked in the same direction by encouraging their followers to
take an active role in their own judgment, translating what was essentially
an invitation to self-incrimination into an admirable endeavor through a
variety of means, such as invoking famous penitents from scripture, whom
they not only held up as role models but also criticized by comparison
with living Christians. This all was oriented toward a clear and common
goal: that Christians as individuals would anticipate the Final Judgment
not with fear, but with a rational, even lawyerly comprehension of how to
build a strong case for themselves.

An Inward Turn

Up until the time when emotions spilled over in the ceremony of reconciliation, penance was mostly an invisible process—in Dom Jean Leclercq's

words, "an inner song, a slight murmur, a silent word."[80] This was the phase to which most scholars of penance have paid the least attention, but it is where the expectations bishops and ordinary Christians had of each other interacted most intimately, and where the promise of mercy replaced the fear of justice.[81] To understand how bishops addressed these unseen movements when communicating with their followers, we should look to Gregory the Great, the bishop who launched his primacy in Rome with a massive penitential procession, but who was also the "father of compunction." Poised on the edge of Late Antiquity and the Early Middle Ages, Gregory explained how souls passed from shame, through punishment and the temptation to relent or relapse, finally to a true longing for eternal salvation. The moment of turning away from sin was marked by a sharp, painful prick as of a thorn (*spina*), a process Latin authors generally termed compunction (*compunctio*).[82] Echoing a Stoic distinction between ostentatious lament and genuine grief, Gregory described how shame and suffering produced fearful tears while desire for God produced joyful tears. Compunction was more than a momentary disposition, it was a sort of *machina ad Deum*, which might lift the penitent's soul up toward divine mercy.[83]

The father of compunction was a late antique pastor, whose theology moved easily across boundaries between philosophical and pastoral, religious and secular life. He was not the first to blur these distinctions. In Augustine's time John Cassian (360–436), although he had traveled the world and counted powerful ecclesiastics among his friends, settled to write in an explicitly monastic environment. Cassian, too, distinguished between tears shed out of sorrow over past sins and those shed in joyful expectation of the good things to come after the final reckoning with the divine judge.[84] In the *Dialogues*, he described the emphasis Pinufius, an Egyptian abbot and presbyter, placed on the "compunction of humility," which came only when the sinner held his sins before his face for judgment. For Pinufius, according to Cassian, absolution was obtained when the memory of past sins no longer aroused any emotion and when the *spina* of the conscience were dug out of the spirit's marrow, letting "the storm cloud of tears rising from confession of guilt extinguish the fire of the conscience."[85] Scripture, especially the psalms, provided these two monks with an expansive catalog of "instruments" of repentance other than baptism, martyrdom, and liturgical penance.[86]

Compunction itself was expansive, and certainly not reserved for monks alone. All of human life was a form of prolonged penance, and people should not have been surprised that "this life abounds in weeping"; so Augustine exhorted laypeople in his congregation to live what they all sang in Psalm 125, "They that sow in tears shall reap in joy."[87] Tears had a voice God could hear, as he had heard the spilled blood of Abel; they were the heart's blood and those who wished to turn from a sinful life should "cry out, gush interior blood, sacrifice your heart to God."[88]

FRAGILITY PREVAILS

As the first chapter of this book emphasized, ordinary people were sensitive to secret, unpredictable, or unintelligible intentions of their neighbors and themselves, for these provided the seedbed for calumny. Christianity offered no novel solution but a language for expressing these concerns: *cogitationes*, one's innermost thoughts, were the site where people had the best chance of preparing themselves to face divine justice, for it was also their front line against sin.[89] Bishops guided their followers through the combat, but laypeople had to prepare themselves by probing and evaluating their own cogitations—engaging in a sort of corollary to episcopal scrutiny. Every Christian was a target for "spirits of iniquity" (*spiritalia nequitiae in caelestibus*), just as every person was a target of calumny on earth. The struggle over control of secret thoughts was no mythical melee, not for Augustine: only "stupid people think we should fight against the air."[90] There was more danger from the "secret waylayer," preached Leo I, than from any "manifest enemy."[91] Everyone must fight "interior battles," and the victors would be those who had invoked divine mercy on their side by doing penance.[92] It was a frightening struggle that exposed human vulnerability at its most intimate, but it was not different in nature from what people experienced living in human society. Thus, the authority of the churchmen bonded most strongly with the expectations of their congregations in the realm of cogitations.

Curiosity about the way things worked beyond the ordinary range of human perception pervaded other forms of literature besides sermons and treatises. In his preeminent study of postclassical poetry, Jacques Fontaine devoted much of his commentary on fifth-century Latin verse to a section entitled, "les examens de conscience."[93] While he acknowledged the historical, penitential, and eschatological setting for much of this literature, Fontaine's analysis also highlighted influential literary traditions. Surely other traditions were at work as well, including the sort of judicial uncertainty we explored in the first chapter—that popular anxiety over the ways that unknowable plots and maneuvers might move beneath an otherwise apparently uniform surface, the widespread concern for personal security whose evidence survives from generation after generation on tombstones and curse tablets. Once provided with a vehicle for expression in religious literature, such traditions could scarcely stop from influencing the way people looked at the world. Thus we find in one verse rendition of Genesis God dwelling before time in the "black chaos . . . intermingled as a secret power, mov[ing] within this concealed mass,"[94] while the fourth-century poet Proba, with the help of Virgil, recalled in the proemium to her *Cento* how, "to me, trying everything, it seemed a better decision to reveal profound matters submerged in earth and darkness."[95] The prospect of introspection could be harrowing: when Leo I preached on the terror gripping Jesus's disciples after they heard that one of them would turn traitor, he explained that what unsettled them was "the uncertainty of human mutability, the fear that what anyone knew about himself had been less correct than truth itself foresaw."[96] Christianity did not change what poets and sorcerers alike had long speculated about the unseen world, but penance provided a channel for directing their energies and sharing them with a broad community.

For the somber poetry of introspection, blended with images of apocalypse, affected bishops too. In the Latin sermon literature, the tone becomes even more insistent after Augustine. "A fire burns in the flesh from the inside out," preached Peter Chrysologus (d. 460), who had become bishop of Ravenna in 433. He described how that fire "vaporizes the veins, inflames the guts, boils in the marrow, and continually incenses the whole interior of man." Lay people could take solace in the fact that even the prophets had experienced difficulty in expressing that which burned so fiercely within. Peter offered that reassurance to his congregation: "For what one conceives in the scope of his mind, he is unable to pull out from his mouth, to pour through his lips, to articulate with his tongue, to condense in any of his speech."[97] Human faculties were scarcely adequate for the task and failed proportionately as the piety of the individual increased. For ordinary Christians, therefore, the assistance of their bishops was essential to survival. Peter understood cogitations less as the product of rational thought than as the main stage for each individual's spiritual progress or regress; they were a battleground, they were like a sea where fearsome storms raged, and they represented the profoundest secrets of the human spirit.[98] Humans found themselves unable to escape sin and injustice—the unrighteousness that would condemn them in the Final Judgment—because these destructive depth charges already were sunk deep in their cogitations, where they could lurk, linger, but inevitably would explode. Therefore, Peter warned, while humans were alive on earth, "fragility prevails in us" (*fragilitas dominatur in nobis*).[99] Although clearly he was talking about sin and encouraging introspection and penitential devotion, his pastoral obligations had led this bishop deep into the area of social insecurity and judicial uncertainty, important matters in the lives of Christians and non-Christians alike. Even while he talked religious psychology, Peter was negotiating between episcopal and popular expectations of justice.

The administration of penance changed episcopal justice. Not only a charismatic judge like the prophets, not only a pastor watching out for defenseless sheep, but now a mentor training people to become their own best sentinels, the bishop shared some of his spiritual gifts and relinquished part of his burden. We see this in the sermons of Maximus of Turin (ca. 380–ca. 466), the first known bishop of that city. Turin was firmly in the orbit of Milan, but Maximus's outlook on divine justice and the pastoral role of bishops was much closer to that of Augustine than Ambrose. Preachers like Maximus drew an important difference between the Hebrew leaders, who governed by what Christians followed Paul in calling the "Old Law," and bishops like himself. The "New Law" embodied in the sacraments they administered shattered the "hardness of sins" and extracted "from secret cogitations the marrow of a pure heart" (*ex occultis cogitationibus medullam mundi cordis*).[100] Paul was the "most powerful lover of justice," as Augustine had once written, and so his writings perfectly encapsulated the ideology of justice bishops now propagated through penance:[101] love God's mercy, fear God's justice, and look long and deep into one's own conscience.[102] Penance was the means not only of introspection, but of communicating this philosophy of justice to ordinary Christians. To this end, Maximus invoked the apostolic keys, that crucial symbol of episcopal authority, in what seems to be a unique and extraordinary fashion for his congregation. The passage is worth quoting at length, for its juxtapositions are intricate.

[God] gave to Peter, the good steward, the key to the kingdom of heaven, and Paul, like an able teacher, he charged with the care of the ecclesiastical institution. Thus, those whom one cultivates towards salvation, the other may receive into tranquility. Paul opens their hearts to the doctrine of the word, that Peter may open the kingdoms of heaven to their souls. Therefore, in a way, Paul received the key of knowledge from Christ. For it must be called a key: with it, the hard places of the breast are unlocked to faith, and secrets of the mind are laid bare. Anything kept shut up within is produced in a form easily comprehensible. It is a key, I say, which opens the conscience to confession of sin, and encloses grace in the eternity of the salvational mystery. So both of them received keys from the Lord, this one of knowledge and that one of power. One dispenses the riches of immortality; the other bestows the treasures of knowing.[103]

Maximus situated the apostolic keys, whose primary function was to facilitate penance by making the actions of a bishop binding in heaven, within a broader ecclesiastical and spiritual order, where penance joined individual Christians together into a communal plea for mercy. Although episcopal power was not diminished in theory at least, this configuration represented a shift in the relationship between bishops and their followers based on a shared responsibility for those things that were beyond the control of juridical rules and procedures. Although Maximus may have been alone in expressing this post-Ambrosian balance of accountability with precisely this image of the shared keys, other bishops reflected it in other ways.

The Balance of Mercy and Justice

Eutropius of Orange, the widower who did penance before becoming a bishop, was one of the many bishops of this period with professional roots in monasticism, particularly in Gaul, who helped change the idea of episcopal authority. The ascetic discipline they brought with them into office not only changed the pedigree and style of being a bishop; it also affected the way bishops related to their followers. All bishops who administered penance well also did penance, though preferably without humiliating themselves. For Caesarius, the bishop of Arles (502–43), penance was another tool of pastoral care like charismatic scrutiny, the spiritual sword, and the power to bind and loose sinners. So he preached to the people of Arles about both "slight sins" and "even greater offenses" that constantly threatened to catch them unawares, unless they kept themselves always vigilant through daily penance. Then he broadened his appeal to explain that "this practice should be observed continuously, not only by the laity and clerics, but even by priests and monks. Indeed, a bishop who does penance every day can pray for me, but one who presumes upon his dignity and sanctity, refusing to do penance, will have to find someone to pray for him."[104] Penance was not only for criminals and professionals but also for everyone capable of being provoked to think about mercy and justice.[105]

The role of bishops was to identify those who could be reached and to draw them free from whatever was holding them back, including complacency. People who enjoyed themselves on earth, for example, indulging in luxuries instead of focusing on alms and penitential devotion, needed persuading to realize that their lifestyle was harmful most of all to themselves—nourishing their bodies only to fatten the worms while their spirits starved. Caesarius used evocative language to carry those who would listen outside the city walls to Les Alyscamps, where he draped a shroud of despair over the splendid graves of the wealthy, whose bodies and treasures together "pass away like a shadow and only leave eternal recriminations and crimes to remain," unless they had done penance.[106] "Let the proud laugh at us, but let us implore God's mercy for their salvation with shouting and groaning both day and night," he urged fellow pastors.[107] Such Christians might even need more forceful persuasion, for which Caesarius trusted "in the ineffable goodness of God, that He will deign to punish them immediately as his children"—a divine slap of some sort to focus their wits, not the death blow that allegedly felled Saggitius of Lerida.[108]

Caesarius called the complacent sinners and the reluctant penitents proud (*superbi*), but they were likely to be happily active members of the community.[109] They were not contemptuous of society with their church, far from it. These same people obsessed over the appearance of their clothes when Sundays came, and although a pastor might prefer they launder their souls with as much thorough attention to detail, Caesarius did not criticize their fastidiousness in and of itself: "you well know, brothers, all people follow this habit."[110] Vanity was not what kept them from repentance; more likely their somber respect for penance held them back. Although ordinary Christians might be aware of their own shortcomings, the crimes and debauchery they saw or suspected to be going on around them could lead them to believe that the pettiness of their own sins insulated them from a community of more dangerous criminals.[111] Reasonable people were careful with whom they associated themselves when it came to admitting guilt.

Provoking sinners to repentance could also be impeded by the fact that repeated harangues grew annoying and dispiriting for preacher and audience alike. Caesarius's followers grumbled, why must they all endure sermon after sermon against men who kept concubines, when their bishop could simply excommunicate them?[112] Why should they hear Caesarius lecture time and again on the evils of phylacteries and other magical devices?[113] As we saw in the first chapter, this same sort of frustration, clear evidence of failed expectations in episcopal leadership, had provoked Augustine to return fire: a conscientious bishop would use every means at his disposal to ensure "that discipline does not sleep," if only accusers would supply him with viable evidence against the sinners they so readily denounced.[114] Caesarius instead admitted that something as simple as the popularity of a vice or bad habit—everybody's doing it!—had the power to render excommunication useless; one could alienate only so many members of a community before there was no viable community left.[115] A good bishop instead must wait in tolerant expectation (*tolerat et exspectat*) for God to "provide them with fruitful penance."[116] As for their resentful neighbors, upset that the bishop's "severity and discipline" failed to deliver due comeuppance, Caesarius invited them to imagine "what sort of sentence" would fall on unrepentant sinners in the divine judgment to come.[117]

Sin was something all Christians—laity and clergy, monks and widows, men and women, young and old—shared in common whether they liked it or not, while penance could be their common solution, but only if they were willing. The list of "the devil's displays" (*pompae diaboli*) was too long and inclusive, Caesarius insisted, for anyone not to have tried some of them at some point. Penance, almsgiving, and making peace with enemies offered both redemption and emendation for the failures of daily life, for as long as the soul remained trapped in "this paltry body."[118] Penance was a way of life that united lay and religious members of the church with not only a common goal of redemption but also a common regimen based on introspection and self-discipline. Before addressing the differences between the three "professions" of virgins, widows, and married people, for example, Caesarius described a penitential lifestyle that would reward them all. His plan for "cultivating" the soul could have been composed by the desert fathers or by Cassian for a community of monks, but Caesarius was addressing laypeople. "First, the thorns should be torn out, that is, evil thoughts (*cogitationes*). Next," he continued, "the stones should be removed, that is, all malice and harshness ought to be taken away. Then, our heart should be broken up and cultivated by the plough of the Gospel and the ploughshare of the Cross: shattered by repentance, softened by almsgiving, and prepared by charity for the Lord's sowing."[119] It is surprising, but also appropriate, that the word *penance* itself is absent from the chapter headings, subheadings, and index to William Klingshirn's rich biography of Caesarius, even though the bishop's sermons are among the most important sources for pastoral care and penance in sixth-century Gaul.[120] Although modern commentators on his sermons are at pains to distinguish what Caesarius often called the "medicine" of penance from liturgical penance, and so to draw clear boundaries between liturgical, professional, and daily penance, Caesarius would have rejected their intrusive glosses, for they diminish a point he made often: penance balanced daily sins with daily remedies.[121]

Caesarius of Arles exhorted his congregation to think about the Final Judgment and not to connive at avoiding the reproach of their neighbors or the censure of their priests. A bishop likewise needed long-term perspective to look past the obstructions of judicial process and focus instead on his own, unique prominence. "Let no one say they were not warned," Caesarius warned his listeners. "See us clamor, see us grapple, see us preach: do not let yourself disdain the herald if you hope to escape the judge."[122] The bishop remained the sentinel, the *episkopos*, of scripture and texts like the *Didascalia*, and Caesarius disclosed his own accountability for the souls of his followers "before the tribunal of the eternal judge." His part as a pastor was to urge his followers toward "lots of charity and hard, long penance," or else he would "render an evil account" for their sin and his negligence alike at the Final Judgment; whatever sins Christians did not recognize and confess in this life, the devil would raise as charges against them before the tribunal.[123] But he encouraged Christians to be on guard themselves against the more subtle, less predictable thoughts and urges that neither their bishop nor even their most watchful neighbors could notice. These were the sins that would surprise them on Judgment Day, and for which they alone were accountable.[124] Whereas bishops and emperors before them blamed procedural blockage and calumnious maneuverings for the failure of justice, Caesarius directed Christians' attention to the secret whisperings of sin within their own hearts.

The final reason Christians were reluctant to do penance was the most difficult to correct, because it troubled philosophers and theologians as well: human beings misunderstood—or perhaps better, did not know how to comprehend—the relationship between divine mercy and divine justice. God's mercy was great but not so great that it interfered with God's justice. So "let us not despair of His mercy because we fear His justice," Caesarius counseled, "nor love His mercy so much that we disregard His justice." He also offered a practical solution: the balance between God's mercy and God's justice might be impossible for a human to figure out intellectually, but penance struck it just right.[125] It might even be possible to tilt the scales of mercy and justice toward mercy, if Christians "make [mercy] our patron in this world."[126] This ceded considerable autonomy to the sinner, along with responsibility, for, as Caesarius insisted, "each must return to his own conscience," examining and judging what sins there required treatment.[127]

Caesarius invited ordinary Christians to become judges of their own consciences. The language of disputes and trials, complete with their rules and procedures as well as their pitfalls and injustices, all of which figured large in the professional experience of bishops, became a means for joining together the mutual expectations of religious professionals and laypeople. While deferring justice until the hereafter, penance provided a rationale for coping with the most paralyzing fear of all: that the justice people look forward to eagerly will turn out to ruin them. One example from Caesarius' sermons may suffice here to convey just how fully penance engaged what people knew about justice from this world and should expect from the next:

Dearest brothers, every person knowing he will plead a case before an earthly judge seeks useful patrons for himself and tries to arrange for the most skilled advocates. If this is what he does to plead a case before that kind of judge—one he can get around, he can surprise or deceive, he can lure away from justice with the eloquence of particular arguments, and perhaps even corrupt with bribes or pervert with false praise and phony flattery—if this is how a man prepares himself to plead a case before a man, how much more should we [prepare ourselves] to plead our case before the eternal judge, not only for our deeds but also our words, not only for our words but also our cogitations—before that judge before whom the heart's secrets are not hidden, who lacks no witness, seeks no arguments, to whose eyes "all things are bare and naked" (Heb 4:13)? Because we shall plead our cases before such a judge, let us make mercy our patron, so that it may always intercede on our behalf to plead our cases. . . . If [mercy] will come there with us, it will defend us from the devil's accusation and lead [us] into eternal bliss.[128]

The public call to introspection marked a major shift in the relationship between popular expectations and episcopal responsibility for the provision of justice. "Attend to your own conscience, each and every one of you," Caesarius begged his followers. The *Didascalia* had charged bishops to "judge like God"; by the sixth century, at least some bishops were charging the ordinary Christian to judge himself like a bishop would and to "cleanse whatever he finds defiled in himself. He should illuminate what is dark, restore what was lost, and with the help of Christ Himself revive by repentance what was dead."[129] Ordinary Christians joined bishops as spiritual judges, distinguished from the latter by their narrower jurisdiction, limited to their own, individual souls. Like the ideal bishop-judge, moreover, they now would have to face the problems raised by calumny and social bond. Justice was the sum of its procedural parts, and bishops like Caesarius let Christians know that attentive preparation for those procedures would determine whether they earned God's mercy or suffered divine justice at the Final Judgment.

An End to the Scholarly Myth of Decline and Rigorism

Pious Christians and successful penitents expected forgiveness, but certainty
came only on their day of judgment. Penance ultimately oriented minds
and hearts toward the Final Judgment, so some of the most important
studies on late antique penance, especially those by Éric Rebillard and Peter
Brown, have focused on exit strategies and endgames—how Christians
died a good death, and what sort of a hearing they expected in the afterlife.[130] Meanwhile, among the living, pastors shaped mundane attitudes
toward penance around two fundamental truths. On one side was human
fallibility, which accounted for not only why people sinned, but why penance needed to be a daily devotion, a disposition, a "frame of mind."[131]
On the other, divine mercy was at work. Prudent Christians invoked mercy
now, not waiting to face the unerring accuracy of divine justice, which would
make no allowance for weakness or for people who misjudged their own
capacities.

Even before authors such as Gregory the Great began asking Christians to focus their attention beyond the evidence of justice working or
failing on earth and toward "the looming immensity of the world beyond
the grave," where each secret thought would be weighed and judged,[132]
ordinary people thought of salvation as a trial. In the most influential
visionary text of the late antique and medieval periods, the *Vision* or *Apocalypse of Paul*, the "most powerful lover of justice" served as a guide to what
everyone would discover at death: angels had reported daily on all their
actions directly to God, and although the Final Judgment might take a while
to come, they would experience divine justice immediately.[133] Those who
had not prepared themselves for trial and made "mercy their advocate," as
Caesarius recommended, would find no mercy in death. Instead of "angels
of justice," their attendants would be "angels without mercy (*sine misericordia*), without pity, their faces full of furor and teeth protruding from their
mouths, whose eyes shone like morning stars in the east, and out from their
hair or mouths shot fiery sparks."[134] Without mercy, divine justice would
feel like worldly justice at its worst, its rules perverted and ensaring, but
the problem was with people's expectations, not with their judge: "Why
do you weep?" asked Paul's angelic guide when the apostle recoiled at the
sight of so many souls condemned. "Are you more merciful than God?
Although God is good, he also understands that there are punishments;
he patiently endures humanity, leaving each one to act according to his
own will for the time he dwells on earth."[135]

While modern medievalists have worried over the rise of purgatory and theologians have grappled with the problem of free will, people in our period who thought at all about salvation were likely to focus on the best way to increase their odds of surviving the barrage of accusations demons would launch at them in the afterlife. Penance in all its manifestations and behaviors, ranging from the reconciliation of homicides and heretics to private prayer and alms, provided the most effective channels for reconciling common expectations of justice and Christian eschatology. This argument, that penance had broad and effective utility, runs counter to a longstanding model of how penance functioned during this period—what Mayke de Jong and others have criticized sharply as the "grand narrative," a model whose persuasive power draws in large part on the scholarly myth of decline and rigor mentioned in the introduction to this book.[136]

Respectable historians not long ago described how a Golden Age of penitential devotion, when Christian communities had been rarefied environments—small, tightly knit, and hardened either by pride in membership or by fear of persecution—slipped away after Constantine's conversion, as those once heroic congregations steadily swelled with droves of half-hearted, reluctant, or spiritless converts. For their part, bishops refused to give any slack by adjusting the rigors of penance to accommodate the new Christian majority. Penance asked too much of such communities; as a result, by the fifth century across the west, according to Bernhard Poschmann, "there was no sacramental remedy at their disposal."[137] Liturgical penance was "unapplied because [it was] inapplicable," explained Vogel later. "The systematic refusal of any indulgence adapted to human weakness caused an almost complete abandonment of penance on the part of the faithful. It quickly reached an untenable situation for the spiritual life of Christians."[138] Everyone, it would seem, contributed to this "untenable situation." Lay people were the agents of "grave moral declension," while church officials clung to rigid standards that had been outdated since before the conversion of Constantine.[139] What was left, in Vogel's surmise, was "a complete 'penitential void'?"[140]

The real penitential void, however, is created by this myth, whose principal agents—bishops—bear little or no resemblance to the flesh-and-blood officials we have been examining throughout this study. Pastors used biblical and hagiographic models of penance, such as Adam's mixed performance in Genesis and Peter's immoderate self-confidence in the narrative of the Passion, to create a community of penitents more inclusive than the living subjects of liturgical penance alone. The performance of penance contributed to the fluidity of boundaries between lay, religious, and clerical spirituality. Late antique bishops cast penance in a vista so broad that its challenges and pitfalls, while foreboding, became wholly natural contours in a vaster landscape of sin and redemption.[141] In the end, although we can assess the contributions and responses of bishops as administrators and pastors, we can only imagine how ordinary Christians responded to this prospect, and whether it might have fired or cooled their penitential zeal.

It is not that there were no meaningful differences between liturgical, professional, and daily penance, between public demonstrations of humility and private acts of devotion, or between crimes such as homicide and light sins such as profanity.[142] Rather, we find an extension of penance beyond the ordinary limits of juridical administration and pastoral care. As a social and juridical problem, bishops had learned that calumny contaminated positive expectations of justice because it cut across the neat boundaries established by law codes, administrative jurisdictions, and social bonds. By similarly cutting across the same sorts of boundaries—juridical, administrative, and social—penance offered an effective solution to something we might call *spiritual calumny*: the concern over not only notorious sins or even secret sins that people had committed, but the insidious possibility of sin lurking in every community, in every heart. Penance was neither rigid nor impossible. It was the most promising means bishops in this period had discovered for directing the expectations of their followers, past the reality of failure and fragility around them, toward the enduring ideal of divine justice.

Conclusion

"IDEOLOGY HAS CONFRONTED REALITY, and ideology has bent." So a modern political analyst commented on the "exhaustion of power" within a contemporary presidential administration whose ideological convictions, he believed, had fouled its effectiveness.[1] One and a half millennia ago, bent ideology and exhausted power helped to shape Christian society in the west. The ideology in question involved a particular conception of justice, which the realities of judicial process and religious life forced to bend but not to break. The essence of this ideology was the belief that divine justice, infallible and inescapable, would reward deserving Christians with eternal salvation in the hereafter. Meanwhile in this life, discrepancies between ideology and reality taxed the power of leaders, above all Christian bishops— the rulers and caretakers of the church, whose power rested on the promise of justice. Their ideology was inseparable from their power, so that the exhaustion of episcopal power would mean the exhaustion of justice, while the contortion of justice meant the same for bishops' rule. Because their power derived explicitly and conditionally from an omnipotent ruler, bishops knew a culture of accountability much sterner than what modern democratic leaders face. For that reason, bishops worked hard at reshaping ideology to make it fit reality.

This task of reconciliation was entirely of bishops' own making, for no Christians who lived in the transition from antiquity to the Middle Ages would confuse worldly and divine justice. Worldly justice had shown them its lethal edge since the trial of Jesus of Nazareth and through the trials of the martyrs, so it inspired little confidence. By contrast, the divine justice to come in the Final Judgment promised more than fire and brimstone. Fear of the end time signified a "lucid conscience," well-ordered priorities, and an appreciation of the "ambiguous frontier" between earthly and heavenly justice.[2] Whereas human judges were quick to punish, God was quick to forgive.[3] Compared to divine justice, what humans conceived and experienced as righteousness was tattered and polluted, a used menstrual rag.[4] Among humans, things like justice, mercy, and piety were dispositions or affectations, "things that happen" and therefore less natural, less real, less permanent than divine justice.[5] Bishops worked hard to convince their followers that justice and salvation were conjoined within the church: without justice, salvation would be arbitrary; without salvation, justice would be shallow, short-lived, and meaningless.

However, divine justice and salvation both required certainty and precision. As theologians and pastors, bishops tried to sanitize the categories of justice—to sharpen the boundaries between right and wrong doctrine, between essential and illicit forms of worship, between salvation and damnation.[6] Early leaders had often exuded confidence that these distinctions would be readily discernible, at least to themselves. So Cyprian of Carthage (died 258), who coined the maxim, "no salvation outside the church," additionally staked out truth and justice for the exclusive purview of the church.[7] But a century later, even the most basic boundaries had begun to blur. Only God knew which Christians were "inwardly and secretly" among those who truly loved justice and deserved salvation, while God's earthly representatives were left to struggle over detecting "the position of the heart, not that of the body."[8] Neither certainty nor precision were guaranteed, and this was a difficult admission for Christian leaders, whose involvement in the procedures of worldly justice was meanwhile growing steadily more intimate.

By the end of the fourth century, with congregations swollen by the influx of forced or reluctant converts and Christians wary of the behavior or beliefs of other Christians, bishops like Augustine of Hippo, who were stalwart defenders of the Christian ideology of justice, were also the first to admit that the absolute categories of divine justice and salvation made little sense of the present world. Although ostensibly Christian by that time, the world still teemed with dangers, including the influence of heresy and superstition, the possibility of being wrongly accused of heresy or superstition, the allure of sin, the pressure to lie and cheat in order to survive and prosper, and the fear of one's own latent weaknesses. The distance separating theory from practice and certainty from doubt opened widest in the realm of justice. This gap between the letter of the law and its execution was an old and obvious fact of governance in secular and religious communities alike, but by the fifth century it had become a fact that church leaders confronted on a daily basis. The many failings of worldly justice, as they cropped up in the mundane interactions of bishops with their congregants, shaped what the Christian community expected of its leaders.

These expectations, moreover, affected the way bishops handled justice in theory and in practice, in both human and divine terms.

The history of justice, much like the history of the episcopal office during our period, must include all its failings, imperfections, and ambiguities, as much as its single point of clarity, always prominent in the minds of Christians: God's ultimate reckoning. Representing divine justice while administering worldly justice, dealing in timeless truths and absolute categories of salvation while neck deep in the treachery of human society, bishops could not do everything their occupation required with uniform success. In the final analysis, they were "ineffective . . . in the face of a confidently profane world" that measured the wages of justice in tangible results.[9] All the while, at the same time that they saw justice bend, twist, and crack under the pressure of social necessity, bishops hammered out the law. Their practical experience, which sometimes absorbed and other times reacted against the expectations of ordinary Christians, shaped the theology of justice. The result then resonated in Christian philosophy, liturgy, and eschatology, as well as legal and political culture, for centuries to come, while its distinctive pitch never lost a disturbing resonation of uncertainty.

Abbreviations

AASS	Jean Bolland et al., eds. *Acta Sanctorum quotquot toto orbe coluntur*. 3rd ed. 60 vols. Paris: Victor Palme, 1863–.
BHL	*Bibliotheca hagiographica latina*. 2 vols. Repr. ed. Brussels: Socii Bollandiani, 1949.
CAH 13	Averil Cameron and Peter Garnsey, eds. *Cambridge Ancient History*. Vol. 13, *The Late Empire, A.D. 337–425*. Cambridge: Cambridge University Press, 1998.
CAH 14	Averil Cameron, Michael Whitby, and Bryan Ward-Perkins, eds. *Cambridge Ancient History*. Vol. 14, *Late Antiquity: Empire and Successors, A.D. 425–600*. Cambridge: Cambridge University Press, 2000.
CCL	Corpus Christianorum Series Latina. Turnhout: Brepols.
CLA	E. A. Lowe, ed. *Codices latini antiquiores: A Paleographical Guide to Latin Manuscripts Prior to the Ninth Century*. 11 vols. Oxford: Clarendon Press, 1934–66.
Cod. Just.	P. Krüger, ed. *Corpus iuris civilis*. Vol. 2, *Codex Iustinianus*. 11th ed. Berlin: Weidmann, 1929.
Const. Sirm.	*Constitutiones Sirmondianes*, in C.Th.
CPL³	Eligius Dekkers. *Clavis Patrum Latinorum*. 3rd ed. CCL (1995).
CSEL	Corpus scriptorum ecclesiasticorum latinorum.
C.Th.	Theodor Mommsen and Paul M. Meyer, eds. *Theodosiani libri XVI cum Constitutionibus Sirmondianis et Leges novellae ad Theodosianum pertinentes*. Berlin, 1905. English: *The Theodosian Code and Novels, and the Sirmondian Constitutions*, trans. Clyde Pharr. Princeton, N.J.: Princeton University Press, 1952.
DACL	Fernand Cabrol and Henri Leclercq, eds. *Dictionnaire d'archéologie chrétienne et de liturgie*. 15 vols. Paris: Letouzey et Ané, 1907–53.
Dig.	Theodor Mommsen and Paul Krueger, eds. *Corpus iuris Civilis*. Vol. 1, *Institutiones, Digesta*. 16th ed. Berlin: Weidmann,

1928. Reprint *The Digest of Justinian*, with English trans. Alan Watson. 4 vols. Philadelphia: University of Pennsylvania Press, 1985; 2-volume rev. ed. English, 1998.

FOTC — Fathers of the Church, a New Translation. Washington, D.C.: Catholic University of America Press.

ICGA — Edmond Le Blant, ed. *Inscriptions chrétiennes de la Gaule antérieures au VIIIe siècle*. Repr. ed. 2 vols. Hildesheim: Georg Olms, 1999.

ILCV — Ernst Diehl, ed. *Inscriptiones Latinae Christianae Veteres*. Emendations by Jacques Moreau and Henri Irénée Marrou. 4 vols. Repr. ed. Berlin: Weidmann, 1961–67.

Inst. — P. Krueger, ed. *Corpus iuris Civilis*. Vol. 1, *Institutiones, Digesta*. 16th ed. Berlin: Weidmann, 1928. English: *Justinian's Institutes*, trans. P. Birks and G. MacLeod. Ithaca, N.Y.: Cornell University Press, 1987.

JECS — Journal of Early Christian Studies.

Loeb — Loeb Classical Library. Cambridge, Mass.: Harvard University Press.

MGH AA — Monumenta Germaniae Historica. Auctores antiquissimi.

MGH Epist. — Monumenta Germaniae Historica. Epistulae.

MGH SRM — Monumenta Germaniae Historica. Scriptores rerum Merovingicarum.

Migne, PG — J.-P. Migne, ed. *Patrologiae cursus completus, Series graeca*. Paris, 1857–66.

Migne, PL — J.-P. Migne, ed. *Patrologiae cursus completus, Series latina*. Paris, 1844–64.

Nov. Just. — R. Schöll and G. Kroll, eds. *Corpus iuris Civilis: Novellae*. 7th ed. Berlin: Weidmann, 1957.

Nov. Theod. and Nov. Val. — Paul M. Meyer, ed. *Theodosiani libri XVI cum Constitutionibus Sirmondianis et Leges novellae ad Theodosianum pertinentes*. Vol. 2. Berlin, 1905. English: *The Theodosian Code and Novels, and the Sirmondian Constitutions*, trans. Clyde Pharr. Princeton, N.J.: Princeton University Press, 1952.

PCBE 1 — André Mandouze, ed. *Prosopographie chrétienne du Bas-Empire: Prosopographie de l'Afrique chrétienne (303–533)*. Paris: Centre national de la recherche scientifique, 1982.

PCBE 2 — Charles Pietri, Luce Pietri, and Janine Desmulliez, eds. *Prosopographie chrétienne du Bas-Empire*. Vol. 2, *Prosopographie de l'Italie chrétienne (313–604)*. Rome: École française de Rome, 1999–2000.

PLRE   A. H. M. Jones, J. R. Martindale, and J. Morris, eds. *The Prosopography of the Later Roman Empire*. 3 vols. Cambridge: Cambridge University Press, 1971–92.

RICG 15   Françoise Descombes, ed. *Recueil des inscriptions chrétiennes de la Gaul antérieures à la Renaissance carolingienne XV: Viennoise du nord*. Paris: Centre national de la recherche scientifique, 1985.

SC   Sources Chrétiennes. Paris: Éditions du Cerf.

TTH   Translated Texts for Historians. Liverpool: Liverpool University Press.

ZPE   *Zeitschrift für Papyrologie und Epigraphik*.

ZRG KA   *Zeitschrift der Savigny-Stiftung für Rechtsgeschichte Kanonistiche Abteilung*.

ZRG RA   *Zeitschrift der Savigny-Stiftung für Rechtsgeschichte Romanistische Abteilung*.

Notes

Introduction

1. S. J. B. Barnish, "The Work of Cassiodorus After His Conversion," *Latomus* 48 (1989):157–87.

2. M. Vessey, "From *Cursus* to *Ductus*: Figures of Writing in Western Late Antiquity (Augustine, Jerome, Cassiodorus, Bede)," in *European Literary Careers: The Author from Antiquity to the Renaissance*, ed. P. Cheney and F. A. de Armas (Toronto, 2002), 47–103, esp. 89–92.

3. F. Troncarelli, *Vivarium: I libri, il destino* (Turnhout, 1998), 39–66, with bibliog. at 44 n. 8, and plate 15 for samples of Cassiodorus's script.

4. R. Dodaro, *Christ and the Just Society in the Thought of Augustine* (Cambridge, 2004).

5. Her book, *Orthodoxy and the Courts in Late Antiquity* (Oxford, forthcoming), did not appear in time for consideration here, but see C. Humfress, "Roman Law, Forensic Argument and the Formation of Christian Orthodoxy (III–VI Centuries)," in *Orthodoxie, christianisme, histoire*, ed. S. Elm, É. Rebillard, and A. Romano (Rome, 2001), 125–47; Humfress, "A New Legal Cosmos: Late Roman Lawyers and the Early Medieval Church," in *The Medieval World*, ed. P. Linehan and J. Nelson (London, 2001), 557–75.

6. See P. Brown, "The Study of Elites in Late Antiquity," *Arethusa* 33 (2000): 321–46; "sub-Roman," less a commonplace than the others named here, appears most among historians of Britain; e.g., D. N. Dumville, "The Idea of Government in Sub-Roman Britain," in *After Empire: Towards an Ethnology of Europe's Barbarians*, ed. G. Ausenda (Woodbridge, 1995), 177–216; C. A. Snyder, *Sub-Roman Britain (AD 400–600): A Gazetteer of Sites*, BAR British Series 247 (Oxford, 1996); Snyder, *An Age of Tyrants: Britain and the Britons, A.D. 400–600* (University Park, Pa., 1998); but also W. E. Klingshirn, "Charity and Power: The Ransoming of Captives in Sub-Roman Gaul," *Journal of Roman Studies* 75 (1985): 183–203.

7. Bibliography in M. Vessey, "The Demise of the Christian Writer and the Remaking of 'Late Antiquity': From H.-I. Marrou's Saint Augustine (1938) to Peter Brown's Holy Man (1983)," *JECS* 6, 3 (1998): 377–411 at 378 n. 5; for one recent history of this particular periodization among historians, see W. Liebeschuetz, "The Birth of Late Antiquity," *Antiquité Tardive* 12 (2004): 253–61.

8. For this chronology, see, e.g., A. Cameron, B. Ward-Perkins, and M. Whitby, eds., *The Cambridge Ancient History*, vol. 14, *Late Antiquity: Empire and Successors A.D. 425–600* (Cambridge, 2000); R. A. Markus, *The End of Ancient Christianity* (Cambridge, 1990), 222; W. Hartmann, "Der Bischof als Richter nach den

kirchenrechtlichen Quellen des 4. bis 7. Jahrhunderts," in *La giustizia nell'alto medio-evo (secoli V–VIII)*, Settimane di Studio del Centro Italiano di Studi sull'Alto Medio-evo 42, 2 vols. (Spoleto, 1995), 805–42 at 805; M. Innes, *State and Society in the Early Middle Ages: The Middle Rhine Valley, 400–1000* (Cambridge, 2001), 23–25, 155–56, 177–78.

9. For one strain of the historiographical debate between change and conti-nuity see F. Lifshitz, review of Innes, *State and Society*, TMR 02.11.17 (2002), playing with the difficult vocabulary ("hyperromanist," "hyporomanist") introduced by A. J. Stoclet, review of M. de Jong, *In Samuel's Image: Child Oblation in the Early Medi-eval West*, Speculum 73, 3 (1998): 828–30.

10. J. B. Bury, *The Invasion of Europe by the Barbarians*, ed. F. J. C. Hearnshaw (New York, 2000).

11. E.g., T. S. Burns, *Barbarians Within the Gates of Rome: A Study of Roman Military Policy and the Barbarians, ca. 375–425 A.D.* (Bloomington, Ind., 1994); P. Heather, *The Fall of the Roman Empire* (London, 2005); B. Ward-Perkins, *The Fall of Rome and the End of Civilization* (Oxford, 2005).

12. Pacian, *Sermo de paenitentibus*, ed. C. Granado, trans. C. Epitalon and M. Lestienne, SC 410 (1995), 118–47, with C. Vogel, *Le pécheur et la pénitence dans l'église ancienne* (Paris, 1966), 88–101; for Caesarius and more on the Golden Age, see M. de Jong, "Transformations of Penance," in *Rituals of Power from Late Antiquity to the Early Middle Ages*, ed. F. Theuws and J. L. Nelson (Leiden, 2000), 185–224.

13. Jonas of Bobbio, *Vita Columbani*, 1.5, ed. B. Krusch, MGH SRG 37 (1905), 161: "Fides tantum manebat christiana, nam penitentiae medicamenta et mortificati-onis amor vix vel paucis in ea repperiebatur locis"; with De Jong, "Transformations of Penance," 215–16; I. N. Wood, *The Missionary Life: Saints and the Evangelisation of Europe, 400–1050* (Harlow, 2001), 31–35; P. Brown, *The Rise of Western Christendom*, 2nd ed. (Oxford, 2003), 248–52.

14. A. Angenendt, *Frühmittelalter: Die abendländische Christenheit von 400–900*, 2nd ed. (Stuttgart, 1995), 147–59 ("Die Dekomposition der Alten Welt"), 155–56 ("verdunkelte Theologie"); J. Le Goff, *The Birth of Purgatory*, trans. A. Goldham-mer (Chicago, 1984), chs. 2–3.

15. Le Goff, *Birth of Purgatory*, 87; J. C. Russell, *The Germanization of Early Medieval Christianity: A Sociohistorical Approach to Religious Transformation* (Oxford, 1994).

16. Dodaro, *Christ and the Just Society*, 14–15.

17. C. Vogel, "La discipline pénitentielle en Gaule des origines au IXe siècle: Le dossier hagiographique," Revue des sciences religieuses 30 (1956): 1–26, 157–86 at 23; Vogel, *Pécheur et la pénitence*, 27–28; B. Poschmann, *Penance and the Anointing of the Sick*, trans. F. Courtney (New York, 1964), 123.

18. Esp. M. C. Mansfield, *The Humiliation of Sinners: Public Penance in Thirteenth-Century France* (Ithaca, N.Y., 1995); S. Hamilton, *The Practice of Pen-ance, 900–1050* (Woodbridge, 2001); K. Cooper and J. Gregory, eds., *Retribution, Repentance, and Reconciliation*, Studies in Church History 40 (Woodbridge, 2004); A. Firey, ed., *A New History of Penance* (Leiden, 2006).

19. De Jong, "Transformations of Penance"; De Jong, "What Was Public About Public Penance? *Paenitentia Publica* and Justice in the Carolingian World,"

in *La giustizia nell'alto medioevo (secoli IX–XI)*, 2 vols. (Spoleto, 1997), 2: 863–904; P. Brown, "Vers la naissance du Purgatoire: Amnistie et pénitence dans le christianisme occidental de l'Antiquité tardive au Haut Moyen Age," *Annales HSS* 52 (1997): 1247–61; Brown, "The Decline of the Empire of God: Amnesty, Penance, and the Afterlife from Late Antiquity to the Middle Ages," in *Last Things: Death and the Apocalypse in the Middle Ages*, ed. C. W. Bynum and P. Freedman (Philadelphia, 2000), 41–59; Brown, *Rise of Western Christendom*, 255–57; R. Meens, "The Frequency and Nature of Early Medieval Penance," in *Handling Sin: Confession in the Middle Ages*, ed. P. Biller and A. J. Minnis (Woodbridge, 1998), 35–61.

20. P. Garnsey and C. Humfress, *Evolution of the Late Antique World* (Cambridge, 2001), 58, 88.

21. P. Wormald, *The Making of English Law: King Alfred to the Twelfth Century*, vol. 1, *Legislation and its Limits* (Oxford, 1999); shared culture, common law: M. Lupoi, *The Origins of the European Legal Order*, trans. A. Belton (Cambridge, 2000), 23–24 and passim.

22. Recent studies focusing on a distinctively episcopal impact in areas of early medieval law include A. Wiesheu, "Bischof und Gefängnis: Zur Interpretation der Kerkerbefreiungswunder in der merowingischen Hagiographie," *Historisches Jahrbuch* 121 (2001): 1–23; I. Wood, "Incest, Law and the Bible in Sixth-Century Gaul," *Early Medieval Europe* 7, 3 (1998): 291–304; B. Jussen, "Über 'Bischofsherrschaft' und die Prozeduren politisch-sozialer Umordnung in Gallien zwischen 'Antike' und 'Mittelalter'," *Historische Zeitschrift* 260 (1995): 673–718; M. Vessey, "The Origins of the *Collectio Sirmondiana*: A New Look at the Evidence," in *The Theodosian Code: Studies in the Imperial Law of Late Antiquity*, ed. J. Harries and I. Wood (London, 1993), 178–99; S. Esders, "Rechtsdenken und Traditionsbewusstsein in der gallischen Kirche zwischen Spätantike und Frühmittelalter: Zur Anwendbarkeit soziologischer Rechtsbegriffe am Beispiel des kirchlichen Asylrechts," *Francia* 20 (1993): 97–135.

23. R. H. Helmholz, *The Oxford History of the Laws of England*, vol. 1, *The Canon Law and Ecclesiastical Jurisdiction from 597 to the 1640s* (Oxford, 2004), 1.

24. D. Liebs, *Römische Jurisprudenz in Gallien (2. bis 8. Jahrhundert)*, Freiburger Rechtsgeschichtliche Abhandlungen, neue Folge 38 (Berlin, 2002).

25. E. James, "'Beati pacifici': Bishops and the Law in Sixth-Century Gaul," in *Disputes and Settlements: Law and Human Relations in the West*, ed. J. Bossy (Cambridge, 1983), 25–46; P. J. Geary, "Extra-Judicial Means of Conflict Resolution," in *La giustizia nell'alto medioevo (secoli V–VIII)*, Settimane di Studio del Centro Italiano di Studi sull'Alto Medioevo 42, 2 vols. (Spoleto, 1995), 1: 569–605.

26. Cf. B. D. Shaw, "Judicial Nightmares and Christian Memory," *JECS* 11, 4 (2003): 533–66 at 537: "We know that judicial processes constituted a social field of rule-driven behavior that seems to have necessitated all sorts of recourse to 'illogical' devices, from formulaic magical prayers to the use of magical curse tablets, to have some effect on, or perhaps merely to cope with, a process that seemed so formally removed from day-to-day logic." J. A. Bowman, *Shifting Landmarks: Property, Proof, and Dispute in Catalonia Around the Year 1000* (Ithaca, N.Y., 2004), 9–13. Recent literature on dispute resolution mostly addresses the medieval period, especially W. Davies and P. Fouracre, eds., *The Settlement of Disputes in Early*

Medieval Europe (Cambridge, 1986); W. Brown, *Unjust Seizure: Conflict, Interest, and Authority in an Early Medieval Society* (Ithaca, N.Y., 2001), 5–11 with refs.

27. Cicero, *De officiis* 1.43.153–54, 44.158 and Augustine, *De Civitate Dei* 19.3, 5, 17, with S. MacCormack, "Sin, Citizenship, and the Salvation of Souls: The Impact of Christian Priorities on Late-Roman and Post-Roman Society," *Comparative Studies in Society and History* 39 (1997): 644–73.

28. M. C. Nussbaum, *Hiding from Humanity: Disgust, Shame, and the Law* (Princeton, N.J., 2004), 7.

29. *Empsuchos nomos*: references to sources and scholarship in C. Rowe and M. Schofield, eds., *The Cambridge History of Greek and Roman Political Thought* (Cambridge, 2000), 663–64 n. 12. C. Rapp, *Holy Bishops in Late Antiquity: The Nature of Christian Leadership in an Age of Transition* (Berkeley, Calif., 2005); also see Rapp, "Bishops in Late Antiquity: A New Social and Urban Elite?" in *Elites Old and New in the Byzantine and Early Islamic Near East*, ed. J. F. Haldon and L. I. Conrad, Studies in Late Antiquity and Early Islam 6 (Princeton, N.J., 2004), 144–73; Rapp, "The Elite Status of Bishops in Late Antiquity in Ecclesiastical, Spiritual, and Social Contexts," *Arethusa* 33, 3 (2000): 379–99; P. Allen and W. Mayer, "Through a Bishop's Eyes: Towards a Definition of Pastoral Care in Late Antiquity," *Augustinianum* 4, 2 (2000): 345–97; H. A. Drake, *Constantine and the Bishops: The Politics of Intolerance* (Baltimore, Md., 2000); *Vescovi e pastori in epoca teodosiana: XXV Incontro di studiosi dell'antichità cristiana*, Studia Ephemeridis Augustinianum 58, 2 vols. (Rome, 1997); P. Brown, *Power and Persuasion in Late Antiquity: Towards a Christian Empire* (Madison, Wis., 1992); R. Lizzi, *Il potere episcopale nell'oriente romano: Rappresentazione ideologica e realtà politica (IV–V sec. d.C.)* (Rome, 1987); H. von Campenhausen, *Ecclesiastical Authority and Spiritual Power in the Church of the First Three Centuries*, trans. J. A. Basker (Stanford, Calif., 1969).

30. *C. Th.* 16.2.31; Lupoi, *Origins of the European Legal Order*, 28.

31. Possidius, *Vita s. Augustini*, 19, ed. A. A. R. Bastiaensen, intro. C. Mohrmann, trans. L. Canali, *Vita di Agostino*, Vite dei Santi 3 (Milan, 1975), trans. F. R. Hoare in *Soldiers of Christ: Saints and Saints' Lives from Late Antiquity and the Early Middle Ages*, ed. T. F. X. Noble and T. Head (University Park, Pa., 1995), 31–73 at 52; L. I. Hamilton, "Possidius' Augustine and Post-Augustinian Africa," *JECS* 12, 1 (2004): 85–105.

32. J. Harries, *Law and Empire in Late Antiquity* (Cambridge, 1999); Harries and I. Wood, eds., *The Theodosian Code: Studies in the Imperial Law of Late Antiquity* (London, 1993); T. Honoré, *Law in the Crisis of Empire, 379–455 AD: The Theodosian Dynasty and Its Quaestors* (Oxford, 1998); C. Kelly, *Ruling the Later Roman Empire* (Cambridge, Mass., 2004); D. Liebs, *Die Jurisprudenz im spätantiken Italien (260–640 n. Chr)*, Freiburger rechtsgeschichtliche Abhandlungen, neue Folge 8 (Berlin, 1987); J. F. Matthews, *Laying Down the Law: A Study of the Theodosian Code* (New Haven, Conn., 2000); for Harries, Honoré, and Matthews see the review essay by A. D. Lee, "Decoding Late Roman Law," *JRS* 92 (2002): 185–93; Garnsey and Humfress, *Evolution of the Late Antique World*, ch. 4; C. Humfress, "Civil Law and Social Life," in *The Cambridge Companion to the Age of Constantine*, ed. N. Lenski (Cambridge, 2006), 205–25.

33. Paulinus of Nola, *Ep.* 45.7 = Augustine, *Ep.* 94.7 (a. 408), ed. A. Goldbacher,

CSEL 34:2, p. 504 ("inluminatum spiritu revelationis"); Paulinus of Nola, *Ep.* 6.2 = Augustine, *Ep.* 30.2 (a. 395), CSEL 34:1, p. 123 ("frater spiritalis omnia iudicans").

34. Ulpian, Inst. 1 = Dig. 1.1.1.

35. Augustine, *Ep.* 261.2, CSEL 57, p. 618 ("oraculum autem legis quo modo sum").

36. R. Somerville and B. C. Brasington, trans., *Prefaces to Canon Law Books in Latin Christianity: Selected Translations, 500–1245* (New Haven, Conn., 1998), 49.

37. Const. Sirm. 1 (a. 333).

38. P. Rousseau, *Ascetics, Authority and the Church in the Age of Jerome and Cassian* (Oxford, 1978); C. Leyser, *Authority and Asceticism from Augustine to Gregory the Great* (Oxford, 2000); A. Sterk, *Renouncing the World Yet Leading the Church: The Monk-Bishop in Late Antiquity* (Cambridge, Mass., 2004); Rapp, *Holy Bishops in Late Antiquity*; G. Demacopoulos, *Five Models of Spiritual Direction in the Early Church* (Notre Dame, Ind., 2006).

39. Among a vast, recent bibliography, see Amory, *People and Identity*, and the following collections: H. Goetz, J. Jarnut, and W. Pohl, eds., *Regna and Gentes: The Relationship Between Late Antique and Early Medieval Peoples and Kingdoms in the Transformation of the Roman World*, Transformation of the Roman World 13 (Leiden, 2003); A. Gillet, ed., *On Barbarian Identity: Critical Approaches to Ethnicity in the Early Middle Ages* (Turnhout, 2002); W. O. Frazer and A. Tyrell, eds., *Social Identity in Early Medieval Britain* (London, 2000). Also see Brown, "Study of Elites," 334.

40. C. Lepelley, "La diabolisation du paganisme et ses conséquences psychologiques: les angoisses de Publicola, correspondant de saint Augustin," in *Impies et païens entre Antiquité et Moyen Ages*, ed. L. Mary and M. Sot (Paris, 2002), 81–96.

41. L. Kolmer, *Promissorische Eide im Mittelalter*, Regensburger Historische Forschungen 12 (Kallmünz, 1989); P. Prodi, *Il sacramento del potere: Il giuramento politico nella storia costituzionale dell'Occidente* (Bologna, 1992); S. Esders and H. J. Mierau, *Der althochdeutsche Klerikereid: Bischöfliche Diözesangewalt, kirchliches Benefizialwesen und volkssprachliche Rechtspraxis im frühmittelalterlichen Baiern*, MGH Studien und Texte 28 (Hannover, 2000), addressing vernacular oaths from the ninth century onward.

42. R. Chartier, *On the Edge of the Cliff: History, Language, and Practices*, trans. L. G. Cochrane (Baltimore, 1997), 4.

43. Analogous transgressions of ideal social boundaries by oath swearers are found in the recent reassessment of high medieval aristocratic women, e.g., F. Cheyette, "Women, Poets, and Politics in Occitania," in *Aristocratic Women in Medieval France*, ed. T. Evergates (Philadelphia, 1999), 138–77; M. Bruckner, L. Shepard, and S. White, eds., *Songs of the Women Troubadours*, rev. ed. (New York, 2000), xli–xlii.

44. I have benefited from articles in *Le Serment: Recueil d'études anthropologiques, historiques et juridiques, Seminaire 1985–1988*, Droits et Cultures (Paris, 1989), and from sociological models for understanding trust, especially K. S. Cook, ed., *Trust in Society*, Russel Sage Foundation Series on Trust 2 (New York, 2001), and R. Hardin, *Trust and Trustworthiness*, Russel Sage Foundation Series on Trust 4 (New York, 2002).

45. E. A. Meyer, *Legitimacy and Law in the Roman World: Tabulae in Roman Belief and Practice* (Cambridge, 2004).

46. Dodaro, *Christ and the Just Society*, 27.

47. Garnsey and Humfress, *Evolution of the Late Antique World*, 187 regarding Christian treatment of children in texts versus practice: "Theology smothers social history."

48. Marseilles (a. 533), *Concilia Galliae, a.511–a. 695*, ed. C. de Clercq, CCL 148A (1963), 85; De Jong, "Transformations of Penance," 201–2.

49. Brown, *Power and Persuasion*, 156; with É. Rebillard, "La 'conversion' de l'empire romain selon Peter Brown (note critique)," *Annales HSS* 54 (1999): 813–23 at 816.

50. Cyprian, *Ep.* 73.21.2, ed. G. F. Diercks, CCL 3C (1996): "salus extra ecclesiam non est."

51. Lactantius, *Divinae* Institutiones 5–6, ed. and trans. P. Monat, *Institutions Divines, Livre V*, 2 vols., SC 204–5 (1973), trans. A. Bowen and P. Garnsey, *Divine Institutions*, TTH 40 (2003), 281–329, with the introduction and references (29–35); Dodaro, *Christ and the Just Society*, 13–16; E. T. Hermanowicz, "Numa's Laws and the Meaning of Justice in the *Divinae Institutiones*," in *The First Christian Humanist: Lactantius in Late Antiquity and the Renaissance*, ed. O. Nicholson (forthcoming), which the author kindly shared with me in advance of publication.

Chapter 1. Calumny:
Well-Known Reasons Why Justice Fails

1. C. Rapp and M. R. Salzman, eds., *Elites in Late Antiquity* = *Arethusa* 33.3 (2000); R. Teja, "La cristianización de los modelos clásicos: el obispo," in *Modelos ideales y prácticas de vida en la antigüedad clásica*, ed. E. Falque and F. Gascò, Serie Filosofía y Letras 166 (Seville, 1993), 181–230; R. Lizzi, *Il potere episcopale nell'Oriente romano: Rappresentazione ideologica e realtà politica (IV–V secolo d.C.)*, Filologia e critica 53 (Rome, 1987).

2. ICGA, 1: 60–61, no. 26 = *Corpus Inscriptionum Latinarum* 13, no. 2399; PLRE 3.2, p. 1052, s.v. "Priscus 3"; M. Heinzelmann, *Bischofsherrschaft in Gallien: Zur Kontinuität römischer Führungsschichten vom 4. bis zum 7. Jahrhundert; Soziale, prosopographische und bildungsgeschichtliche Aspekte* (Munich, 1976), 177–79.

3. The major studies include references to earlier scholarship: F. Prinz, "Die bischöfliche Stadtherrschaft im Frankenreich vom 5. bis zum 7. Jahrhundert," *Historische Zeitschrift* 217 (1973): 1–35; Heinzelmann, *Bischofsherrschaft in Gallien*; F. Prinz, ed., *Herrschaft und Kirche: Beiträge zur Entstehung und Wirkungsweise episkopaler und monastischer Organisationsformen*, Monographien zur Geschichte des Mittelalters 33 (Stuttgart, 1988); for a concise summary, see R. W. Mathisen, *Roman Aristocrats in Barbarian Gaul: Strategies for Survival in an Age of Transition* (Austin, Tex., 1993), 89–104.

4. C. Lepelley, "Le patronat épiscopal aux IVe et Ve siècles: continuités et ruptures avec le patronat classique," in *L'évêque dans la cité du IVe au Ve siècle: image et autorité. Actes de la table ronde organisée par l'Istituto patristico Augustinianum et l'École française de Rome (Rome, 1er et 2 décembre 1995)*, ed. É. Rebillard and C. Sotinel, Collection de l'Ecole française de Rome 248 (Rome, 1998), 17–33.

5. N. B. McLynn, *Ambrose of Milan: Church and Court in a Christian Capital* (Berkeley, Calif., 1994), 376.

6. C. Humfress, "Roman Law, Forensic Argument and the Formation of Christian Orthodoxy (III–VI Centuries)," in *Orthodoxie, christianisme, histoire*, ed. S. Elm, É. Rebillard, and A. Romano (Rome, 2000), 125–47; Humfress, *Orthodoxy and the Courts in Late Antiquity* (Oxford, forthcoming).

7. Priscus, *Fragmenta*, 8, trans. in C. D. Gordon, *The Age of Attila: Fifth-Century Byzantium and the Barbarians* (Ann Arbor, Mich., 1960), 87.

8. Cf. Isidore of Seville, *Etymologiae* 5.26.8: "Calumnia est iurgium alienae litis, a calvendo, id est decipiendo dicta"; ibid., 10.42: "Calumniator, falsi criminis accusator; a calvendo, id est frustrando et decipiendo, dictus."

9. J. Harries, *Law and Empire in Late Antiquity* (Cambridge, 1999), e.g., 5, 160; in a similar vein, P. Garnsey and C. Humfress, *Evolution of the Late Antique World* (Cambridge, 2001), ch. 4.

10. Culture and rhetoric also figure in the vast scholarship on *delatio* and *delatores* under the empire, e.g., S. H. Rutledge, "'Delatores' and the Tradition of Violence in Roman Oratory," *AJPh* 120, 4 (1999): 555–73.

11. Basil, *Homilia in divites* = *Homilia* 7.57A, in *Homélies sur la richesse*, ed. and trans. Y. Courtonne (Paris, 1935), 39–71, with C. R. Whittaker and P. Garnsey, "Rural Life in the Later Roman Empire," in CAH 13, 277–312 at 299; Ambrosiaster (ca. 380s), *Quaestiones Veteris et Novi Testamenti*, 4.2, ed. A. Souter, CSEL 1 (1908), with Harries, *Law and Empire*, 153.

12. Among general works, see especially J. G. Camiñas, "Le *crimen calumniae* dans la *lex Remmia de calumniatoribus*," *Revue internationale des droits de l'antiquité* 3rd ser. 37 (1990): 117–33; A. D. Manfredini, *La diffamazione verbale nel diritto romano, I. Età repubblicana*, Pubblicazioni della Facoltà Giuridica dell'Università di Ferrara, 2nd ser. 12 (Milan, 1979); M. Lemosse, "Accusation calomnieuse et action d'injures à propos d'une incription récent," repr. in Lemosse, *Études romanistiques*, Annales de la Faculté de Droit et de Science Politique 26 (Clermont-Ferrand, 1991), 361–70; Harries, *Law and Empire*, 101, 119–22, 160.

13. C.Th., *Gesta senatus Romani de Theodosiano publicando*, 5: "Extinctores delatorum, extinctores calumniarum. Dictum XXVIII."

14. C.Th. 9.39.3, *interpretatio*: "Calumniatores sunt, qui falsa deferentes contra cuiuscumque innocentis personam principum animos ad iracundiam commovere praesumunt." On the Breviary, see recently J. F. Matthews, *Laying Down the Law: A Study of the Theodosian Code* (New Haven, Conn., 2000), 87–88, and P. Stein, *Roman Law in European History* (Cambridge, 1999), 31–32, both with references.

15. C.Th. 9.39.1 (a. 383) ("alienam innocentiam securitatemque sine crimine damnabili adpetitione terreri").

16. C.Th. 9.39.2 (a. 385).

17. W. Mossakowski, "The Introduction of an Interdiction of Oral Accusation in the Roman Empire," *Revue internationale des droits de l'antiquité* 3rd ser. 43 (1996): 269–81, addressing C. Th. 9.1.5, which required written accusations in all cases; for *inscriptio* and accusations generally, see Harries, *Law and Empire*, 101, 119–22.

18. C.Th. 9.34.8 (a. 368).

19. Inst., preface ("princeps Romanus uictor existat . . . per legitimos tramites calumniantium iniquitates expellens"); C. Pazdernik, "Justinianic Ideology and the Power of the Past," in *The Cambridge Companion to the Age of Justinian*, ed. M. Maas (Cambridge, 2005), 185–212.

20. J. G. Camiñas, "Régimen jurídico del *iusiurandum calumniae*," *Studia et Documenta Historiae et Iuris* 60 (1994): 457–68.

21. J. G. Camiñas, *Ensayo de reconstrucción del título IX del Edicto Perpetuo:* de calumniatoribus (Santiago de Compostela, 1994); M. Lemosse, "Recherches sur l'histoire du serment de calumnia," repr. in Lemosse, *Études romanistiques*, 335–59.

22. Dig. 10.44.4 (Paul); Inst. 4.172 (Gaius).

23. Dig. 39.2.13.3 (Ulpian).

24. Dig. 2.13.6.2 (Ulpian); Camiñas, "Régimen jurídico," 463–65.

25. E.g., N. Sarti, *Maximum dirimendarum causarum remedium: Il giuramento di calumnia nella dottrina civilistica dei secoli XI–XIII*, Seminario giuridico della Universita di Bologna 160 (Milan, 1995); R. H. Helmholz, *Select Cases on Defamation to 1600*, Publications of the Selden Society 101 (London, 1985), xiv–xlvii; F. Lot and R. Fawtier, *Histoire des institutions francaises au moyen âge*, 3 vols. (Paris, 1958), 2: 386–92. With Camiñas and Lemosse, also L. Charvet, "Les serments contre la calomnie dans la procédure au temps de Justinien," *Revue des Études Byzantines* 8 (1950–51): 130–42.

26. Cod. Just. 2.58 (59).1; cf. Inst. 4.16: "Idque eo maxime fieri potest, quod temeritas tam agentium quam eorum cum quibus ageretur modo pecuniaria poena, modo iusiurandi religione, modo metu infamiae coercetur."

27. Nov. Just. 49.3.

28. Cod. Just. 2.58 (59).2.

29. Cod. Just. 2.58 (59).2.6–7.

30. Cod. Just. 2.58 (59).2.8.

31. P. Brown, *Augustine of Hippo: A Biography*, 2nd ed. (Berkeley, Calif. and Los Angeles, 2000), 457, with Augustine, *Enarrationes in psalmos* 136.3; also D. Potter, "Performance, Power and Justice in the High Empire," in *Roman Theater and Society: E. Togo Salmon Papers I*, ed. W. J. Slater (Ann Arbor, Mich., 1996), 129–59.

32. For what follows, see F. Pergami, *L'appello nella legislazione del tardo impero* (Milan, 2000); D. Johnston, *Roman Law in Context* (Cambridge, 1999), 122–32; J. A. Crook, *Legal Advocacy in the Roman World* (Ithaca, N.Y., 1995), 62–69; Harries, *Law and Empire*, 99–113; P. Garnsey, "The *Lex Iulia* and Appeal Under the Empire," *Journal of Roman Studies* 56 (1966): 167–89.

33. Harries, *Law and Empire*, 173; cf. A. D. Lee, "Decoding Late Roman Law," *Journal of Roman Studies* 92 (2002): 185–93 at 191.

34. On imperial law under Justinian in general, see now C. Humfress, "Law and Legal Practice in the Age of Justinian," in *The Cambridge Companion to the Age of Justinian*, ed. M. Maas (Cambridge, 2005), 161–84; Pazdernik, "Justinianic Ideology and the Power of the Past."

35. J. E. Grubbs, *Law and Family in Late Antiquity: The Emperor Constantine's Marriage Legislation* (Oxford, 1995), 124–27.

36. C.Th., *Gesta senatus Romani de Theodosiano publicando* 5: "Constitutionum ambiguum removistis. Dictum XXIII."

37. Nov. Theod. 1.1 pr. (a. 438), with Harries, *Law and Empire*, 9; Lee, "Decoding Late Roman Law," 187.

38. Cod. Just. 2.58 (59).2.4 (a. 534).

39. Themistius, *Or.* 19.227d–228a, trans. F. Dvornik, in *Readings in Late Antiquity: A Sourcebook*, ed. M. Maas (London, 2000), 5.

40. G. M. Browne, "The Origin and Date of the *Sortes Astrampsychi*," *Illinois Classical Studies* 1 (1976): 53–58; Browne, ed., *Sortes Astrampsychi*, 2 vols. (Leipzig, 1983, 2001); Browne, *The Papyri of the Sortes Astrampsychi*, Beiträge zur klassichen Philologie 58 (Meisenheim-am-Glan, 1974).

41. Text and introduction: A. Dold with R. Meister, *Die Orakelsprüche im St. Galler Palimpsestcodex 908 (die sogenannten "Sortes Sangallenses")*, Österreichische Akademie der Wissenschaften, Philosophisch-historische Klasse 225.4 (Vienna, 1948), with register of contents at 11–14; emendations by A. Kurfess in *Sacris Erudiri* 5 (1953), 143–46; facsimiles: CLA 7 (1956), no. 961 (identified as Italian uncial); DACL 6.1, cols. 162–63; CPL³, p. 188, no. 536 identifies it as "e Gallia meridionali; saec iv [sic] exeunte."

42. W. E. Klingshirn, "Defining the *Sortes Sanctorum*: Gibbon, Du Cange, and Early Christian Lot Divination," *JECS* 10, 1 (2002): 77–130 at 96–97 and passim.

43. *Sortes Sangallensis* 51.3, 8, 9, 39–40: "Mereris quidem, sed non habes calumniam; securus esto", "Suspectus es; modo non calumniaris; aliud age", "Tu tibi molestus es; non calumniaris in nullo."

44. *Sortes Sangallensis* 52.10, p. 40: "Noli timere; Deus auertit malla tua et calumniam quam pateris."

45. *Sortes Sangallensis* 7.8 and 10, p. 23: "Quid uereris? De quo suspicaris, non te lacerat, sed magis bonum testimonium de te reddet", "In absenti multum lacerat, de quo consulis"; 73.3, p. 51: "Societas incerta est et non stat fid[es]"; 131.7, p. 71: "Accipies pignus, sed non cum inuidia", "Iuste accipies pignus; noli uereri"; 2.11, p. 21: "Quid prom[ittis bona] religiosus et aliut in [mente habes] quid cogitas?"; 1.12, p. 21: "Quare h[omines f]alles? Sed deum non potes [fallere per] insposturam." *Fallere* here may well have a more specific meaning, to lie under oath.

46. G. Frank, *The Memory of the Eyes: Pilgrims to Living Saints in Christian Late Antiquity* (Berkeley, Calif., 2000), 168.

47. Recent bibliography: D. R. Jordan, "New Greek Curse Tablets (1985–2000)," *Greek, Roman, and Byzantine Studies* 41 (2000): 5–46; Jordan, "A Survey of Greek Defixiones Not Included in the Special Corpora," *Greek, Roman, and Byzantine Studies* 26 (1985): 151–97. Among analyses of classical and Hellenistic Greek judicial curse tablets: Jordan, "A Curse Tablet Against Opponents at Law," in A. L. Boegehold, *The Lawcourts at Athens: Sites, Buildings, Equipment, Procedure, and Testimonia*, The Athenian Agora 28 (Princeton, 1995), 55–57; A. Chaniotis, "Watching a Lawsuit: A New Curse Tablet from Southern Russia," *Greek, Roman, and Byzantine Studies* 33 (1992): 69–73.

48. In 46 BCE, Cicero reported that one of his own opponents became tongue-tied in the middle of a trial and blamed "spells and incantations": *Brutus* 217, in D. Ogden, *Magic, Witchcraft, and Ghosts: A Sourcebook* (New York, 2002), 212 no. 172.

49. C. A. Faraone, "The Agonistic Context of Early Greek Binding Spells," in *Magika Hiera: Ancient Greek Magic and Religion*, ed. C. A. Faraone and D. Obbink

(New York, 1991), 3–32 at 15–16; J. G. Gager, ed., *Curse Tablets and Binding Spells from the Ancient World* (New York, 1992), 116–22.

50. Gager, *Curse Tablets*, 132–36, no. 45.

51. Gager, *Curse Tablets*, 144–45, no. 54.

52. R. S. O. Tomlin, "The Curse Tablets," in *The Temple of Sulis Minerva at Bath 2: The Finds from the Sacred Spring*, ed. B. Cunliffe (Oxford, 1988), 59–277, with J. N. Adams, "British Latin: The Text, Interpretation and Language of the Bath Curse Tablets," *Britannia* 23 (1992): 1–26; Gager, *Curse Tablets*, ch. 5, esp. 94–100; H. S. Versnel, "Beyond Cursing: The Appeal to Justice in Judicial Prayers," in *Magika Hiera: Ancient Greek Magic and Religion*, ed. C. A. Faraone and D. Obbink (New York, 1991), 60–106.

53. *Tab. Sulis* no. 44, in Ogden, *Magic, Witchcraft, and Ghosts*, 220, no. 186.

54. The injunction enjoys historical force in late antique scholarship far too often, especially considering the positive evidence that Christians ignored even those imperatives that seem most unambiguous, such as "Do not swear at all" (Mt 5:34–37; Jas 5:12): see ch. 3.

55. J.-P. Laporte, "Tigzirt: saint Paul contre l'*inuidus*," in *L'Afrique, la Gaule, la religion à l'époque romaine: Mélanges à la mémoire de Marcel Le Glay*, ed. Y. Le Bohec, Collection Latomus 226 (Brussels, 1994), 285–87; É. Rebillard, *In hora mortis: Evolution de la pastorale chrétienne de la mort aux IVe et Ve siècles dans l'occident latin* (Rome, 1994), 152.

56. T. Lehmann, "Eine spätantike Inschriftensammlung und der Besuch des Papstes Damasus an der Pilgerstätte des Hl. Felix in Cimitile/Nola," *ZPE* 91 (1992): 243–81, at 251–53; on the Epigrammata Damasiana generally see J. R. Curran, *Pagan City and Christian Capital: Rome in the Fourth Century*, Oxford Classical Monographs (Oxford, 2000), 148–55 with references.

57. Augustine, *Epp.* 77–78, CSEL 34.2, 329–45.

58. Cf. B. D. Shaw, review of J. E. Grubbs, *Law and Family in Late Antiquity*, in *BMCR* 96.8.12: "The Roman law was a pragmatic discourse that was impervious to magical imperatives and religious transcendences, including those of Christianity."

59. Cf. W. Hartmann, "Der Bischof als Richter nach den kirchenrechtlichen Quellen des 4. bis 7. Jahrhunderts," in *La giustizia nell'alto medioevo (secoli V–VIII)*, Settimane di Studio del Centro Italiano di Studi sull'Alto Medioevo 42, 2 vols. (Spoleto, 1995), 2:805–42 at 807.

60. M. R. Cimma, *L'episcopalis audientia nelle costituzioni imperiali da Costantino a Giustiniano* (Turin, 1989); along with additional references below, J. Lamoreaux, "Episcopal Courts in Late Antiquity," *JECS* 3 (1995): 143–67; J. D. Harries, "Resolving Disputes: The Frontiers of Law in Late Antiquity," and N. E. Lenski, "Evidence for the *Audientia episcopalis* in the New Letters of Augustine," both in *Law, Society, and Authority in Late Antiquity*, ed. R. W. Mathisen (Oxford, 2001), 68–82 and 83–97.

61. E.g., C.Th. 2.1.10 (a. 398): arbitration in Jewish courts; Cod. Just. 1.9.14 (a. 418): Jewish leaders do not decide Christian-Jewish disputes.

62. With W. Selb, "Episcopalis audientia von der Zeit Konstantins bis zur Nov. XXXV Valentinians III," *ZRG RA* 84 (1967): 162–217, see now O. Huck, "A propos de *CTh* 1,27,1 et *CSirm* 1: Sur deux textes controversés relatifs à l'episcopalis

audientia constantinienne," ZRG RA 120 (2003): 78–105; Huck, "Encore à propos des *Sirmondiennes:* arguments présentés à l'appui de la thèse de l'authenticité, en réponse à une mise en cause récente," *Antiquité tardive* 11 (2003): 181–96.

63. Esp. Harries, *Law and Empire*, ch. 10 (191–211), who argues forcefully that Constantine "inflicted" adjudicating powers upon a venue of informal mediation.

64. Const. Sirm. 1 (a. 333). The common legal usage of *praescriptio* at this time was to indicate an opponent's defense: A. Berger, *Encyclopedic Dictionary of Roman Law* (Philadelphia, Penn., 1953), 645, s.v. "Praescriptio"; C. Pharr, *The Theodosian Code and Novels and The Sirmondian Constitutions* (Princeton, N.J., 1952), 477 translates it loosely as "legal technicality."

65. Const. Sirm. 1.

66. Huck, "A propos de *CTh* 1,27,1 et *CSirm* 1"; Huck, "Encore à propos des *Sirmondiennes."*

67. Const. Sirm. 1.

68. Nov. Val. 35.1 (a. 452).

69. Elvira (ca. 506), c. 52, 73–75, in *Concilios Visigóticos e Hispano-Romanos,* ed. and trans. J. Vives, T. M. Martínez, and G. Martínez Díez (Barcelona, 1963); S. G. Rivas, *La penitencia en la primitiva Iglesia española,* Consejo Superior de Investigaciones Científicas (Salamanca, 1949), 44–46; J. Orlandis and D. Ramon-Lissón, *Historia de los concilios de la España romana y visigoda* (Pamplona, 1986), 45–46.

70. Clergy: Arles I (a. 314) c. 15 (14), in *Concilia Galliae, a. 314–a. 506,* ed. C. Munier, CCL 148 (1963), 12, trans. J. Gaudemet, *Conciles gaulois du IVe siècle,* SC 241 (1977), 54; *traditores:* ibid., c. 14 (13); S. Scholz, "Die Rolle der Bischöfe auf den Synoden von Rom (313) und Arles (314)," in *Köln: Stadt und Bistum in Kirche und Reich des Mittelalters; Festschrift für Odilo Engels zum 65. Geburtstag,* ed. H. Vollrath and S. Weinfurter (Köln, 1993), 1–21.

71. *Breviarium Hipponense* c. 7c and *Register Carthaginensis* c. 129c, ed. C. Munier, *Concilia Africae, a. 345–a.525,* CCL 149 (1974), 35, 231.

72. Carthage (a. 390) c. 6, *Concilia Africae, a. 345–a. 525,* p. 15 = *Canones in causa Apiarii* c. 8, *Concilia Africae, a. 345–a. 525,* p.135; cf. Mâcon (a. 581–83), c. 18 (17)–19 (18), *Concila Galliae, a. 511–a. 695,* ed. C. de Clercq, CCL 148A (1963), 227–28, trans. J. Gaudemet and B. Basdevant, *Les canons des conciles mérovingiens (VIe–VIIe siècles),* 2 vols., SC 353–54 (1989).

73. Carthage (a. 419), cc. 128–31, *Concilia Africae, a. 345–a. 525,* 230–31; S. Dagemark, "Examples of *excommunicatio, paenitentia* and *reconciliatio* in the African Councils," in *I Concili della cristianità occidentale secoli III–V,* Studia Ephemeridis Augustinianum 78 (Rome, 2002), 167–234 at 183–86; G. May, "Anklage- und Zeugnisfähigkeit nach der zweiten Sitzung des Konzils zu Karthago vom Jahre 419," *Theologische Quartalschrift* 140 (1960): 163–205; cf. C.Th. 9.39.1 (a. 383): "Nec enim patimur frequenter iterari, quae consistere prima actione non quiuerint, atque alienam innocentiam securitatemque sine crimine damnabili adpetitione terreri."

74. Hippo (a. 427), cc. 6–7, *Concilia Africae, a. 345–a. 525,* p. 252; E. Vodola, *Excommunication in the Middle Ages* (Berkeley, Calif., 1986), 73–78.

75. Vaison (a. 442), c. 8, *Concilia Galliae, a. 314–a. 506,* p. 100.

76. "Arles II" (ca. 501) c. 24, *Concilia Galliae, a. 314–a. 506,* p. 119: "Eos qui falso fratribus suis capitalia obiecisse conuicti fuerint, placuit eos usque ad exitum

non communicare, sicut magna synodus ante constituit, nisi digna satisfactione paenituerint"; cf. Arles (a. 314), c. 15 (14), *Concilia Galliae, a. 314–a. 506*, p. 12. On "Arles II," see R. Mathisen, "The 'Second Council of Arles' and the Spirit of Compilation in Late Roman Gaul," *JECS* 5, 4 (1997): 511–54.

77. Vannes (461–91), c. 1, *Concilia Galliae, a. 314–a. 506*, p. 151: "Itaque censuimus homicidas et falsos testes a communione ecclesiastica submouendos, nisi paenitentiae satisfactione crimina admissa diluerint"; repeated in Agde (506), c. 37, *Concilia Galliae, a. 314–a. 506*, p. 208.

78. Agde (506), c. 32, *Concilia Galliae, a. 314–a. 506*, p. 207.

79. Orléans V (a. 549), c. 22, *Concila Galliae, a. 511–a. 695*, p. 156.

80. Clichy (a. 626–7), c. 17, *Concila Galliae, a. 511–a. 695*, pp. 294–95.

81. Clichy (a. 626–7), c. 7, *Concila Galliae, a. 511–a. 695*, pp. 292–93.

82. Mâcon II (a. 585), c. 7, *Concila Galliae, a. 511–a. 695*, p. 242, concerning external claims on freedmen of the church.

83. Cf. Lenski, "Evidence for the *Audientia episcopalis*," 84–87.

84. Vaison I (a. 442), c. 9, *Concilia Galliae, a. 314–a. 506*, 100–101; J. Boswell, *The Kindness of Strangers: The Abandonment of Children in Western Europe from Late Antiquity to the Renaissance* (New York, 1988), 172–73.

85. Vaison I (a. 442), c. 9, *Concilia Galliae, a. 314–a. 506*, 100–101: ". . . eos non misericordiae iam sed canibus exponi, quos colligere calumniatorum metu, quamuis inflexa praeceptis misericordiae mens humana detrectat . . ."; ibid. c. 10: ". . . collectorum repetitor uel calumniator extiterit, ut homicida ecclesiastica districtione feriatur."

86. Clichy (a. 626–7), c. 19, *Concila Galliae, a. 511–a. 695*, p. 295: "Si quis ingenuum aut libertum ad seruitium inclinare uoluerit et fortasse iam fecit et commonitus ab episcopo se de inquitudine eius reuocare neglexerit aut emendare noluerit, tamquam calumniae reum placuit sequestrari."

87. Augustine, *Contra Faustum Manichaeum* (a. 397/99), 19.11, ed. J. Zycha, CSEL 25.1 (1891), 249–797; cf. P. Buc, *The Dangers of Ritual: Between Early Medieval Texts and Social Scientific Theory* (Princeton, N.J., 2001), 118: "a very Durkheimian Augustine."

88. M. Meslin, *La fête des Kalendes de Janvier dans l'empire romain*, Collection Latomus 115 (Brussels, 1970).

89. Augustine, *Serm. Mayence* 62 (Dolbeau 26, "Contra paganos") 7, ed. F. Dolbeau, *Vingt-six sermons au peuple d'Afrique*, Collection des Études Augustiniennes Série Antiquité 147 (Paris, 1996), 366–417 at 371.

90. Augustine, *Serm. Mayence* 15 (Dolbeau 7, "de sepultura catechumenorum"), *Vingt-six sermons au peuple d'Afrique*, 302–3; Brown, *Augustine of Hippo*, 461.

91. On the problem of integrating the Donatists, see Brown, *Augustine of Hippo*, 212–13 and 218–19, who cites previous scholarship; B. D. Shaw, "African Christianity: Disputes, Definitions, and 'Donatists'," in *Orthodoxy and Heresy in Religious Movements: Discipline and Dissent*, ed. M. R. Greenshields and T. A. Robinson (Lewiston, Pa., 1992), 5–34; for a dossier of the pivotal council, *Gesta conlationis Carthaginiensis, anno 411*, ed. S. Lancel, CCL 149A (1974).

92. Augustine, *Contra Faustum Manichaeum*, 12.15.

93. Augustine, *De Civitate Dei* 2.25.2: "Haeretici et schismatici ab huius unitate

corporis separati possunt idem percipere sacramentum, sed non sibi utile, immo uero etiam noxium."

94. Augustine, *Serm.* 17.6, ed. C. Lambot, CCL 41, rev. ed. (1991), 242.

95. Augustine, *Serm.* 164.6.8, PL 38, col. 899.

96. Augustine, *Serm.* 164.6.8, PL 38, col. 899: "Quem nosti talem, et fidelis est, uel potius fidelis uocatur, non eum potes de ecclesia pellere, non habes aliquem aditum castigando et corripiendo corrigere, accesurus est tecum ad altare . . . Portet ergo sarcinam suam, et tu tuam. . . ."

97. Augustine, *Serm.* 4.35, CCL 41, p. 46.

98. [Pseudo-]Augustine, *Serm.* 351.10. On the authenticity of this sermon, see P. Verbraken, *Études critiques sur les sermons authentique de Saint Augustin*, Instrumenta Patristica 12 (Steenbrugis, 1974), 147.

99. Carthage (30 May 419), cc. 132–33, *Concilia Africae, a. 345–a. 525*, p. 232 ("ut magis caueat episcopus ne dicat in quemquam quod aliis documentis conuincere non potest").

100. Possidius, *Vita s. Augustini*, 19, ed. A. A. R. Bastiaensen, intro. C. Mohrmann, trans. L. Canali, *Vita di Agostino*, Vite dei santi 3 (Milan, 1975); Augustine, *Enarrationes in psalmos* 118.24.3.

101. Augustine, *Serm.* 164.11, PL 38, col. 900.

102. E.g. L. Dossey, "Judicial Violence and the Ecclesiastical Courts in Late Antique North Africa," in *Law, Society and Authority in Late Antiquity*, ed. R. W. Mathisen (Oxford, 2001), 98–114.

103. John Donne, *The Sermons*, ed. G. R. Potter and E. M. Simpson, 10 vols. (Berkeley, Calif., 1953–1962), 5:267; Harries, "Resolving Disputes," 73: "The effectiveness of expulsion, or excommunication, should not be underrated."

104. E.g. Dossey, "Judicial Violence," 113; Lenski, "Evidence for *Audientia episcopalis*," 90–91.

105. See the classic essay by P. Brown, "Religious Coercion in the Later Roman Empire: The Case of North Africa," *History* 48 (1963): 283–305, repr. in Brown, *Religion and Society in the Age of Saint Augustine* (New York, 1972), 301–31; more recently, P. I. Kaufman, "Augustine, Macedonius, and the Courts," *Augustinian Studies* 34, 1 (2003): 67–82 is descriptive; for a very different approach, L. Barnard, "The Criminalization of Heresy in the Later Roman Empire: A Sociopolitical Device?" *Journal of Legal History* 16 (1995): 121–46.

106. C.Th. 16.2.31.

107. N. H. Baynes, *Byzantine Studies and other Essays* (London, 1955), 56–57 referring to Themistius.

108. R. M. Frakes, "Late Roman Social Justice and the Origin of the Defensor Civitatis," *Classical Journal* 89 (1994): 337–48; Frakes, *Contra Potentium Iniurias: The Defensor Civitatis and Late Roman Justice* (Munich, 2001).

109. Augustine, *Ep.* 22*.3. He seems ignorant or unsure of the relevant legislation (C. Th. 1.29): F. Jacques, "Le defenseur de cité d'après la lettre 22* de Saint Augustine," *Revue des Études Augustiniennes* 32 (1986) : 56–73; Lenski, "Evidence for the *Audientia episcopalis*," 92; cf. *Reg. Eccl. Carthag. Exc.* 75 (a. 410), *Concilia Africae, a. 345–a. 525*, p. 202.

110. No torture: C.Th. 1.29.7 (a. 392); C.Th. 1.29.8 (a. 392) ("probatissimi quique atque districtissimi defensores").

111. The evidence comes from two letters by Augustine, whose information was second-hand: *Epp.* 1*, 250, 250A (a fragment of 1*).

112. G. Folliet, "Le Dossier de l'affaire Classicianus (*Epistulae* 250 et 1*)," in *Les Lettres de saint Augustin découvertes par Johannes Divjak* (Paris, 1982), 129–46 at 140–43.

113. Folliet, "Le Dossier de l'affaire Classicianus," 132–37.

114. Augustine, *Ep.* 1*.3.

115. C. Th. 9.45.1 (a. 392): "Publicos debitores, si confugiendum ad ecclesias crediderint, aut ilico extrahi de latebris oportebit aut pro his ipsos, qui eos occultare probantur, episcopos exigi."

116. A. Ducloux, *Ad ecclesiam confugere: naissance du droit d'asile dans les églises (IVe–milieu du Ve s.)* (Paris, 1994); S. Esders, "Rechtsdenken und Traditionsbewusstsein in der gallischen Kirche zwischen Spätantike und Frühmittelalter: Zur Anwendbarkeit soziologischer Rechtsbegriffe am Beispiel des kirchlichen Asylrechts," *Francia* 20 (1993): 97–135; Rapp, *Holy Bishops in Late Antiquity*, 253–60.

117. A. Chaniotis, "Conflicting Authorities: Asylia between Secular and Divine Law in the Classical and Hellenistic Poleis," *Kernos* 9 (1996): 65–86.

118. As Rapp observes in *Holy Bishops in Late Antiquity*, 253–54.

119. Augustine, *Ep.* 9*; Lenski, "Evidence for the *Audientia episcopalis*," 85, 89; Dossey, "Judicial Violence," 111.

120. Augustine, *Epp.* 14* and 15*, at 15*.3; cf. Augustine, *Serm.* 351.10 ("nisi aut sponte confessum").

121. Augustine, *Ep.* 15*.3–4. *Raptus* encompassed elopement, which is one reason why canons often address the possible willingness of the female. Nevertheless, unwilling victims were also liable to punishment under late Roman law. Chalcedon added deposition for rapist-priests, and anathema for laymen. In 533 Justinian assigned the death penalty to rapists of women of any age, rank, or marital or religious status, and added forfeiture of the rapist's property to the church in the case of nuns. C. Th. 9.24.1.2–3; Cod. Just. 9.13.1; ibid. 1.3.53(54); Chalcedon (a. 451), c. 27, ed. G. Alberigo et al., *Conciliorum oecumenicorum decreta* (Freiburg, 1962), 69–70; Orléans (a. 511), c. 2, *Concilia Galliae, a. 511–a. 695*, p. 5 (rapists who seek asylum); Orléans III (a. 538), c. 19 (16), *Concilia Galliae, a. 511–a. 695*, p. 121; Lérida (a. 546), c. 6, *Concilios Visigóticos e Hispano-Romanos*, p. 57; Tours II (567), c. 21 (20), *Concilia Galliae, a. 511–a. 695*, 184–88; Paris (a. 614) = *Edictum Clotarii*, c. 18, *Concilia Galliae, a. 511–a. 695*, p. 285; Clichy (a. 626/27), c. 26, *Concilia Galliae, a. 511–a. 695*, p. 296; Berger, *Encyclopedic Dictionary*, p. 667, s.v. "Raptus"; J. A. Brundage, *Law, Sex, and Christian Society in Medieval Europe* (Chicago, 1987), 107, 119–20.

122. Clichy (a. 626/27), c. 6, *Concilia Galliae, a. 511–a. 695*, p. 292: "Episcopus non temere quemquam excommunicare debet; nam excommunicatus si se existimat iniuste damnatum, in proxima synodo habeat licentiam reclamandi et, si iniuste damnatus fuerit, absoluatur, si autem iuste, impositae paenitentiae tempus exsoluat."

123. Vodola, *Excommunication in the Middle Ages*, 35–38.

124. Augustine, *Serm.* 180.3.3, PL 38, col. 973: "inter ista multa tua cogitata

incerta, uolatica, coniecturas humanas, fallacias humanas, quando non subrepit tibi quod falsum est, posito in regione falsitatis?"

125. Isaiah 64: 6 (Vulgate: "quasi pannus menstruatae universae iustitiae nostrae").

Chapter 2. "Judge like God":
What Bishops Claimed to Expect of Themselves

1. C. Leyser, *Authority and Asceticism from Augustine to Gregory the Great* (Oxford, 2000), vii.

2. N. McLynn, "Seeing and Believing: Aspects of Conversion from Antoninus Pius to Louis the Pious," in *Conversion in Late Antiquity and the Early Middle Ages: Seeing and Believing*, ed. K. Mills and A. Grafton, Studies in Comparative History: Essays from the Shelby Cullom Davis Center for Historical Studies (Rochester, N.Y., 2003), 224–70 at 236.

3. H. Chadwick, *The Role of the Christian Bishop in Ancient Society: Protocol of the Thirty-Fifth Colloquy, 25 February 1979*, ed. E. C. Hobbs and W. Wuellner (Berkeley, Calif., 1980), 13–14.

4. For asceticization see G. E. Demacopoulos, "A Monk in Shepherd's Clothing: Pope Gregory I and the Asceticizing of Pastoral Direction" (Ph.D. diss., University of North Carolina at Chapel Hill, 2002) and now Demacopoulos, *Five Models of Spiritual Direction in the Early Church* (Notre Dame, Ind., 2006).

5. P. Rousseau, *Ascetics, Authority, and the Church in the Age of Jerome and Cassian* (Oxford, 1978), 33, a work that I shall refer to frequently in this chapter.

6. G. Schöllgen, *Die Anfänge der Professionalisierung des Klerus und das kirchliche Amt in der syrischen Didaskalie*, JAC Ergänzungsband 27 (Munster, 1998).

7. For patristic commentary on this assembly, see H. J. Sieben, *Die Konzilsidee der Alten Kirche*, Konziliengeschichte Reihe B, Untersuchungen (Paderborn, 1979), 407–23.

8. The only complete version of the original *Didascalia* is in Syriac: *Didascalia et constitutiones apostolorum*, ed. F. X. Funk, vol. 1 (Paderborn, 1905); see C. E. Fonrobert, "The Didascalia Apostolorum: A Mishnah for the Disciples of Jesus," *JECS* 9, 4 (2001): 483–509, detecting a rabbinic "voice" in the text. Julian "the Arian" compiled the *Apostolic Constitutions* in Greek: *Les Constitutions apostoliques*, ed. and trans. M. Metzger, 3 vols., SC 320, 329, 336 (1985–87); Dionysius Exiguus's Latin translation (ca. 500) was influential in canon law: W. Hartmann, "Der Bischof als Richter nach den kirchenrechtlichen Quellen des 4. bis 7. Jahrhunderts," in *La giustizia nell'alto medioevo (secoli V–VIII)*, Settimane di Studio del Centro Italiano di Studi sull'Alto Medioevo 42, 2 vols. (Spoleto, 1995), 2:805–42 at 809; R. Somerville and B. C. Brasington, trans., *Prefaces to Canon Law Books in Latin Christianity: Selected Translations, 500–1245* (New Haven, Conn., 1998), 10, 47.

9. The *Didascalia* itself was also translated into various languages, including a Latin translation made in the 370s, whose lengthy fragments survive in thirty-two palimpsest leaves of a text transcribed in the later fifth century, written over with

the text of Isidore of Seville's *Sententiae* in the eighth century, and preserved now in Verona. Quotes here are from the Verona text as printed in *Didascalia Apostolorum: The Syriac Version Translated and Accompanied by the Verona Latin Fragments*, ed. R. H. Connolly (Oxford, 1969), with discussion of the manuscript at xviii–xx; text also available in *Didascaliae Apostolorum, canonum ecclesiasticorum, traditionis apostolicae versiones latinae*, ed. E. Tidner (Berlin, 1963).

10. Juvencus, *Evangeliorum libri quattuor* 3.283–87, ed. J. Huemer, CSEL 24 (1891).

11. Mt 16:13–20, 18:15–18; Jn 20:22–23; K. Hein, *Eucharist and Excommunication: A Study in Early Christian Doctrine and Discipline*, European University Papers Series 23, Theology 19 (Bern and Frankfurt, 1973), 69–77; J. Gross, "Die Schlüsselgewalt nach Haimo von Auxerre," *Zeitschrift für Religions- und Geistesgeschichte* 9 (1957): 30–41, is a good point of entry to the medieval ecclesiological significance of the keys; P. Galtier, *L'Église et la rémission des péchés aux premiers siècles* (Paris, 1932), viii, highlights their use as the one constant element between eastern and western penitential theology.

12. References are to the Latin version, with the more familiar chapter numbers to the Syriac Didascalia in parentheses: Latin Didascalia 27 (2.34), ed. Connolly, p. 97; C. Rapp, *Holy Bishops in Late Antiquity* (Berkeley, Calif., 2005), 29–32.

13. Latin Didascalia 27 (2.34), ed. Connolly, p. 97; for bishops' attendance to both "body and soul" elsewhere see e.g., Constantius of Lyon, *Vita Germani* 6.32 (a. 475–480), ed. W. Levison, MGH SRM 7 (1920), 247–83 at 275, trans. R. Borius, *Vie de Saint Germain d'Auxerre*, SC 112 (1965), 182 ("et animas curabat et corpora").

14. Latin Didascalia 25 (2.26), ed. Connolly, pp. 87–89 ("sacerdos Leuita," "in typum Dei" [Greek "epigeios theos"]); cf. Ignatius of Antioch (ca. 140); e.g., *Ep. ad Magnesios* 6, in *The Apostolic Fathers*, ed. and trans. B. D. Ehrman, Loeb 24 (2003), 240–55 ("prokathêmenou tou episkopou eis topon theou "), with J. Gaudemet, "Charisme et droit: Le domaine de l'évêque," ZRG KA 74 (1988): 44–70 at 45, and Chadwick, *Role of the Christian Bishop*, 2: "Hence [the bishop's] monarchical presidency"; on hierarchy, see, e.g., R. Lizzi, "I vescovi e i potentes della terra: definizione e limite del ruolo episcopale nelle due partes imperii fra IV e V secolo d.C.," in *L'évêque dans la cité du IVe au Ve siècle: image et autorité*, ed. É. Rebillard and C. Sotinel (Rome, 1998), 81–104 at 84 n. 9.

15. Latin Didascalia 24 (2.24), ed. Connolly, p. 77.

16. J. Lienhard, "On Discernment of Spirits in the Early Church," *Theological Studies* 41 (1980): 505–29.

17. Latin Didascalia 13 (2.13), ed. Connolly, p. 45 ("seditioso homini"); ibid. 12 (2.12), p. 24 ("iudica, episcope, cum fiducia ut Deus"). The most extensive treatment of procedure and accusations in the *Didascalia* (2.37–56, ed. Connolly, 101–19) is not extant in the Latin version and so is not addressed here, but see J. Harries, *Law and Empire in Late Antiquity* (Cambridge, 1999), 193–95; Harries, "Resolving Disputes: The Frontiers of Law in Late Antiquity," in *Law, Society, and Authority in Late Antiquity*, ed. R. W. Mathisen (Oxford, 2001), 68–82 at 73; K. Rahner, "Bußlehre und Bußpraxis der Didascalia Apostolorum," *Zeitschrift für katholische Theologie* 72 (1950): 257–81.

18. Ambrose, *De officiis* 2.8.46, ed. and trans. I. J. Davidson, Oxford Early Christian Studies, 2 vols. (Oxford, 2001), 294: "Quid autem occultius internorum viscerum testimonio? In quae sapientis intellectus velut quidam pietatis descendit arbiter et velut quamdam genitalis alvi vocem meruit."

19. Ibid. 2.8.47, p. 294: "Sapientiae igitur fuit latentes distinguere conscientias, ex occultis eruere ueritatem; et uelut quadam machaera, ita spiritus gladio penetrare non solum uteri, sed etiam animae et mentis uiscera."

20. Ibid. 2.8.40–43, 290–92, at 43: "Facit enim iustitia ut nullus sit fraudis metus; facit etiam prudentia ut nulla erroris suspicio sit."

21. References to *gladius ultor* in the Theodosian Code: Harries, *Law and Empire*, 136 n. 7; also see the comment by G. Caspary in Chadwick, *Role of the Christian Bishop*, 44.

22. Sidonius, *Ep.* IV 11.2 and 5, ed. A. Loyen, Collection des Universités de France, 2 vols. (Paris, 1970); M. Heinzelmann, "Bischof und Herrschaft von spätantiken Gallien bis zu den karolingischen Hausmeiern: Die institutionellen Grundlagen," in *Herrschaft und Kirche: Beiträge zur Entstehung und Wirkungsweise episkopaler und monastischer Organisationsformen*, ed. F. Prinz, Monographien zur Geschichte des Mittelalters 33 (Stuttgart, 1988), 23–82 at 43–44.

23. Sidonius, *Ep.* 4.11.6 to Petreius ("doctus soluere uincla quaestionum et uerbi gladio secare sectas"); cf. Augustine, *Ep.* 22.2 ("conciliorum graui ense"), with F. L. Cross, "History and Fiction in the African Canons," *Journal of Theological Studies* n.s. 12 (1961): 227–47 at 229.

24. Tours II (a. 567) c. 21 (20), *Concilia Galliae, a. 511–a. 695*, 184–88 ("tunc perimendi sunt oris gladio [cf. Ap. 2.16] et a communione priuandi"); for medieval uses of the sword in the context of excommunication, see R. H. Helmholz, "Excommunication and the Angevin Leap Forward," *Haskins Society Journal* 7 (1995): 133–49 at 136–38.

25. P. Brown, "Asceticism: Pagan and Christian," in CAH 13, 601–31 at 612 on Ambrose enhancing his image with pagan philosophical traditions.

26. See generally Rapp, *Holy Bishops*, ch. 2 ("Pragmatic Authority").

27. Fortitude and temperance were the other half of the "classical tetrad": I. J. Davidson, "Staging the Church? Theology as Theater," *JECS* 8, 3 (2000): 413–51 at 416 with refs.

28. Ambrose, *De officiis* II.8.42, p. 292, with Davidson's comments (p. 728); cf. Cicero, *De officiis*, 2.33, ed. M. Winterbottom, Oxford Classical Texts (Oxford, 1994); generally, R. Gryson, *Le prêtre selon saint Ambroise* (Louvain, 1968).

29. "Cultural takeover": Davidson, "Staging the Church?" 420–21; on a possible pagan readership see N. B. McLynn, *Ambrose of Milan: Church and Court in a Christian Capital*, Transformation of the Classical Heritage 22 (Berkeley, Calif., 1994), 272.

30. Ambrose, *De officiis* I.29.142, p. 198 ("ecclesia autem quaedam forma iustitiae est").

31. Paulinus of Nola, *Ep.* 45.7 = Augustine, *Ep.* 94.7 (a. 408), CSEL 34.2, p. 504 ("inluminatum spiritu revelationis"); Paulinus of Nola, *Ep.* 6.2 = Augustine, *Ep.* 30.2 (a. 395), CSEL 34.1, p. 123 ("frater spiritalis omnia iudicans"); D. Trout, *Paulinus of Nola: Life, Letters, and Poems*, Transformation of the Classical Heritage

27 (Berkeley, Calif., 1999), 200–18; more generally see C. Conybeare, *Paulinus Noster: Self and Symbols in the Letters of Paulinus of Nola*, Oxford Early Christian Studies (Oxford, 2000), and É. Rebillard, "Augustin et le rituel épistolaire de l'élite sociale et culturelle de son temps: Éléments pour une analyse processuelle des relations de l'évêque et de la cité dans l'Antiquité tardive," in *L'évêque dans la cité du IVe au Ve siècle: image et autorité*, ed. É. Rebillard and C. Sotinel (Rome, 1998), 127–52.

32. K. Thraede, *Grundzüge griechisch-römischer Brieftopik*, Zetemata 48 (Munich, 1970), 120–25.

33. Augustine, *Ep.* 119.1, CSEL 34.2, p. 699: "Tamen tu, uir admirabilis, si tibi ille pater noster solus conscius secretorum, qui 'habet clauem Dauid' (Rv 3:7), serenissimo cordis obtutu caelorum machinam penetrare concessit et reuelata, ut scriptum est, 'facie gloriam domini speculari' (2 Cor 3:18), in quantum tibi ille qui huius modi cogitationem dedit, promendi dederit facultatem, enuntia nobis aliquam ineffabilis substantiae portionem et imaginem similitudinis eius ipso adiuuante exprimere"; cf. Paulinus of Nola, *Ep.* 50.18 = Augustine, *Ep.* 121.18, CSEL 34.2, p. 741 ("de interioris oculi puritate").

34. P. Brown, *Augustine of Hippo: A Biography*, 2nd ed. (Berkeley, Calif., 2000), 467 with refs.; R. Van Dam, "'Sheep in Wolves' Clothing': The Letters of Consentius to Augustine," *Journal of Ecclesiastical History* 37 (1986): 515–35.

35. Ulpian, *Inst.* 1 = Dig. 1.1.1; Harries, *Law & Empire*, 7.

36. Augustine, *Ep.* 261.2, CSEL 57, p. 618 ("oraculum autem legis quo modo sum").

37. Augustine, *Ep.* 95.3, CSEL 34.2, 508–9: "Ego in his cotidie peccare me fateor. . . . Quis in his omnibus tremor, mi Pauline, sancte homo dei. Quis tremor, quae tenebrae."

38. C. Lepelley, "Le patronat épiscopal aux IVe et Ve siècles: continuités et ruptures avec le patronat classique," in *L'évêque dans la cité du IVe au Ve siècle: image et autorité*, ed. É. Rebillard and C. Sotinel, Collection de l'Ecole française de Rome 248 (Rome, 1998), 17–33 at 20 (the social importance of legal knowledge) and 27–29 (Augustine's frustration when his connections failed).

39. C. Gallagher, *Church Law and Church Order in Rome and Byzantium: A Comparative Study*, Birmingham Byzantine and Ottoman Monographs 8 (Aldershot, 2002), 9–18; Somerville and Brasington, *Prefaces to Canon Law Books*, 23–27.

40. Dionysius Exiguus, *Praefationes latinae genuinae in variis suis translationibus ex graeco* 4.2 (ad Hormisdam papam) = Hormisdas, *Ep.* 148 (a. 514–23), ed. F. Glorie, *Scriptores 'Illyrici' Minores*, CCL 85 (1972), 51: "Sed quorundam supercilium—qui se graecorum canonum peritissimos esse iactitant, quique sciscitati de quolibet ecclesiastico constituto responderse se uelut ex occulto uidentur oraculo—ueneratio uestra non sustinens"; trans. in Somerville and Brasington, *Prefaces to Canon Law Books*, 49.

41. Const. Sirm. 1 (a. 333): "Multa enim, quae in iudicio captiosa praescriptionis vincula promi non patiuntur, investigat et publicat sacrosanctae religionis auctoritas"; O. Huck, "A propos de *CTh* 1,27,1 et *CSirm* 1: Sur deux textes controversés relatifs à l'episcopalis audientia constantinienne," ZRG RA 120 (2003): 78–105; Huck, "Encore à propos des *Sirmondiennes:* arguments présentés à l'appui de la thèse de l'authenticité, en réponse à une mise en cause récente, *Antiquité*

tardive 11 (2003): 181–196; Chadwick, *Role of the Christian Bishop*, 6–7 rightly associates this passage with bishops' "charismatic powers," but goes too far when he infers "freedom from [evidentiary] restriction."

42. *Epistola Romani concilii sub Damaso habiti* ("Et hoc gloriae"), ed. Migne, PL 13, cols. 575D–584B at 578A: "qui postremo dum iniuriam religionis ulciscitur, non eam in lateribus innocentium, sed accusati quaerat in moribus? Quam multos etenim saepe patuit, quos absoluerint iudicia, ab episcopis esse damnatos, et quos iudicia damnauerint, absolutos?"; cf. Ambrose, *Ep.* 21.2 with C. Pietri, *Roma Christiana: Recherches sur l'Église de Rome, son organisation, sa politique, son idéologie de Miltiade à Sixte III (311–440)*, Bibliothèque des Écoles Françaises d'Athènes et de Rome, 2 vols. (Rome, 1976), 1: 736–45; H. Chadwick, *Priscillian of Avila: The Occult and the Charismatic in the Early Church* (Oxford, 1976), observes similar arguments here and in the appeal by Priscillian and his colleagues Damasus refused two years later (39 and 128–29). For vivid depictions of judicial torture, P. Brown, *Power and Persuasion in Late Antiquity: Towards a Christian Empire*, Curti Lectures 1988 (Madison, Wis., 1992), 52; Harries, *Law and Empire*, 122–34; B. D. Shaw, "Judicial Nightmares and Christian Memory," *JECS* 11, 4 (2003): 533–66, esp. 538–40.

43. E.g., the early history of the canons from Serdica (342/43), included in Dionysius's first collection: C. Munier, "La question des appels à Rome d'après la Lettre 20* d'Augustin," in *Les Lettres de saint Augustin découvertes par Johannes Divjak* (Paris, 1983), 287–99 at 293–94; H. Hess, *The Early Development of Canon Law and the Council of Serdica* (Oxford, 2002).

44. C. Mohrmann, "Quelques observations sur 'sacramentum' chez Tertullien," in W. den Boer et al., eds., *Romanitas et Christianitas* (1973), 233–242 with refs.; Mohrmann, "Sacramentum dans les plus anciens textes chrétiens," *Harvard Theological Review* 47 (1954): 141–52, esp. 146 ; cf. D. Burton-Christie, *The Word in the Desert: Scripture and the Quest for Holiness in Early Christian Monasticism* (New York, 1993), 82–83, for discernment and interpretation of scripture in the Latin (Systematic) *Sayings of the Desert Fathers*.

45. Rufinus, *Historia ecclesiastica* 1.14, ed. Migne, PL 21, col. 487A ("videt ab his geri quaedam etiam secretiora et mystica"); cf. Socrates Scholasticus, *Historia ecclesiastica* 1.15, ed. G. C. Hansen, *Kirchengeschichte*, Die griechischen christlichen Schriftsteller der ersten Jahrhunderte, Neue Folge 1 (Berlin, 1995), 53–54; Sozomen, *Historia ecclesiastica* 2.17.6–10, ed. J. Bidez, trans. A.-J. Festugière, *Histoire ecclésiastique*, 2 vols., SC 306, 418 (1983, 1996), 1:300–302; T. M. Shaw, "Wolves in Sheeps' Clothing: The Appearance of True and False Piety," *Studia Patristica* 29 (1997): 127–32.

46. Priscillian of Avila, *Tractatus* 1.7.26–8.8, ed. G. Schepss, CSEL 18 (1889); V. Burrus, "Priscillianist Duplicity Reconsidered," *Studia Patristica* 33 (1997): 401–6 at 402–3; Chadwick, *Priscillian of Avila*, 91–94.

47. *Epigrammata Damasiana* 15, line 17, in D. E. Trout, "Damasus and the Invention of Early Christian Rome," *Journal of Medieval and Early Modern Studies* 33, 3 (2003): 517–36 at 521–22, where Damasus substitutes the *sacramenta Christi* for Ovid's *ritus Cereris*; for similar gatekeeping based on penetrating divine mysteries in a monastic community, see Cassian, *Conlationes* 10.9, with Rousseau, *Ascetics, Authority, and the Church*, 199–205.

48. Ambrose, *De officiis* I.50.251, p. 262.

49. Hippolytus, *Traditio Apostolica* 4, ed. and trans. B. Botte, 2nd ed., SC 11[bis] (1968); *Constitutiones Apostolorum* 8.11; Cyprian, *De dominica oratione*, 31. While most often *corda*, in Augustine the refrain is always *sursum cor*: e.g., Augustine, *Ep.* 131, CSEL 44, p. 78 and ibid. 263.2, CSEL 57, p. 632.

50. T. Klauser, *A Short History of the Western Liturgy: An Account and Some Reflections*, trans. J. Halliburton (London, 1969), 189; cf. G. de Nie, "Poetics of Wonder: Dream-Consciousness and Transformational Dynamics in Sixth-Century Miracle Stories," repr. in de Nie, *Word, Image and Experience: Dynamics of Miracle and Self-Perception in Sixth-Century Gaul* (Aldershot, 2003), no. XIV at p. 7; G. Frank, "'Taste and See': The Eucharist and the Eyes of Faith in the Fourth Century," *Church History* 70, 4 (2001): 619–43 at 629.

51. Augustine to Consentius (a. 410), *Ep.* 120.14, CSEL 34.2, p. 716 ("hic maxime in caelis sunt, ubi et nostra est conuersatio"); cf. Augustine to Count Boniface, *Ep.* 189.7, CSEL 57, p. 135 ("cum audimus ut cor sursum habeamus, non mendaciter respondere debemus").

52. Caesarius of Arles, *Serm.* 82.2 ("ualde pauci et rari in ecclesia fiducialiter et cum ueritate dicere possunt"); N. Adkins, "A Problem in the Early Church: Noise during Sermon and Lesson," *Mnemosyne* ser. 4, 38 (1985): 161–63.

53. Jerome, *Ep.* 52.8 (a. 394), in *Select Letters*, trans. F. A. Wright, Loeb 262 (1933), p. 210; Rousseau, *Ascetics, Authority, and the Church*, 127.

54. Gregory of Nazianzus, *Or.* 2.92; N. B. McLynn, "A Self-Made Holy Man: The Case of Gregory Nazianzen," *JECS* 6, 3 (1998): 463–83 at 475; Palladius, *Dialogus de vita Iohannis Chrysostomi*, 17.206–8, 20.523–28, ed. and trans. A.-M. Malingrey and P. Leclercq, *Dialogue sur la vie de Jean Chrysostome*, SC 341–42, 2 vols. (1988), 1:348–50, 438–40; A. Sterk, *Renouncing the World Yet Leading the Church: The Monk-Bishop in Late Antiquity* (Cambridge, Mass., 2004), 124–25, 156–58, et passim.

55. Jerome, *Ep.* 52.7, *Select Letters*, p. 208 ("monachus, pontifex, avunculus").

56. Jerome, *Ep.* 117.1, "Ad matrem et filiam in Gallia" (a. 405), *Select Letters*, pp. 370–72.

57. Rousseau, *Ascetics, Authority, and the Church*, 102–4.

58. Jerome, *Ep.* 14.9, *Select Letters*, p. 46.

59. Jerome, *Ep.* 14.8, *Select Letters*, p. 42 ("quodammodo ante iudicii diem iudicant").

60. Jerome, *Ep.* 14.9, *Select Letters*, p. 48.

61. Rousseau, *Ascetics, Authority, and the Church*, 106–8.

62. Sterk, *Renouncing the World*; S. Elm, "Orthodoxy and the True Philosophical Life: Julian and Gregory of Nazianzus," *Studia Patristica* 38 (1999): 69–85; P. Rousseau, "The Spiritual Authority of the 'Monk-Bishop': Eastern Elements in Some Western Hagiography of the Fourth and Fifth Centuries," *Journal of Theological Studies* n.s. 23.2 (1971): 380–419 remains fundamental; D. Brakke, *Athanasius and the Politics of Asceticism*, Oxford Early Christian Studies (Oxford, 1995), 99–110, for episcopal appointments in Egypt.

63. Gregory of Nyssa, *Vita Gregorii Thaumaturgi* 10.14.18–15.1, 40.25–41.1, ed. Migne, PG 46, cols. 908CD, 940A; Sterk, *Renouncing the World*, 60 (Basil), 107, and 109–10 (Gregory).

64. Sterk, *Renouncing the World*, ch. 6 with quote at p. 156.

65. Sterk, *Renouncing the World*, 150–52; Ambrose, *Ep. extra collectionem* 14 [63].71, ed. M. Zelzer CSEL 82 (1982), 273 ("haec velut in quodam theatro, illa in secreto, spectatur ista, illa absconditur"); Davidson, "Staging the Church?," 433–34; cf. Jerome on barking bishops, *Ep.* 69.8, CSEL 54, pp. 695–96.

66. John Chrysostom, *De sacerdote* 6.4.22–24, trans. A. Malingrey, *Sur le Sacerdoce (Dialogue et Homélie)*, SC 272 (1980), 314; ibid. 6.2.5–6, p. 306: "Kai gar tôn aktinôn autôn katharôteran tôi hieri tên psychên einai dei"; cf. Lizzi, "I vescovi e i potenti della terra," 91–92; Brakke, *Athanasius and the Politics of Asceticism*, 252–53; C. Rapp, "The Elite Status of Bishops in Late Antiquity in Ecclesiastical, Spiritual, and Social Contexts," *Arethusa* 33, 3 (2000): 379–99 at 385.

67. Palladius, *Dialogus de vita Iohannis Chrysostomi*, 8.226–31, 11.120–56; vol. 1, pp. 176–78, 224–30; Sterk, *Renouncing the World*, 157–58.

68. Text from *The Life of Pachomius (Vita Prima Graeca)* 22, trans. A. N. Athanassakis, Society of Biblical Literature Texts and Translations 7, Early Christian Literature Series 2 (Missoula, Mont., 1975), p. 28: "kai ên hôs horôn ton aoraton theon têi katharotêti tês kardias hôs en esoptrôi"; also translated in *Pachomian Koinonia I: The Life of Saint Pachomius and his Disciples*, trans. A. Veilleux, Cistercian Studies 45 (Kalamazoo, Mich., 1980); Bishop Athanasius's relationship with Pachomius and Pachomian foundations: Brakke, *Athanasius and the Politics of Asceticism*, 111–29.

69. *Life of Pachomius* 112, trans. Athanassakis, pp. 152–54.

70. Rousseau, "Spiritual Authority of the 'Monk-Bishop'," 386–87, does not read Pachomius's explanation of his discernment as hedging in any way, but rather says he "laid claim to it without fear"; see Rousseau, *Ascetics, Authority, and the Church*, 30–31; Rousseau, *Pachomius: The Making of a Community in Fourth-Century Egypt*, Transformation of the Classical Heritage 6 (Berkeley, Calif., 1985), 171–72; Sterk, *Renouncing the World*, 19; P. Brown, *Making of Late Antiquity*, Carl Newell Jackson Lectures (Cambridge, Mass., 1978), 96; Brakke, *Athanasius and the Politics of Asceticism*, 115–16 with n. 157, 124–25, notes Pachomius's previous confrontations with the bishop of Latopolis.

71. C. E. Straw, *Gregory the Great: Perfection in Imperfection*, Transformation of the Classical Heritage 14 (Berkeley, Calif., 1988), 15–16 n. 60.

72. Ibid. with ample bibliography, also p. 50; N. Caciola, *Discerning Spirits: Divine and Demonic Possession in the Middle Ages*, Conjunctions of Religion & Power in the Medieval Past (Ithaca, N.Y., 2003), 3–9; Brown, *Making of Late Antiquity*, 95; Brakke, *Athanasius and the Politics of Asceticism*, 250–52.

73. Leyser, *Authority and Asceticism*, is the most thorough analysis of this subject to emphasize its relationship to episcopal authority; Leyser, "Expertise and Authority in Gregory the Great: The Social Function of *Peritia*," in *Gregory the Great: A Symposium*, ed. J. C. Cavadini, Notre Dame Studies in Theology 2 (Notre Dame, Ind., 1995), 38–61; Demacopoulos, "A Monk in Shepherd's Clothing," all with refs. to vast bibliog. R. A. Markus, *Gregory the Great and his World* (Cambridge, 1997), 17–33, and P. Brown, *The Rise of Western Christendom: Triumph and Diversity, A.D. 200–1000*, 2nd ed. (Oxford, 2003), 190–215, both contextualize Gregory's pastoralism deftly and concisely.

74. P. Brown, *Society and the Holy in Late Antiquity* (Berkeley, Calif., 1982), 103–65; Brown, "The Saint as Exemplar in Late Antiquity," *Representations* 1.2 (1983): 1–25, repr. in *Saints and Virtues*, ed. J. S. Hawley (Berkeley, Calif., 1987), 3–14; Brown, *Authority and the Sacred: Aspects of the Christianisation of the Roman World* (Cambridge, 1995), ch. 3; J. Howard-Johnston and P. A. Hayward, eds., *The Cult of Saints in Late Antiquity and the Early Middle Ages: Essays on the Contribution of Peter Brown* (Oxford, 2002).

75. Rousseau, "Spiritual Authority of the 'Monk-Bishop'," 381.

76. Rousseau, "Spiritual Authority of the 'Monk-Bishop'," 71–74, 384 with J. Fontaine, "Une clé littéraire de la *Vita Martini* de Sulpice Sévère: la typologie prophétique," in *Mélanges Christine Mohrmann: nouveau recueil, offert par ses anciens élèves* (Utrecht, 1963), 84–95; by contrast, some pagan ascetic philosophers had no problem generating a family tree "a thousand years" old: Brown, "Asceticism: Pagan and Christian," 602–3.

77. Burton-Christie, *Word in the Desert*, 203–7; for a much broader perspective, see the classic study by P. Courcelle, *Connais-toi toi-même, de Socrate à saint Bernard*, 3 vols. (Paris, 1974–75).

78. Esp. C. Rapp, "Storytelling as Spiritual Communication in Early Greek Hagiography: The Use of *Diegesis*," *JECS* 6, 3 (1998): 431–62, esp. 423, 434–35, 441; also P. Brown, "Enjoying the Saints in Late Antiquity," *Early Medieval Europe* 9, 1 (2000): 1–24.

79. P. Brown, review of H.-J. Diesner, *Kirche und Stadt im spätrömischen Reich: Aufsätze zur Spätantike und zur Geschichte der Alten Kirche*, repr. in Brown, *Religion and Society in the Age of Saint Augustine* (New York, 1972), 334. See T. Urbainczyk, *Theodoret of Cyrrhus: The Bishop and the Holy Man* (Ann Arbor, Mich., 2002); J. Binns, *Ascetics and Ambassadors of Christ: The Monasteries of Palestine, 314–631* (Oxford, 1994); *Lives of the Monks of Palestine*, trans. R. M. Price, intro. J. Binns, Cistercian Studies 114 (Kalamazoo, Mich., 1991); B. Flusin, *Miracle et histoire dans l'oeuvre de Cyrille de Scythopolis* (Paris, 1983).

80. Brakke, *Athanasius and the Politics of Asceticism*, 254–65; Rousseau, *Ascetics, Authority, and the Church*, 192–93.

81. Greek *Apophthegmata patrum* (Macarius) 32, ed. Migne, PG 65, col. 273D, trans. B. Ward, *The Sayings of the Desert Fathers*, Cistercian Studies 59 (Kalamazoo, Mich., 1975), 134; see above for Latin Didascalia 25 (2.26), ed. Connolly, p. 89.

82. *Historia Monachorum* 28, ed. Migne, PL 21, col. 451AB.

83. Ibid. cols. 450B–451A; Rousseau, *Ascetics, Authority, and the Church*, 53–54.

84. Rousseau, "Spiritual Authority of the 'Monk-Bishop'," 406–19 esp. 407.

85. Sulpicius Severus, *Vita Martini Turonensis* 11, ed. and trans. J. Fontaine, 3 vols., SC 133–35 (1967–69).

86. Rousseau, *Ascetics, Authority, and the Church*, 152–65.

87. Gregory of Tours, *De virtibus sancti Martini*, 2.43, ed. B. Krusch, MGH SRM 1.2 (1885), 584–661 ("O quotiens hic prophetarum et sublimium uirorum uirtutes"); R. Van Dam, "Images of Saint Martin in Late Roman and Early Medieval Gaul," *Viator* 19 (1988): 1–27; B. Brennan, "'Being Martin': Saint and Successor in Sixth-Century Tours," *Journal of Religious History* 21, 2 (1997): 121–35; M. Heinzelmann, "Histoire, rois et prophètes: le rôle des éléments autobiographiques dans les

Histoires de Grégoire de Tours: un guide épiscopal à l'usage du roi chrétien," in *De Tertullien aux Mozarabes: mélanges offerts à Jacques Fontaine*, ed. L. Holtz and J.-C. Fredouille, 3 vols. (Paris, 1992), 1:537–50 at 546–48 ; B. Jussen, "Liturgy and Legitimation, or How the Gallo-Romans Ended the Roman Empire," in *Ordering Medieval Society: Perspectives on Intellectual and Practical Modes of Shaping Social Relations*, ed. B. Jussen, trans. P. Selwyn (Philadelphia, Penn., 2001), 147–99 at 179–80 with refs.

88. J. R. Curran, *Pagan City and Christian Capital: Rome in the Fourth Century*, Oxford Classical Monographs (Oxford, 2000), 142–55 and Trout, "Damasus and the Invention of Early Christian Rome," both with references to earlier scholarship; McLynn, *Ambrose of Milan*, 209–19; G. Clark, "Victricius of Rouen: *Praising the Saints*," *JECS* 7, 3 (1999): 365–99; more generally, P. Brown, *The Cult of the Saints: Its Rise and Function in Latin Christianity* (Chicago, 1981); Howard-Johnston and Hayward, *Cult of Saints in Late Antiquity*.

89. Victricius, *De laude sanctorum* 1, ed. I. Mulders and R. Demeulenaere, CCL 64 (1985), 70 ("ut peccata nostra pia miseratione aduocationis excusent, non animo iudicantis inquirant"); cf. ibid. 12, p. 88 ("semper iudices quia semper apostoli"); trans. Clark, "Victricius of Rouen," 377; cf. Paulinus of Pella, *Vita Ambrosii* 39.2, intro. C. Mohrmann, ed. A. A. R. Bastiaensen, and trans. L. Canali, *Vita di Ambrogio*, Vite dei Santi 3 (Milan, 1975), 102 (my italics): "Causas autem criminum quae ille confitebatur nulli nisi Domino soli, apud quem intercedebat, loquebatur, bonum relinquens exemplum posteris sacerdotibus, *ut intercessores magis apud Deum sint quam accusatores apud homines*."

90. D. G. Hunter, "Vigilantius of Calagurris and Victricius of Rouen: Ascetics, Relics, and Clerics in Late Roman Gaul," *JECS* 7, 3 (1999): 401–30.

91. Augustine, *Serm.* 224, ed. C. Lambot, *Revue Bénédictine* 79 (1969), 193–205 ("erogatorem me dominus posuit, non exactorem"); R. Teja, "La cristanización de los modelos clásicos: el obispo," in *Modelos ideales y prácticas de vida en la antigüedad clásica*, ed. E. Falque and F. Gascò (Seville, 1993), 181–230 at 221–22; cf. F. Bellentani, "*Episcopus . . . est nomen suscepti officii*: Il vocabolario del servizio episcopale in alcuni testi agostiniani," in *Vescovi e pastori in epoca teodosiana*, 2 vols. (Rome, 1997), 667–81.

92. Jerome, *Commentarii in Ezechielem* 10.33, ed. F. Glorie, CCL 75 (1964): "Speculator terrae Iudae, uel rex potest intelligi, uel propheta. Speculator autem ecclesiae, uel episcopus, uel presbyter, quia a populo electus est, et scripturarum lectione cognoscens, et praeuidens quae futura sint, annuntiet populo et corrigat delinquentem."

93. Julian Pomerius, *De vita contemplativa* 1.20.2, ed. Migne, PL 59, col. 435; also Augustine, *De civitate Dei* 1.9.3; cf. Rapp, "Elite Status of Bishops," 380–81 and, on *episkopos*, Rapp, *Holy Bishops*, 24–25; M. H. Hoeflich, "The Speculator in the Governmental Theory of the Early Church," *Vigiliae Christianae* 34 (1980): 120–29 at 124.

94. Gregory the Great, *Homiliae in Hiezechielem* 1.11.4, ed. and trans. C. Morel, 2 vols., SC 327, 360 (1986, 1990); Morel notes that *speculator* was often associated with Sion, which some translated as *speculatio*, for which see Gregory, *Moralia in Iob* 33.26, ed. M. Adriaen, 2 vols., CCL 143–143A (1979, 1985); Augustine, *De civitate Dei* 17.16.2; Augustine, *Enarrationes in psalmos* 68.31; Hilarius of Poitiers, *Tractatus*

super psalmos 68.31, ed. J. Doignon, CCL 61 (1997). Cf. Gregory the Great's use of the term *rector* to refer to bishops, influenced by Gregory of Nazianzus: R. A. Markus, "Gregory the Great's *Rector* and His Genesis," in *Grégoire le Grand*, ed. J. Fontaine, R. Gillet, and S. Pellistrandi (Paris, 1987), 137–46.

95. For the following, Gregory of Tours, *Vita patrum* 17, ed. B. Krusch, MGH SRM 1.2 (1885), 661–744 at 727–33, trans. E. James, *Life of the Fathers*, 2nd ed. (Liverpool, 1991), 105–113, although I have used my own translations here; on Trier see E. Ewig, *Trier im Merowingerreich: Civitas, Stadt, Bistum* (Trier, 1954), esp. 11–111; N. Gauthier, *L'évangélisation des pays de la Moselle: La province romaine de Première Belgique entre Antiquité et Moyen-Ages (IIIe–VIIIe siècles)* (Paris, 1980), 35–89, 123–38, 169–207; Gauthier, *Province ecclésiastique de Treves (Belgica Prima)*, Topographie chrétienne des cités de la Gaule 1 (Paris, 1986); M. A. Handley, "Beyond Hagiography: Epigraphic Commemoration and the Cult of Saints in Late Antique Trier," in *Society and Culture in Late Antique Gaul: Revisiting the Sources*, ed. R. W. Mathisen and D. Shanzer (Aldershot, 2001), 187–200; H. Heinen, *Frühchristliches Trier: Von den Anfängen bis zur Völkerwanderung* (Trier, 1996) provides good coverage of the earlier period.

96. Gregory of Tours, *Vita patrum* 17.1, p. 728 ("saepius vitia eius nudaret, ac crimina castigatus emendatior redderetur"); C. Vogel, "La discipline pénitentielle en Gaule des origines au IXe siècle: Le dossier hagiographique," *Revue des Sciences Religieuses* 30 (1956): 1–26, 157–186 at 185.

97. Venantius Fortunatus, *Carmina* 3.12, ed. F. Leo, MGH AA 4.1 (1881), 64–65; Gauthier, *L'évangélisation des pays de la Moselle*, 181–89; S. Coates, "Venantius Fortunatus and the Image of Episcopal Authority in Late Antique and Early Merovingian Gaul," *English Historical Review* 115 (2000): 1109–37 at 1122 et passim.

98. N. Gauthier, "Le réseau de pouvoirs de l'évêque dans la Gaule du haute moyen-âge," in *Towns and Their Territories Between Late Antiquity and the Early Middle Ages*, ed. G. P. Brogiolo, N. Gauthier, and N. Christie, Transformation of the Roman World 9 (Leiden, 2000), 173–207 at 182.

99. *Ep. Austrasiacae* 7 (pre-535), ed. W. Gundlach, MGH Epist. 3 (1892), 118–19.

100. Gregory of Tours, *Vita patrum* 1, p. 729 ("non enim honorabat personam potentis").

101. Coates, "Venantius Fortunatus and the Image of Episcopal Authority," 1134–35; K. Uhalde, "Proof and Reproof: The Judicial Component of Episcopal Confrontation," *Early Medieval Europe* 8 (1999): 1–11.

102. Gregory of Tours, *Vita patrum*, prologue, p. 662: "Manifestus est, melius dici uitam patrum quam uitas, quia, cum sit diuersitas meritorum uirtutumque, una tamen omnes uita corporis alit in mundo."

103. Gregory of Tours, *Vita patrum* 17, pp. 727–78.

104. Gregory of Tours, *Vita patrum* 17.4–5, pp. 731–32.

105. Perjury at the tomb: Gregory of Tours, *Gloria confessorum* 92, ed. B. Krusch, MGH SRM 1.2 (1885), 744–820 at 807; also see *Glory of the Confessors*, trans. R. Van Dam (Liverpool, 1988), 96–97; holding a king to his oath: *Ep. Austrasiacae* 6 (ca. 550) from Abbot Florianus, MGH Epist. 3, p. 117.

106. Venantius Fortunatus, *Carmina* 3.11.15–16 (ca. 564), MGH AA 4.1, p. 63: "Tristibus inponis curas purgando querellas, / et sanat cunctos una medella uiros."

107. *Ep. Austrasiacae* 5.7 ("conversatio in caelis est"); Gregory of Tours, *Vita patrum* 17, pp. 727–8 ("cum summa conuersans innocentia cordis").

108. Ennodius of Pavia, *Vita Epifani* 31, ed. F. Vogel, MGH AA 7 (1885), 84–109 at 88, trans. R. J. Deferrari, *Early Christian Biographies*, FOTC 15 (1952), 301–51 at 309–10: "si propheta fuisset in manibus, prophetantem videres codice amisso lectorem; si testamenti veteris recensuisset volumina, Moysi dignus aemulator incedebat, taliter ac si illum Israhelitica per desertum agmina sequerentur; si apostolicum lac verborum et mel dominicae passionis severitatem legis condiens scriptura index revelasset, continuo ex ore ipsius dulciora favis verba fluxerunt"; Rapp, "Storytelling as Spiritual Communication," 431.

109. *Passio Praiecti*, prologue, ed. B. Krusch, MGH SRM 5 (1910), 225–48 at 225 ("cui etiam secreta caeli patuerunt"); trans. with a good introduction in P. Fouracre and R. A. Gerberding, *Late Merovingian France: History and Hagiography, 640–720*, Manchester Medieval Sources Series (Manchester, 1996), 254–300.

110. The standard discussion is H. H. Anton, "Pseudo-Cyprian, De duodecim abusivis saeculi und sein Einfluß auf den Kontinent, insbesonders auf die karolingischen Fürstenspiegel," in *Die Iren und Europa im früheren Mittelalter*, ed. H. Löwe, Veröffentlichungen des Europa Zentrums Tübingen, Kulturwissenschaftliche Reihe, 2 vols. (Stuttgart, 1982); also see CPL³, p. 357, no. 1106; M. Esposito, "Notes on Latin Learning and Literature in Medieval Ireland—III," *Hermathena* 48 (1933): 221–49 at 221–36; A. Breen, "The Date, Provenance and Authorship of the Pseudo-Patrician Canonical Materials," ZRG KA 81 (1995): 83–129 at 109–11; Breen, "*De XII Abusiuis*: Text and Transmission," in *Ireland and Europe in the Early Middle Ages: Texts and Transmission*, ed. P. Ní Chatháin and M. Richter (Dublin, 1998), 78–94.

111. Pseudo-Cyprianus, *De XII abusivis saeculi*, ed. S. Hellman, *Texte und Untersuchungen zur Geschichte der altchristlichen Literatur* 34, 1 (Leipzig, 1910), 53–54.

112. For a convenient survey, Fouracre and Gerberding, *Late Merovingian France*, 43–52.

113. Audoenus, *Vita Eligii*, 1.31, ed. B. Krusch, MGH SRM 4 (1902), 687 ("vir venerabilis sensit forte operandum"), ibid. 2.15, pp. 703–4 ("stimulabat enim animum eius," "concessam sibi virtutem quasi nihil ad se simulans pertinere," "'Dominus enim operatus est, sicut voluit'"); cf. ibid. 1.2, p. 670: a priest coming to pray with Eligius's mother is compelled "quasi prophetico mox usurpans verbo" to reveal the unborn child's blessed future.

114. Audoenus, *Vita Eligii*, 2.12, pp. 701–2 ("adiuro te").

115. Audoenus, *Vita Eligii*, 2.15, p. 704 ("cum prophetica fiducia exaltans vocem"), 2.32, pp. 717–18 ("familiariter loquens saepe prophetando praedixit," "plerumque Eligius prophetiae gratia afflatus praenuntiavit").

116. Audoenus, *Vita Eligii*, 2.41, 58, and 62, pp. 724–5 and 730–32.

117. Audoenus, *Vita Eligii*, 2.66, pp. 733–34.

118. Eligius of Noyon, *Sermo de supremo iudicio*, 1, ed. B. Krusch, MGH SRM 4 (1902), 749–61 at 751.

119. Augustine, *Ep.* 133.2 (a. 411) to Count Marcellinus, officiating over the trial of Donatists: "Inquirendi quam puniendi necessitas maior est; ad hoc enim et mitissimi homines facinus occultatum diligenter atque instanter examinant, ut inueniant quibus parcant"; cf. Harries, *Law and Empire*, 132.

120. North African bishops to the emperors, *Registri ecclesiae Carthaginensis excerpta* no. 93 = Carthage (16 June 404), *commonitorium*, *Concilia Africae*, a. 354–a. 525, p. 212: "impletum est erga eos episcopale officium."

121. Ambrose, *E*56 (5)–57 (6), ed. O. Faller and M. Zelzer, *Epistulae et Acta*, 4 vols., CSEL 82 (1968–86); F. Martroye, "L'affaire *Indicia*: Une sentence de saint Ambroise," in *Mélanges Paul Fournier de la Bibliothèque d'Histoire du Droit* (Paris, 1929), 503–10; H. Jaeger, "La preuve judiciaire d'après la tradition rabbinique et patristique," *La Preuve*, Receuil de la Société Jean Bodin 16–19, 4 vols. (Brussels, 1963–65), 1:415–594 at 516–22; R. Lizzi, "Una società esortata all'ascetismo: misure legislative e motivazioni economiche nel IV–V secolo d. C.," *Studi Storici* 30 (1989): 129–52 at 142; J. C. Lamoreaux, "Episcopal Courts in Late Antiquity," *JECS* 3, 2 (1995): 143–67 at 160–61; J. E. Grubbs, *Law and Family in Late Antiquity: The Emperor Constantine's Marriage Legislation* (Oxford, 1995), 200.

122. Cf. J. McNamara, "Muffled Voices: The Lives of Consecrated Women in the Fourth Century," in *Medieval Religious Women*, vol. 1, *Distant Echoes*, ed. J. A. Nichols and L. T. Shank (Kalamazoo, Mich., 1984), 11–29 at 19: no implication of the brother-in-law.

123. Ambrose, *Ep.* 56 (5).5 ("patebit ut genitalium secretorum petant inspectionem"); the midwife's social status (ibid. 6: "uile mancipium, procacem uernulam") was clearly an aggravating factor.

124. M. Himmelfarb, *Tours of Hell: An Apocalyptic Form in Jewish and Christian Literature* (Philadelphia,, 1983), 72–73.

125. V. Lozito, *Il corvo: Calunnie, accuse e lettere anonime nei primi secoli dell'era cristiana* (Bari, 1996), ch. 1 (Tacitus) and 92–119 (Ammianus)—this is an odd study; H. Sivan, "Le corps d'une pécheresse, le prix de la piété: La politique de l'adultère dans l'Antiquité tardive," *Annales HSS* 53, 2 (1998): 231–53 at 246; M.-A. Marié, "Deux sanglants épisodes de l'accession au pouvoir d'une nouvelle classe politique: Les grands procès de Rome et d'Antioche chez Ammien Marcellin, *Res Gestae* XXVIII, 1; XXIX, 1 et 2," in *De Tertullien aux Mozarabes: mélanges offerts à Jacques Fontaine*, ed. L. Holtz and J.-C. Fredouille, 3 vols. (Paris, 1992), 1: 349–60; Gregory of Tours, *Historiarum libri X*, 2.20, 4.7, 5.18. 5.48–49, 9.34, 10.15, ed. B. Krusch and W. Levison, MGH SRM 1.1, rev. ed. (1937–51).

126. Gregory of Tours, *Gloria confessorum* 91, pp. 806–7.

127. Grubbs, *Law and Family*, 205–16, with Sivan, "Le corps d'une pécheresse," occasionally correcting Grubbs on technical points; C. Léglu, "Defamation in the Troubadour *Sirventes*: Legislation and Lyric Poetry," *Medium Aevum* 66 (1997): 28–41, is good on the damage such slander might do within small communities; A. Richlin, "Approaches to the Sources on Adultery at Rome," *Women's Studies* 8 (1981): 225–50 for republican and imperial literary evidence; generally, see T. Fenster and D. L. Smail, eds., *Fama: The Politics of Talk and Reputation in Medieval Europe* (Ithaca, N.Y., 2003).

128. Grubbs, *Law and Family*, 211; C. Dupont, "La procédure civile dans les constitutions de Constantin: Traits caractéristiques," *Revue internationale des droits de l'antiquité* 3rd ser. vol. 21 (1974): 191–213; edicts by Constantine and Licinius: C.Th. 9.5.1, 10.1.3, 10.10.1–2, 13.10.1, with S. Corcoran, *Empire of the Tetrarchs: Imperial Pronouncements and Government, AD 284–324*, Oxford Classical Monographs,

rev. ed. (Oxford, 2000), 188–91, 194; good overview of Roman republican and imperial sources: S. Treggiari, *Roman Marriage: Iusti Coniuges from the Time of Cicero to the Time of Ulpian* (Oxford, 1991), esp. 262–98.

129. C.Th. 3.2.1, 4.12.3, 8.16.1, *CJ* 6.9.9, 6.23.15, 6.37.21; Grubbs, *Law and Family*, 118–23, and 124–7 for Nazarius; cf. P. Stein, *Roman Law in European History* (Cambridge, 1999), 24.

130. T. A. J. McGinn, *Prostitution, Sexuality, and the Law in Ancient Rome* (New York, 1998), chs. 5–6 with refs.; also see H. Sivan, "Revealing the Concealed: Rabbinic and Roman Legal Perspectives on Detecting Adultery," ZRG RA 116 (1999): 112–46.

131. C.Th. 9.7.2 (a. 326): "nonnulli tamen proterue id faciunt et falsis contumeliis matrimonia deformant."

132. C.Th. 9.7.2; C. Venturini, "'*Accusatio Adulterii*' e politica constantiniana (Per un riesame di CTH 9, 7, 2)," *Studia et Documenta Historiae et Iuris* 54 (1988): 66–109.

133. E.g., C.Th. 9.7.4 (a. 385): torture of slaves belonging to both husband and the wife; ibid. 9.7.7 (a. 392): no civil litigation until after the criminal trial; ibid. 9.7.9 (a. 383): prohibit soldiers from avoiding the forum where an adultery accusation was filed; see J. Beaucamp, *Le statut de la femme à Byzance (4e–7e siècle)*, Travaux et Mémoire du centre de Recherche d'Histoire et Civilisation de Byzance, Monographies 5, 2 vols. (Paris, 1990), 1:139–70.

134. C.Th. 9.7.8.

135. Grubbs, *Law and Family*, 217–21.

136. C.Th. 11.36.1 (a. 314).

137. C.Th. 11.36.4.

138. *P. Lips.* 43 = *M. Christian.* 98 = FIRA III, 574–76, with R. Bagnall, *Egypt in Late Antiquity* (Princeton, 1993), 224–25; S. Elm, "An Alleged Book-Theft in Fourth-Century Egypt: P. Lips. 43," *Studia Patristica* 18 (1989): 209–15; Harries, *Law and Empire*, 197–98.

139. Jerome, *Ep.* 54.13 to the widow Furia (a. 394), *Select Letters*, p. 252.

140. Jerome, *Ep.* 127.3 (a. 412), *Select Letters*, p. 442.

141. Rousseau, *Ascetics, Authority, and the Church*, 109, referring to Jerome, *Ep.* 22.13 to Eustochium, written before Jerome had left Rome; Jerome's departure: J. N. D. Kelly, *Jerome: His Life, Writings, and Controversies* (London, 1975), 91–115.

142. D. G. Hunter, "The Virgin, the Bride, and the Church: Reading Psalm 45 in Ambrose, Jerome, and Augustine," *Church History* 69.2 (2000): 281–303; for similar advice from another bishop, see Brakke, *Athanasius and the Politics of Asceticism*, 22–44.

143. Paulinus of Pella, *Vita Ambrosii* 4.1, *Vita di Ambrogio*, p. 58.

144. T. M. Shaw, "*Askesis* and the Appearance of Holiness," *JECS* 6, 3 (1998): 485–99 at 487–89 and 493, quoting P. Bourdieu, *Distinction: A Social Critique of the Judgement of Taste*, trans. R. Nice (Cambridge, Mass., 1984), 191; cf. Brown, "Saint as Exemplar," 4–5; B. Leyerle, "John Chrysostom on the Gaze," *JECS* 1 (1993): 159–74.

145. Ambrose, *De bono mortis* 2.4, ed. and trans. W. T. Wiesner, Patristic Studies 100 (Washington, D.C., 1970), 89.

146. Ambrose, *De Nabuthae* 11.47, ed. C. Schenkl, CSEL 32.2 (1897), 469–516 at 494.

147. *Protoevangelium of James*, chs. 19–20, with G. Clark, *Women in Late*

Antiquity: Pagan and Christian Lifestyles (Oxford, 1993), 73–75; Grubbs, *Law and Family*, 199–201; cf. Jaeger, "Preuve judiciaire," 529–30; T. J. Horner, "Jewish Aspects of the *Protoevangelium of James*," *JECS* 12, 3 (2004): 313–35, arguing that emphasis on postpartum virginity reflects Mishnaic influence.

148. Ambrose, *Ep.* 56 (5).8, p. 88; Ambrose, *De uiduis* 4.26, ed. Migne, PL 16, cols. 233–62 at 255.

149. Ambrose, *Ep.* 56 (5).6, p. 87: "se uirginem probet, nec abditorum occultorumque inspectio, sed obuia omnibus modestia adstipulatur integritati."

150. Novatian, *De bono pudicitiae* 8.4–5, ed. G. F. Diercks, CCL 4 (1972), trans. R. J. DeSimone, *Novatian*, FOC 67 (1972), 171 (I change his "foolhardiness" to "temerity").

151. Marcianus, *Senatus Consultum Turpillianum* = Dig. 48.16.1: "Accusatorum temeritas tribus modis detegitur et tribus poenis subiuitur: aut enim calumniantur aut praeuaricantur aut tergiuersantur."

152. Novatian, *De bono pudicitiae*, 9.2.

153. Ambrose, *De fuga saeculi*, 9.53, ed. C. Schenkl, CSEL 32.2 (1897), 163–207.

154. *Liber Sacramentorum Gellonensis* ch. 486, 2893, ed. A. Dumas, 2 vols., CCL 159–159A (1981), 461.

155. See especially K. A. Smith, "Inventing Marital Chastity: The Iconography of Susanna and the Elders in Early Christian Art," *Oxford Art Journal* 16 (1993): 3–24; C. Boehden, "Der Susannensarkophag von Gerona: Ein Versuch zur typologischen Deutung des Susannenzyklus," *Römische Quartalschrift für christliche Altertumskunde und Kirchengeschichte* 89 (1994): 1–25; H. Leclerq, "Suzanne," in DACL 15.2, cols. 1742–52. C. B. Tkacz has argued forcefully for interpreting Susanna as a Christ figure in a number of studies, including *The Key to the Brescia Casket: Typology and the Early Christian Imagination*, Collection des Études Augustiniennes Série Antiquité 165 (Notre Dame, Ind., 2002), 74–81; Tkacz, "Susanna as a Type of Christ," *Studies in Iconography* 20 (1999): 101–53; Tkacz, "Women as Types of Christ: Susanna and Jephthah's Daughter," *Gregorianum* 85, 2 (2004): 278–311 at 278–92. Such "type"-casting, of course, runs the risk of missing other nuances, including judicial ones, at play in any given text or material: see e.g., G. A. Kornbluth, "The Susanna Crystal of Lothar II: Chastity, the Church, and Royal Justice," *Gesta* 31, 1 (1992): 25–39; V. I. J. Flint, "Susanna and the Lothar Crystal: A Liturgical Perspective," *Early Medieval Europe* 4, 1 (1995): 61–86.

156. Not Athanasius, who blamed Susanna for her predicament because she bathed in the garden (her own!): Brakke, *Athanasius and the Politics of Asceticism*, 42–43.

157. Ambrose, *Ep.* 56 (5).3, 85–86.

158. Ambrose, *Ep.* 68 (26).17–19, 176–77; J. D. M. Derret, "Law in the New Testament: The Story of the Woman Taken in Adultery," *New Testament Studies* 10 (1964): 1–26.

159. P. Hyams, "Due Process versus the Maintenance of Order in European Law: The Contribution of the *ius commune*," in *The Moral World of the Law*, ed. P. Coss (Cambridge, 2000), 62–90 at 75–76.

160. Ambrose, *Exameron*, 6.4.22, ed. Schenkl, CSEL 32.1 (1897), 3–261.

161. Ambrose, *De fuga saeculi*, 9.53.

162. Cf. Ambrose, *Ep.* 20 (77).11–12, 151–2: "Respondet ei iudex: 'Non possum a me facere quisquam. Iustitia in iudicando, non potentia est in iudicando. Ego non iudico, sed facta tua de te iudicant, ipsa te accusant, et ipsa condemnant. . . . Nihil ego ex me profero, sed ex te forma iudicii in te procedit.'"

163. Shaw, "Judicial Nightmares and Christian Memory," 556–57.

164. Ambrose, *Expositio de Psalmo 118* 7.17, ed. M. Petschenig, CSEL 62 (1913); É. Rebillard, *In hora mortis: Evolution de la pastorale chrétienne de la mort aux IVe et Ve siècles dans l'occident latin* (Rome, 1994), is outstanding on this topic (quotation at p. 134).

165. P. Brown, *The Body and Society: Men, Women and Sexual Renunciation in Early Christianity* (New York, 1988), 347.

166. McLynn, *Ambrose of Milan*, 275.

167. E.g., McLynn, *Ambrose of Milan*, 276–90; Davidson, "Staging the Church?" 432–43; É. Rebillard, "La 'conversion' de l'empire romain selon Peter Brown (note critique)," *Annales HSS* 54 (1999): 813–23 at 823 n. 70.

Chapter 3. Christian Oaths:
A Case Study in Practicality over Doctrine

1. R. Hardin, *Trust and Trustworthiness*, Russell Sage Foundation Series on Trust 4 (New York, 2002); K. S. Cook, ed., *Trust in Society*, Russell Sage Foundation Series on Trust 2 (New York, 2001).

2. H. Jaeger, "La preuve judiciaire d'après la tradition rabbinique et patristique," in *La Preuve*, Recueils de la Société Jean Bodin pour l'histoire comparative des institutions 16–19, 4 vols. (Brussels, 1963–65), 1:415–594 at 529.

3. M. Gerwing, "Eid," in *Lexikon des Mittelalters* (Munich, 1986), 3: 1673–74.

4. The best extensive treatment is L. Kolmer, *Promissorische Eide im Mittelalter*, Regensburg Historische Forschungen 12 (Kallmünz, 1989).

5. J. J. O'Donnell, *Augustine: A New Biography* (New York, 2005), 319; M. Vessey, "From *Cursus* to *Ductus*: Figures of Writing in Western Late Antiquity (Augustine, Jerome, Cassiodorus, Bede)," in *European Literary Careers: The Author from Antiquity to the Renaissance*, ed. P. Cheney and F. A. de Armas (Toronto, 2002), 47–103.

6. Augustine, *Serm.* 180.8.9, ed. Migne, PL 38, col. 977: "Tanquam in specula ita te posuit contra te."

7. A. Ducloux, *Ad ecclesiam confugere: naissance du droit d'asile dans les églises (IVe–milieu du Ve s.)* (Paris, 1994).

8. Jerome, *Commentarii in Evangelium Matthaei*, 1.5.34, ed. D. Hurst and M. Adriaen, CCL 77 (1969), 32; Kolmer, *Promissorische Eide*, 48, 276.

9. Jerome, *In Hieremiam prophetam*, 1.69, ed. S. Reiter, CCL 74 (1961), 40: "veritatem, iudicium atque iustitiam; si ista defuerint, nequaquam erit iuramentum, sed periurium"; Kolmer, *Promissorische Eide*, 277; Gerwing, "Eid," with Thomas Aquinas, *Summa Theologica* 2.2 q. 89 a.3.

10. For example M. Lemosse, *Cognitio: Étude sur le role du juge dans l'instruction du procès civil antique* (Paris, 1944), 11.

11. To access vast literature: R. Bartlett, *Trial by Fire and Water: The Medieval Judicial Ordeal* (Oxford, 1986).

12. T. Frymer-Kensky, "The Tribulations of Marduk: The So-Called 'Marduk Ordeal Text," *Journal of the American Oriental Society* 103 (1983): 131–41; K. van der Toorn, "Herem-Bethel and Elephantine Oath Procedure," *Zeitschrift für die Alttestamentliche Wissenschaft* 98 (1986): 282–85; G. Ries, "Altbabylonische Beweisurteile," ZRG RA 106 (1989): 56–80. Also see U. Kaplony-Heckel, *Die Demotischen Tempeleide*, Ägyptologische Abhandlungen 6 (Weisbaden, 1963).

13. Homer, *Iliad* 18.497–508; D. C. Mirhady, "The Oath-Challenge in Athens," *Classical Quarterly* 41 (1991): 78–83; G. Thür, "Oaths and Dispute Settlements in Ancient Greek Law," in *Greek Law in Its Political Setting: Justifications Not Justice*, ed. L. Foxhall and A. D. E. Lewis (Oxford, 1996), 57–72, is an excellent entry into the abundant literature on archaic Greek oaths.

14. *Pace* Bartlett, *Trial by Fire and Water*, 4–12.

15. Augustine, *Enarrationes in psalmos*, 7.3, ed. E. Dekkers and J. Fraipont, 3 vols., CCL 38–40 (1956), 1:38.

16. H. S. Versnel, "Beyond Cursing: The Appeal to Justice in Judicial Prayers," in *Magika Hiera: Ancient Greek Magic and Religion*, ed. C. A. Faraone and D. Obbink (New York, 1991), 60–106.

17. W. Speyer, "Fluch," *Reallexikon für Antike und Christentum* 7 (Stuttgart, 1969), 1160–1288, esp. 1161–64.

18. J. Assman, "When Justice Fails: Jurisdiction and Imprecation in Ancient Egypt and the Near East," *Journal of Egyptian Archaeology* 78 (1992): 149–62 at 150.

19. For most of the following evidence, L. Robert, *Hellenica: Recueil d'épigraphie, de numismatique, et d'antiquités grecques*, vols. 11–12 (Limoges, 1960), 381–413; Robert, "Malédictions funéraires grecques," *Comptes rendus de l'Académie des Inscriptions et Belles-Lettres* (1978): 241–89; J. Strubbe, ed., *Arai epitumbioi: Imprecations against Desecrators of the Grave in the Greek Epitaphs of Asia Minor: A Catalogue*, Inschriften griechischer Städte aus Kleinasien 52 (Bonn, 1997). For nearly verbatim Latin examples of some of the Greek inscriptions here, see, e.g., B. D. Shaw, "Judicial Nightmares and Christian Memory," *JECS* 11, 4 (2003): 533–66 at 559–60.

20. W. M. Ramsay, *Cities and Bishoprics of Phrygia* 1.2 (Oxford, 1897), 499 n. 5.

21. References in E. Gibson, *"Christians for Christians" Inscriptions of Phrygia*, Harvard Theological Studies 32 (Ann Arbor, Mich., 1978), 2–3, including Lydian inscriptions.

22. J. H. M. Strubbe, "Curses against Violation of the Grave in Jewish Epitaphs of Asia Minor," in *Studies in Early Jewish Epigraphy*, ed. J. W. van Henten and P. W. van der Horst, Arbeiten zum Geschichte des antiken Judentums und Urchristentums 21 (Leiden, 1994), 70–128 at 84–46; D. R. Seely, "The Raised Hand of God as an Oath Gesture," in *Fortunate the Eyes that See: Essays in Honor of David Noel Freedman*, ed. A. Beck et al. (Grand Rapids, Mich., 1995), 411–25.

23. J. H. M. Strubbe, "Cursed be he that moves my bones," in *Magika Hiera: Ancient Greek Magic and Religion*, ed. C. A. Faraone and D. Obbink (New York, 1991), 33–59, on pagan epitaphs; P. W. van der Horst, *Ancient Jewish Epitaphs: An Introductory Survey of a Millennium of Jewish Epigraphy (300 BCE–700 CE)*, Contributions to Biblical Exegesis and Theology 2 (Kampen, 1991), 124–46 and 54–60

more generally; P. R. Trebilco, *Jewish Communities in Asian Minor*, Society for New Testament Studies, Monograph Series 60 (Cambridge, U.K., 1991), 78–81, and the following note for "Eumeneian" type in Jewish epitaphs of Acmonia. For physiological repercussions, A. Chaniotis, "Illness and Cures in the Greek Propitiatory Inscriptions and Dedications of Lydia and Phrygia," in *Ancient Medicine in its Socio-Cultural Context*, ed. P. H. van der Eijk, H. F. J. Horstmanshoff, and P. H. Schrijvers, 2 vols. (Amsterdam, 1995), 2:323–44. On juridical language in ritual texts, see R. Gordon, "Raising a Sceptre: Confession-Narratives from Lydia and Phrygia," *Journal of Roman Archaeology* 17, 1 (2004): 177–96.

24. Best known is the "Eumeneian" formula: Gibson, *"Christians for Christians,"* 4 n. 4, 125–44. On Eumeneia (a well-known early Christian community), Robert, *Hellenica*, 413–39; R. L. Fox, *Pagans and Christians* (New York, 1987), 295, 302.

25. E. Seidl, *Der Eid im römisch-ägyptischen Provinzialrecht*, Münchener Beiträge zur Papyrusforschung und antiken Rechtsgeschichte 17, 24, 2 vols. (Munich, 1933, 1935) 1:8–39, and 2:4–33; R. Taubenschlag, *Law of Greco-Roman Egypt in the Light of the Papyri (332 B.C.–640 A.D.)* (New York, 1944), 315–16; K. A. Worp, "Byzantine Imperial Titulature in the Greek Documentary Papyri: The Oath Formulas," *ZPE* 45 (1982): 199–226.

26. Worp, "Byzantine Imperial Titulature," 217. Robert, *Hellenica*, 401–4 with 403 n. 5 (esp. nos. 10, 11, 14), from ca. late 4th c. R. S. Bagnall, *Egypt in Late Antiquity* (Princeton, N.J., 1993), 194 n. 77 (*P. Cair. Masp.* II 67154).

27. Basil, *Ep.* 85, ed. R. J. Deferrari, 4 vols., Loeb 190, 215, 243, 270 (Cambridge, Mass., 1926–34), 2:108–11.

28. J. A. Crook, *Law and Life of Rome, 90 B.C.–A.D. 212* (Ithaca, N.Y., 1967), 208; R. Zimmerman, *Law of Obligations: Roman Foundations of the Civilian Tradition* (Oxford, 1990, 1996), 72 et passim; F. Pastori, *Il negozio verbale in diritto romano* (Bologna, 1994); R. C. Stacey, *Road to Judgment: From Custom to Court in Medieval Ireland and Wales* (Philadelphia, Pa., 1994), 29, 33, and ch. 8; J. A. Harrill, "The Influence of Roman Contract Law on Early Baptismal Formulae (Tertullian, *Ad Martyras* 3)," *Studia Patristica* 36 (2001): 275–82, suggests there are echoes of *stipulatio* in the catechumenical words, *verba respondimus*.

29. Virgil, *Georgics*, 1.42, ed. R. A. B. Mynors, *Opera* (Oxford, 1969), 30: "uotis iam nunc adsuesce uocari."

30. C. Castillo, "El nuevo juramento a Augusto encontrado en la Bética," in *L'Afrique, la Gaule, la religion à l'époque romaine*, ed. Y. Le Bohec, Collection Latomus 226 (Brussels, 1994), 681–86; J. González, "The First Oath *pro salute Augusti* found in Baetica," *ZPE* 72 (1988): 113–27.

31. Tertullian, *Apologeticum*, 32.2–3, ed. E. Dekkers, CCL 1 (1954), 77–171 at 143; R. Beare, "The Meaning of the Oath by the Safety of the Roman Emperor," *American Journal of Philology* 99.1 (1978): 106–10.

32. D. Fishwick, *Imperial Cult in the Latin West: Studies in the Ruler Cult of the Western Provinces of the Roman Empire*, Études Préliminaires aux Religions Orientales dans l'Empire Romain, 2 vols. in 4 parts (Leiden, 1987–92), 2.1: 395–96.

33. E.g., Fishwick, *Imperial Cult*, 1.1: 130 n. 233; Y. Le Bohec, *Imperial Roman Army*, repr. ed. (London, 2000), 74, 239; N. Lewis and M. Reinhold, eds., *Roman Civilization: Selected Readings*, vol. 2, *The Empire*, 3rd ed. (New York, 1990), 7–10;

J. Moralee, *"For Salvation's Sake"*: *Provincial Loyalty, Personal Religion, and Epigraphic Production in the Roman and Late Antique Near East* (New York, 2004).

34. M. Euzennat, "Le *clipeus* de Tamuda (Maroc): *Imagines* impériales et serment militaire," in *L'Afrique, le Gaule, la religion à l'époque romaine*, ed. Y. Le Bohec, Collection Latomus 226 (Brussels, 1994), 111–15. More on military oaths: W. Seston, "Fahneneid (*sacramentum militiae*)," Reallexikon für Antike und Christentum 7 (Stuttgart, 1969), 277–84; J. B. Campbell, *The Emperor and the Roman Army, 31 BC–AD 235* (Oxford, 1984), 19–32.

35. Found in Maryport (2nd c.): Fishwick, *Imperial Cult*, 2.1:418, 595–96.

36. M. H. Crawford, ed., *Roman Statutes*, 2 vols., BICS Supplement 64 (London, 1996), 23.

37. Vegetius, *Epitoma rei militari*, 2.5, ed. M. D. Reeve (Oxford, 2004), with M. Meslin, *La fête des Kalendes de Janvier dans l'empire romain*, Collection Latomus 115 (Brussels, 1970), 63.

38. M. Becher, *Eid und Herrschaft: Untersuchungen zum Herrscherethos Karls des Großen*, Vorträge und Forschungen 39 (Sigmaringen, 1993), esp. 94–111.

39. *Sacramentum* had utility for doctrinal writers because of its multivalent meaning ("symbol" or "mystery," "oath," and "ritual" as in baptism most of all). Augustine, for example, explored the full range in *De consensu evangelistarum* (a. 399/400), ed. F. Weihrich, CSEL 43 (1904), 452, s.v. "sacramentum"; elsewhere in his early works: Augustine, *Contra Adimantum*, 21 (a. 393/94), ed. J. Zycha, CSEL 25.1 (1891), 113–90 at 180: "huic sacramento ipse dominus adtestatus est"; Augustine, *Contra Faustum Manichaeum*, 3.3, ed. J. Zycha, CSEL 25.1 (1891), 249–797 at 264: "in nostrae fidei sacramento apostolica doctrina testatur," 12.11, 19.25; Augustine, *Contra litteras Petiliani*, 2.30.69 (a. 401–3), ed. M. Petschenig, CSEL 52 (1909), 1–227 at 58: "quisque uerus sacerdos, oportet ut non solo sacramento, sed iustitia induatur (cf. Ps. 131.9)"; E. J. Cutrone, "Sacraments," in *Augustine through the Ages: An Encyclopedia*, ed. A. D. Fitzgerald et al. (Grand Rapids, Mich., 1999), 741–47.

40. J. Crehan, *Early Christian Baptism and the Creed: A Study in Ante-Nicene Theology*, Bellarmine Series 13 (London, 1950), 96–110.

41. Augustine, *Ep.* 23.5, CSEL 34.1, p. 69: "Nonne ingemescimus, quod uir et uxor, ut fideliter coniungant corpora sua, iurant sibi plerumque per Christum et ipsius Christi corpus diuersa communione dilaniant?"; dotal contracts: D. G. Hunter, "Augustine and the Making of Marriage in Roman North Africa," *JECS* 11, 1 (2003): 63–85; generally, P. L. Reynolds, *Marriage in the Western Church: The Christianization of Marriage During the Patristic and Early Medieval Periods* (Leiden, 1994); J. K. Leonard, "Rites of Marriage in the Western Middle Ages," in *Medieval Liturgy: A Book of Essays*, ed. L. Larson-Miller (New York, 1997), 165–202.

42. Cf. S. Elm, *"Virgins of God": The Making of Asceticism in Late Antiquity*, Oxford Classical Monographs (Oxford, 1994), 26–28 with n. 4.

43. Augustine, *Ep.* 127.8, CSEL 44, pp. 27–28; ibid. 262.2, CSEL 57, pp. 622–23 (to Ecdicia).

44. Ibid., 127.1, CSEL 44, p. 19.

45. E.g., Council of Valence (a. 374), c. 2, *Concilia Galliae, a. 314–a. 506*, ed. C. Munier, CCL 148 (1963), 39: "De puellis uero quae se uouerint"; P. Brown, *Body*

and Society: Men, Women, and Sexual Renunciation in Early Christianity (New York, 1988), 259–84; E. A. Clark, *Reading Renunciation: Asceticism and Scripture in Early Christianity* (Princeton, N.J., 1999), 14–42.

46. B. Kötting, "Gelübde," *Reallexikon für Antike und Christentum* 9 (Stuttgart, 1976), 1055–99 esp. 1093–99; A. Stuiber, "Contra votum," *Reallexikon für Antike und Christentum* 3 (Stuttgart, 1955), 421–22; DACL 12.2, s.v. "Graffites"; ICLV 3: 419–20, s.v. "votum", including inscriptions in the name of deacons and (not necessarily Christian) presbyters. A recent regional study, G. Schörner, *Votive im römischen Griechenland: Untersuchungen zur späthellenistischen und kaiserzeitlichen Kunst- und Religionsgeschichte*, Altertumswissenschaftliches Kolloquium 7 (Stuttgart, 2003), includes 1240 inscriptions in its catalogue.

47. The meaning of *contra votum* in this and similar epitaphs may not be literal but mean simply, "against the [deep] wish"; even so, the sense of betrayal implies expectation, if not a contract: *L'année épigraphique* (1991), no. 0688 = *Inscriptiones Latinae Selectae*, ed. H. Dessau, 3 vols. (Berlin, 1892–1916), no. 9093: ". . . M(arco) Ant(onio) Augustanio Phileto filio / inocentiss(imo) q(ui) v(ixit) ann(os) III mens(es) VIII / dies X cui dii nefandi parvulo contra / vot(um) genitor(um) vita privaverunt. . . ."

48. D. R. Worley, "Fleeing to Two Immutable Things, God's Oath-Taking and Oath-Witnessing: The Use of the Litigant Oath in Hebrews 6.12–20," *Restoration Quarterly* 36 (1994): 223–36.

49. Ambrose, *De officiis* 3.12.79, ed. and trans. I. J. Davidson, Oxford Early Christian Studies, 2 vols. (Oxford, 2001), 402: "Denique ipse dominus frequenter suam mutat sententiam, sicut scriptura indicat."

50. Ambrose, *De officiis* 3.12.77–78, pp. 400–402.

51. Basil, *Ep.* 199.29, ed. Deferrari, 3: 118–23.

52. Basil, *Ep.* 217.82, ed. Deferrari, 3: 262; ibid., 64, ed. Deferrari, 3:252, where the full penance is ten years.

53. Ambrose, *Ep.* 17.9, ed. Migne, PL 16, col. 963: "Te ergo imperatore, christiani in aram iurare cogentur? Quid est iurare, nisi eius quem testaris fidei tuae praesulem, diuinam potentiam confiteri?"

54. Brown, *Body and Society*, 355.

55. Ambrose, *De officiis* 3.12.76, p. 400: "Purum igitur ac sincerum oportet esse affectum, ut unusquisque simplicem sermonem proferat, uas suum in sanctitate possideat, nec fratrem circumscriptione uerborum inducat, nihil promittat inhonestum: ac si promiserit, tolerabilius est promissum non facere, quam facere quod turpe sit"; cf. Ambrose, *Exhortatio virginitatis*, 11.74, ed. Migne, PL 16, cols. 335–64 at 358: "Qui autem non iurat, utique non peierat; qui autem iurat, aliquando necesse est incidat in periurium; quia omnis homo mendax (Psalm 115.11). Noli ergo iurare, ne incipias peierare."

56. Cf. Kolmer, *Promissorische Eide*, 277: "Diese etwas gebrochen anmutende Argumentation resultiert ohne Zweifel aus dem auch für Augustinus problematischen Zwiespalt zwischen der Zulassung von Eiden im Alten und deren Verbot im Neuen Testament."

57. Ambrose, *Ep.* 50 (= 28 in CSEL edition), ed. Migne, PL 16, cols. 1155–59.

58. Chromatius, *Tractatus* 24 (*in Matthaeum 5.31–37*), 3–4, ed. R. Étaix and J. Lemarié, 2 vols., CCL 9A (1974, 1977), 309–12. Also see *Chromace d'Aquilée: Sermons*, ed. J. Lemarié, trans. H. Tardif, 2 vols., SC 154, 164 (1969, 1971).

59. Chromatius, *Tractatus* 24.2.5.

60. Chromatius, *Tractatus* 24.3.1, 3.

61. Non-Jewish traditions, for example, had influenced Philo of Alexandria: J. Heinemann, "Philos Lehre vom Eid," in *Judaica: Festschrift zu Hermann Cohens siebzigstem Geburtstage* (Berlin, 1912), 109–18.

62. Chromatius, *Tractatus* 24.2.4; Gratian, *Caus.* XXII, q. 5, c. 12.

63. Chromatius, *Tractatus* 24.2.3; cf. Jerome, *Commentarii in Evangelium Matthaei* 1.5.34, quoted above.

64. Augustine, *De sermone Domini in monte* 1.17.52, ed. A. Mutzenbecher, CCL 35 (1967), 59.

65. Ibid., 1.17.52, pp. 59–60.

66. Augustine, *De beata vita* (a. 386), 3.18, ed. W. M. Green, CCL 29 (1970), 63–85 at 75; Augustine, *Ep.* 23.5 (a. 392).

67. Augustine, *De sermone Domini in monte* 1.17.53, p. 61.

68. Augustine, *Mayence* 61 (Dolbeau 25, "Cum pagani ingrederentur," a. 404) 7, ed. F. Dolbeau, *Vingt-six sermons au peuple d'Afrique*, Collection des Études Augustiniennes Série Antiquité 147 (Paris, 1996), 248–67 at 252: "Si ergo caelum sedes est dei, esto caelum ut portes deum. Cum portare coeperis deum, caelum eris"; see Augustine, *Serm.* 53.14; *Enarrationes in psalmos*, 121.9.

69. Augustine, *De sermone Domini in monte* 1.18.54, p. 61.

70. Augustine, *De mendacio* 15.28, ed. J. Zycha, CSEL 41 (1900), 411–66 at 448–49: "ne scilicet iurando ad facilitatem iurandi ueniatur, ex facilitate ad consuetudinem, atque ita ex consuetudine in periurium decidatur."

71. Augustine, *De sermone Domini in monte* 1.18.54.

72. See now P. J. Griffiths, *Lying: An Augustinian Theology of Duplicity* (Grand Rapids, Mich., 2004).

73. Augustine, *Ep.* 40.3.3, CCL 34.2, pp. 71–72: "Si enim ad scripturas sanctas admissa fuerint uelut officiosa mendacia, quid in eis remanebit auctoritatis?"; J. N. D. Kelly, *Jerome: His Life, Writings, and Controversies* (London, 1975), 217–18; on their correspondence, see P. Brown, *Augustine of Hippo: A Biography*, 2nd ed. (Berkeley, Calif., 2000), 274–75.

74. Augustine, *De sermone Domini in monte* 1.17.51, pp. 57–58.

75. Augustine, *De mendacio* 15.28: "Et ideo non inuenitur iurasse, nisi scribens, ubi consideratio cautior non habet linguam praecipitatem. Nam quod loquens iurasset, dum non scriberet, nescio utrum aliqua de illo scriptura narrauerit. Et tamen dominus ait 'omnino non iurare'; non enim concessit ut id liceret scribentibus."

76. E.g., Augustine, *Ep.* 30.2 (a. 395), CSEL 34.1, p. 123 ("dominus enim testis est"); ibid. 66.2 (a. 402) ("adiuro te per Christum ut ad ista respondeas"); ibid. 85.1 (ca. 405), CSEL 34.2, p. 394 ("ecce iterum et testor deum").

77. Augustine, *Ep.* 21.6, CSEL 34.1, p. 53: "Sic autem mihi dominum et Christum testem facis innoventiae et caritatis et sinceri affectus quem circa nos habes, quasi ego non de his iurare omnibus possum."

78. Augustine, *Ep.* 40.6.9, CSEL 34.2, p. 81 ("bonum coram deo testimonium perhibemus").

79. Augustine, *Ep.* 67.2.2, CSEL 34.2, p. 238; ibid. 72, CSEL 34.2, pp. 255–62 for Jerome's reply.

80. Augustine, *De mendacio* 15.28.

81. Augustine, *De sermone Domini in monte* 1.17.51, pp. 58–9: "Quapropter qui intellegit non in bonis sed in necessariis iurationem habendam, refrenet se quantum potest, ut non ea utatur nisi necessitate, cum uidet pigros esse homines ad credendum quod eis utile est credere, nisi iuratione . . . id est si iurare cogeris, scias de necessitate uenire infirmitatis eorum quibus aliquid suades. Quae infirmitas utique malum est, unde nos cotidie liberari deprecamur, cum dicimus: *Libera nos a malo* (Mt. 6.13)."

82. Augustine, *De mendacio* 15.28: "Et hoc utique a malo, sicut dictum est: 'Quod autem amplius est, a malo est'; non tamen suo, sed eorum infirmitatis, quibus etiam sic fidem facere conabatur."

83. Augustine, *De mendacio* 15.28: "[I]ntelligendum est illud quod positum est 'omnino,' ad hoc positum, ut quantum in te est, non affectes, non ames, non quasi pro bono cum aliqua delectione appetas iusiurandum."

84. Augustine, *De civitate Dei* 14.11, 19.3, 5, 17; Cicero, *De officiis* 1.43.153–54, 44.158; S. MacCormack, "Sin, Citizenship, and the Salvation of Souls: The Impact of Christian Priorities on Late-Roman and Post-Roman Society," *Comparative Studies in Society and History* 39 (1997): 644–73.

85. Augustine, *De sermone Domini in monte* 1.17.51, p. 59: "Sed nemo nouit nisi qui expertus est, quam sit difficile et consuetudinem iurandi extinguere, et numquam temere facere quod nonnumquam facere necessitas cogit."

86. Augustine, *Ep.* 46, CSEL 34.2, pp. 123–29; see most recently C. Lepelley, "La diabolisation du paganisme et ses conséquences psychologiques: les angoisses de Publicola, correspondant de saint Augustin," in *Impies et païens entre Antiquité et Moyen Ages*, ed. L. Mary and M. Sot (Paris, 2002), 81–96; K. Uhalde, "Barbarian Traffic, Demon Oaths, and Christian Scruples (Aug. *Ep.* 46–47)," in *Romans and Barbarians*, ed. R. W. Mathisen, D. Shanzer (Aldershot, U.K., forthcoming).

87. Augustine, *Ep.* 47, CSEL 34.2, pp. 129–36; O. Perler, *Les voyages de Saint Augustin* (Paris, 1969), 393, dates the letter to Autumn 399. Y. Modéran, *Les Maures et l'Afrique romaine: IVe–VIIe siècle* (Rome, 2003), 364–74; Lepelley, "La diabolisation du paganisme," 86–87; F. Van der Meer, *Augustine the Bishop: Church and Society at the Dawn of the Middle Ages* (London, 1961), 153–56; convention follows Orosius, *Historiae adversum paganos* 1.2.90, ed. C. Zangemeister, CSEL 5 (1882), 32, but note the broad location: "Tripolitana prouincia, quae et Subuentana uel regio Arzugum dicitur . . . quamuis Arzuges per longum Africae limitem generaliter uocenter (Tripolitania, also called Subventana or the region of the Arzuges . . . although [they] are called the Arzuges generically the whole length of the African border)."

88. Hearsay informed him (*audivi*, repeated four times): N. Moine, "Melaniana," *Recherches augustiniennes* 15 (1980): 3–79 at 57; A. Mandouze, PCBE 1, pp. 932–93, s.v. "Publicola," at p. 932 nn. 3–4; same evidence, opposite inference: E. A. Clark (trans.), *Life of Melania the Younger* (New York, 1984), 87–88.

89. E.g., Augustine, *Ep.* 199.46 (to Bishop Hesychius of Salona, ca. 419), CSEL 57, pp. 284–5.

90. E.g., C. R. Whittaker, "Land and Labour in North Africa," *Klio* 60 (1978): 331–62; P. Trousset, "Pénétration romaine et organisation de la zone frontière dans le prédésert tunisien," in *Ai confini dell'Impero: contatti, scambi, conflitti* (= *L'Africa romana* 15), ed. M. Khanoussi, P. Ruggeri, and C. Vismara, 3 vols. (Rome, 2004), 1:59–88 with references; E. W. B. Fentress, *Numidia and the Roman Army: Social, Military and Economic Aspects of the Frontier Zone*, BAR International Series 53 (Oxford, 1979), 183–86; P. Leveau, "Le pastoralisme dans l'Afrique antique," in *Pastoral Economies in Classical Antiquity*, ed. C. R. Whittaker (Cambridge, U.K., 1988), 177–95; B. Shaw, "Rural Markets in North Africa and the Political Economy of the Roman Empire," *Antiquités africaines* 17 (1981): 37–83; C. Grey, "Letters of Recommendation and the Circulation of Rural Laborers in the Late Roman West," in *Travel, Communication and Geography in Late Antiquity: Sacred and Profane*, ed. L. Ellis and F. L. Kidner (Aldershot, 2004), 25–40.

91. Augustine, *Ep.* 46.2–3, CSEL 34.2, pp. 125–25: "Si, cum illi ergo iurant per daemones suos, ut custodiant fruges, non polluunt ipsas fruges, ut, si inde manducauerit Christianus sciens uel de pretio ipsarum rerum *usus* [editor: "ex coniectura addidi"] fuerit, coinquinetur, significare dignare. . . . Quid debeo de ipsis frugibus uel de pretio ipsarum facere?"

92. Augustine, *Ep.* 46.1, p. 124: "Quacumque enim condicione etiam auro dato et obsidibus datis, ut audiui, tamen iuramentum iniquum medium intercessit."

93. Augustine, *Ep.* 46.6–18, pp. 126–8.

94. Cf. Van der Meer, *Augustine the Bishop*, p. 153: he inquired "for the benefit of his petty tenants."

95. Van der Meer, *Augustine the Bishop*, 153 ("victim of scruples," "pathologically concerned") and 56 ("a pitiful performance, as also is his style, and both express a purely formalistic type of Christianity"); D. Gorce, ed. and trans., *Vie de sainte Mélanie*, SC 90 (1962), 26 n. 2 ("délicatesse de conscience allant jusqu'au scrupule"); A. Mandouze, *Saint Augustin, l'aventure de la raison et de la grace* (Paris, 1968), 575 n. 5 ("son étroitesse d'esprit et sa maladi du scrupule"), and the same in his entry for Publicola in PCBE 1, pp. 932–93; Clark, *Life of Melania*, 88 ("the nugatory concerns of epistle 46"); Lepelley, "La diabolisation du paganisme," passim, follows the same tenor ("une religiosité fruste et une intelligence fort médiocre," "tempérament anxieux," "névrotiques"), while also asserting that these concerns reflect "l'imaginaire de beaucoup de ses contemporains" (90).

96. *Pace* Clark, *Life of Melania*, 88: "Far from attempting to limit conflict between pagan and Christian so that social life could proceed in a normal fashion, as did many late ancient men of cultivation, [he] exacerbates it."

97. Van der Meer, *Augustine the Bishop,* 156, called his Latin "execrable," and thus Clark, *Life of Melania*, 88; in her translation of *Ep.* 46, W. Parsons declared (220 n. 1): "The writer is evidently one whose native language is not Latin. He handles the language awkwardly, constructs his sentences clumsily, and moves uneasily within the circle of a restricted vocabulary"; Lepelley, "La diabolisation du paganisme," 85–86 and 95, follows M. Moreau, "Sur un correspondant d'Augustin: qui est donc Publicola," *Revue des études augustiniennes* 28 (1982): 225–38, in denigrating

his Latin but not in Moreau's suggestion that bad Latin might not preclude Publicola from being a senator. Others have allowed for greater diversity in literary style and elite culture, e.g., G. Haverling, *Studies on Symmachus' Language and Style* (Göteborg, 1988); M. R. Salzman, "Elite Realities and *Mentalités*: The Making of a Western Christian Aristocracy," *Arethusa* 33 (2000): 347–62.

98. Augustine, *Ep.* 46.1, CSEL 34.2, p. 124: "Dignare autem mihi definitiue rescribere et non suspense, quod, si ipse scribas dubitanter, ego in maiores dubitationes incidere possum, quam antequam interrogassem."

99. Thomas Aquinas, *Summa theologica*, 2.2 q. 78 a.4 response.

100. He addressed pollution in relation to some questions, for example, whether a Christian could bathe in a bathhouse where there was an idol, or benefit from a peace established by pagan oaths (yes to both).

101. Augustine, *Ep.* 47.2, CSEL 34.2, p. 130: "Nunc uero, quia et iurauit perquos non debuit, et contra pollicitam fidem fecit quod non debuit, bis utique peccauit."

102. Augustine was quick to distinguish this *fides* from the Christian article, *Ep.* 47.2, p. 130: "[Christian faith] enim longe alia est longeque discreta a fide humanorum placitorum et pactorum."

103. Augustine, *Ep.* 47.2, CSEL 34.2, p. 130: "Verum tamen sine ulla dubitatione minus malum est per deum falsum iurare ueraciter, quam per Deum uerum fallaciter. Quanto enim per quod iuratur magis est sanctum, tanto magis est poenale periurium."

104. E.g., O'Donnell, *Augustine*, 150–52.

105. P. Brown, "Enjoying the Saints in Late Antiquity," *Early Medieval Europe* 9 (2000): 1–24, in the abstract.

106. Paulinus of Nola, *Carmina* 28.1–2, ed. W. de Hartel, CSEL 30 (1894), 284, quoted in A. van den Hoek and J. J. Herrman Jr., "Paulinus of Nola, Courtyards, and Cantharii," *Harvard Theological Review* 93, 3 (2000): 173–219 at 178.

107. D. Trout, "Christianizing the Countryside: Animal Sacrifice at the Tomb of St. Felix," *JECS* 3 (1995): 281–98; Trout, *Paulinus of Nola: Life, Letters, and Poems*, Transformation of the Classical Heritage 27 (Berkeley, 1999), esp. 160–97; S. Mratschek-Halfmann, "*Multis enim notissima est sanctitas loci*: Paulinus and the Gradual Rise of Nola as a Center of Christian Hospitality," *JECS* 9, 4 (2001): 511–53.

108. C. Conybeare, *Paulinus Noster: Self and Symbols in the Letters of Paulinus of Nola* (New York, 2000).

109. PLRE 1, pp. 592–93, s.v. "Melania (1)"; PCBE 2, pp. 1480–83 s.v. "Melania (1)."

110. Moine, "Melaniana"; PLRE 1, p. 593, s.v. "Melania (2)"; ibid. p. 702, s.v. "Valerius Pinianus (2)"; PCBE 2, pp. 1483–90, s.v. "Melania (2)"; ibid. pp. 1798–1802, s.v. "Pinianus (2)."

111. PLRE 1, pp. 681–83, s.v. "Paulinus (21)": either consular or proconsul (official designation changed); Trout, *Paulinus of Nola*, 33–45.

112. Explicit support: Gorce, in *Vie de sainte Mélanie*, 26; Moine, "Melaniana," 57–58; Moreau, "Sur un correspondant d'Augustin." Tacit support: Van der Meer, *Augustine the Bishop*, 153–56 (remarkable, because his contempt for the individual is reason for others to reject the identification); Brown, *Augustine of Hippo*, 274; PLRE 1, p. 753. Uncertain: Mandouze, *Saint Augustin*, 562 n. 2; Mandouze, PCBE

1, p. 932. C. Pietri and L. Pietri in PCBE 2, pp. 1863–64 s.v. "Publicola," give no comment on this issue.

113. Against the identification: R. Thouvenot, "Saint Augustin et les païens d'après Epist. XLVI et XLVII," in *Hommages à Jean Bayet*, ed. M. Renard and R. Schilling, Collection Latomus 70 (Brussels, 1964), 682–90 at 683; Clark, *Life of Melania the Younger*, 87–88; Lepelley, "La diabolisation du paganisme," 85 n.7.

114. Other circumstantial evidence is the fact that Melania and Pinianus inherited property throughout Numidia, Mauritania, and Africa Proconsularis: Gerontius, *Life of Melania the Younger*, 20, *Vie de sainte Mélanie*, pp. 168–71 (my emphasis): "aragenamenoi de ekeise, eutheôs pôlountes ta ktêmata en têi Noumidiai kai Mauritaniai *kai en autêi têi Aphrikêi*, apesteilan ta chrêmata"; Clark, *Life of Melania*, interprets this as a telling omission of any reference to property in the region of the Arzuges (88), but one might recall Orosius, *Historiae adversum paganos* 1.2.90 ("per longum Africae limitem"), quoted above; also J. Matthews, *Western Aristocracies and Imperial Court, A.D. 364–425*, repr. ed. (New York, 1990), 25–30, on Romans holding North African property. The cognomen Publicola appears peculiar to the *gens Valeria*: Moine, "Melaniana," 57.

115. Clark, *Life of Melania the Younger*, 85.

116. For the following episode: Mandouze, *Saint Augustin*, 629–34; PCBE 1, pp. 53–65, s.v. "Alypius" at 60–61; PCBE 2, pp. 1798–1802, s.v. "Pinianus 2"; G. A. Cecconi, "Un evergete mancato: Piniano a Ippona," *Athenaeum* 66 (1988): 371–89; L. J. Swift, "Augustine on the Oath of Pinianus," *Studia Ephemeridis "Augustinianum"* 24 (Rome, 1987): 371–79; Swift, "Augustine on *Fama*: The Case of Pinianus," in *Nova et Vetera: Patristic Studies in Honor of Thomas Patrick Halton*, ed. J. Petruccione (Washington, D.C., 1998), 196–205; O'Donnell, *Augustine*, 230–33.

117. Gerontius, *Life of Melania the Younger*, 32–33; for the Latin version, see now P. Laurence, ed. and trans., *Gérontius, La Vie Latine de Sainte Mélanie: Édition critique, traduction et commentaire*, Studium Biblicum Franciscanum Collectio Minor 41 (Jerusalem, 2002); V. A. Sirago, "Incontro di Agostino con Melania e Piniano," in *L'umanesimo di Sant'Agostino: Atti del congresso internazionale*, ed. M. Fabris (Bari, 1988), 629–48; Matthews, *Western Aristocracies*, 290.

118. Augustine, *Ep.* 125, CSEL 44, pp. 3–7.

119. Mandouze, *Saint Augustin*, 634 n. 3.

120. Augustine, *Enarrationes in psalmos*, 88, *serm.* 1.4 (late 411/early 412), CCL 39, p. 1222: "Dei quippe iuratio, promissionis est confirmatio. Bene prohibetur homo iurare, ne consuetudine iurandi, quia potest homo falli, etiam in periuriam prolabatur. Deus solus securus iurat, quia falli non potest."

121. Augustine, *Ep.* 125.3, CSEL 44, p. 5; also Augustine, *De civitate Dei*, 1.15, 24 (a. 413), CCL 47, pp. 16–17, 25.

122. Zach. 5.1–3; Trebilco, *Jewish Communities*, 74–77; Strubbe, "Curses," p. 87 nos. 5–6.

123. E.g., *P. SB* 5273 (a. 487, Fayum) in Seidl, *Der Eid*, 2:34: "kata touto homologô hekousia gnômêi, epomnumenos theon pantokratora kai tên eusebeian kai nikên tês kallinikou kai athanatou [gra]phês. . . ."

124. Augustine, *Epp.* 62–63 (a. 401), CSEL 34.2, pp. 224–9.

125. Swift, "Augustine on *Fama*," 197; cf. C. Lepelley, "Le patronat épiscopal

aux IVe et Ve siècles: continuités et ruptures avec le patronat classique," in *L'évêque dans la cité du IVe au Ve siècle: image et autorité*, ed. É. Rebillard and C. Sotinel (Rome, 1998), 17–33 at 24–26 ("très embarrassée").

126. Augustine, *Ep.* 126.8–9, CSEL 44, pp. 14–15: "Quid ergo faciemus? Qua nos, si apud inimicos non possumus, saltem apud uos ratione purgamus? Res haec animi est, intus est, procul ab oculis secreta mortalium, Deo tantummodo nota est. Quid ergo restat, nisi Deum testari cui nota est? [O]mnino cogitis ut iuremus . . . intentato metu mortis existimationis nostrae, quae propter infirmos quibus nos praebere ad exemplum bonorum operum qualicumque conuersatione conamur, etiam uitae carnis huius utique praeponenda est. . . . Deus testis est, istam omnem rerum ecclesiasticarum procurationem, quarum credimur amare dominatum, propter seruitutem quam debeo charitati fratrum et timori Dei, tolerare me, non amare. . . . Nec aliud me de fratre meo Alypio sentire, ipse Deus testis est."

127. The episode clearly had little bearing for the Palestinian audience of the *Life*, but see Gorce in *Vie de sainte Mélanie*, 173 n. 3; Moine, "Melaniana," 57; Clark, *Life of Melania the Younger*, 110–11.

128. In 418, a letter from the three pilgrims notified Augustine of Pelagius's activity in Jerusalem, Augustine dedicated two anti-Pelagian treatises to them, and Pinianus and Melania sent salutations through Jerome: *PCBE* 2, p. 1801.

129. Also Swift, "Augustine on *Fama*," 202–3.

130. As perhaps did bishops: Augustine, *Ep.* 151.10 (a. 413), CSEL 44, p. 390, regarding the exculpatory oath Caecilian swore in front of a group of bishops in Carthage: "cordis inuisibilia paene oculis cerneremus."

131. Pelagius, *Ep. ad Demetriadem*, 19.4, ed. Migne, PL 30, cols. 15–45, trans. in B. R. Rees, *Pelagius: Life and Letters*, repr. in 1 vol. (Woodbridge, 1998), 57.

132. Pelagius, *Ep. ad Celentiam matronam*, 19, ed. Migne, PL 22, cols. 1204–29, *Pelagius: Life and Letters*, p. 137. The authorship of this letter is not certain. Also see the anonymous *Ep. ad virginem devotam* 3.1, ed. Migne, PL 17, cols. 579–84, *Pelagius: Life and Letters*, p. 343, which substitutes "in truth and in lying" for "by heaven" and "by earth" in a paraphrase of Matthew 5:34.

133. Brown, *Augustine of Hippo*, 340–53, 400–410; B. R. Rees, *Pelagius: A Reluctant Heretic* (Suffolk 1988), repr. in *Pelagius: Life and Letters*; also R. H. Weaver, *Divine Grace and Human Agency: A Study of the Semi-Pelagian Controversy*, Patristic Monograph Series 15 (Macon, Ga., 1996); full bibliography: E. TeSelle, "Pelagius, Pelagianism," in *Augustine through the Ages: An Encyclopedia*, ed. A. D. Fitzgerald et al. (Grand Rapids, Mich., 1999), 633–40.

134. Augustine, *Serm.* 180.2.2, ed. Migne, PL 38, cols. 972–79 at 973: "Et tamen iuratio ab ore non discedit, frequentatur; plura sunt plerumque iuramenta, quam uerba."

135. Ibid., 180.8.9, col. 977: "Non aperis os, nisi ad talem iurationem."

136. Ibid., 180.2.2, col. 973: "Si discutiat homo quoties iuret per totum diem, quoties se uulneret, quoties gladio linguae se feriat et transfigat, quis in illo locus inuenitur sanus?"

137. Augustine, *Ep.* 156 (a. 414), CSEL 44, pp. 448–49: "[C]hristiani apud Syracusas exponunt dicentes . . . non debere iurare omnino. . . ."

138. Augustine, *Ep.* 157.4.40, CSEL 44, pp. 487–48: "Sed illi, quantum aliquos

eorum audiui, quid sit iurare, prorsus ignorant"; he goes on to identify the oaths Paul swore.

139. Augustine, *Serm.* 180, 307–8, cols. 972–79, 1406–10; P. Verbraken, *Études critiques sur les sermons authentiques de Saint Augustin*, Instrumenta patristica 12 (Steenbrugis, 1976), 97.

140. Augustine, *Serm.* 180.3.3, col. 974: "Periuriam praecipitium. Qui iurat, iuxta est; qui non iurat, longe est. . . . Fac te ambulare in aliquo loco, ubi a parte dextera spatiosa sit terra, nec usquam angustias patiaris; a sinistra praeceps locus est. Ubi eligis ambulare? Super finem terrae in labio praecipitii, an inde longe? Puto quia inde longe. Sic et qui iurat, in fine ambulat; et ambulat pedibus infirmis, quia humanis"; cf. *Apostolic Constitutions* 2.15.3, ed. and trans. M. Metzger, *Les Constitutions apostoliques*, 3 vols., SC 320, 329, 336 (1985–7), 1:182, where humans walk precariously along the edge of a river.

141. Augustine, *Serm.* 180.2.2–3.3, cols. 972–74.

142. Ibid., 180.6.7, col. 975: "Si aliquid teste filio tuo faceres, et amico uel proximo tuo uel cuilibet homini diceres, 'Non feci,' et tangeres filio tuo caput, quo teste fecisti, et diceres, 'Per huius salutem, qua non feci.' Exclameret forte filius tuus sub paterna manu tremens, nec tamen paternam manum, sed diuinam tremens, 'Noli pater, non tibi uilis sit salus mea. Deum super me inuocasti. Ego te uidi, fecisti. Noli peierare. Te quidem habeo genitorem, sed plus et tuum et meum timeo Creatorem'."

143. Ibid., 180.3; *regio falsitatis, regio dissimilitudinis*, and neo-Platonism: Augustine, *Confessiones*, 7.10.16, ed. L. Verheigen, CCL 27 (1981), 103–4; P. Courcelle, *Les "Confessions" de saint Augustine dans la tradition littéraire* (Paris, 1963), 623–45; Courcelle, *Recherches sur les Confessions de Saint Augustin*, 2nd ed. (Paris, 1968), 405–40; B. Stock, *Augustine the Reader: Meditation, Self-Knowledge, and the Ethics of Interpretation* (Cambridge, Mass., 1996), 72 with n. 266 for a partial bibliography.

144. Augustine, *Serm.* 180.9.10, col. 977: "Cum uidero non mihi credi nisi faciam, et ei qui mihi non credit non expedire quod non credit, hac perpensa ratione et consideratione librata, cum magno timore dico, 'coram Deo,' aut 'testis est Deus,' aut 'scit Christus sic esse in animo meo'."

145. E.g., Caesarius of Arles, *Serm.* 14.3, ed. G. Morin, 2 vols., CCL 103–4 (1953), CCL 103, p. 71: "non solum periurare, sed nec iurare consuescite"; ibid. 23.2, CCL 103, p. 105: "numquam iurare"; ibid. 130.5, CCL 103, p. 538: "[the recently baptized] non solum a periurio sed etiam a iuramento abstineant"; ibid. 200.5, CCL 104, p. 810: "Nec solum a periurio, sed etiam a iuramento abstineant. . . ." John Chrysostom was also a hardliner: J. Maxwell, *Christianization and Communication in Late Antiquity: John Chrysostom and Lay Christians in Antioch* (Cambridge, 2006), 149–51; but see Dayna Kalleres's nuanced analysis of how spells and oaths influenced his explanation of the catechumenate and *exorkizein* in "Exorcizing the Devil to Silence Christ's Enemies: Ritualized Speech Practices in Late Antique Christianity" (Ph.D. diss., Brown University, 2002), 42–71.

146. Assman, "When Justice Fails," 150–53.

147. Augustine, *Epp.* 77–78 (a. 402), CSEL 34.2, pp. 329–45; date: Perler, *Les voyages*, 244–45; PCBE 1, p. 148, s.v. "Bonifatius (5)" (the priest), and p. 1091, s.v. "Spes" (the monk); Trout, *Paulinus of Nola*, 235–38, who emphasizes Paulinus's

influence: "Augustine's recourse to the tomb . . . signals the powerful pull that Paulinus might exercise even on a hesitant mind . . ."; Brown, *Augustine of Hippo*, 196: "[W]e are now entering the medieval world of the ordeal."

148. A. Ferrua, "Graffiti di pellegrini alla tomba di San Felice," *Palladio* 13 (1963): 17–19; P. Testini, "Note per servire allo studio del complesso paleocristiano di S. Felice a Cimitile (Nola)," *Mélanges d'Archéologie et d'Histoire de l'École Française de Rome, Antiquité* 97 (1985), 329–71; some examples in A. Gattiglia, "Paulin de Nole et Nicéta de Rémésiana: Voyages et pèlerinages de rang élevé," in *Akten des XII. Internationalen Kongresses für chritliche Archäologie (Bonn 22.–28. September 1991)*, ed. E. Dassmann and J. Engemann, JbAC Ergänzungsband 20, 2 vols. (Münster, 1995), 805–14 at 806.

Chapter 4. Mercy Not Justice:
How Penance Became a Worthy Act of Self-Incrimination

1. Gregory of Tours, *Historiarum libri X*, 10.1, ed. B. Krusch and W. Levison, MGH SRM 1.1, rev. ed. (1937–51), 477–81; R. Webb, "Imagination and the Arousal of the Emotions," in *The Passions in Roman Thought and Literature*, ed. S. M. Braund and C. Gill (Cambridge, 1997), 112–27 at 117–21.

2. Salvian of Marseille, *Ep.* 9.10–11, ed. G. Lagarrigue, 2 vols., SC 176, 220 (1971, 1974), 1:126; M. de Jong, "Transformations of Penance," in *Rituals of Power from Late Antiquity to the Early Middle Ages*, ed. F. Theuws and J. L. Nelson (Leiden, 2000), 185–224 at 205–7.

3. G. Nathan, "The Rogation Ceremonies of Late Antique Gaul: Creation, Transmission and the Role of the Bishop," *Classica et Mediaevalia* 40 (1998), 275–303.

4. Gregory of Tours, *Historiarum libri X*, 6.5, pp. 248–49 ("ipsos praedicatores paenitentiae") and 1.20, p. 43 ("Domino autem Deo nostro Iesu Christo paenitentiam praedicante"); cf. *Vita S. Marcellini episcopi Ebredunensis* 1.6, AASS April II, p. 751, probably written in the late fourth century (CPL³, no. 2122): "Ite, inquit, filii, Domini custodientes praeceptum, quoniam ipse misit discipulos suos binos et binos praedicare poenitentiam in remissionem peccatorum."

5. Gregory of Tours, *Historiarum libri X*, 4.36, p. 168 ("castigator deliquentium poenitentiumque remissor").

6. Honoratus of Marseilles, *Vita Hilarii Arelatensis*, 16, ed. P. Jacob, SC 404 (1995), 126–28; P. Brown, *The Rise of Western Christendom: Triumph and Diversity, A.D. 200–1000*, 2nd ed. (Oxford, 2003), 111–13.

7. Julian Pomerius, *De vita contemplativa* 2.7.3, ed. Migne, PL 59, cols. 452A–B. See P. Brown, "*Gloriosus Obitus*: The End of the Ancient Other World," in *The Limits of Ancient Christianity: Essays on Late Antique Thought and Culture in Honor of R. A. Markus*, ed. W. E. Klingshirn and M. Vessey (Ann Arbor, Mich., 1999), 289–314 at 308–10 on *crimina / peccata levia*.

8. Orléans IV (a. 541) c. 28, *Concilia Galliae, a. 511–a. 695*, ed. C. de Clercq. CCL 148A (1963), 139.

9. R. Somerville and B. C. Brasington (trans.), *Prefaces to Canon Law Books in Latin Christianity: Selected Translations, 500–1245* (New Haven, Conn., 1998), 28.

10. C. Vogel, *La discipline pénitentielle en Gaule des origines à la fin du VIIe siècle* (Paris, 1952), 32–33; P. Saint-Roch, *La pénitence dans les conciles et les lettres des papes des origines à la mort de Grégoire le Grand* (Vatican City, 1991), 29–31; Brown, *Rise of Western Christendom*, 255.

11. *Statuta Ecclesiae Antiqua* c. 19 (LXXV), *Concilia Galliae, a. 314–a. 506*, ed. C. Munier, CCL 148 (1963), 169: "ut negligentiores paenitentes tardius recipiantur"; Lérida (a. 546) c. 9 ("moderatione et clementia episcopi"), with J. Orlandis and D. Ramon-Lissón, *Historia de los concilios de la España romana y visigoda* (Pamplona, 1986), 129–30; "Arles II" (ca. 501) c. 10, *Concilia Galliae, a. 314–a. 506*, pp. 115–16 ("pro ecclesiastica humanitate"), with R. Mathisen, "The 'Second Council of Arles' and the Spirit of Compilation in Late Roman Gaul," *JECS* 5, 4 (1997): 511–54.

12. Innocent I, *Ep.* 27.7.10, ed. Migne, PL 20, col. 559; Angers (a. 453) c. 12, *Concilia Galliae, a. 314–a. 506*, p. 138; Leo I, *Ep.* 108.3–4 (a. 432), ed. Migne, PL 54, cols. 1012–13, with P. Adnès, "Pénitence," in *Dictionnaire de Spiritualité* 14 (Paris, 1984), cols. 943–1010, on *sacerdotalis supplicatio*.

13. Mâcon I (a. 581–3) c. 12, *Concilia Galliae, a. 511–a. 695*, p. 226 ("quamdiu episcopo . . . uisum fuerit"); *Breviarium Hipponense* (a. 393) c. 30a, *Concilia Africae, a. 345–a. 525*, p. 41 ("episcopi arbitrio paenitentiae"); Eauze (a. 551) c.1, *Concilia Galliae, a. 511–a. 695*, p. 163 ("sacerdotis . . . arbitrium"); Orléans IV (a. 541) c. 21, *Concilia Galliae, a. 511–a. 695*, p. 137 ("iuxta pontificis districtionem"); Orléans IV (a. 541) c. 8, *Concilia Galliae, a. 511–a. 695*, p. 134 ("in episcoporum potestatem"); and ibid., c. 28, p. 139 ("in sacerdotis potestate").

14. Tours II (a. 567), *Epistula ad plebem*, par. 1, *Concilia Galliae, a. 511–a. 695*, pp. 197–98; cf. Ez 34:10.

15. Leo I, *Ep.* 108.2 to Bishop Theodore of Fréjus, ed. Migne, PL 54, cols. 1011C–1012A.

16. Leo I, *Ep.* 159.5, ed. Migne, PL 54, col. 1138A, trans. E. Hunt, FOC 34 (1957), 250.

17. É. Rebillard, *In hora mortis: Évolution de la pastorale chrétienne de la mort aux IVe et Ve siècles dans l'occident latin* (Rome, 1994), 185–98; also J. Gaudemet, *L'Église dans l'empire romain (IVe–Ve siècles)* (Paris, 1958), 678–79; C. Vogel, *Le pécheur et la pénitence dans l'église ancienne* (Paris, 1966), 167–76.

18. Épaone (a. 517) c. 36, *Concilia Galliae, a. 511–a. 695*, pp. 33–34.

19. "Arles II" (ca. 501) c. 50, *Concilia Galliae, a. 314–a. 506*, p. 124; Vogel, *Discipline pénitentielle en Gaule*, 66; Adnès, "Pénitence," col. 962. Augustine, *Serm.* 77A.3, ed. G. Morin, *Miscellanea agostiniana* (Rome, 1930), 1:578.

20. Anonymous Archdeacon of Rome, *Serm.* 1.1, ed. F. Heylen, CCL 9 (1957), 355; more on this text below. Among many similar treatments see Julian Pomerius, *De vita contemplativa* 2.7.3, ed. Migne, PL 59, col. 451B; Caesarius of Arles, *Serm.* 59.6, ed. G. Morin, 2 vols., CCL 103–4 (1953), vol. 1 (103), pp. 261–62, trans. M. Delage, *Sermons au peuple*, 3 vols., SC 175, 243, 330 (1971–86), 3:42–43 with n. 1: in this case as elsewhere, Delage, following Poschmann, is at pains to insist that Caesarius was not speaking of liturgical penance.

21. Peter Chrysologus, *Serm.* 41.2, ed. A. Olivar, 3 vols., CCL 24–24B (1975–82), 232, with Rebillard, *In hora mortis*, 169–85 at 170–71.

22. E.g., Gerona (a. 517) c. 9, *Concilios Visigóticos e Hispano-Romanos*, ed. and

trans. J. Vives, T. M. Martínez, and G. Martínez Díez (Barcelona, 1963) ("poenitentiae benedictionem quod uiaticum deputamus"); Barcelona II (a. 599) c. 4, with E. Göller, "Das spanisch-westgotische Bußwesen vom 6. bis 8. Jahrhundert," *Römische Quartalschrift für christliche Altertumskunde und Kirchengeschichte* 37 (1929): 245–313 at 247–50. See Rebillard, *In hora mortis*, 199–224.

23. E.g., *Breviarium Hipponense* (a. 393) c. 32, *Concilia Africae, a. 345–a. 525*, p. 42; Leo I, *Ep.* 108.5 (a. 432); Orange I (a. 441) c. 3 and 11 (12), *Concilia Galliae, a. 314–a. 506*, pp. 78–79 and 81; *Statuta Ecclesiae Antiqua* c. 20 (LXXVI), *Concilia Galliae, a. 314–a. 506*, p. 170; "Arles II" (ca. 501) c. 28 (27), *Concilia Galliae, a. 314–a. 506*, p. 120; Barcelona I (a. 540) c. 8.

24. E.g., Caesarius of Arles, *Serm.* 19.4–5 and 50.1, vol. 1, pp. 89–91 and 224–25.

25. Gerona (a. 517) c. 9; ibid. c. 10 [= Toledo IV (a. 633) c. 54] clarified who were and were not eligible for clerical service by identifying the nature of the sin: "Hi qui in discrimine constituti poenitentiam accipiunt nulla manifesta scelera confitentes, sed tantum peccatores se praedicantes, huiusmodi si reualuerint, possunt etiam per morum probitatem ad gradus ecclesiasticos peruenire; qui uero ita poenitentiam accipiunt, ut aliquod mortale peccatum perpetrasse publice fateantur, ad clerum uel honores ecclesiasticos peruenire nullatenus possunt, quia se confessione propria notauerunt"; Orlandis and Ramon-Lissón, *Historia de los concilios*, 111–12, 283, 288.

26. Nicaea (a. 325) c. 13; *Statuta ecclesiae antiqua* (ca. 475) c. 84–5 (LXVIII–LXIX); "Arles II" (ca. 501) c. 25; Agde (a. 506) c. 43, *Concilia Galliae, a. 314–a. 506*, p. 211, rather than grouping penitents with bigamists, orders penitents who are ordained "ut sicut bigami aut internuptarum mariti locum teneant"; Épaon (a. 517) c. 3, *Concilia Galliae, a. 511–a. 695*, p. 24 ("paenitentiam professi"); Caesarius of Arles, *Serm.* 1.14, SC 175, pp. 252–5 with notes; Arles IV (a. 524) c. 3, *Concilia Galliae, a. 511–a. 695*, p. 44; Orléans III (a. 538) c. 6, *Concilia Galliae, a. 511–a. 695*, pp. 116–17, adding those physically or publicly possessed to the list of ineligible.

27. Toledo I (a. 400) c. 2; Göller, "Spanisch-westgotische Bußwesen," 246; Orlandis and Ramon-Lissón, *Historia de los concilios*, 85.

28. Vaison (a. 442) c. 8, *Concilia Galliae, a. 314–a. 506*, p. 100: a bishop should *discretely* admonish a sinful colleague to repent ("cum ipso ad compunctionem eius secretis correptionibus elaboret"); Tours II (a. 567) c. 2, *Concilia Galliae, a. 511–a. 695*, pp. 177–78, where a bishop who rejected the mediation settled upon by a council of his peers "etiam congruae poenitentiae intelligat uindictam subire."

29. Chalons (ca. 647–53), *Epistula synodi ad Theudorium, Concilia Galliae, a. 511–a. 695*, pp. 309–10; significantly, Theudorius had not appeared at the council, even though its members knew he was in town and waited expectantly for him to show.

30. E.g., Augustine, *Ep.* 10*.1 (a. 428), ed. J. Divjak, *Lettres 1*–29**, Bibliothèque Augustinienne 46B (Paris, 1987), 166, regarding the reconciliation of Bishop Turbantius after his alleged involvement with Pelagianism: "Hunc enim eandem haeresem satis humili confessione damnantem et in pacem catholicam a papa Coelestino esse susceptum a tali homine audiui quem non possum dicere fuisse mentitum."

31. Augustine, *Ep.* 11*.22, p. 222: "Sed numquid sine crimine possimus adfirmare episcopum qui catholicus uidebatur plaga domini fuisse percussum?" Also

see R. B. Eno, trans., vol. 6, *Saint Augustine: Letters (1*–29*)*, FOC 81 (1989), 81–98. Augustine, *Ep.* 11*.21, p. 220.

32. Augustine, *Ep.* 11*.14, p. 208 ("cum intimis malae conscientiae ignibus ureretur").

33. Augustine, *Ep.* 11*.16, p. 212 ("iure quidem potens et liberalibus litteris eruditus").

34. Augustine, *Ep.* 11*.15, p. 210: "[D]omini nostri Iesu Christi mirabili uisione perterritus uidit se ante tribunal metuendi iudicis constitutum tristem pro tanto conscientiae crimine suscepisse sententiam"; M. Moreau's translation in the Divjak edition, "pour avoir participé à un si grand crime" (p. 211), works but Eno's, "for so great a crime" (p. 92), does not. For the dream, see B. D. Shaw, "Judicial Nightmares and Christian Memory," *JECS* 11, 4 (2003): 533–63 at 549–50.

35. Augustine, *Ep.* 11*.15, pp. 210–12 ("tantaque animi consternatione percussus est"); ibid. 18, ed. Divjak, p. 216.

36. See Moreau's commentary and bibliography in the Divjak edition, pp. 479–88; M. Kulikowski, "Fronto, the Bishops, and the Crowd: Episcopal Justice and Communal Violence in Fifth-Century Tarraconensis," *Early Medieval Europe* 11, 4 (2002): 295–320.

37. Penance with loss of office: Elvira (a. 306) c. 76; Riez (a. 439) c. 7, *Concilia Galliae, a. 314–a. 506*, p. 70; Orléans II (a. 533) c. 8, *Concilia Galliae, a. 511–a. 695*, p. 117. Retain office with restrictions: Orléans I (a. 511) c. 12, *Concilia Galliae, a. 511–a. 695*, p. 8; Lérida (a. 546) c. 5. Retain office without explicit restrictions: Orange I (a. 441) c. 4, *Concilia Galliae, a. 314–a. 506*, p. 79; Agde (a. 506) c. 2, *Concilia Galliae, a. 314–a. 506*, p. 193; Orléans I (a. 511) c. 7, *Concilia Galliae, a. 511–a. 695*, p. 7.

38. Possidius, *Vita S. Augustini* 21, ed. A. A. R. Bastiaensen, intro. C. Mohrmann, trans. L. Canali, Vite dei santi 3 (Milan, 1975): "siue per fas siue per nefas excommunicati, uel absoluentur uel abicerentur."

39. Orléans III (a. 538) c. 22 (19), *Concilia Galliae, a. 511–a. 695*, pp. 122–23.

40. Orléans III (a. 538) c. 2, 7, *Concilia Galliae, a. 511–a. 695*, pp. 114–15, 117: penance for bishops who wrongly ordain or readmit clergy; Orange I (a. 441) c. 4 = "Arles II" (ca. 501) c. 29 (28), *Concilia Galliae, a. 314–a. 506*, p. 120: penance must be given to clergy who request it.

41. Marseilles (a. 533) , *Concilia Galliae, a. 511–a. 695*, p. 85; de Jong, "Transformations of Penance," 201–2 and also 210–15 for other penitent bishops in Gregory of Tours.

42. Gregory of Tours, *Historiarum libri X*, 1.44; the couple and their daughter were buried *iuxta aggerem publicum*.

43. Gregory of Tours, *Historiarum libri X*, 5.20, 27, pp. 218, 222.

44. Gregory of Tours, *Historiarum libri X*, 8.20: "accepto huiusmodi placito, ut paenitenciam tribus annis agens, neque capillum neque barbam tonderit, uino et carnibus abstineret, missas celebrare, clericos ordinare aeclesiasque et crisma benedicere, eulogias dare paenitus non auderet; utilitas tamen aeclesiae per eius ordinationem, sicut solita erat, omnino exerceretur."

45. Gregory of Tours, *Historiarum libri X*, 7.16 (escapes deposition) and 8.31 (assassinated).

46. Ruricius, *Ep.* 2.4 (c. 485/95), ed. B. Krusch, MGH AA 8 (1887), p. 314, *Ruricius of Limoges and Friends: A Collection of Letters from Visigothic Gaul*, trans. R. W. Mathisen, TTH 30 (1999), 140.

47. Ruricius, *Ep.* 2.13 (c.490/500), p. 322, *Ruricius of Limoges and Friends*, pp. 155–57; PLRE 2, p. 903.

48. Ruricius, *Ep.* 2.12 (c.490/500), p. 321, *Ruricius of Limoges and Friends*, pp. 154–55; quotation is James 2:13.

49. RICG 15, pp. 724–27, no. 283, from Saint-Sixte-Merlas, canton de Saint-Geoire-en-Valdaine, Isère: "In huc loco requiescit / penitens ERVALDE te- / mens Deum femena C / domena, in spe resurexi- / onis uite aeterne, / quae uixit annos qua- / draginta et duos, min- / ses sex; obiet quinto / kalendas nouembris, / indixione XIIII."

50. Ruricius, *Ep.* 1.13 (c. 475/85), p. 307, *Ruricius of Limoges and Friends*, pp. 124–25. In some cases, "professional" penitents (*professa paenitentia, professio,* or similar) might in fact be liturgical penitents: e.g., Tours I (a. 461) c. 8; Avitus of Vienne, *Ep.* 17 (c.516/17), ed. R. Peiper, MGH AA 6.2 (1883), 49, *Avitus of Vienne: Letters and Selected Prose*, trans. D. Shanzer and I. Wood, TTH 38 (2001), 287–29; Épaone (a. 517) c. 3, 23, *Concilia Galliae, a. 511–a. 695*, pp. 25, 30; J. Gaudement, "Épaone (concile d')," *Dictionnaire d'histoire et de géographie ecclésiastiques*, ed. R. Aubert and É. Van Cauwenbergh, vol. 5 (Paris, 1963), cols. 524–45.

51. Ruricius, *Ep.* 2.32 (c. 502/6), p. 335, *Ruricius of Limoges and Friends*, pp. 190–91; Agricola's father: Gregory of Tours, *Historiarum libri X*, 2.11, pp. 60–61; PLRE 2, pp. 196–98, s.v. "Eparchius AVITUS 5."

52. Ruricius, *Ep.* 1.1–2 (c. 475/77), pp. 299–301, *Ruricius of Limoges and Friends*, pp. 86–92; Faustus, *Ep.* 2 (ca. 477), ed. R. Demeulenaere, CCL 64 (1985), pp. 408–12 at 409, *Ruricius of Limoges and Friends*, pp. 96–101 at 97; the idea that Ruricius professed penance discomforted H. G. J. Beck, *The Pastoral Care of Souls in South-East France During the Sixth Century*, Analecta Gregoriana 51 (Rome, 1950), 212–13; for more on *conversi* see, e.g., Orléans III (a. 538) c. 27 (24), *Concilia Galliae, a. 511–a. 695*, p. 124, in Vogel, *Discipline pénitentielle en Gaule*, 128–38; for Faustus, see D. J. Nodes, "*De Subitanea Paenitentia* in the Letters of Faustus of Riez and Avitus of Vienne," *Recherches de théologie ancienne et médiévale* 55 (1988): 30–40; R. Barcellona, "La questione antropologica nell'epistolario di Fausto di Riez: la penitenza, l'anima, la salvezza," *Cassiodorus* 4 (1998): 83–123.

53. Vogel, *Discipline pénitentielle en Gaule*, 117; Rebillard, *In hora mortis*, 226.

54. E.g., Elvira (c. 306) c. 7; Tours I (a. 461) c. 8, *Concilia Galliae, a. 314–a. 506*, p. 146; Vannes (461–91) c. 3, *Concilia Galliae, a. 314–a. 506*, p. 152; "Arles II" (ca. 501) c. 21 (penitent widow) and c. 25, *Concilia Galliae, a. 314–a. 506*, pp. 118–19; Agde (a. 506) c. 15, *Concilia Galliae, a. 314–a. 506*, p. 201; Orléans I (a. 511) c. 11; Épaone (a. 517) c. 23, *Concilia Galliae, a. 511–a. 695*, p. 30; Orléans III (a. 538) c. 28 (25), *Concilia Galliae, a. 511–a. 695*, p. 124; Eauze (a. 551) c. 1, *Concilia Galliae, a. 511–a. 695*, p. 163; Paris III (a. 556–73) c. 5, *Concilia Galliae, a. 511–a. 695*, pp. 207–8, along with lay religious and virgins; Toledo III (a. 589) c. 11, most famous for condemning repetition of liturgical penance ("quotienscumque peccare . . . totiens a presbytero reconciliari"), treats those who "vel infra poenitentiae tempus vel post reconciliationem relabuntur"; Barcelona II (a. 599) c. 4.

55. RICG 15, pp. 401–4, no. 98A (a. 557/8); ibid., pp. 609–11, no. 227 (a. 527); ibid., pp. 724–27, no. 283, (quoted above); *Corpus Inscriptionum Latinarum* II².5, p. 95, no. 358 (late 6th / early 7th c.); ibid. II².7, p. 39, no. 136 (a. 650) = *Inscriptiones cristianas de la España romana y visigoda*, ed. D. J. Vives (Barcelona, 1969), pp. 21–22, 163–64, no. 42 = 480 (a. 588); ibid., p. 22, no. 44 (a. 657); ibid., p. 27, no. 66 (a. 662); ibid., p. 45, no. 142 (a. 636); ibid., p. 54, no. 178 (a. 650); ibid., pp. 324–25, no. 586; further examples cited in M. A. Handley, *Death, Society and Culture: Inscriptions and Epitaphs in Gaul and Spain, AD 300–750*, BAR International Series 1135 (Oxford, 2003), 10 n. 26; also C. Vogel, "La discipline pénitentielle dans les inscriptions paléochrétiennes," *Rivista di Archeologia Cristiana* 42 (1966): 317–25.

56. Vaison I (a. 442) c. 2, *Concilia Galliae, a. 314–a. 506*, p. 96; *Statuta Ecclesiae Antiquae* (compiled ca. 475) c. 22 (LXXIX), *Concilia Galliae, a. 314–a. 506*, p. 170.

57. M. Heinzelmann, *Bischofsherrschaft in Gallien: Zur Kontinuität römischer Führungsschichten vom 4. bis zum 7. Jahrhundert. Soziale, prosopographische und bildungsgeschichtliche Aspekte*, Beihefte der Francia 5 (Munich, 1976), 94–98.

58. Verus, *Vita Eutropii* 4, Acta Sanctorum May VI (27 May), pp. 700F–701E at 701B, also ed. J. H. Albanés and U. Chevalier, *Gallia Christiana novissima* (Montebéliard, 1916), 6:10–18 at 11–12: "Accidit ergo ut quadam nocte, post orationis vigilias, in soporem depressus, visione terribili frangeretur. Videbat namque se supinum terra prostratum, et in columna a locis genitalibus nigrarum avium multitudinem conglobatam usque ad nubes extendi. Cumque tantae rei stupor etiam dormientem invaderet, vidit e caelo ignem usque genitalia sua avium multitudinem consumentem." On this text see BHL, no. 2782; CPL³, p. 690, no. 2099.

59. Peter in penitential exegesis: A. Fitzgerald, *Conversion through Penance in the Italian Church of the Fourth and Fifth Centuries: New Approaches to the Experience of Conversion from Sin* (New York, 1988), 99–130, 489–90; Fitzgerald, "Christ, Peter and the Rooster," *Augustinianum* 41.2 (2001): 409–23.

60. Augustine, *Serm.* 229P, ed. C. Lambot, *Revue Bénédictine* 49 (1937): 252–57.

61. Augustine, *Serm.* 229O.1, ed. G. Morin, *Miscellanea agostiniana* (Rome, 1930), 1:495–96.

62. Ambrose, *Expositio evanggelii secundum Lucam*, 10.88, ed. M. Adriaen, CCL 14 (1957), 371.

63. Maximus of Turin, *Serm.* 59.1, ed. A. Mutzenbecher, CCL 23 (1962), p. 236 ("actus paenitentia refuderit uenditionis praetium, sed conscientiae suae non resoluerit scelus"); also see ibid., 25, 61, and the series 75–77; Fitzgerald, *Conversion through Penance*, 251–57; A. Merkt, *Maximus I von Turin: Die Verkündigung eines bischofs der frühen Reichskirche im zeitgeschichtlichen, gesellschaftlichen und liturgischen Kontext*, Supplements to Vigiliae Christianae 40 (Leiden, 1997), 204–11.

64. Verecundus, *Commentarii super cantica ecclesiastica*, 2 (*Deut*) 21, ed. R. Demeulenaere, CCL 93 (1976), 36; cf. ibid. 5 (*Ez*) 1, p. 117.

65. Cassiodorus, *Expositio Psalmorum*, 50.11, ed. M. Adriaen, CCL 97 (1958), 461.

66. Jerome, *Ep.* 77.4 ("Ad Oceanum, de morte Fabiolae," a. 400), ed. J. Labourt, *Lettres*, 8 vols. (Paris, 1949–63), 4:43 ("qui me prius docuerat uirtutibus suis, quomodo stans non caderem, doceret per paenitentiam, quomodo cadens resurgerem").

67. E.g., Cassiodorus, *Expositio Psalmorum*, 50.3, p. 454; Gregory the Great,

Regula pastoralis 3.2, ed. and trans. B. Judic, F. Rommel, and C. Morel, *Règle pastorale*, 2 vols., SC 381–82 (1992), 2:272.

68. Augustine, *Enarrationes in psalmos* 50.5, ed. E. Dekkers and J. Fraipont, 3 vols., CCL 38–40, rev. ed. (1990), 602: "Ad te Nathan propheta non est missus, ipse Dauid ad te missus est. Audi eum clamantem, et simul clama; audi gementem, et congemisce; audi flentem, et lacrimas iunge; audi correctum, et condelectare"; M. P. Kuczynski, *Prophetic Song: The Psalms as Moral Discourse in Late Medieval England*, Middle Ages Series (Philadelphia, Penn., 1995), 51–56.

69. Cassiodorus, *Expositio Psalmorum* 50.12, p. 462: "Sed paenitens iste bonorum auidus, uenturi praemii amore succensus, quod in futuro prouenire poterat, hoc sibi concedi praesenti tempore postulabat."

70. Kuczynski, *Prophetic Song*, 48.

71. Kuczynski, *Prophetic Song*, 37–38.

72. Peter Chrysologus, *Serm.* 115.1, p. 699 ("Dauiticam citharam spiritalis intelligentiae plectro et modulatione tangentes"); P. F. Bradshaw, *Daily Prayer in the Early Church: A Study of the Origin and Early Development of the Divine Office*, Alcuin Club Collections 63 (London, 1981), chs. 6–7.

73. W. Meyer, "Vita Adae et Evae," *Abhandlungen der philosophisch-philologischen Classe der königlich bayerischen Akademie der Wissenschaften* 14.3 (1878): 185–250; G. A. Anderson and M. E. Stone, eds., *A Synopsis of the Books of Adam and Eve* (Atlanta, Ga., 1994); M. E. Stone, *A History of the Literature of Adam and Eve* (Atlanta, Ga., 1992), esp. 53–58; *forsitan*: J. R. Levison, *Portraits of Adam in Early Judaism, from Sirach to 2 Baruch* (Sheffield, U.K., 1988), 163–90 at 175. Also see B. O. Murdoch, *The Irish Adam and Eve Story from Saltair na Rann*, vol. 2, *Commentary* (Dublin, 1976); C. Ireland, "Penance and Prayer in Water: An Irish Practice in Northumbrian Hagiography," *Cambrian Medieval Celtic Studies* 34 (1997): 51–66 at 52–53 ("a precursor of the cold shower"); R. Pettazzoni, "Confession of Sins and the Classics," *Harvard Theological Review* 30 (1937): 1–14; E. C. Quinn, *The Penitence of Adam: A Study of the Andrius MS. (Bibliothèque Nationale Fr. 95 Folios 380r–394v)* (University, Miss., 1980), 30–31.

74. Anonymous Archdeacon of Rome, *Sermones tres de reconciliandis paenitentibus*, ed. F. Heylen, CCL 9 (1957), 349–63; CPL³, p. 93, no. 238; F. Bussini, "L'intervention de l'assemblée des fideles au moment de la réconciliation des pénitents d'après les trois 'Postulationes' d'un archidiacre romain du Ve–VIe siècle," *Revue des sciences religieuses* 41 (1967): 29–38; Adnès, "Pénitence," 962–63.

75. Anonymous Archdeacon of Rome, *Serm.* 1.1 and 4–5, pp. 355–56 ("ostendentes tibi uulnera sua, et ferinis morsibus cruentas conscientias renudantes"); cf. Ruricius, *Ep.* 1.32 (c. 502/6), p. 335 (my italics): "[N]ec simus quasi timentes deum, aliud sermonibus praetendentes, aliud habentes in moribus, aliud ostentantes in vestibus, aliud actibus comprobantes, ne nos mordeat sermo ille dominicus, *sub vestitu ouium luporum rabiem contegentes.* . . ."

76. Anonymous Archdeacon of Rome, *Serm.* 2.9, p. 359.

77. Anonymous Archdeacon of Rome, *Serm.* 1.6, p. 356: "Hi sunt quibus in ecclesia stantibus tamquam in paradiso constitutis uetustus ille inimicus inuidit. . . . Sed et hi tandem respicientes et reformidantes antiquae damnationis exemplum non a facie dei refugiuent, non se umbraculo excusationis occultant, non inani

defensione uerborum tamquam infructuoso uelamento foliorum contegunt pudenda commissa. . . ."

78. Anonymous Archdeacon of Rome, *Serm.* 2.10, p. 359: "Neque enim fugiunt deum, nec sterilibus uerbis tamquam siluis operiunt, sed fructuosis lacrimis aperiunt quod fecerunt, obicientes sibi ipsi crimina sua criminaturum inimicum praeueniendo superant, non negando."

79. Gaudemet, *L'Église dans l'empire romain*, 669: "La pénitence exige donc une manifestation de volonté. Mais le muet pourrait d'une façon quelconque faire connaître cette volonté."

80. J. Leclerq, *The Love of Learning and the Desire for God: A Study of Monastic Culture*, trans. C. Misrahi, 3rd ed. (New York, 1982), 37–39.

81. Scholars have not ignored this phase entirely; e.g., Vogel, *Discipline pénitentielle en Gaule*, 68, 157–58, et passim, and J. Gaudemet, *Sources du droit de l'Église en Occident du IIe au VIIe siècle* (Paris, 1985), 675–76 on *thérapeutique spirituelle*.

82. J. Pegon, "Componction," in *Dictionnaire de spiritualité* 2 (Paris, 1937), cols. 1312–21; cf. Ps 31:4.

83. E.g., Gregory I, *Moralia in Iob*, 1.47bis, ed. M. Adriaen, 2 vols., CCL 143–143° (1979, 1985): "mens per quandam compunctionis machinam ad alta sustollitur"; P. Courcelle, *Connais-toi toi-même, de Socrate à Saint Bernard*, 3 vols. (Paris, 1974–75), 215; M. Wilson, "The Subjugation of Grief in Seneca's 'Epistles'," in *The Passions in Roman Thought and Literature*, ed. S. M. Braund and C. Gill (Cambridge, 1997), 48–67 at 52, 60; Brown, *Rise of Western Christendom*, 256; cf. T. O'Loughlin and H. Conrad-O-Briain, "The 'Baptism of Tears' in Early Anglo-Saxon Sources," *Anglo-Saxon England* 22 (1993): 65–83 at 73–74.

84. Cassian, *Conlationes* 20.8, ed. and tr. E. Pichery, SC 64 (1959): "Et ita iam non recordatione ueteris admissi, sed spe futurorum flere incipiet gaudiorum, nec tam de praeteritis malis quam de uenturis cogitans bonis non ex peccatorum maerore lacrimas, sed ex aeternae illius laetitiae alacritate profundet, atque 'obliuiscens ea quae posteriora sunt,' id est carnalia uitia, 'ad ea quae in ante sunt' extendetur (Phil. 3.13), hoc est spiritalia dona atque uirtutes."

85. Ibid., 20.6–7: "Dum ergo agimus paenitentiam et adhuc uitiosorum actuum recordatione mordemur, necessarium est ut ignem conscientiae nostrae obortus ex confessione culparum lacrimarum imber extinguat."

86. Ibid., 20.8.

87. Augustine, *Serm.* 313D.3 = Morin Guelferbytana 27, *Miscellanea agostiniana*, 1:533–34 ("fletu enim abundat haec uita").

88. Augustine, *Serm.* 77B.7, ed. G. Morin, *Miscellanea agostiniana*, 1:655–57, in reference to Psalm 38 ("Exaudi orationem meam, auribus percipe lacrimas meas"): "Ita uero [lacrimae] habent uoces suas, sicut sanguis Abel habuit uocem suam. Si habuit ad dominum sanguis occisi, habent etiam lacrimae precantis, habent omnino. Nam et lacrimae sanguis cordis est. Ergo, quando postulas uitam aeternam, quando dicis, 'Adueniat regnum tuum' (Mt 6.10), ubi securus uiuas, ubi semper uiuas, ubi numquam doleas amicum, numquam timeas inimicum, quando hoc poscis, plora, funde sanguinem interiorem, immola deo tuo cor tuum. . . ."

89. Rebillard, *In hora mortis*, 140–43; see the entry *De cogitacione* in the 7th-century florilegium by Defensor, *Liber scintillarum*, ed. H. M. Rochais, CCL 117

(1957), 38; on this text, L. S. B. MacCoull, "More Sources for the *Liber Scintillarum* of Defensor of Ligugé," *Revue Bénédictine* 112, 3–4 (2002): 291–300 with refs.

90. Augustine, *De agone Christiano* 5.5: "Quamuis ille locus ubi ait, 'Spiritalia nequitiae in caelestibus' (Eph 6:12) possit et aliter intelligi, ut non ipsos praeuaricatores angelos in caelestibus esse dixerit, sed nos potius, de quibus alio loco dicit, 'Conversatio nostra in caelis est,' ut nos in caelestibus constituti, id est in spiritalibus praeceptis Dei ambulantes, dimicemus aduersus spiritalia nequitiae, quae nos inde conantur abstrahere. Magis ergo illud quaerendum est, quomodo aduersus eos, quos non uidemus, pugnare possibus et uincere: ne putent stulti aduersus aerem nos debere certare."

91. Leo I, *Sermo* 47.1, ed. Migne, PL 54, col. 295 ("plus plerumque periculi est in insidiatore occulto quam in hoste manifesto").

92. Rebillard, *In hora mortis*, 186–89.

93. J. Fontaine, *Naissance de la poésie dans l'occident chrétien: Esquisse d'une histoire de la poésie latine chrétienne du IIIe au VIe siècle* (Paris, 1981).

94. Pseudo-Hilarius, *Metrum in Genesim*, ll. 23–29, ed. R. Peiper, CSEL 23.1 (1891), 1–208: "Omnia cum tegeret nigrum chaos altaque moles / desuper urgeret informis corpora mundi / et caliganti premeret serotina morte, / nec species nec forma foret, deus intus agebas / corporibus tectis mixtus, secreta potestas, / iam tum disponens nascentia moenia mundi / et uarias rerum facies animasque futuras"; I have used the translation of D. J. Nodes, *Doctrine and Exegesis in Biblical Latin Poetry*, ARCA Classical and Medieval Texts, Papers and Monographs 31 (Leeds, 1993), 88–89.

95. Proba, *Cento virgilianus (Carmen Sacrum)*, ll. 9–12, 35–37, 50–51, ed. K. Schenkl, CSEL 16 (1888), 569–609, trans. Nodes, *Doctrine and Exegesis*, 13–14: "Omnia temptanti potior sententia uisa est / pandere res altas terra et caligne mersas"; cf. Augustine, *Confessiones*, 10.32.38; E. A. Clark and D. F. Hatch, *The Golden Bough, the Oaken Cross: The Virgilian Cento of Faltonia Betitia Proba*, American Academy of Religion, Texts and Translations Series 5 (Chico, CA, 1981); H. Sivan, "Anician Women, the Cento of Proba, and Aristocratic Conversion in the Fourth Century," *Vigiliae Christianae* 47 (1993): 140–57.

96. Leo I, *Serm.* 58.3, ed. Migne, PL 54, col. 334: "Contristati enim sunt, non de conscientiae reatu, sed de humanae mutabilitatis incerto, timentes ne minus uerum esset quod in se quisque nouerat, quam quod ipsa ueritas praeuidebat."

97. Peter Chrysologus, *Serm.* 57.1, p. 318, in reference to Isaiah 6.5: "Semper humano percellitur hoc dolore, qui quod de deo sentit et uidet, loqui non ualet, adnuntiare non potest, non potest confiteri. Quanto caro angusta est animo suo, artarta sunt labia tantum, lingua tantum breuis est suae mentis interpres. In carne ignis anhelat inclusus, uaporat uenas, inflammat uiscera, exaestuat in medullis, totaque hominis interna semper incendit, quia quod montis contemplatur aspectu, ore depromere, effundere labiis, lingua distinguere, et in totum non sufficit euaporare sermonem."

98. Ibid., 15.4, 81.4, 83.2, 84.4, 88.2, 91.3, with Rebillard, *In hora mortis*, 172–73.

99. Peter Chrysologus, *Serm.* 34.4, p. 197; cf. ibid., 91.3: "Estne homo qui corde non peccet, non cogitatione delinquat, non offendat dubitatione, non lapsum reputationis incurrat?"; see Rebillard, *In hora mortis*, 163–64, 171–72, 194; G. Bartelink,

"Fragilitas (infirmitas) humana chez Augustin," in *Collecteana Augustiniana: Mélanges T. J. van Bavel*, ed. B. Bruning, M. Lamberigts, and J. van Houten, 2 vols. (Leuven, 1991), 2: 815–28.

100. Maximus of Turin, *Sermo* 20.4, p. 76: "Harum igitur molarum operatione, id est noui ac ueteris testamenti, hoc agit sancta ecclesia cura peruigili, ut peccatorum asperitate discussa ex occultis cogitationibus medullam mundi cordis eliceat; et caelestibus mandatis mundata ex intimis spiritalia alimenta producat"; cf. Ambrose, *Expositio evangelii secundum Lucam*, 8.48–52.

101. Augustine, *Ep.* 145.6.

102. A common antithesis, which Fulgentius for one condenses in *De remissione peccatorum ad Euthymium* 1.8, ed. J. Fraipoint, CCL 91A (1968), 649–707: "His igitur atque innumeris huiusmodi testimoniis, quibus Dominus Deus noster misericors praedicatur et iustus, ostenditur quantum diligenda sit eius misericordia, quantumque iustitia metuenda monstratur."

103. Maximus of Turin, *Serm.* 1.1, p. 2: "[N]am Petro sicut bono dispensatori clauem regni caelestis dedit, Paulo tamquam idoneo doctori magisterium ecclesiasticae insitutionis iniunxit; scilicet ut quos iste erudierit ad salutem, ille suscipiat ad quietem; et quorum corda Paulus patefecerit doctrina uerborum, eorum animabus Petrus aperiat regna caelorum. Clauem ergo quodammodo a Christo scientiae et Paulus accepit [cf. Lk 11:52]; clauis enim dicenda est qua ad fidem pectorum dura reserantur mentium secreta panduntur; et quidquid intrinsecus clausum tenetur in palam rationabili manifestatione producitur. Clauis, inquam, est quae et conscientiam ad confessionem peccati aperit, et gratiam ad aeternitatem mysterii salutaris includit. Ambo igitur claues a domino perceperunt, scientiae iste ille potentiae; diuitias inmortalitatis ille dispensat, scientiae thesauros iste largitur."

104. Caesarius, *Serm.* 61.1, CCL 103, p. 267, trans. M. M. Mueller, FOC 31 (1956), p. 300.

105. Caesarius, *Serm.* 56.3, SC 330 p. 16 ("generaliter omnes ad paenitentiam provocamus").

106. Caesarius, *Serm.* 31.2, SC 243, p. 144: "Certe transierunt omnia tamquam umbra; et si paenitentia non subvenerit, sola in perpetuum obprobria et crimina remanserunt."

107. Caesarius, *Serm.* 5.4, SC 175, pp. 312: "Inrideant ergo nos superbi: nos tamen pro eorum salute, licet minus digni, die noctuque cum rugitu et gemitu dei misericordiam supplicemus. . . ."

108. Caesarius, *Serm.* 5.4, SC 175, pp. 312–14: "Confidentes de illius ineffabili pietate, quod eos cito inter filios suos ita dignabitur castigare, ut per ipsam castigationem ab omnium peccatorum praecipitio revocentur, et dignam paenitentiam agentes cum sanctis mereantur praemia aeterna percipere."

109. Also Caesarius, *Serm.* 22.5, SC 243, p. 38: "Et licet haec ita sint, attamen nec peccatores superbi debent desperare, nec humiles iusti in aliquo quasi de suis meritis superbire: quia et iusti si de se praesumpserint, cito perdunt radicem caritatis; et peccatores si ad paenitentiam convertuntur, evulsa cupiditate cito plantam recipiunt caritatis."

110. Caesarius, *Serm.* 14.1, SC 175, pp. 430–32; cf. Caesarius, *Serm.* 56.3, SC

330, p. 16: *vera conversio* is not reliant on change of clothes and hairstyle for penitential garb.

111. E.g., Caesarius, *Serm.* 5.4, SC 175, p. 312 (my emphasis): "Haec ergo diligentius et adtentius cogitet, *qui se in conparatione peiorum minus peccare putat*, et dum adhuc anima ista peccatrix in isto fragili corpuscolo continetur, remedia sibi in aeternum mansura provideat."

112. Caesarius, *Serm.* 43.5, SC 243, p. 318: "'Quare, qui hoc agunt, a communione non suspenduntur?' Ideo enim tantum scelus a sacerdotibus minime vindicatur, quia a multis admittitur."

113. Caesarius, *Serm.* 184.5: "Sed forte dicit aliquis: quid est quod nos tam frequenter de hac re admonet episcopus noster?"; support for the complaint is found, e.g., in Caesarius, *Serm.* 1.12 and 50.1.

114. Augustine, *Serm.* 164.11, ed. Migne, PL 38, col. 900.

115. Caesarius, *Serm.* 43.5, SC 243, p. 318.

116. Caesarius, *Serm.* 42.5, SC 243, pp. 304–5: "Et quia grandis multitudo est, excommunicare omnes non potest episcopus, sed cum gemitu et suspiriis multis tolerat et expectat, si forte pius et misericors Dominus det illis fructuosam poenitentiam per quam possint ad indulgentiam pervenire. Et quia hoc malum in consuetudinem est missum, ut putetur non esse peccatum."

117. Caesarius, *Serm.* 43.5, SC 243, p. 318: "Iam videte, si paenitentiae remedium non subvenerit, quid de illo erit, vel quali sententiae eum necesse erit in futuro iudicio subiacere. . . ."

118. Caesarius, *Serm.* 12.4, SC 175, p. 408: "et dum adhuc anima eius in hoc corpusculo continetur, quicquid in se de supradictis malis aut fuisse aut esse cognoscit, per paenitentiam et elemosinam et praecipue per indulgentiam inimicorum suorum redimere vel emendare festinet."

119. Caesarius, *Serm.* 6.7, SC 175, p. 332: "Primum eradicentur spinae, id est, cogitationes malae. Postea lapides auferantur, hoc est, omnis malitia vel duritia expurgetur. Deinde cor nostrum evangelico aratro et crucis vomere proscindatur et aretur, et confringatur per paenitentiam, molliatur per elemosinam, per caritatem sementi dominicae praeparetur: ut tunc purgata et bene culta cordis nostri terra cum gaudio semen verbi dei possit excipere."

120. W. E. Klingshirn, *Caesarius of Arles: The Making of a Christian Community in Late Antique Gaul* (Cambridge, 1994); Beck, *Pastoral Care of Souls*, 187–222.

121. Caesarius, *Serm.* 59.1, CCL 103, p. 259 ("quomodo enim nobis peccatorum vulnera numquam deesse possunt, sic et confessionis medicamenta deesse non debent"), with commentary at SC 330: 42–43 n. 1; ibid., 162.4, CCL 104, p. 666 ("quomodo non nobis desunt cotidiana peccata, sic per paenitentiam numquam debent deesse cotidiana remedia").

122. Caesarius, *Serm.* 53.3: "Non dicat aliquis, se non fuisse ammonitum. Ecce clamamus, ecce contestamur, ecce praedicamus: nolite contemnere praeconem, si vultis evadere iudicem."

123. Caesarius, *Serm.* 54.1, CCL 103, p. 235–36.

124. Caesarius, *Serm.* 57.1–2, SC 330, pp. 18–22: "Quotiens vobis durum aliquid praedicamus, non hoc ideo dicimus, quod a vobis tale aliquid fieri suspicemur;

sed ideo etiam illa quae non facitis denuntiamus, ut illa, in quibus forte praeventi fueritis, sanare possimus."

125. Caesarius, *Serm.* 12.5, SC 175, p. 410: "Nec iustitiam metuentes de misericordia desperemus, nec sic amemus misericordiam ut iustitiam neglegamus. . . Male sperat, qui se sine paenitentia et bonis operibus putat promereri misericordiam; et male desperat, si post bona opera non se credit recepturum esse misericordiam."

126. Caesarius, *Serm.* 26.1, SC 243, p. 82: "[Fa]ciamus illam [misericordiam] patronam in hoc saeculo, ut nos illa dignetur susceptos habere et defendere in futuro."

127. Caesarius, *Serm.* 12.4, SC 175, p. 406–8 ("unusquisque . . . recurrat ad conscientiam suam").

128. Caesarius, *Serm.* 26.2, SC 243, pp. 82–84: "Omnis homo, fratres dilectissimi, qui causam ante terrenum iudicem se dicturum esse cognoverit, patronos sibi utiles requirit, et advocatos studet peritissimos providere. Et si hoc ille facit, qui ante illum iudicem dicturus est causam, quem et circumvenire, cui et subripere et fallere potest, quem per eloquentiam quibusdam argumentis a iustitia potest avertere, et muneribus forte corrumpere, vel falsis laudibus et fictis adulationibus depravare: si sic se praeparat homo ante hominem causam dicturus, quanto magis nos dicturi causam ante aeternum iudicem, non solum de operibus sed etiam de sermonibus nostris, nec solum de sermonibus sed etiam de cogitationibus, ante illum utique iudicem cui cordis secreta non latent, qui teste non indiget, qui argumenta non quaerit, cuius oculis 'exposita et nuda sunt omnia' (Heb 4:13)? Dicturi ergo causas ante talem iudicem, faciamus nobis patronam misericordiam, ut ipsa causas nostras dicere, immo ipsa pro nobis intercedere dignetur. . . . Si illa nobis cum ibi venerit, ipsa nos de diaboli accusatione defendet, et in aeterna beatitudine introducet."

129. Caesarius, *Serm.* 26.4, SC 243, p. 88: "Et ideo admoneo, fratres, et rogo ac supplicio, ut unusquisque adtendat conscientiam suam, et quia christum ab homine opera mala repellunt, quicquid in se sordidum unusquisque reppererit, per dei adiutorium mundet: quicquid tenebrosum, inluminet: quicquid perditum, reparet: quicquid mortuum, per paenitentiam ipso christo adiuvante resuscitet. . . ."

130. Rebillard, *In hora mortis*; P. Brown, "Vers la naissance du Purgatoire: Amnistie et pénitence dans le christianisme occidental de l'Antiquité tardive au Haut Moyen Âge," *Annales HSS* 52 (1997): 1247–61; Brown, "The Decline of the Empire of God: Amnesty, Penance, and the Afterlife from Late Antiquity to the Middle Ages," in *Last Things: Death and the Apocalypse in the Middle Ages*, ed. C. W. Bynum and P. Freedman (Philadelphia, 2000), 41–59.

131. Brown, *Rise of Western Christendom*, 256.

132. Brown, "*Gloriosus Obitus*," esp. 298–99.

133. I cite from the Paris manuscript: *Visio Pauli* 7, ed. M. R. James, *Apocrypha Anecdota: A Collection of Thirteen Apocryphal Books and Fragments* (Cambridge, 1893), 1–42 at 13; on this text, see M. Himmelfarb, *Tours of Hell: An Apocalyptic Form in Jewish and Christian Literature* (Philadelphia, 1983), 16–19.

134. *Visio Pauli* 11–12, *Apocrypha Anecdota*, p. 15.

135. *Visio Pauli* 33, *Apocrypha Anecdota*, p. 29.

136. The phrase is from de Jong, "Transformations of Penance"; also see Brown, *Rise of Western Christendom*, 255–56.

137. B. Poschmann, *Penance and the Anointing of the Sick*, trans. F. Courtney (New York, 1964): "No amount of pastoral care . . . could make up for the privation of the sacrament" (123).

138. C. Vogel, "La discipline pénitentielle en Gaule des origines au IXe siècle: Le dossier hagiographique," *Revue des sciences religieuses* 30 (1956): 1–26, 157–86 at 23; Vogel, *Pécheur et la pénitence*, 27–28.

139. O. D. Watkins, *History of Penance: Being a Study of the Authorities*, 2 vols., repr. ed. (New York, 1961), 412–13; Orlandis and Ramon-Lissón, *Historia de los concilios*, 61–63.

140. C. Vogel, "Penance," in *Encyclopedia of the Early Church*, ed. A. Di Berardino, trans. A. Walford, 2 vols. (Oxford, 1992), 667.

141. Brown, *Rise of Western Christendom*, 261.

142. Recent scholarship tends to question boundaries in early medieval penance as well; e.g., R. Meens, "The Frequency and Nature of Early Medieval Penance," in *Handling Sin: Confession in the Middle Ages*, ed. P. Biller and A. J. Minnis (Woodbridge, 1998), 35–61 at 54 on later penance ("a mixture of public and private acts"). T. Tentler reacts against such arguments for ambiguity, especially between public and private, in his review of S. Hamilton, *The Practice of Penance, 900–1050* (Woodbridge, 2001) in *The Medieval Review*, 2 July 2002.

Conclusion

1. D. Milbank and J. Weisman, "Conservatives Restive About Bush Policies. Fresh Initiatives Sought On Iraq, Domestic Issues," *Washington Post*, 10 May 2004, A01 (the anonymous commentator was identified as a "veteran of conservative think tanks").

2. É. Rebillard, *In hora mortis: évolution de la pastorale chrétienne de la mort aux IVe et Ve siècles dans l'occident latin* (Rome, 1994), pp. 131–33, 146–48, 225.

3. Victor of Cartenna (5th century), *De paenitentia*, 1, ed. Migne, PL 17, cols. 971–1004: "Et cum quid saeculi iudices confessus mox dirigatur ad poenam, apud Dominum confitens statim pergit ad ueniam."

4. John Cassian (a. 360–435), *Conlationes*, 23.4, ed. and trans. E. Pichery, SC 64 (1959): "Denique sicut bonitas nostra supernae bonitatis intuitu in malitiam uertitur, ita etiam iustitia nostra diuinae conlata iustitae panno menstruatae similis deputatur dicente Esaia propheta (Is 64.6)."

5. Faustus of Riez (active ca. 455–90), *Ep.* "Quaeris a me," ed. B. Krusch, MGH AA 8 (1887), 293: "In homine diversae affectiones, id est iustitia, misericordia, sanctitas, benevolentia, pietas, res accidentes sunt et ideo affectus vocantur, deus vero his non possibiliter afficitur, quia ei inesse iugiter et naturaliter dinoscuntur. Ergo quod in homine affectus et gratia, in deo virtus est et natura"; see *Ruricius of Limoges and Friends: A Collection of Letters from Visigothic Gaul*, trans. R. W. Mathisen, TTH 30 (Liverpool, 1999), 239–40.

6. See recently S. Elm, É. Rebillard, and A. Romano, eds., *Orthodoxie, Christianisme, Histoire*, Collection de l'École Française de Rome 270 (Rome, 2000).

7. Cyprian, *Ep.* 73.21.2, ed. G. F. Diercks, CCL 3C (1996): "salus extra ecclesiam non est."

8. Augustine, *De baptismo contra Donatistas*, 5.38–39, ed. M. Petschenig, CSEL 51 (1908), 143–375; R. Crespin, *Ministère et sainteté: pastorale du clergé et solution de la crise donatiste dans la vie et la doctrine de saint Augustin* (Paris, 1965), 252–61.

9. P. Brown, *Augustine of Hippo: A Biography*, 2nd ed. (Berkeley, Calif., 2000), 492.

Bibliography

Primary Sources

Ambrose. *De bono mortis*. Ed. and trans. William Theodore Wiesner. Washington, D.C.: Catholic University Press of America, 1970.

——. *De fuga saeculi*. Ed. Carolus Schenkl. CSEL 32.2 (1897), 163–207.

——. *De Nabuthae*. Ed. Carolus Schenkl. CSEL 32.2 (1897), 469–516.

——. *De officiis*. Ed. and trans. Ivor J. Davidson. Oxford Early Christian Studies. 2 vols. Oxford: Oxford University Press, 2001.

——. *De uiduis*. Ed. Migne. PL 16, cols. 233–62.

——. *Epistulae*. Ed. Otto Faller and Michaela Zelzer. 4 vols. CSEL 82 (1968–86).

——. *Exameron*. Ed. Carolus Schenkl. CSEL 32.1 (1897), 3–261.

——. *Exhortatio virginitatis*. Ed. Migne. PL 16, cols. 335–64.

——. *Expositio de Psalmo 118*. Ed. Michael Petschenig. CSEL 62 (1913).

——. *Expositio evangelii secundum Lucam*. Ed. M. Adriaen. CCL 14 (1957), 1–400.

Ambrosiaster. *Quaestiones Veteris et Novi Testamenti*. Ed. Alexander Souter. CSEL 1 (1908).

Ammianus Marcellinus. *Rerum Gestarum libri*. Ed. and trans. John C. Rolfe. Loeb 300, 315, 331 (1935–39).

Anonymous Archdeacon of Rome. *Sermones tres de reconciliandis paenitentibus*. Ed. F. Heylen. CCL 9 (1957), 349–63.

Apophthegmata patrum (Greek). Ed. Migne. PG 65, cols. 71–442. English: *The Sayings of the Desert Fathers: The Alphabetical Collection*, trans. Benedicta Ward. Cistercian Studies 59. Rev. ed. Kalamazoo, Mich.: Cistercian Publications, 1984.

Apostolic Constitutions. Ed. and trans. Marcel Metzger. *Les Constitutions apostoliques*. 3 vols. SC 320, 329, 336 (1985–87).

Audoenus. *Vita Eligii*. Ed. B. Krusch. MGH SRM 4 (1902).

Augustine. *Contra Adimantum*. Ed. Joseph Zycha. CSEL 25, 1 (1891), 113–90.

——. *Contra Faustum Manichaeum*. Ed. Joseph Zycha. CSEL 25, 1 (1891), 249–797.

——. *Contra litteras Petiliani*. Ed. Michael Petschenig. CSEL 52 (1909), 1–227.

——. *Confessiones*. Ed. Lucas Verheijen. CCL 27 (1981).

——. *De agone christiano*. Ed. Joseph Zycha. CSEL 41 (1900), 99–138.

——. *De baptismo contra Donatistas*. Ed. Michael Petschenig. CSEL 51 (1908), 143–375.

——. *De beata vita*. Ed. W. M. Green. CCL 29 (1970), 63–85.

——. *De Civitate Dei*. Ed. Bernard Dombart and Alphons Kalb. 2 vols. CCL 47–48 (1955).

——. *De consensu evangelistarum*. Ed. Francis Weihrich. CSEL 43 (1904).

——. *De mendacio*. Ed. Joseph Zycha. CSEL 41 (1900), 411–66.

——. *De sermone Domini in monte*. Ed. Almut Mutzenbecher. CCL 35 (1967).

——. *Enarrationes in psalmos*. Ed. Eligius Dekkers and Johannes Fraipont. 3 vols. CCL 38–40. Rev. ed. (1990).

——. *Epistulae*. Ed. Alois Goldbacher. 4 vols. CSEL 34, 44, 57, 58 (1894–1923). *Lettres 1*–29**, ed. J. Divjak. Bibliothèque Augustinienne 46B (Paris, 1987). English: *Letters Volume VI (1*–29*)*, trans. R. B. Eno. FOC 81 (1989).

——. *Sermones*. Ed. Migne, PL 38–39. Sermons 1–50 = *Sermones de Vetere Testamento*, ed. C. Lambot. CCL 41. Rev. ed. (1997). Sermons 77A, 77B, 229O, 313D: vol. 1, *Miscellanea agostiniana*, ed. Germain Morin. (Rome, 1930). Sermons 224, 229P: Cyril Lambot, ed. *Revue Bénédictine* 79 (1969): 193–205; ibid. 49 (1937): 252–57. Mayence Sermons = *Vingt-six sermons au peuple d'Afrique*, ed. François Dolbeau. Collection des Études Augustiniennes. Série Antiquité 147. Paris: Institut d'Études augustiniennes, 1996.

Avitus of Vienne. *Epistulae*. Ed. Rudolph Peiper. MGH AA 6.2 (1883), 35–103. English: *Avitus of Vienne: Letters and Selected Prose*, trans. D. Shanzer and I. Wood. TTH 38 (2001).

Basil. *Epistulae*. Ed. and trans. Roy J. Deferrari. 4 vols. Loeb 190, 215, 243, 270 (1926–34).

——. *Homilia in divites = Homilia 7*. In *Homélies sur la richesse*. Ed. and trans. Yves Courtonne. Paris: Firmin-Didot, 1935: 39–71.

Caesarius of Arles. *Sermones*. Ed. Germain Morin. 2 vols. CCL 103–4 (1953). French: *Sermons au peuple*, trans. Marie-José Delage. SC 175, 243, 330 (1971–1986). English: *Sermons*, trans. Mary Magdeleine Mueller. 3 vols. FOC 31, 47, 66 (1956–73).

Cassian. *Conlationes*. Ed. and trans. E. Pichery. SC 64 (1959).

Cassiodorus. *Expositio Psalmorum*. Ed. M. Adriaen. CCL 97 (1958).

Chromatius. *Tractatus*. Ed. R. Étaix and J. Lemarié. 2 vols. CCL 9A (1974, 1977). French: *Chromace d'Aquilée: Sermons*, trans. Henri Tardif. 2 vols. SC 154, 164 (1969, 1971).

Cicero. *De officiis*. Ed. Michael Winterbottom. Oxford Classical Texts. Oxford: Oxford University Press, 1994.

Concilia Africae. a. 345–a. 525. Ed. Charles Munier. CCL 149 (1974).

Concilia Galliae. a. 314–a. 506. Ed. Charles Munier. CCL 148 (1963). *Concilia Galliae, a. 511–a. 695*. Ed. C. de Clercq. CCL 148A (1963). French: *Conciles gaulois du IVe siècle*, trans. Jean Gaudemet. SC 241 (1977). *Les canons des conciles mérovingiens (VIe–VIIe siècles)*, trans. Jean Gaudemet and Brigitte Basdevant. 2 vols. SC 353–54 (1989).

Concilios Visigóticos e Hispano-Romanos. Ed. and trans. José Vives, Tomás Marín Martínez, and Gonzalo Martínez Díez. Barcelona: Consejo Superior de Investigaciones Científicas, 1963.

Conciliorum oecumenicorum decreta. Ed. Giuseppe Alberigo. 3rd ed. Bologna: Istituto per le scienze religiose, 1973.

Constantius of Lyon. *Vita Germani*. Ed. Wilhelm Levison. MGH SRM 7 (1920), 247–83. French: *Vie de Saint Germain d'Auxerre*, trans. René Borius. SC 112 (1965).

Cyprian. *Epistulae*. Ed. G. F. Diercks. 2 vols. CCL 3B–3C (1994–96).

Defensor. *Liber scintillarum*. Ed. H. M. Rochais. CCL 117 (1957).

Didascalia Apostolorum: The Syriac Version Translated and Accompanied by the Verona Latin Fragments. Ed. R. Hugh Connolly. Oxford: Clarendon Press, 1969.

Didascalia et constitutiones apostolorum. Ed. F. X. Funk. Vol. 1. Paderborn: Shoeningh, 1905.

Didascaliae Apostolorum, canonum ecclesiasticorum, traditionis apostolicae versiones latinae. Ed. Erik Tidner. Berlin: Akademie Verlag, 1963.

Dionysius Exiguus. *Praefationes latinae genuinae in variis suis translationibus ex graeco*. Ed. F. Glorie in *Scriptores 'Illyrici' Minores*, CCL 85 (1972), 33–81.

Eligius of Noyon. *Sermo de supremo iudicio*. Ed.Bruno Krusch. MGH SRM 4 (1902), 749–61.

Ennodius of Pavia. *Vita Epifani*. Ed. Friedrich Vogel. *Magni Felicis Ennodi opera*. MGH AA 7 (1885), 84–109. English: Roy J. Deferrari in *Early Christian Biographies*. FOTC 15 (1952), 301–51.

Epistola Romani concilii sub Damaso habiti ("Et hoc gloriae"). Ed. Migne, PL 13, cols. 575D–584B.

Epistulae Austrasiacae. Ed. Wilhelm Gundlach. MGH Epist. 3 (1892), 110–53.

Faustus of Riez. *Epistulae*. Ed. Bruno Krusch. MGH AA 8 (1887), 265–98.

Fulgentius. *De remissione peccatorum ad Euthymium*. Ed. Johannes Fraipont. *Opera*. CCL 91–91A (1968), 2:649–707.

Gerontius. *Vie de sainte Mélanie*. Edited and trans. D. Gorce. SC 90 (1962). English: *Life of Melania the Younger*, trans. Elizabeth A. Clark. Studies in Women and Religion 14. New York: E. Mellen Press, 1984. Latin version: *Gérontius, La Vie Latine de Sainte Mélanie*, ed. P. Laurence. Studium Biblicum Franciscanum Collectio Minor 41. Jerusalem: Franciscan Printing Press, 2002.

Gesta conlationis Carthaginiensis, anno 411. Ed. Serge Lancel. CCL 149A (1974).

Gregory of Nazianzus. *Orationes. Grégoire de Nazianze: Discours 1–3*. Ed. and trans. Jean Bernardi. SC 247 (1978).

Gregory of Nyssa. *Vita Gregorii Thaumaturgi*. Ed. Migne, PG 46, cols. 893–957. English: *St. Gregory Thaumaturgus: Life and Works*, trans. Michael Slusser. FOC 98 (1998), 41–90.

Gregory of Tours. *De virtutibus sancti Martini*. Ed. Bruno Krusch. MGH SRM 1.2 (1885), 584–661.

———. *Gloria confessorum*. Ed. Bruno Krusch. MGH SRM 1.2 (1885), 744–820. English: *Glory of the Confessors*, trans. Raymond Van Dam. TTH 4 (1988).

———. *Gloria martyrum*. Ed. Bruno Krusch. MGH SRM 1.2 (1885), 484–561. English: *Glory of the Martyrs*, tran. Raymond Van Dam. TTH 3 (1988).

———. *Historiarum libri X*. Ed. Bruno Krusch and Wilhelm Levison. MGH SRM 1.1. Rev. ed. 1937–51.

———. *Vita patrum*. Ed. Bruno Krusch. MGH SRM 1.2 (1885), 661–744. English: *Life of the Fathers*, trans. E. James. 2nd ed. TTH 1 (1991).

Gregory the Great. *Homiliae in Hiezechielem*. Ed. and trans. Charles Morel. 2 vols. SC 327, 360 (1986, 1990).

———. *Moralia in Iob*. Ed, Marc Adriaen. 2 vols. CCL 143–143A (1979, 1985).

———. *Regula pastoralis*. Ed. and trans. Bruno Judic, Floribert Rommel, and Charles Morel. 2 vols. SC 381–82 (1992).

Hilary of Poitiers. *Tractatus super psalmos*. Ed, Jean Doignon. CCL 61 (1997).

Hilary of Poitiers (pseudo). *Metrum in Genesim*. Ed. Rudolf Peiper. CSEL 23.1 (1891), 1–208.

Hippolytus. *Traditio Apostolica*. Ed. and trans. Bernard Botte. 2nd ed. SC 11bis (1968).

Honoratus of Marseille. *Vita Hilarii Arelatensis*. Ed. Paul-André Jacob. SC 404 (1995).

Ignatius of Antioch. *Epistula ad Magnesios*. In vol. 1, *The Apostolic Fathers*, ed. and trans. Bart D. Ehrman. Loeb 24 (2003), 240–55.

Innocent I. *Epistulae*. Ed. Migne, PL 20, cols. 463–608.

Jerome. *Commentarii in Ezechielem*. Ed. F. Glorie, CCL 75 (1964).

——. *Commentarii in Evangelium Matthaei*. Ed. D. Hurst and M. Adriaen, CCL 77 (1969).

——. *Epistulae*. Ed. and trans. Jérôme Labourt. *Lettres*. 8 vols. Paris: Les Belles Lettres, 1949–63. English: *Select Letters*. Ed. and trans. F. A. Wright. Loeb 262 (1933).

——. *In Hieremiam prophetam*. Ed. Siegfried Reiter. CCL 74 (1961).

John Chrysostom. *De sacerdote*. Ed. and trans. A. Malingrey. SC 272 (1980).

Jonas of Bobbio. *Vita Columbani*. Ed. Bruno Krusch. MGH SRG 37 (1905), 144–294.

Julian Pomerius. *De vita contemplativa*. Ed. Migne, PL 59, cols. 415–520.

Juvencus. *Evangeliorum libri quattuor*. Ed.J. Huemer. CSEL 24 (1891).

Lactantius. *Divinae institutiones*. Ed. and trans. P. Monat. 2 vols. SC 204–5 (1973). English: *Divine Institutes*, trans. Anthony Bowen and Peter Garnsey. TTH 40 (2003).

Leo I. *Epistulae*. Ed. Migne, PL 54, cols. 593–1218.

——. *Sermones*. Ed. Antoine Chavasse. 2 vols. CCL 138–138A (1973). French: trans. René Dolle. 2nd ed. 4 vols. SC 22bis, 49bis, 74, 200 (1964–73).

Liber Sacramentorum Gellonensis. Ed. Antoine Dumas. 2 vols. CCL 159–159A (1981).

Life of Pachomius (Vita Prima Graeca). Trans. A. N. Athanassakis. Society of Biblical Literature Texts and Translations 7, Early Christian Literature Series 2. Missoula, Mont.: Scholars Press, 1975; also in *Pachomian Koinonia I: The Life of Saint Pachomius and his Disciples*, trans. A. Veilleux. Cistercian Studies 45. Kalamazoo, Mich.: Cistercian Publications, 1980.

Lives of the Monks of Palestine. Trans. R. M. Price; intro.J. Binns. Cistercian Studies 114. Kalamazoo, Mich.: Cistercian Publications, 1991.

Novatian. *De bono pudicitiae*. Ed. G. F. Diercks. CCL 4 (1972). English: trans. Russell J. DeSimone. FOC 67 (1972).

Orosius. *Historiae adversum paganos*. Ed. Charles Zangemeister. CSEL 5 (1882).

Pacian. *Sermo de paenitentibus*. Ed. Carmelo Granado; trans. Chantal Epitalon and Michel Lestienne. *Écrits*. SC 410 (1995).

Palladius. *Dialogus de vita Iohannis Chrysostomi*. Ed. and trans. Anne-Marie Malingrey and Philippe Leclercq. *Dialogue sur la vie de Jean Chrysostome*. 2 vols. SC 341–42 (1988).

Passio Praiecti. Ed. Bruno Krusch. MGH SRM 5 (1910), 225–48. English: *Late Merovingian France: History and Hagiography, 640–720*, trans. P. Fouracre and R. A. Gerberding. Manchester Medieval Sources Series. Manchester: Manchester University Press, 1996: 254–300.

Paulinus of Nola. *Carmina*. Ed. Wilhelm de Hartel. CSEL 30 (1894), 1–338.

Paulinus of Pella. *Vita Ambrosii*. Ed. A. A. R. Bastiaensen; intro. C. Mohrmann; trans. L. Canali. *Vita di Ambrogio*. Vite dei Santi 3. Milan: Mondadori, 1975.

Pelagius (pseudo). *Epistula ad virginem devotam*. Ed. Migne, PL 17, cols. 579–84. English: Rees, *Pelagius: Life and Letters*, 338–44.

Pelagius. *Ep. ad Celentiam matronam*. Ed. Migne, PL 22, cols. 1204–29. English: Rees, *Pelagius: Life and Letters*, 127–44.

———. *Ep. ad Demetriadem*. Ed. Migne, PL 30, cols. 15–45. English: Rees, *Pelagius: Life and Letters*, 29–70.

Peter Chrysologus. *Sermones*. Ed. Alexandre Olivar. 3 vols. CCL 24–24B (1975–82).

Possidius. *Vita s. Augustini*. Ed. A. A. R. Bastiaensen; intro C. Mohrmann; trans. L. Canali. *Vita di Agostino*. Vite dei Santi 3. Milan: Mondadori, 1975. English: in *Soldiers of Christ: Saints and Saints' Lives from Late Antiquity and the Early Middle Ages*, trans. F. R. Hoare, ed. Thomas F. X. Noble and Thomas Head, 31–73. University Park: Pennsylvania State University Press, 1995.

Priscillian of Avila. *Tractatus*. Ed. Georg Schepss. CSEL 18 (1889), 3–106.

Priscus. *Fragmenta*. Trans. Colin D. Gordon in *The Age of Attila: Fifth-Century Byzantium and the Barbarians*. Ann Arbor: University of Michigan Press, 1960.

Proba. *Cento virgilianus (Carmen Sacrum)*. Ed. Karl Schenkl. CSEL 16 (1888), 569–609.

Protoevangelium of James. In *The Infancy Gospels of James and Thomas*, by Ronald F. Hock. Scholars Bible 2. Santa Rosa, Calif.: Polebridge Press: 32–77.

Pseudo-Cyprianus. *De XII abusivis saeculi*. Ed. Siegmund Hellman. Texte und Untersuchungen zur Geschichte der altchristlichen Literatur 34.1. Leipzig: Hinrichs, 1910.

Rufinus of Aquileia. *Historia ecclesiastica*. Ed. Migne, PL 21, cols. 465–540.

———. *Historia monachorum*. Ed. Migne, PL 21, cols. 387–462.

Ruricius of Limoges. *Epistulae*. Ed. Bruno Krusch. MGH AA 8 (1887), 299–350. English: *Ruricius of Limoges and Friends: A Collection of Letters from Visigothic Gaul*, trans. Ralph W. Mathisen, TTH 30 (1999).

Salvian of Marseille. *Epistulae*. Ed. and trans. George Lagarrigue. *Œuvres*. 2 vols. SC 176, 220 (1971, 1974), 1: 76–133.

Sidonius. *Epistulae*. Ed. André Loyen. Collection des Universités de France. 2 vols. Paris: Les Belles Lettres, 1970.

Socrates Scholasticus. *Historia ecclesiastica*. Ed. G. C. Hansen. *Kirchengeschichte*. Die griechischen christlichen Schriftsteller der ersten Jahrhunderte, Neue Folge 1. Berlin, 1995. French: book 1, *Histoire ecclésiastique*, trans. Pierre Périchon and Pierre Maraval. SC 477 (2004).

Sozomen. *Historia ecclesiastica*. Ed. J. Bidez. Trans. André-Jean Festugière. 2 vols. SC 306, 418 (1983, 1996).

Statuta Ecclesiae Antiqua. Ed. Charles Munier. Paris: Presses universitaires de France, 1960.

Sulpicius Severus. *Vita Martini Turonensis*. Ed. and trans. Jacques Fontaine. 3 vols. SC 133–35 (1967–69).

Tertullian. *Apologeticum*. Ed. Eligius Dekkers. CCL 1 (1954), 77–171.

Themistius. *Orationes*. Ed. H. Schenkl, G. Downey, and A. F. Norman. 3 vols. Leipzig: Teubner, 1965–74.

Vegetius. *Epitoma rei militari*. Ed. M. D. Reeve. Oxford: Oxford University Press, 2004.

Venantius Fortunatus. *Carmina*. Ed. and trans. Marc Reydellet. 3 vols. Paris: Les Belles Lettres, 1994–2004.

Verecundus. *Commentarii super cantica ecclesiastica*. Ed. R. Demeulenaere, CCL 93 (1976), 3–203.

Verus. *Vita Eutropii*, AASS May VI (27 May), 700F–701E. Also *Gallia Christiana novissima*, ed. J. H. Albanés and U. Chevalier, 6:10–18. Montebéliard: Société anonyme, 1916.

Victor of Cartenna. *De paenitentia*. Ed. Migne, PL 17, cols. 971–1004.

Victricius. *De laude sanctorum*. Ed. I. Mulders and R. Demeulenaere. CCL 64 (1985), 69–93. English: Gillian Clark, "Victricius of Rouen: *Praising the Saints*," JECS 7, 3 (1999): 365–99.

Virgil. *Georgics*. Ed. R. A. B. Mynors. *Opera*. Oxford: Clarendon Press, 1969.

Visio Pauli. In *Apocrypha Anecdota: A Collection of Thirteen Apocryphal Books and Fragments*, ed. Montague Rhodes James. Cambridge: Cambridge University Press, 1893: 1–42.

Vita S. Marcellini episcopi Ebredunensis, AASS April II, 749–51.

SECONDARY SOURCES

Adams, J. N. "British Latin: The Text, Interpretation and Language of the Bath Curse Tablets." *Britannia* 23 (1992): 1–26.

Adkins, N. "A Problem in the Early Church: Noise during Sermon and Lesson." *Mnemosyne* 4th ser. 38 (1985): 161–63.

Adnès, Pierre. "Pénitence." In *Dictionnaire de Spiritualité* 14, cols. 943–1010. Paris: Beauchesne, 1984.

Allen, Pauline and Wendy Mayer. "Through a Bishop's Eyes: Towards a Definition of Pastoral Care in Late Antiquity." *Augustinianum* 4, 2 (2000): 345–97.

Anderson, Gary A. and Michael E. Stone, eds. *A Synopsis of the Books of Adam and Eve*. Atlanta: Scholars Press, 1994.

Angenendt, Arnold. *Frühmittelalter: Die abendländische Christenheit von 400–900*. 2nd ed. Stuttgart: Kohlhammer, 1995.

Anton, H. H. "Pseudo-Cyprian, De duodecim abusivis saeculi und sein Einfluß auf den Kontinent, insbesonders auf die karolingischen Fürstenspiegel." In *Die Iren und Europa im früheren Mittelalter*, ed. H. Löwe. Veröffentlichungen des Europa Zentrums Tübingen, Kulturwissenschaftliche Reihe. 2 vols. Stuttgart: Klett-Cotta, 1982.

Assman, Jan. "When Justice Fails: Jurisdiction and Imprecation in Ancient Egypt and the Near East." *Journal of Egyptian Archaeology* 78 (1992): 149–62.

Bagnall, Roger S. *Egypt in Late Antiquity*. Princeton, N.J.: Princeton University Press, 1993.

Barcellona, Rossana. "La questione antropologica nell'epistolario di Fausto di Riez: la penitenza, l'anima, la salvezza." *Cassiodorus* 4 (1998): 83–123.

Barnard, L. "The Criminalization of Heresy in the Later Roman Empire: A Sociopolitical Device?" *Journal of Legal History* 16 (1995): 121–46.

Barnish, S. J. B. "The Work of Cassiodorus After His Conversion." *Latomus* 48 (1989): 157–87.

Bartelink, G. "Fragilitas (infirmitas) humana chez Augustin." In *Collectanea Augustiniana: Mélanges T. J. van Bavel*, ed. B. Bruning, M. Lamberigts, and J. van Houten. 2 vols. Leuven: University Press, 1991. 2: 815–28.

Bartlett, Robert. *Trial by Fire and Water: The Medieval Judicial Ordeal.* Oxford: Oxford University Press, 1986.

Baynes, Norman H. *Byzantine Studies and Other Essays.* London: University of London Press, 1955.

Beare, Rhona. "The Meaning of the Oath by the Safety of the Roman Emperor." *American Journal of Philology* 99, 1 (1978): 106–10.

Beaucamp, Joëlle. *Le statut de la femme à Byzance (4e–7e siècle).* Travaux et Mémoire du centre de Recherche d'Histoire et Civilisation de Byzance, Monographies 5. 2 vols. Paris: De Boccard, 1990–92.

Becher, Matthias. *Eid und Herrschaft: Untersuchungen zum Herrscherethos Karls des Großen.* Vorträge und Forschungen 39. Sigmaringen: Thorbecke, 1993.

Beck, Henry G. J. *The Pastoral Care of Souls in South-East France During the Sixth Century.* Analecta Gregoriana 51. Rome: Gregorian University, 1950.

Bellentani, F. "*Episcopus . . . est nomen suscepti officii*: Il vocabolario del servizio episcopale in alcuni testi agostiniani." In *Vescovi e pastori in epoca teodosiana*, 667–81. Studia ephemeridis Augustinianum 58. 2 vols. Rome: Institutum Patristicum Augustinianum, 1997.

Berger, Adolf. *Encyclopedic Dictionary of Roman Law.* Philadelphia: American Philosophical Society, 1953.

Binns, John. *Ascetics and Ambassadors of Christ: The Monasteries of Palestine, 314–631.* Oxford: Oxford University Press, 1994.

Boehden, Christiane. "Der Susannensarkophag von Gerona: Ein Versuch zur typologischen Deutung des Susannenzyklus." *Römische Quartalschrift für christliche Altertumskunde und Kirchengeschichte* 89 (1994): 1–25.

Boswell, John. *The Kindness of Strangers: The Abandonment of Children in Western Europe from Late Antiquity to the Renaissance.* New York: Pantheon Books, 1988.

Bourdieu, Pierre. *Distinction: A Social Critique of the Judgement of Taste.* Trans. R. Nice. Cambridge, Mass.: Harvard University Press, 1984.

Bowman, Jeffrey A. *Shifting Landmarks: Property, Proof, and Dispute in Catalonia around the Year 1000.* Ithaca, N.Y.: Cornell University Press, 2004.

Bradshaw, Paul F. *Daily Prayer in the Early Church: A Study of the Origin and Early Development of the Divine Office.* New York: Oxford University Press, 1981.

Brakke, David. *Athanasius and the Politics of Asceticism.* Oxford Early Christian Studies. Oxford: Oxford University Press, 1995.

Breen, Aidan. "The Date, Provenance and Authorship of the Pseudo-Patrician Canonical Materials." *ZRG KA* 81 (1995): 83–129.

———. "*De XII Abusiuis*: Text and Transmission." In *Ireland and Europe in the Early Middle Ages: Texts and Transmission*, ed. P. Ní Chatháin and M. Richter Dublin: Four Courts Press, 1998. 78–94.

Brennan, Brian. "'Being Martin': Saint and Successor in Sixth-Century Tours." *Journal of Religious History* 21, 2 (1997): 121–35.

Brown, Peter. "Asceticism: Pagan and Christian." In *CAH* 13, 601–31.

———. *Authority and the Sacred: Aspects of the Christianisation of the Roman World*. Cambridge: Cambridge University Press, 1995.

———. *The Body and Society: Men, Women and Sexual Renunciation in Early Christianity*. New York: Columbia University Press, 1988.

———. *The Cult of the Saints: Its Rise and Function in Latin Christianity*. Chicago: University of Chicago Press, 1981.

———. "The Decline of the Empire of God: Amnesty, Penance, and the Afterlife from Late Antiquity to the Middle Ages." In *Last Things: Death and the Apocalypse in the Middle Ages*, ed. Caroline Walker Bynum and Paul Freedman. Philadelphia: University of Pennsylvania Press, 2000. 41–59.

———. "Enjoying the Saints in Late Antiquity." *Early Medieval Europe* 9, 1 (2000): 1–24.

———. "*Gloriosus Obitus*: The End of the Ancient Other World." In *The Limits of Ancient Christianity: Essays on Late Antique Thought and Culture in Honor of R. A. Markus*, ed. William E. Klingshirn and Mark Vessey. Ann Arbor: University of Michigan Press, 1999. 289–314.

———. *Making of Late Antiquity*. Carl Newell Jackson Lectures. Cambridge, Mass.: Harvard University Press, 1978.

———. *Poverty and Leadership in the Later Roman Empire*. Menahem Stern Jerusalem Lectures. Hanover, N.H.: University Press of New England, 2002.

———. *Power and Persuasion in Late Antiquity: Towards a Christian Empire*. Madison: University of Wisconsin Press, 1992.

———. *Religion and Society in the Age of Saint Augustine*. New York: Harper and Row, 1972.

———. "Religious Coercion in the Later Roman Empire: The Case of North Africa." *History* 48 (1963): 283–305. Reprinted in *Religion and Society in the Age of Saint Augustine*, 301–31.

———. *The Rise of Western Christendom*. 2nd ed. Oxford: Blackwell, 2003.

———. "The Saint as Exemplar in Late Antiquity." *Representations* 1, 2 (1983): 1–25. Reprinted in *Saints and Virtues*, ed. John Stratton Hawley. Berkeley: University of California Press, 1987. 3–14.

———. *Society and the Holy in Late Antiquity*. Berkeley: University of California Press, 1982).

———. "The Study of Elites in Late Antiquity." *Arethusa* 33 (2000): 321–46.

———. "Vers la naissance du Purgatoire: Amnistie et pénitence dans le christianisme occidental de l'Antiquité tardive au Haut Moyen Age." *Annales HSS* 52 (1997): 1247–61.

Brown, Warren. *Unjust Seizure: Conflict, Interest, and Authority in an Early Medieval Society*. Ithaca, N.Y.: Cornell University Press, 2001.

Browne, Gerald M. "The Origin and Date of the *Sortes Astrampsychi*." *Illinois Classical Studies* 1 (1976): 53–58.

———. *The Papyri of the Sortes Astrampsychi*. Beiträge zur klassichen Philologie 58. Meisenheim-am-Glan: Verlag Anton Hain, 1974.

———, ed. *Sortes Astrampsychi*. 2 vols. Leipzig: Teubner, 1983, 2001.

Bruckner, Matilda Tomaryn, Laurie Shepard, and Sarah White, eds. *Songs of the Women Troubadours*. Rev. ed. New York and London: Garland, 2000.

Brundage, James A. *Law, Sex, and Christian Society in Medieval Europe*. Chicago: University of Chicago Press, 1987.

Buc, Philippe. *The Dangers of Ritual: Between Early Medieval Texts and Social Scientific Theory*. Princeton, N.J.: Princeton University Press, 2001.

Burns, Thomas S. *Barbarians within the Gates of Rome: A Study of Roman Military Policy and the Barbarians, ca. 375–425 A.D.* Bloomington: Indiana University Press, 1994.

Burrus, Virgina. "Priscillianist Duplicity Reconsidered." *Studia Patristica* 33 (1997): 401–6.

Burton-Christie, Douglas. *The Word in the Desert: Scripture and the Quest for Holiness in Early Christian Monasticism*. New York: Oxford University Press, 1993.

Bury, J. B. *The Invasion of Europe by the Barbarians*. Ed. F. J. C. Hearnshaw. New York: Norton, 2000.

Bussini, François. "L'intervention de l'assemblée des fideles au moment de la réconciliation des pénitents d'après les trois 'Postulationes' d'un archidiacre romain du Ve-VIe siècle." *Revue des sciences religieuses* 41 (1967): 29–38.

Caciola, Nancy. *Discerning Spirits: Divine and Demonic Possession in the Middle Ages*, Conjunctions of Religion & Power in the Medieval Past. Ithaca, N.Y.: Cornell University Press, 2003.

Camiñas, J. G. "Le *crimen calumniae* dans la *lex Remmia de calumniatoribus*." *Revue internationale des droits de l'antiquité* 3rd ser. 37 (1990): 117–33.

———. *Ensayo de reconstrucción del título IX del Edicto Perpetuo*: de calumniatoribus. Santiago de Compostela, 1994.

———. "Régimen jurídico del *iusiurandum calumniae*." *Studia et Documenta Historiae et Iuris* 60 (1994): 457–68.

Campbell, J. B. *The Emperor and the Roman Army, 31 BC-AD 235*. Oxford: Oxford University Press, 1984.

Campenhausen, Hans von. *Ecclesiastical Authority and Spiritual Power in the Church of the First Three Centuries*. Trans. J. A. Basker. Stanford, Calif.: Stanford University Press, 1969.

Castillo, C. "El nuevo juramento a Augusto encontrado en la Bética." In *L'Afrique, le Gaule, la religion à l'époque romaine*, ed. Yann Le Bohec. Collection Latomus 226. Brussels, 1994. 681–86.

Cecconi, Giovanni Alberto. "Un evergete mancato: Piniano a Ippona." *Athenaeum* 66 (1988): 371–89.

Chadwick, Henry. *Priscillian of Avila: The Occult and the Charismatic in the Early Church*. Oxford: Oxford University Press, 1976.

———. *The Role of the Christian Bishop in Ancient Society: Protocol of the Thirty-Fifth Colloquy, 25 February 1979*. Ed. Edward C. Hobbs and Wilhelm Wuellner. Berkeley: University of California Press, 1980.

Chaniotis, Angelos. "Conflicting Authorities: Asylia Between Secular and Divine Law in the Classical and Hellenistic Poleis." *Kernos* 9 (1996), 65–86.

———. "Illness and Cures in the Greek Propitiatory Inscriptions and Dedications of Lydia and Phrygia." In *Ancient Medicine in Its Socio-Cultural Context*, ed. P. H. van der Eijk, H. F. J. Horstmanshoff, and P. H. Schrijvers, 2 vols. Amsterdam: Rodopi, 1995. 2: 323–44.

———. "Watching a Lawsuit: A New Curse Tablet from Southern Russia." *Greek, Roman, and Byzantine Studies* 33 (1992): 69–73.

Chartier, Roger. *On the Edge of the Cliff: History, Language, and Practices.* Trans. L. G. Cochrane. Baltimore, Md.: Johns Hopkins University Press, 1997.

Charvet, Louis. "Les serments contre la calomnie dans la procédure au temps de Justinien." *Revue des Études Byzantines* 8 (1950–51): 130–42.

Cheyette, Fredric. "Women, Poets, and Politics in Occitania." In *Aristocratic Women in Medieval France*, ed. Theodore Evergates, 138–77. Philadelphia: University of Pennsylvania Press, 1999.

Cimma, Maria Rosa. *L'episcopalis audientia nelle costituzioni imperiali da Costantino a Giustiniano.* Turin: Giapichelli, 1989.

Clark, Elizabeth A. *Reading Renunciation: Asceticism and Scripture in Early Christianity.* Princeton, N.J.: Princeton University Press, 1999.

Clark, Elizabeth A. and Diane F. Hatch. *The Golden Bough, the Oaken Cross: The Virgilian Cento of Faltonia Betitia Proba.* American Academy of Religion, Texts and Translations Series 5. Chico, Calif.: Scholars Press 1981.

Clark, Gillian. *Women in Late Antiquity: Pagan and Christian Lifestyles.* Oxford: Oxford University Press, 1993.

Coates, Simon. "Venantius Fortunatus and the Image of Episcopal Authority in Late Antique and Early Merovingian Gaul," *English Historical Review* 115 (2000), 1109–37.

Conybeare, Catherine. *Paulinus Noster: Self and Symbols in the Letters of Paulinus of Nola*, Oxford Early Christian Studies. Oxford: Oxford University Press, 2000.

Cook, Karen S., ed. *Trust in Society.* Russell Sage Foundation Series on Trust 2. New York: Russell Sage Foundation, 2001.

Cooper, Kate and Jeremy Gregory, eds. *Retribution, Repentance, and Reconciliation.* Studies in Church History 40. Woodbridge: Boydell, 2004.

Corcoran, Simon. *Empire of the Tetrarchs: Imperial Pronouncements and Government, AD 284–324.* Oxford Classical Monographs. Rev. ed. Oxford: Oxford University Press, 2000.

Courcelle, Pierre. *Les 'Confessions' de saint Augustine dans la tradition littéraire: antécédents et postérité.* Paris: Études augustiniennes, 1963.

———. *Connais-toi toi-même, de Socrate à saint Bernard.* 3 vols. Paris: Études augustiniennes, 1974–75.

———. *Recherches sur les Confessions de Saint Augustin.* 2nd ed. Paris: Éditions de Boccard, 1968.

Crawford, M. H., ed. *Roman Statutes.* 2 vols. BICS Supplement 64. London: Institute of Classical Studies, 1996.

Crehan, Joseph. *Early Christian Baptism and the Creed: A Study in Ante-Nicene Theology*, Bellarmine Series 13. London: Burns, Oates & Washbourne, 1950.

Crespin, Remi. *Ministère et sainteté: pastorale du clergé et solution de la crise donatiste dans la vie et la doctrine de saint Augustin.* Paris: Études augustiniennes, 1965.

Crook, J. A. *Law and Life of Rome, 90 B.C.–A.D. 212.* Ithaca, N.Y.: Cornell University Press, 1967.

———. *Legal Advocacy in the Roman World.* Ithaca, N.Y.: Cornell University Press, 1995.

Cross, F. L. "History and Fiction in the African Canons," *Journal of Theological Studies* n.s. 12 (1961): 227–47.

Curran, John R. *Pagan City and Christian Capital: Rome in the Fourth Century.* Oxford Classical Monographs. Oxford: Oxford University Press, 2000.

Cutrone, E. J. "Sacraments," in *Augustine Through the Ages: An Encyclopedia,* ed. A. D. Fitzgerald. Grand Rapids, Mich., 1999. 741–47.

Dagemark, Siver. "Examples of *excommunicatio, paenitentia* and *reconciliatio* in the African Councils." In *I Concili della cristianità occidentale secoli III–V.* Studia Ephemeridis Augustinianum 78. Rome: Institutum patristicum Augustinianum, 2002. 167–234.

Davidson, Ivor J. "Staging the Church? Theology as Theater," JECS 8, 3 (2000): 413–51.

Davies, Wendy and Paul Fouracre, eds. *The Settlement of Disputes in Early Medieval Europe.* Cambridge: Cambridge University Press, 1986.

De Jong, Mayke. "Transformations of Penance." In *Rituals of Power from Late Antiquity to the Early Middle Ages,* ed. Frans Theuws and Janet L. Nelson. Leiden: E.J. Brill, 2000. 185–224.

———. "What Was Public About Public Penance? *Paenitentia Publica* and Justice in the Carolingian World." In *La giustizia nell'alto medioevo (secoli IX–XI).* Spoleto: Centro Italiano di Studi sull'Alto Medioevo, 1997. 2: 863–904.

Demacopoulos, G. E. *Five Models of Spiritual Direction in the Early Church.* Notre Dame, Ind.: University of Notre Dame Press, 2006.

———. "A Monk in Shepherd's Clothing: Pope Gregory I and the Asceticizing of Pastoral Direction." Ph.D. dissertation, University of North Carolina at Chapel Hill, 2002.

de Nie, Giselle. "Poetics of Wonder: Dream-Consciousness and Transformational Dynamics in Sixth-Century Miracle Stories," reprinted in *Word, Image and Experience: Dynamics of Miracle and Self-Perception in Sixth-Century Gaul.* Aldershot, U.K.: Ashgate, 2003.

Derret, J. Duncan M. "Law in the New Testament: The Story of the Woman Taken in Adultery." *New Testament Studies* 10 (1964): 1–26.

Dodaro, Robert. *Christ and the Just Society in the Thought of Augustine.* Cambridge: Cambridge University Press, 2004.

Dold, Alban with Richard Meister. *Die Orakelsprüche im St. Galler Palimpsestcodex 908 (die sogenannten "Sortes Sangallenses").* Österreichische Akademie der Wissenschaften, Philosophisch-historische Klasse 225, 4. Vienna: R.M. Rohrer, 1948.

Donne, John. *The Sermons.* Ed. George R. Potter and Evelyn M. Simpson. 10 vols. Berkeley: University of California Press, 1953–62.

Dossey, Leslie. "Judicial Violence and the Ecclesiastical Courts in Late Antique North Africa." In *Law, Society and Authority in Late Antiquity,* ed. Ralph W. Mathisen. Oxford: Oxford University Press, 2001. 98–114.

Drake, H. A. *Constantine and the Bishops: The Politics of Intolerance.* Baltimore, Md.: Johns Hopkins University Press, 2000.

Ducloux, Anne. *Ad ecclesiam confugere: naissance du droit d'asile dans les églises (IVe–milieu du Ve s.* Paris: De Boccard, 1994.

Dumville, David N. "The Idea of Government in Sub-Roman Britain." In *After Empire: Towards an Ethnology of Europe's Barbarians*, ed. G. Ausenda. Woodbridge: Boydell, 1995. 177–216.

Dupont, C. "La procédure civile dans les constitutions de Constantin: traits caractéristiques." *Revue internationale des droits de l'antiquité* 3rd ser. 21 (1974): 191–213.

Elm, Susanna. "An Alleged Book-Theft in Fourth-Century Egypt: P. Lips. 43." *Studia Patristica* 18 (1989): 209–15.

——. "Orthodoxy and the True Philosophical Life: Julian and Gregory of Nazianzus." *Studia Patristica* 37 (2001): 69–85.

——. *"Virgins of God": The Making of Asceticism in Late Antiquity*. Oxford Classical Monographs. Oxford: Oxford University Press, 1994.

Esders, Stefan. "Rechtsdenken und Traditionsbewusstsein in der gallischen Kirche zwischen Spätantike und Frühmittelalter: Zur Anwendbarkeit soziologischer Rechtsbegriffe am Beispiel des kirchlichen Asylrechts." *Francia* 20 (1993): 97–135.

Esders, Stefan, and Heike Johanna Mierau. *Der althochdeutsche Klerikereid: Bischofliche Diozesangewalt, kirchliches Benefizialwesen und volkssprachliche Rechtspraxis im frühmittelalterlichen Baiern*. MGH Studien und Texte 28. Hannover: Hahnsche Buchhandlung, 2000.

Esposito, Mario. "Notes on Latin Learning and Literature in Medieval Ireland— III." *Hermathena* 48 (1933): 221–49.

Euzennat, Maurice. "Le *clipeus* de Tamuda (Maroc): *Imagines* impériales et serment militaire." In *L'Afrique, la Gaule, la religion à l'époque romaine*, ed. Yann Le Bohec. Collection Latomus 226. Brussels: Latomus, 1994. 111–15.

Ewig, Eugen. *Trier im Merowingerreich: Civitas, Stadt, Bistum*. Trier: Paulinus-Verlag, 1954.

Faraone, Christopher A. "The Agonistic Context of Early Greek Binding Spells." In *Magika Hiera: Ancient Greek Magic and Religion*, ed. Christopher A. Faraone and Dirk Obbink. New York: Oxford University Press, 1991. 3–32.

Fenster, Thelma and Daniel Lord Smail, eds. *Fama: The Politics of Talk and Reputation in Medieval Europe*. Ithaca, N.Y.: Cornell University Press, 2003.

Fentress, Elizabeth W. B. *Numidia and the Roman Army: Social, Military and Economic Aspects of the Frontier Zone*. BAR International Series 53. Oxford, B.A.R., 1979.

Ferrua, Antonio. "Graffiti di pellegrini alla tomba di San Felice." *Palladio* 13 (1963): 17–19.

Firey, Abigail, ed. *A New History of Penance*. Leiden: E.J. Brill, 2006.

Fishwick, Duncan. *Imperial Cult in the Latin West: Studies in the Ruler Cult of the Western Provinces of the Roman Empire*. Études Préliminaires aux Religions Orientales dans l'Empire Romain. 2 vols. in 4 parts. Leiden: E.J. Brill, 1987–92.

Fitzgerald, Alan. "Christ, Peter and the Rooster." *Augustinianum* 41, 2 (2001): 409–23.

——. *Conversion Through Penance in the Italian Church of the Fourth and Fifth Centuries: New Approaches to the Experience of Conversion from Sin*. New York: Mellen, 1988.

Flint, Valerie I. J. "Susanna and the Lothar Crystal: A Liturgical Perspective." *Early Medieval Europe* 4, 1 (1995): 61–86.

Flusin, Bernard. *Miracle et histoire dans l'oeuvre de Cyrille de Scythopolis*. Paris: Études augustiniennes, 1983.

Folliet, Georges. "Le Dossier de l'affaire Classicianus (*Epistulae* 250 et 1*)." In *Les Lettres de saint Augustin découvertes par Johannes Divjak*. Paris: Études augustiniennes, 1982. 129–46.

Fonrobert, Charlotte Elisheva. "The Didascalia Apostolorum: A Mishnah for the Disciples of Jesus." JECS 9, 4 (2001): 483–509.

Fontaine, Jacques. "Une clé littéraire de la *Vita Martini* de Sulpice Sévère: la typologie prophétique." In *Mélanges Christine Mohrmann: nouveau recueil, offert par ses anciens élèves*. Utrecht: Spectrum, 1963. 84–95.

———. *Naissance de la poésie dans l'occident chrétien: Esquisse d'une histoire de la poésie latine chrétienne du IIIe au VIe siècle*. Paris: Études augustiniennes, 1981.

Fox, Robin Lane. *Pagans and Christians*. New York: Knopf, 1987.

Frakes, Robert M. *Contra Potentium Iniurias: The Defensor Civitatis and Late Roman Justice*. Münchener Beiträge zur Papyrusforschung und antiken Rechtsgeschichte 90. Munich: C.H. Beck, 2001.

———. "Late Roman Social Justice and the Origin of the Defensor Civitatis." *Classical Journal* 89 (1994): 337–48.

Frank, Georgia. *The Memory of the Eyes: Pilgrims to Living Saints in Christian Late Antiquity*. Berkeley: University of California Press, 2000.

———. "'Taste and See': The Eucharist and the Eyes of Faith in the Fourth Century." *Church History* 70, 4 (2001): 619–43.

Frazer, William O. and Andrew Tyrell, eds. *Social Identity in Early Medieval Britain*. London: Leicester University Press, 2000.

Frymer-Kensky, Tikva. "The Tribulations of Marduk: The So-Called 'Marduk Ordeal Text'." *Journal of the American Oriental Society* 103 (1983): 131–41.

Gager, John G., ed. *Curse Tablets and Binding Spells from the Ancient World*. New York: Oxford University Press, 1992.

Gallagher, Clarence. *Church Law and Church Order in Rome and Byzantium: A Comparative Study*. Birmingham Byzantine and Ottoman Monographs 8. Aldershot: Ashgate, 2002.

Galtier, Paul. *L'Église et la rémission des péchés aux premiers siècles*. Paris: Beauchesne, 1932.

Garnsey, Peter. "The *Lex Iulia* and Appeal Under the Empire." *Journal of Roman Studies* 56 (1966): 167–89.

Garnsey, Peter and Caroline Humfress. *Evolution of the Late Antique World*. Cambridge: Cambridge University Press, 2001.

Gattiglia, A. "Paulin de Nole et Nicéta de Rémésiana: Voyages et pèlerinages de rang élevé." In *Akten des XII. Internationalen Kongresses für christliche Archäologie (Bonn 22.–28. September 1991)*, ed. Ernst Dassmann and Josef Engemann, JbAC Ergänzungsband 20. 2 vols. Münster: Aschendorffsche Verlagsbuchhandlung, 1995. 805–14.

Gaudemet, Jean. "Charisme et droit: Le domaine de l'évêque." ZRG KA 74 (1988): 44–70.

———. *L'Église dans l'empire romain (IVe–Ve siècles)*. Paris: Sirey, 1958.

———. "Épaone (concile d')." *Dictionnaire d'histoire et de géographie ecclésiastiques*, ed.

R. Aubert and É. Van Cauwenbergh, vol. 5, cols. 524–45. Paris: Letouzey et Ané, 1963.

———. *Sources du droit de l'Eglise en Occident du IIe au VIIe siècle*. Paris: Éditions du Cerf, 1985.

Gauthier, Nancy. *L'évangélisation des pays de la Moselle: la province romaine de Première Belgique entre Antiquité et Moyen-Ages (IIIe–VIIIe siècles)*. Paris: De Boccard, 1980.

———. *Province ecclésiastique de Treves (Belgica Prima)*. Topographie chrétienne des cités de la Gaule 1. Paris: De Boccard, 1986.

———. "Le réseau de pouvoirs de l'évêque dans la Gaule du haute moyen-âge." In *Towns and Their Territories Between Late Antiquity and the Early Middle Ages*, ed. G. P. Brogiolo, N. Gauthier, and N. Christie. Transformation of the Roman World 9. Leiden: E.J. Brill, 2000. 173–207.

Geary, Patrick J. "Extra-Judicial Means of Conflict Resolution." In *La giustizia nell'alto medioevo (secoli V–VIII)*. Settimane di Studio del Centro Italiano di Studi sull'Alto Medioevo 42. Spoleto: Centro Italiano di Studi sull'Alto Medioevo, 1995. 1: 569–605.

Gerwing, Manfred. "Eid." In *Lexikon des Mittelalters*, 3: 1673–74. Munich: Artemis-Verlag, 1986.

Gibson, Elsa. *"Christians for Christians": Inscriptions of Phrygia*. Harvard Theological Studies 32. Missoula, Mont.: Scholars Press, 1978.

Gillet, Andrew, ed. *On Barbarian Identity: Critical Approaches to Ethnicity in the Early Middle Ages*. Turnhout: Brepols, 2002.

Goetz, Hans-Werner, Jörg Jarnut, and Walter Pohl, eds. *Regna and Gentes: The Relationship between Late Antique and Early Medieval Peoples and Kingdoms in the Transformation of the Roman World*. Transformation of the Roman World 13. Leiden: E.J. Brill, 2003.

Göller, Emil. "Das spanisch-westgotische Bußwesen vom 6. bis 8. Jahrhundert." *Römische Quartalschrift für christliche Altertumskunde und Kirchengeschichte* 37 (1929): 245–313.

González, J. "The First Oath *pro salute Augusti* found in Baetica." ZPE 72 (1988): 113–27.

Gonzalez Rivas, Severino. *La penitencia en la primitiva Iglesia española*. Consejo Superior de Investigaciones Cientificas. Salamanca: Instituto San Raimundo de Peñafort, 1949.

Gordon, Richard. "Raising a Sceptre: Confession-Narratives from Lydia and Phrygia." *Journal of Roman Archaeology* 17, 1 (2004): 177–96.

Grey, Cam. "Letters of Recommendation and the Circulation of Rural Laborers in the Late Roman West." In *Travel, Communication and Geography in Late Antiquity: Sacred and Profane*, ed. Linda Ellis and Frank L. Kidner, Aldershot: Ashgate, 2004. 25–40.

Griffiths, Paul J. *Lying: An Augustinian Theology of Duplicity*. Grand Rapids, Mich.: Brazos Press, 2004.

Gross, Julius. "Die Schlüsselgewalt nach Haimo von Auxerre." *Zeitschrift für Religions- und Geistesgeschichte* 9 (1957): 30–41.

Grubbs, Judith Evans. *Law and Family in Late Antiquity: The Emperor Constantine's Marriage Legislation*. Oxford: Oxford University Press, 1995.

Gryson, Roger. *Le prêtre selon saint Ambroise*. Louvain: Edition orientaliste, 1968.

Hamilton, Louis. I. "Possidius' Augustine and Post-Augustinian Africa." *JECS* 12, 1 (2004): 85–105.

Hamilton, Sarah. *The Practice of Penance, 900–1050*. Woodbridge: Boydell, 2001.

Handley, Mark A. "Beyond Hagiography: Epigraphic Commemoration and the Cult of Saints in Late Antique Trier." In *Society and Culture in Late Antique Gaul: Revisiting the Sources*, ed. Ralph W. Mathisen and Danuta Shanzer. Aldershot: Ashgate, 2001. 187–200.

——. *Death, Society and Culture: Inscriptions and Epitaphs in Gaul and Spain, AD 300–750*. BAR International Series 1135. Oxford: Archaeopress, 2003.

Hardin, Russell. *Trust and Trustworthiness*, Russell Sage Foundation Series on Trust 4. New York: Russell Sage Foundation, 2002.

Harries, Jill. *Law and Empire in Late Antiquity*. Cambridge: Cambridge University Press, 1999.

Harries, Jill and Ian Wood, eds. *The Theodosian Code: Studies in the Imperial Law of Late Antiquity*. London: Duckworth, 1993.

——. "Resolving Disputes: The Frontiers of Law in Late Antiquity." In *Law, Society, and Authority in Late Antiquity*, ed. Ralph W. Mathisen. Oxford: Oxford University Press, 2001. 68–82.

Harrill, J. Albert. "The Influence of Roman Contract Law on Early Baptismal Formulae (Tertullian, *Ad Martyras* 3)." *Studia Patristica* 36 (2001): 275–82.

Hartmann, Wilfried. "Der Bischof als Richter nach den kirchenrechtlichen Quellen des 4. bis 7. Jahrhunderts." In *La giustizia nell'alto medioevo (secoli V–VIII)*. Settimane di Studio del Centro Italiano di Studi sull'Alto Medioevo 42. Spoleto: Centro Italiano di Studi sull'Alto Medioevo, 1995. 2: 805–42.

Haverling, Gerd. *Studies on Symmachus' Language and Style*. Göteborg: Acta Universitatis Gothoburgensis, 1988.

Heather, Peter. *The Fall of the Roman Empire*. London: Macmillan, 2005.

Hein, Kenneth. *Eucharist and Excommunication: A Study in Early Christian Doctrine and Discipline*. European University Papers Series 23, Theology 19. Bern: Lang, 1973.

Heinemann, J. "Philos Lehre vom Eid." In *Judaica: Festschrift zu Hermann Cohens siebzigstem Geburtstage*. Berlin: Cassirer, 1912. 109–18.

Heinen, Heinz. *Frühchristliches Trier: Von den Anfängen bis zur Völkerwanderung*. Trier: Paulinus Verlag, 1996.

Heinzelmann, Martin. *Bischofsherrschaft in Gallien: Zur Kontinuität römischer Führungsschichten vom 4. bis zum 7. Jahrhundert. Soziale, prosopographische und bildungsgeschichtliche Aspekte*. Munich: Artemis Verlag, 1976.

——. "Bischof und Herrschaft von spätantiken Gallien bis zu den karolingischen Hausmeiern: Die institutionellen Grundlagen." In *Herrschaft und Kirche: Beiträge zur Entstehung und Wirkungsweise episkopaler und monastischer Organisationsformen*. Friedrich Prinz, ed. Monographien zur Geschichte des Mittelalters 33. Stuttgart : A. Hiersemann, 1988. 23–82.

———. "Histoire, rois et prophètes: le rôle des éléments autobiographiques dans les Histoires de Grégoire de Tours: un guide épiscopal à l'usage du roi chrétien." In *De Tertullien aux Mozarabes: mélanges offerts à Jacques Fontaine*, ed. Louis Holtz and Jean-Claude Fredouille. Paris: Institut d'études augustiniennes, 1992. 1: 537–50.

Helmholz, R. H. "Excommunication and the Angevin Leap Forward." *Haskins Society Journal* 7 (1995): 133–49.

———. *The Oxford History of the Laws of England*. Vol. 1, *The Canon Law and Ecclesiastical Jurisdiction from 597 to the 1640s*. Oxford: Oxford University Press, 2004.

Hermanowicz, Erika T. "Numa's Laws and the Meaning of Justice in the *Divinae Institutiones*." In *The First Christian Humanist: Lactantius in Late Antiquity and the Renaissance*, ed. O. Nicholson (forthcoming).

———, ed. *Select Cases on Defamation to 1600*. Publications of the Selden Society 101. London: Selden Society, 1985.

Hess, Hamilton. *The Early Development of Canon Law and the Council of Serdica*. Oxford: Oxford University Press, 2002.

Himmelfarb, Martha. *Tours of Hell: An Apocalyptic Form in Jewish and Christian Literature*. Philadelphia: University of Pennsylvania Press, 1983.

Hoeflich, Michael H. "The Speculator in the Governmental Theory of the Early Church." *Vigiliae Christianae* 34 (1980): 120–29.

Hoek, Annewies van den and John J. Herrmann Jr. "Paulinus of Nola, Courtyards, and Cantharii," *Harvard Theological Review* 93, 3 (2000): 173–219.

Honoré, Tony. *Law in the Crisis of Empire, 379–455 AD: The Theodosian Dynasty and its Quaestors*. Oxford: Oxford University Press, 1998.

Horner, Timothy J. "Jewish Aspects of the *Protoevangelium of James*." JECS 12, 3 (2004): 313–35.

Horst, Pieter Willem van der. *Ancient Jewish Epitaphs: An Introductory Survey of a Millennium of Jewish Epigraphy (300 BCE—700 CE)*. Contributions to Biblical Exegesis and Theology 2. Kampen: Kok Pharos, 1991.

Howard-Johnston, James and Paul Antony Hayward, eds. *The Cult of Saints in Late Antiquity and the Early Middle Ages: Essays on the Contribution of Peter Brown*. Oxford: Oxford University Press, 2002.

Huck, Olivier. "A propos de *CTh* 1,27,1 et *CSirm* 1: Sur deux textes controversés relatifs à l'episcopalis audientia constantinienne," ZRG RA 120 (2003): 78–105.

———. "Encore à propos des *Sirmondiennes*: Arguments présentés à l'appui de la thèse de l'authenticité, en réponse à une mise en cause récente. *Antiquité tardive* 11 (2003): 181–96.

Humfress, Caroline. "Civil Law and Social Life." In *The Cambridge Companion to the Age of Constantine*, ed. Noel Lenski, 205–225. Cambridge: Cambridge University Press, 2006.

———. "Law and Legal Practice in the Age of Justinian." In *The Cambridge Companion to the Age of Justinian*, ed. Michael Maas, 161–84. Cambridge: Cambridge University Press, 2005.

———. "A New Legal Cosmos: Late Roman Lawyers and the Early Medieval Church." In *The Medieval World*, ed. Peter Linehan and Janet L. Nelson, 557–75. London: Routledge, 2001.

———. *Orthodoxy and the Courts in Late Antiquity*. Oxford: Oxford University Press, forthcoming.

———. "Roman Law, Forensic Argument and the Formation of Christian Orthodoxy (III–VI Centuries)." In *Orthodoxie, christianisme, histoire*, ed. Susanna Elm, Eric Rebillard, and Antonella Romano. Rome: École française de Rome, 2000. 125–47.

Hunter, David G. "Augustine and the Making of Marriage in Roman North Africa." JECS 11, 1 (2003): 63–85.

———. "Vigilantius of Calagurris and Victricius of Rouen: Ascetics, Relics, and Clerics in Late Roman Gaul." JECS 7, 3 (1999): 401–30.

———. "The Virgin, the Bride, and the Church: Reading Psalm 45 in Ambrose, Jerome, and Augustine." *Church History* 69, 2 (2000): 281–303.

Hyams, Paul. "Due Process Versus the Maintenance of Order in European Law: The Contribution of the *ius commune*." In *The Moral World of the Law*, ed. Peter Coss, 62–90. Cambridge: Cambridge University Press, 2000.

Innes, Matthew. *State and Society in the Early Middle Ages: The Middle Rhine Valley, 400–1000*. Cambridge: Cambridge University Press, 2001.

Ireland, C. "Penance and Prayer in Water: an Irish Practice in Northumbrian hagiography." *Cambrian Medieval Celtic Studies* 34 (1997): 51–66.

Jacques, François. "Le defenseur de cité d'après la lettre 22* de Saint Augustine." *Revue des Études Augustiniennes* 32 (1986): 56–73.

Jaeger, Hasso. "La preuve judiciaire d'après la tradition rabbinique et patristique." In *La Preuve*., 1: 415–594 at 529. Recueils de la Société Jean Bodin pour l'histoire comparative des institutions 16–19. Brussels : Éditions de la Librairie encyclopédique, 1963–65.

James, Edward. "'Beati pacifici': Bishops and the Law in Sixth-Century Gaul." In *Disputes and Settlements: Law and Human Relations in the West*, ed. John Bossy. Cambridge: Cambridge University Press, 1983. 25–46.

Johnston, David. *Roman Law in Context*. Cambridge: Cambridge University Press, 1999.

Jordan, David R. "A Curse Tablet Against Opponents at Law." In *The Lawcourts at Athens: Sites, Buildings, Equipment, Procedure, and Testimonia*, ed. Alan L. Boegehold. Athenian Agora 28. Princeton, N.J.: American School of Classical Studies at Athens, 1995. 55–57.

———. "New Greek Curse Tablets (1985–2000)." *Greek, Roman, and Byzantine Studies* 41 (2000): 5–46.

———. "A Survey of Greek Defixiones Not Included in the Special Corpora." *Greek, Roman, and Byzantine Studies* 26 (1985): 151–97.

Jussen, Bernhard. "Liturgy and Legitimation, or How the Gallo-Romans Ended the Roman Empire." In *Ordering Medieval Society: Perspectives on Intellectual and Practical Modes of Shaping Social Relations*, ed. Bernhard Jussen, trans. Pamela Selwyn, Philadelphia: University of Pennsylvania Press, 2001. 147–99.

———. "Über 'Bischofsherrschaft' und die Prozeduren politisch-sozialer Umordnung in Gallien zwischen 'Antike' und 'Mittelalter'." *Historische Zeitschrift* 260 (1995): 673–718.

Kalleres, Dayna. "Exorcizing the Devil to Silence Christ's Enemies: Ritualized

Speech Practices in Late Antique Christianity." Ph.D. dissertation, Brown University, 2002.

Kaplony-Heckel, Ursula. *Die Demotischen Tempeleide.* Ägyptologische Abhandlungen 6 Weisbaden: O. Harrassowitz, 1963.

Kaufman, Peter Iver. "Augustine, Macedonius, and the Courts." *Augustinian Studies* 34, 1 (2003): 67–82.

Kelly, Christopher. *Ruling the Later Roman Empire.* Cambridge, Mass.: Harvard University Press, 2004.

Kelly, J. N. D. *Jerome: His Life, Writings, and Controversies.* New York: Harper & Row, 1975.

Klauser, Theodor. *A Short History of the Western Liturgy: An Account and Some Reflections.* Trans. John Halliburton. Oxford: Oxford University Press, 1969.

Klingshirn, William E. *Caesarius of Arles: The Making of a Christian Community in Late Antique Gaul.* Cambridge: Cambridge University Press, 1994.

——. "Charity and Power: The Ransoming of Captives in Sub-Roman Gaul." *Journal of Roman Studies* 75 (1985): 183–203.

——. "Defining the *Sortes Sanctorum*: Gibbon, Du Cange, and Early Christian Lot Divination." JECS 10, 1 (2002): 77–130.

Kolmer, Lothar. *Promissorische Eide im Mittelalter.* Regensburger Historische Forschungen 12. Kallmünz: Verlag Michael Laßleben, 1989.

Kornbluth, Genevra A. "The Susanna Crystal of Lothar II: Chastity, the Church, and Royal Justice." *Gesta* 31, 1 (1992): 25–39.

Kötting, Bernhard. "Gelübde." *Reallexikon für Antike und Christentum* 9. Stuttgart: Hiersemann, 1976. 1055–99.

Kuczynski, Michael P. *Prophetic Song: The Psalms as Moral Discourse in Late Medieval England.* Middle Ages Series. Philadelphia: University of Pennsylvania Press, 1995.

Kulikowski, Michael. "Fronto, the Bishops, and the Crowd: Episcopal Justice and Communal Violence in Fifth-Century Tarraconensis." *Early Medieval Europe* 11, 4 (2002): 295–320.

Lamoreaux, John C. "Episcopal Courts in Late Antiquity." JECS 3, 2 (1995): 143–67.

Laporte, Jean-Pierre. "Tigzirt: Saint Paul contre l'*inuidus*." In *L'Afrique, la Gaule, la Religion à l'époque romaine: Mélanges à la mémoire de Marcel Le Glay*, ed. Yann Le Bohec. Collection Latomus 226. Brussels: Latomus, 1994. 285–87.

Le Bohec, Yann. *Imperial Roman Army.* Reprint. London: Routledge, 2000.

Le Goff, Jacques. *The Birth of Purgatory.* Trans. Arthur Goldhammer. Chicago: University of Chicago Press, 1984.

Le Serment: Recueil d'études anthropologiques, historiques et juridiques, Séminaire 1985–1988. Centre Droits et Cultures. Paris: Université Parix-X, 1989.

Leclerq, Henri. "Suzanne." In *DACL* 15, 2, 1742–52.

Leclerq, Jean. *The Love of Learning and the Desire for God: A Study of Monastic Culture.* Trans. by Catharine Misrahi. 3rd ed. New York: Fordham University Press, 1982.

Lee, A. D. "Decoding Late Roman Law." *Journal of Roman Studies* 92 (2002): 185–93.

Léglu, Catherine. "Defamation in the Troubadour *Sirventes*: Legislation and Lyric Poetry." *Medium Aevum* 66, 1 (1997): 28–41.

Lehmann, Tomas. "Eine spätantike Inschriftensammlung und der Besuch des Papstes Damasus an der Pilgerstätte des Hl. Felix in Cimitile/Nola." ZPE 91 (1992): 243–81.

Lemosse, Maxime. "Accusation calomnieuse et action d'injures à propos d'une incription récent." In *Études romanistiques*, 361–70.

———. *Cognitio: Étude sur le role du juge dans l'instruction du procès civil antique*. Paris: A. Lesot, 1944.

———. *Études romanistiques*. Annales de la Faculté de Droit et de Science Politique 26. Clermont-Ferrand: Adosa, 1991.

———. "Recherches sur l'histoire du serment de calumnia." In *Études romanistiques*, 335–59.

Lenski, Noel E. "Evidence for the *Audientia episcopalis* in the New Letters of Augustine." In *Law, Society, and Authority in Late Antiquity*, ed. Ralph W. Mathisen. Oxford: Oxford University Press, 2001. 83–97.

Leonard, John K. "Rites of Marriage in the Western Middle Ages." In *Medieval Liturgy: A Book of Essays*, ed. Lizette Larson-Miller. New York: Garland, 1997. 165–202.

Lepelley, Claude. "La diabolisation du paganisme et ses conséquences psychologiques: les angoisses de Publicola, correspondant de saint Augustin." In *Impies et païens entre Antiquité et Moyen Ages*, ed. Lionel Mary and Michel Sot. Paris: Picard, 2002. 81–96.

———. "Le patronat épiscopal aux IVe et Ve siècles: continuités et ruptures avec le patronat classique." In *L'évêque dans la cité du IVe au Ve siècle: image et autorité: Actes de la table ronde organisée par l'Istituto patristico Augustinianum et l'École française de Rome (Rome, 1er et 2 décembre 1995)*, ed, Éric Rebillard and Claire Sotinel. Collection de l'Ecole française de Rome 248. Rome: École française de Rome, 1998. 17–33.

Leveau, Philippe. "Le pastoralisme dans l'Afrique antique." In *Pastoral Economies in Classical Antiquity*, ed. C. R. Whittaker. Cambridge: Cambridge University Press, 1988. 177–95.

Levison, John R. *Portraits of Adam in Early Judaism, from Sirach to 2 Baruch*. Sheffield: JSOT, 1988.

Leyerle, Blake. "John Chrysostom on the Gaze." JECS 1 (1993): 159–74.

Leyser, Conrad. *Authority and Asceticism from Augustine to Gregory the Great*. Oxford: Oxford University Press, 2000.

———. "Expertise and Authority in Gregory the Great: The Social Function of *Peritia*." In *Gregory the Great: A Symposium*, ed. John C. Cavadini. Notre Dame Studies in Theology 2. Notre Dame, Ind.: University of Notre Dame Press, 1995. 38–61.

Liebeschuetz, Wolf. "The Birth of Late Antiquity." *Antiquité Tardive* 12 (2004): 253–61.

Liebs, Detlef. *Die Jurisprudenz im spätantiken Italien (260–640 n. Chr)*. Freiburger rechtsgeschichtliche Abhandlungen, neue Folge 8. Berlin: Duncker & Humblot, 1987.

———. *Römische Jursprudenz in Gallien (2. bis 8. Jahrhundert)*. Freiburger rechtsgeschichtliche Abhandlungen, neue Folge 38. Berlin: Duncker & Humblot, 2002.

Lienhard, J. "On Discernment of Spirits in the Early Church." *Theological Studies* 41 (1980): 505–29.

Lizzi, Rita. *Il potere episcopale nell'Oriente romano: Rappresentazione ideologica e realtà politica (IV–V secolo d.C.)*. Filologia e critica 53. Rome: Edizioni dell'Ateneo, 1987.

———. "Una società esortata all'ascetismo: misure legislative e motivazioni economiche nel IV–V secolo d. C." *Studi Storici* 30 (1989): 129–52.

———. "I vescovi e i potentes della terra: definizione e limite del ruolo episcopale nelle due partes imperii fra IV e V secolo d.C." In *L'évêque dans la cité du IVe au Ve siècle: image et autorité: Actes de la table ronde organisée par l'Istituto patristico Augustinianum et l'École française de Rome (Rome, 1er et 2 décembre 1995)*, ed. Eric Rebillard and Claire Sotinel Collection de l'Ecole française de Rome 248. Rome: École française de Rome, 1998. 81–104.

Lot, Ferdinand and Robert Fawtier. *Histoire des institutions françaises au moyen âge*. 3 vols. Paris: Presses universitaires de France, 1958.

Lozito, Vito. *Il corvo: Calunnie, accuse e lettere anonime nei primi secoli dell'era cristiana*. Bari: Levante, 1996.

Lupoi, Maurizio. *The Origins of the European Legal Order*. Trans. Adrian Belton. Cambridge: Cambridge University Press, 2000.

MacCormack, Sabine. "Sin, Citizenship, and the Salvation of Souls: The Impact of Christian Priorities on Late-Roman and Post-Roman Society." *Comparative Studies in Society and History* 39 (1997): 644–73.

MacCoull, Leslie S. B. "More Sources for the *Liber Scintillarum* of Defensor of Ligugé." *Revue Bénédictine* 112, 3–4 (2002): 291–300.

Mandouze, André. *Saint Augustin, l'aventure de la raison et de la grace*. Paris: Études augustiniennes, 1968.

Manfredini, Arrigo D. *La diffamazione verbale nel diritto romano*. Vol. 1, *Età repubblicana*. Pubblicazioni della Facoltà Giuridica dell'Università di Ferrara 2nd ser. 12. Milan: A. Giuffrè, 1979.

Mansfield, Mary C. *The Humiliation of Sinners: Public Penance in Thirteenth-Century France*. Ithaca, N.Y.: Cornell University Press, 1995.

Marié, M.-A. "Deux sanglants épisodes de l'accession au pouvoir d'une nouvelle classe politique: Les grands procès de Rome et d'Antioche chez Ammien Marcellin, *Res Gestae* XXVIII, 1; XXIX, 1 et 2." In *De Tertullien aux Mozarabes: mélanges offerts à Jacques Fontaine*, ed. Louis Holtz and Jean-Claude Fredouille. Paris: Institut d'études augustiniennes. 1:349–60.

Markus, R. A. *The End of Ancient Christianity*. Cambridge: Cambridge University Press, 1990.

Gregory the Great and His World. Cambridge: Cambridge University Press, 1997.

———. "Gregory the Great's *Rector* and His Genesis." In *Grégoire le Grand*, ed. J. Fontaine, R. Gillet, and S. Pellistrandi. Paris: Centre de la recherche scientifique, 1987. 137–46.

Martroye, François. "L'affaire *Indicia*: Une sentence de saint Ambroise." In *Mélanges Paul Fournier de la Bibliothèque d'Histoire du Droit*. Paris: Sirey, 1929. 503–10.

Mathisen, Ralph W. *Roman Aristocrats in Barbarian Gaul: Strategies for Survival in an Age of Transition*. Austin: University of Texas Press 1993.

———. "The 'Second Council of Arles' and the Spirit of Compilation in Late Roman Gaul." JECS 5, 4 (1997): 511–54.

Matthews, John F. *Laying Down the Law: A Study of the Theodosian Code*. New Haven, Conn.: Yale University Press, 2000.

———. *Western Aristocracies and Imperial Court, A.D. 364–425*. Reprint. New York: Oxford University Press, 1990.

Maxwell, J. *Christianization and Communication in Late Antiquity: John Chrysostom and Lay Christians in Antioch*. Cambridge: Cambridge University Press, 2006.

May, G. "Anklage- und Zeugnisfähigkeit nach der zweiten Sitzung des Konzils zu Karthago vom Jahre 419." *Theologische Quartalschrift* 140 (1960): 163–205.

McGinn, Thomas A. J. *Prostitution, Sexuality, and the Law in Ancient Rome*. New York: Oxford University Press, 1998.

McLynn, Neil B. *Ambrose of Milan: Church and Court in a Christian Capital*. Transformation of the Classical Heritage 22. Berkeley: University of California Press, 1994.

———. "Seeing and Believing: Aspects of Conversion from Antoninus Pius to Louis the Pious." In *Conversion in Late Antiquity and the Early Middle Ages: Seeing and Believing*, ed. Kenneth Mills and Anthony Grafton. Studies in Comparative History: Essays from the Shelby Cullom Davis Center for Historical Studies. Rochester, N.Y.: University of Rochester Press, 2003. 224–70.

———. "A Self-Made Holy Man: The Case of Gregory Nazianzen." JECS 6, 3 (1998): 463–83.

McNamara, Jo Ann. "Muffled Voices: The Lives of Consecrated Women in the Fourth Century." In *Medieval Religious Women*, vol. 1, *Distant Echoes*, ed. John A. Nichols and Lillian Thomas Shank, 11–29. Kalamazoo, Mich.: Cistercian Publications, 1984.

Meens, Rob. "The Frequency and Nature of Early Medieval Penance." In *Handling Sin: Confession in the Middle Ages*, ed. Peter Biller and A. J. Minnis, 35–61. Woodbridge: York Medieval Press, 1998.

Meer, Frederik van der. *Augustine the Bishop: Church and Society at the Dawn of the Middle Ages*. London: Sheed and Ward, 1961.

Merkt, Andreas. *Maximus I von Turin: Die Verkündigung eines bischofs der frühen Reichskirche im zeitgeschichtlichen, gesellschaftlichen und liturgischen Kontext*. Supplements to Vigiliae Christianae 40. Leiden: E.J. Brill, 1997.

Meslin, Michel. *La fête des Kalendes de Janvier dans l'empire romain*. Collection Latomus 115. Brussels: Latomus, 1970.

Meyer, Elizabeth A. *Legitimacy and Law in the Roman World: Tabulae in Roman Belief and Practice*. Cambridge: Cambridge University Press, 2004.

Meyer, W. "Vita Adae et Evae." *Abhandlungen der philosophisch-philologischen Classe der königlich bayerischen Akademie der Wissenschaften* 14, 3 (1878): 185–250.

Millar, Fergus. *The Emperor in the Roman World, 31 BC-AD 337*. Ithaca, N.Y.: Cornell University Press, 1977.

Mirhady, David C. "The Oath-Challenge in Athens." *Classical Quarterly* 41 (1991): 78–83.

Modéran, Yves. *Les Maures et l'Afrique romaine: IVe-VIIe siècle*. Rome: École française de Rome, 2003.

Mohrmann, Christine. "Quelques observations sur 'sacramentum' chez Tertullien." In *Romanitas et Christianitas*, ed. Willem den Boer et al. Amsterdam: North-Holland, 1973. 233–42.

——. "Sacramentum dans les plus anciens textes chrétiens." *Harvard Theological Review* 47 (1954): 141–152.

Moine, N. "Melaniana." *Recherches augustiniennes* 15 (1980): 3–79.

Moralee, Jason. *"For Salvation's Sake": Provincial Loyalty, Personal Religion, and Epigraphic Production in the Roman and Late Antique Near East.* New York: Routledge, 2004.

Moreau, Madeleine. "Sur un correspondant d'Augustin: qui est donc Publicola." *Revue des études augustiniennes* 28 (1982): 225–38.

Mossakowski, Wieslaw. "The Introduction of an Interdiction of Oral Accusation in the Roman Empire." *Revue internationale des droits de l'Antiquité* 3rd ser. 43 (1996): 269–68.

Mratschek-Halfmann, Sigrid. *"Multis enim notissima est sanctitas loci*: Paulinus and the Gradual Rise of Nola as a Center of Christian Hospitality." JECS 9, 4 (2001): 511–53.

Munier, Charles. "La question des appels à Rome d'apreès la Lettre 20* d'Augustin." In *Les Lettres de saint Augustin découvertes par Johannes divjak.* Paris: Études augustiniennes, 1983. 287–99.

Murdoch, B. O. *The Irish Adam and Eve Story from Saltair na Rann.* Vol. 2, *Commentary.* Dublin: Institute for Advanced Studies, 1976.

Nathan, G. "The Rogation Ceremonies of Late Antique Gaul: Creation, Transmission and the Role of the Bishop." *Classica et Mediaevalia* 40 (1998): 275–303.

Nodes, Daniel J. *"De Subitanea Paenitentia* in the Letters of Faustus of Riez and Avitus of Vienne." *Recherches de théologie ancienne et médiévale* 55 (1988): 30–40.

——. *Doctrine and Exegesis in Biblical Latin Poetry.* ARCA Classical and Medieval Texts, Papers and Monographs 31. Leeds: F. Cairns, 1993.

Nussbaum, Martha C. *Hiding from Humanity: Disgust, Shame, and the Law.* Princeton, N.J.: Princeton University Press, 2004.

O'Donnell, James J. *Augustine: A New Biography.* New York: HarperCollins, 2005.

O'Loughlin, T. and H. Conrad-O-Briain, "The 'Baptism of Tears' in Early Anglo-Saxon Sources." *Anglo-Saxon England* 22 (1993): 65–83.

Ogden, Daniel. *Magic, Witchcraft, and Ghosts: A Sourcebook.* New York: Oxford University Press, 2002.

Orlandis, José and Domingo Ramon-Lissón. *Historia de los concilios de la España romana y visigoda.* Colección Historia de la Iglesia 13. Pamplona: Ediciones Universidad de Navarra, 1986.

Pastori, Franco. *Il negozio verbale in diritto romano.* Bologna: Cisalpino, 1994.

Pazdernik, Charles. "Justinianic Ideology and the Power of the Past." In *The Cambridge Companion to the Age of Justinian*, ed. Michael Maas. Cambridge: Cambridge University Press, 2005. 185–212.

Pegon, J. "Componction." In *Dictionnaire de Spiritualité* 2, cols. 1312–21. Paris: Beauchesne, 1937.

Pergami, Federico. *L'appello nella legislazione del tardo impero.* Milan: A. Giuffrè, 2000.

Perler, Othmar. *Les voyages de Saint Augustin.* Paris: Études augustiniennes, 1969.

Pettazzoni, Raffaele. "Confession of Sins and the Classics." *Harvard Theological Review* 30 (1937): 1–14.

Pietri, Charles. *Roma Christiana: Recherches sur l'Eglise de Rome, son organisation, sa politique, son idéologie de Miltiade à Sixte III (311–440)*. 2 vols. Bibliothèque des Écoles Françaises d'Athènes et de Rome. Rome: École française de Rome, 1976.

Poschmann, Bernhard. *Penance and the Anointing of the Sick*. Trans. Francis Courtney. New York: Herder and Herder, 1964.

Potter, David. "Performance, Power and Justice in the High Empire." In *Roman Theater and Society: E. Togo Salmon Papers I*, ed.William J. SlaterAnn Arbor, Mich.: University of Michigan Press, 1996. 129–59.

Prinz, Friedrich. "Die bischöfliche Stadtherrschaft im Frankenreich vom 5. bis zum 7. Jahrhundert." *Historische Zeitschrift* 217 (1973): 1–35.

———, ed. *Herrschaft und Kirche: Beiträge zur Entstehung und Wirkungsweise episkopaler und monastischer Organisationsformen*. Monographien zur Geschichte des Mittelalters 33. Stuttgart: A. Hiersemann, 1988.

Prodi, Paolo. *Il sacramento del potere: Il giuramento politico nella storia costituzionale dell'Occidente*. Bologna: Il Mulino, 1992.

Quinn, Esther C. *The Penitence of Adam: A Study of the Andrius MS. (Bibliothèque Nationale Fr. 95 Folios 380r–394v)*. University, Miss.: Romance Monographs, 1980.

Rahner, Karl. "Bußlehre und Bußpraxis der Didascalia Apostolorum." *Zeitschrift für katholische Theologie* 72 (1950): 257–81.

Ramsay, William Mitchell. *Cities and Bishoprics of Phrygia* 1.2. Oxford: Clarendon Press, 1897.

Rapp, Claudia. "Bishops in Late Antiquity: A New Social and Urban Elite?" In *Elites Old and New in the Byzantine and Early Islamic Near East*, ed. John F. Haldon and Lawrence I. Conrad, 144–73. Studies in Late Antiquity and Early Islam 6. Princeton, N.J.: Darwin Press, 2004.

———. "The Elite Status of Bishops in Late Antiquity in Ecclesiastical, Spiritual, and Social Contexts." *Arethusa* 33.3 (2000): 379–99.

———. *Holy Bishops in Late Antiquity: The Nature of Christian Leadership in an Age of Transition*. Berkeley: University of California Press, 2005.

———. "Storytelling as Spiritual Communication in Early Greek Hagiography: The Use of *Diegesis*." JECS 6, 3 (1998): 431–62.

Rapp, Claudia and Michele Renee Salzman, eds. *Elites in Late Antiquity = Arethusa* 33.3 (2000).

Rebillard, Éric. "Augustin et le rituel épistolaire de l'élite sociale et culturelle de son temps: Éléments pour une analyse processuelle des relations de l'évêque et de la cité dans l'Antiquité tardive." In *L'évêque dans la cité du IVe au Ve siècle: image et autorité. Actes de la table ronde organisée par l'Istituto patristico Augustinianum et l'École française de Rome (Rome, 1er et 2 décembre 1995)*, ed. Éric Rebillard and Claire Sotinel. Collection de l'École française de Rome 248. Rome: École française de Rome, 1998. 127–52.

———. "La 'conversion' de l'empire romain selon Peter Brown (note critique)." *Annales HSS* 54 (1999): 813–23.

———. *In hora mortis: Evolution de la pastorale chrétienne de la mort aux IVe et Ve siècles dans l'occident latin*. Rome: École française de Rome, 1994.

Rees, B. R. *Pelagius: A Reluctant Heretic*. Reprinted in *Pelagius: Life and Letters*. Woodbridge: Boydell, 1988.

———. *Pelagius: Life and Letters*. Rochester, N.Y.: Boydell, 1998.

Reynolds, Philip Lyndon. *Marriage in the Western Church: The Christianization of Marriage during the Patristic and Early Medieval Periods*. Leiden: E.J. Brill, 1994.

Richlin, Amy. "Approaches to the Sources on Adultery at Rome." *Women's Studies* 8 (1981): 225–50.

Ries, G. "Altbabylonische Beweisurteile." *ZRG RA* 106 (1989): 56–80.

Robert, Louis. *Hellenica: Recueil d'épigraphie, de numismatique, et d'antiquités grecques*. Vols. 11–12. Limoges: Bontemps, 1960.

———. "Malédictions funéraires grecques." *Comptes rendus de l'Académie des Inscriptions et Belles-Lettres* (1978): 241–89.

Rousseau, Philip. *Ascetics, Authority and the Church in the Age of Jerome and Cassian*. Oxford: Oxford University Press, 1978.

———. *Pachomius: The Making of a Community in Fourth-Century Egypt*. Transformation of the Classical Heritage 6. Berkeley: University of California Press, 1985.

———. "The Spiritual Authority of the 'Monk-Bishop': Eastern Elements in Some Western Hagiography of the Fourth and Fifth Centuries." *Journal of Theological Studies* n.s. 23, 2 (1971): 380–419.

Rowe, Christopher and Malcom Schofield, eds. *The Cambridge History of Greek and Roman Political Thought*. Cambridge: Cambridge University Press, 2000.

Russell, James C. *The Germanization of Early Medieval Christianity: A Sociohistorical Approach to Religious Transformation*. Oxford: Oxford University Press, 1994.

Rutledge, Stephen H. "'Delatores' and the Tradition of Violence in Roman Oratory." *American Journal of Philology* 120.4 (1999): 555–73.

Saint-Roch, Patrick. *La pénitence dans les conciles et les lettres des papes des origines à la mort de Grégoire le Grand*. Studi di antichità cristiana 46. Vatican City: Pontificio Istituto di archeologia cristiana, 1991.

Salzman, Michele Renee. "Elite Realities and *Mentalités*: The Making of a Western Christian Aristocracy." *Arethusa* 33 (2000): 347–62.

Sarti, Nicoletta. *Maximum dirimendarum causarum remedium: Il giuramento di calumnia nella dottrina civilistica dei secoli XI–XIII*. Seminario giuridico della Universita di Bologna 160. Milan: A. Giuffrè, 1995.

Schöllgen, Georg. *Die Anfänge der Professionalisierung des Klerus und das kirchliche Amt in der syrischen Didaskalie*. JAC Ergänzungsband 27. Munster: Aschendorffsche Verlagsbuchhandlung, 1998.

Scholz, S. "Die Rolle der Bischöfe auf den Synoden von Rom (313) und Arles (314)." In *Köln: Stadt und Bistum in Kirche und Reich des Mittelalters*, ed. Hanna Vollrath, Stefan Weinfurter, and Odilo Engels. Cologne: Böhlau, 1993. 1–21.

Schörner, Günther. *Votive im römischen Griechenland: Untersuchungen zur späthellenistischen und kaiserzeitlichen Kunst- und Religionsgeschichte*. Altertumswissenschaftliches Kolloquium 7. Stuttgart: Steiner, 2003.

Seely, David R. "The Raised Hand of God as an Oath Gesture." In *Fortunate the*

Eyes That See: Essays in Honor of David Noel Freedman, ed. Astrid B. Beck et al. Grand Rapids, Mich.: Eerdmans, 1995. 411–25.

Seidl, Erwin. *Der Eid im römisch-ägyptischen Provinzialrecht*. 2 vols. Münchener Beiträge zur Papyrusforschung und antiken Rechtsgeschichte 17, 24. Munich: Beck, 1933, 1935.

Selb, Walter. "Episcopalis audientia von der Zeit Konstantins bis zur Nov. XXXV Valentinians III." *ZRG RA* 84 (1967): 162–217.

Seston, William. "Fahneneid (*sacramentum militiae*)." In *Reallexikon für Antike und Christentum* 7 (Stuttgart: Hiersemann, 1969). 277–84.

Shaw, Brent D. "African Christianity: Disputes, Definitions, and 'Donatists.'" In *Orthodoxy and Heresy in Religious Movements: Discipline and Dissent*, ed. Malcom R. Greenshields and Thomas A. Robinson. Lewiston, Pa.: Edwin Mellen, 1992. 5–34.

——. "Judicial Nightmares and Christian Memory." *JECS* 11, 4 (2003): 533–66.

——. "Rural Markets in North Africa and the Political Economy of the Roman Empire." *Antiquités africaines* 17 (1981): 37–83.

Shaw, Teresa M. "*Askesis* and the Appearance of Holiness." *JECS* 6, 3 (1998): 485–99.

——. "Wolves in Sheeps' Clothing: The Appearance of True and False Piety." *Studia Patristica* 29 (1997): 127–32.

Sieben, Hermann Josef. *Die Konzilsidee der Alten Kirche*. Konziliengeschichte Reihe B, Untersuchungen. Paderborn: Schöningh, 1979.

Sirago, Vito A. "Incontro di Agostino con Melania e Piniano." In *L'umanesimo di Sant'Agostino*, ed. Matteo Fabris. Bari: Levante, 1988. 629–48.

Sivan, Hagith. "Anician Women, the Cento of Proba, and Aristocratic Conversion in the Fourth Century," *Vigiliae Christianae* 47 (1993), 140–57.

——. "Le corps d'une pécheresse, le prix de la piété: La politique de l'adultère dans l'Antiquité tardive" *Annales HSS* 53, 2 (1998): 231–53.

——. "Revealing the Concealed: Rabbinic and Roman Legal Perspectives on Detecting Adultery." *ZRG RA* 116 (1999): 112–46.

Smith, Kathryn A. "Inventing Marital Chastity: The Iconography of Susanna and the Elders in Early Christian Art." *Oxford Art Journal* 16 (1993): 3–24.

Snyder, Christopher A. *An Age of Tyrants: Britain and the Britons, A.D. 400–600*. University Park: Pennsylvania State University Press, 1998.

——. *Sub-Roman Britain (AD 400–600): A Gazetteer of Sites*. BAR British Series 247. Oxford: Tempus Reparatum, 1996.

Somerville, Robert and Bruce C. Brasington, trans. *Prefaces to Canon Law Books in Latin Christianity: Selected Translations, 500–1245*. New Haven, Conn.: Yale University Press, 1998.

Speyer, Wolfgang. "Fluch." *Reallexikon für Antike und Christentum*. Stuttgart: Hiersemann, 1969. 7: 1160–1288.

Stacey, Robin Chapman. *Road to Judgment: From Custom to Court in Medieval Ireland and Wales*. Philadelphia: University of Pennsylvania Press, 1994.

Stein, Peter. *Roman Law in European History*. Cambridge: Cambridge University Press, 1999.

Sterk, Andrea. *Renouncing the World Yet Leading the Church: The Monk-Bishop in Late Antiquity*. Cambridge, Mass.: Harvard University Press, 2004.

Stock, Brian. *Augustine the Reader: Meditation, Self-Knowledge, and the Ethics of Interpretation.* Cambridge, Mass.: Harvard University Press, 1996.

Stone, M. E. *A History of the Literature of Adam and Eve.* Atlanta: Scholars Press, 1992.

Straw, Carol E. *Gregory the Great: Perfection in Imperfection.* Transformation of the Classical Heritage 14. Berkeley: University of California Press, 1988.

Strubbe, J. H. M., ed. *Arai epitymbioi: Imprecations against Desecrators of the Grave in the Greek Epitaphs of Asia Minor: A Catalogue.* Inschriften griechischer Städte aus Kleinasien 52. Bonn: Habelt, 1997.

———. "Cursed be he that moves my bones." In *Magika Hiera: Ancient Greek Magic and Religion,* ed. Christopher A. Faraone and Dirk Obbink. New York: Oxford University Press, 1991. 33–59.

———. "Curses Against Violation of the Grave in Jewish Epitaphs of Asia Minor." In *Studies in Early Jewish Epigraphy,* ed. Jan Willem van Henten and Pieter Willem van der Horst. Arbeiten zum Geschichte des antiken Judentums und Urchristentums 21. Leiden: E.J. Brill, 1994. 70–128.

Stuiber, Alfred. "Contra votum." *Reallexikon für Antike und Christentum.* Stuttgart: Hiersemann, 1955. 3: 421–22.

Swift, Louis J. "Augustine on *Fama*: The Case of Pinianus." In *Nova et Vetera: Patristic Studies in Honor of Thomas Patrick Halton,* ed. John Petruccione. Washington, D.C.: Catholic University of America Press, 1998. 196–205.

———. "Augustine on the Oath of Pinianus." *Studia Ephemeridis "Augustinianum"* 24 (1987): 371–79.

Taubenschlag, Rafal. *Law of Greco-Roman Egypt in the Light of the Papyri (332 B.C.-640 A.D.).* New York: Herald Square Press, 1944.

Teja, Ramón. "La cristianización de los modelos clásicos: El obispo." In *Modelos ideales y prácticas de vida en la antigüedad clásica,* ed. Emma Falque and Fernando Gascó. Serie Filosofía y letras 166. Seville: Universidad de Sevilla, 1993. 181–230.

TeSelle, Eugene. "Pelagius, Pelagianism." In *Augustine Through the Ages: An Encyclopedia,* ed. A. D. Fitzgerald et al. Grand Rapids, Mich.: Eerdmans, 1999. 633–40.

Testini, Pasquale. "Note per servire allo studio del complesso paleocristiano di S. Felice a Cimitile (Nola)." *Mélanges d'Archéologie et d'Histoire de l'École Française de Rome, Antiquité* 97 (1985): 329–71.

Thouvenot, Raymond. "Saint Augustin et les païens d'après Epist. XLVI et XLVII." In *Hommages à Jean Bayet,* ed. Marcel Renard and Robert Schilling. Collection Latomus 70. Brussels: Latomus, 1964. 682–90.

Thraede, Klause. *Grundzüge griechisch-römischer Brieftopik.* Zetemata 48. Munich: Beck, 1970.

Thür, Gerhard. "Oaths and Dispute Settlements in Ancient Greek Law." In *Greek Law in its Political Setting: Justifications not Justice,* ed. L. Foxhall and A. D. E. Lewis. Oxford: Oxford University Press, 1996. 57–72.

Tkacz, Catherine Brown. *The Key to the Brescia Casket: Typology and the Early Christian Imagination.* Collection des Études Augustiniennes Série Antiquité 165. Notre Dame, Ind.: University of Notre Dame Press and Institute d'Études augustiniennes, 2002.

——. "Susanna as a Type of Christ." *Studies in Iconography* 20 (1999): 101–53.

——. "Women as Types of Christ: Susanna and Jephthah's Daughter." *Gregorianum* 85, 2 (2004): 278–311.

Tomlin, R. S. O. "The Curse Tablets." In *The Temple of Sulis Minerva at Bath 2: The Finds from the Sacred Spring*, ed. Barry Cunliffe. Oxford: Oxford University Committee for Archaeology, 1988. 59–277.

Toorn, Karel van der. "Herem-Bethel and Elephantine Oath Procedure." *Zeitschrift für die Alttestamentliche Wissenschaft* 98 (1986): 282–85.

Trebilco, Paul R. *Jewish Communities in Asia Minor.* Society for New Testament Studies, Monograph Series 60. Cambridge: Cambridge University Press, 1991.

Treggiari, Susan. *Roman Marriage: Iusti Coniuges from the Time of Cicero to the Time of Ulpian.* Oxford: Oxford University Press, 1991.

Troncarelli, Fabio. *Vivarium: I libri, il destino.* Turnhout: Brepols, 1998.

Trousset, Pol. "Pénétration romaine et organisation de la zone frontière dans le pré-désert tunisien." In *L'Africa Romana: Ai confini dell'Impero: contatti, scambi, conflitti* (= *L'Africa romana* 15), ed. Mustapha Khanoussi, Paola Ruggeri, and Cinzia Vismara. 3 vols. Rome: Carocci, 2004. 59–88.

Trout, Dennis E. "Christianizing the Countryside: Animal Sacrifice at the Tomb of St. Felix." JECS 3 (1995): 281–98.

——. "Damasus and the Invention of Early Christian Rome." *Journal of Medieval and Early Modern Studies* 33.3 (2003): 517–36.

——. *Paulinus of Nola: Life, Letters, and Poems.* Transformation of the Classical Heritage 27. Berkeley: University of California Press, 1999.

Uhalde, Kevin. "Barbarian Traffic, Demon Oaths, and Christian Scruples (Aug. *Ep.* 46–47)." In *Romans and Barbarians*, ed. Ralph W. Mathisen and Danuta Shanzer. Aldershot: Ashgate, forthcoming.

——. "Proof and Reproof: The Judicial Component of Episcopal Confrontation." *Early Medieval Europe* 8 (1999): 1–11.

Urbainczyk, Theresa. *Theodoret of Cyrrhus: The Bishop and the Holy Man.* Ann Arbor: University of Michigan Press, 2002.

Van Dam, Raymond. "Images of Saint Martin in Late Roman and Early Medieval Gaul." *Viator* 19 (1988): 1–27.

——. "'Sheep in Wolves' Clothing': The Letters of Consentius to Augustine." *Journal of Ecclesiastical History* 37 (1986): 515–35.

Venturini, Carlo. "'*Accusatio Adulterii*' e politica constantiniana (Per un riesame di CTH 9, 7, 2)." *Studia et Documenta Historiae et Iuris* 54 (1988): 66–109.

Verbraken, Pierre-Patrick. *Études critiques sur les sermons authentique de Saint Augustin.* Instrumenta Patristica 12. Steenbrugis: Abbatia S. Petri, 1974.

Versnel, H. S. "Beyond Cursing: The Appeal to Justice in Judicial Prayers." In *Magika Hiera: Ancient Greek Magic and Religion*, ed. Christopher A. Faraone and Dirk Obbink. New York: Oxford University Press, 1991. 60–106.

Vescovi e pastori in epoca teodosiana: XXV Incontro di studiosi dell'antichità cristiana. Studia Ephemeridis Augustinianum 58. 2 vols. Rome: Institutum patristicum Augustinianum, 1997.

Vessey, Mark. "The Demise of the Christian Writer and the Remaking of 'Late

Antiquity': From H.-I. Marrou's Saint Augustine (1938) to Peter Brown's Holy Man (1983)." JECS 6, 3 (1998): 377–411.

———. "From *Cursus* to *Ductus*: Figures of Writing in Western Late Antiquity (Augustine, Jerome, Cassiodorus, Bede)." In *European Literary Careers: The Author from Antiquity to the Renaissance*, ed. Patrick Cheney and Frederick A. de Armas. Toronto: University of Toronto Press, 2002. 47–103.

———. "The Origins of the *Collectio Sirmondiana*: A New Look at the Evidence." In *The Theodosian Code: Studies in the Imperial Law of Late Antiquity*, ed. Jill Harries and Ian Wood. London: Duckworth, 1993. 178–99.

Vives, José, ed. *Inscripciones cristianas de la España romana y visigoda*. 2nd ed. Barcelona: A. G. Ponsa, 1969.

Vodola, Elizabeth. *Excommunication in the Middle Ages*. Berkeley: University of California Press, 1986.

Vogel, Cyrille. *La discipline pénitentielle en Gaule des origines à la fin du VIIe siècle*. Paris : Letouzey et Ané, 1952.

———. "La discipline pénitentielle en Gaule des origines au IXe siècle: Le dossier hagiographique." *Revue des sciences religieuses* 30 (1956): 1–26, 157–86.

———. "La discipline pénitentielle dans les inscriptions paléochrétiennes." *Rivista di Archeologia Cristiana* 42 (1966): 317–25.

———. *Le pécheur et la pénitence dans l'église ancienne*. Paris: Éditions du Cerf, 1966.

———. "Penance." In *Encyclopedia of the Early Church*, ed. A. Di Berardino, trans. A. Walford, Oxford, 1992. 2:667.

Ward-Perkins, Bryan. *The Fall of Rome and the End of Civilization*. Oxford: Oxford University Press, 2005.

Watkins, Oscar Daniel. *History of Penance: Being a Study of the Authorities*. 2 vols. Reprint. New York: B. Franklin, 1961.

Webb, Rebecca Harden. *Divine Grace and Human Agency: A Study of the Semi-Pelagian Controversy*. Patristic Monograph Series 15. Macon, Ga.: Mercer University Press, 1996.

———. "Imagination and the Arousal of the Emotions." In *The Passions in Roman Thought and Literature*, ed. Susanna Morton Braund and Christopher Gill. Cambridge: Cambridge University Press, 1997. 112–27.

Whittaker, C. R. "Land and Labour in North Africa." *Klio* 60 (1978): 331–62.

Whittaker, C. R. and Peter Garnsey, "Rural Life in the Later Roman Empire." In CAH 13: 277–312.

Wiesheu, Annette. "Bischof und Gefängnis: Zur Interpretation der Kerkerbefreiungswunder in der merowingischen Hagiographie." *Historisches Jahrbuch* 121 (2001): 1–23.

Wilson, M. "The Subjugation of Grief in Seneca's 'Epistles.'" In *The Passions in Roman Thought and Literature*, ed. Susanna Morton Braund and Christopher Gill. Cambridge: Cambridge University Press, 1997. 48–67.

Wood, Ian N. "Incest, Law and the Bible in Sixth-Century Gaul." *Early Medieval Europe* 7, 3 (1998): 291–304.

———. *The Missionary Life: Saints and the Evangelisation of Europe, 400–1050*. Harlow: Longman, 2001.

Worley, David R. "Fleeing to Two Immutable Things, God's Oath-Taking and

Oath-Witnessing: The Use of the Litigant Oath in Hebrews 6:12–20." *Restoration Quarterly* 36 (1994): 223–36.

Wormald, Patrick. *The Making of English Law: King Alfred to the Twelfth Century.* Vol. 1, *Legislation and Its Limits.* Oxford: Blackwell, 1999.

Worp, K. A. "Byzantine Imperial Titulature in the Greek Documentary Papyri: The Oath Formulas." ZPE 45 (1982): 199–226.

Zimmerman, Reinhard. *Law of Obligations: Roman Foundations of the Civilian Tradition.* Oxford: Oxford University Press, 1990, 1996.

Index

Aaron, 55
Ablabius, 30–31
Adam, 120–22
adultery, 69–70, 114
advice-giving (*usus consiliorum*), 49–53
Agiulf, 105
Agricola, 115
Albina, 97–99, 100–101
Alypius of Thagaste, 38, 97, 98, 99
Ambrose of Milan: on advice-giving, 49–50; on discernment of scriptural mysteries, 54; on discernment and the spiritual sword, 48; on oaths, 85–86; on Peter's contrition, 119; and relics, 61; response to failure of episcopal justice, 10, 73–76; and sense of divine justice, 73–76; and sexual accusations against women, 68, 71–5; *De officiis*, 49–50, 54, 66, 85, 86
Ammianus Marcellinus, 67, 69
Angenendt, Arnold, 6
Apocalypse of Paul, 132
apocalyptic images and penance, 125, 130, 133–34
Apostolic Constitutions, 46, 52
apostolic keys: and episcopal authority, 46–48; and Paul's episcopal justice, 126–27; and penance, 108, 110
Arcadius, 21
Aredius of Limoges, 65
Athanasius, 53
Augustine of Hippo: and advice-giving, 50–52; and Cassiodorus, 2; on curses, 81; on Donatist threats to sacraments, 36–37; and due process, 36–37; on exemplary penitents, 118–20; and group excommunication, 39–40; on Jewish swearing, 88; on judges and process of inquiry, 66–67; and limits of episcopal justice, 38–42, 128–29; on lying, 90–92;

and municipal defenders, 38–40; and oath-swearing, 13, 78–79, 81, 88–104; and oath-swearing scandals, 98–101; and pagan oaths, 93–95; and Pelagian controversy, 102–3; on penance and compunction, 123–24; on perjury, 90, 92, 103; and punishment of priests, 41–42; on role as bishop-judge, 11; Sermon on the Mount commentary, 88–90; on the social bond, 9, 35–36, 92–101; *Against Lying*, 50; *Confessions*, 50; *De civitate Dei*, 3, 102; *On Lying*, 90; *Retractiones*, 78–79
Auxilius, 39–41

baptism, 84
barbarian invasions, 5, 6
Basil of Caesarea, 57, 83, 85
Bede the Venerable, 79
Beweisurteil, 81
bishops and bishop-judge ideal, 10–12, 45; and advice-giving, 49–53; and bishops' courts, 31; crafting image of, 17–18, 31; and discernment of sacred mysteries, 53–55; essential judicial attributes, 65–67; and Gallic hagiographic tradition, 65–66; Jerome on, 55–58, 62; Nicetius and early medieval Trier, 62–65; and penance, 106–7, 109; sexual misconduct accusations and failure of ideal, 67–76; and superior surveillance, 62–63; texts propagating the ideal, 46–49. *See also* spiritual discernment and bishop-judges
Boniface, 104
Bowman, Jeffrey, 9
Breviary of Alaric, 21
Brown, Peter, 7, 14, 75, 132
Bury, J. B., 5
business contracts, Egyptian, 82–83

Acknowledgments

A number of generous institutions, grants, and fellowships made it possible to research and write this book. I am pleased to acknowledge support from the Program in the Ancient World, the Group for the Study of Late Antiquity, a Stanley J. Seeger Fellowship in Hellenic Studies, and a Junior Fellowship at the University Center for Human Values at Princeton University; an Andrew W. Mellon Junior Faculty Fellowship through the American Council of Learned Societies; a summer stipend from Northern Illinois University; and a Humanities Research Fund award from Ohio University and its College of Arts and Sciences.

Many colleagues have provided comments along the way and I thank them all, especially Lisa Bailey, Nikolas Bakirtzis, Dani Botsman, Kim Bowes, Jeffrey Bowman, Scott Bruce, Santiago Castellanos, Adam Davis, Crystal Feimster, Abigail Firey, Michael Gaddis, Ignacio Gallup-Diaz, James Goehring, David Gordon, Patrick Griffin, Evan Haefeli, Erika Thorgerson Hermanowicz, Judith Herrin, Jennifer Hevelone-Harper, William Klingshirn, Tia Kolbaba, Michael Kulikowski, Noel Lenski, Ralph Mathisen, Rob Meens, Leonora Neville, Thomas Noble, Bruce O'Brien, Claudia Rapp, Teofilo Ruiz, Danuta Shanzer, Brent Shaw, Dennis Trout, Raymond Van Dam, and Joel Walker. Peter Brown read more than one "final" version of the manuscript leading to the present book. My debt to him will be obvious throughout these pages, so here I only need to express my deepest gratitude for his kindness and generosity over the past decade. What I owe the medievalist William Jordan is less conspicuous in this study but just as real; above all, he has tried to make me make better sense. I take sole responsibility for the judgments and any remaining errors or infelicities in this book. It would be much poorer without Christopher MacEvitt, Jaclyn Maxwell, Jarbel Rodriguez, Kristina Sessa, and Joshua Sosin, each of whom read the entire manuscript at some point.

I am happy to acknowledge the support of my family, which has waited a long time to see some concrete evidence of my work. My sister Yvette, my brother René and his wife Amanda, and my parents Ruth and Ray are a loving group of people I am proud to call my own. My wife Jackie has been a tolerant friend and prudent advisor, even while finishing her own book and bearing our son, Oscar. I dedicate this book to all of them.